## About the Author

Ian Wishart is an award-winning journalist and author, with a 30 year career in radio, television and magazines, a #1 talk radio show and five #1 bestselling books to his credit. Together with his wife Heidi, they edit and publish the news magazine *Investigate* and the news website www.investigatedaily.com.

*For our newest little princess, Victoria*

# Our Stories
## THE WAY WE USED TO BE
## The New Zealand That Time Forgot...

*Edited by*
**Ian Wishart**

HOWLING AT THE MOON PUBLISHING LTD

Howling At The Moon Publishing Ltd

First edition published 2014
by Howling At The Moon Publishing Ltd
PO Box 188, Kaukapakapa
Auckland 0843, NEW ZEALAND

Email: editorial@howlingatthemoon.com
Web: http://www.ianwishart.com

Copyright © Ian Wishart, 2014
Copyright © Howling At The Moon Publishing Ltd, 2014

The moral rights of the author have been asserted.

*Our Stories* is copyright. Except for the purpose of fair reviewing, no part of this publication may be copied, reproduced or transmitted in any form or by any means, including via technology either already in existence or developed subsequent to publication, without the express written permission of the publisher and authors.
All rights reserved.

ISBN 978-0-9941064-0-7

Cover photo by David Wall, DanitaDelimont.com/Newscom
Typeset in Adobe Garamond Pro and Century Handtooled
Cover concept: Heidi and Ian Wishart
Book design: Bozidar Jokanovic

# Contents

Introduction .................................................................................. 6
Young Auckland: A Portrait In Words ........................................ 8
The Tsunami Menace .................................................................. 24
Life In New Zealand – Part 1 ..................................................... 55
The Telephone Comes To NZ ..................................................... 70
The Last Huia .............................................................................. 81
Ancient Peoples, Ancient Pathways ........................................... 95
New Zealand's Forgotten Dinosaurs ........................................ 113
Life In New Zealand – Part 2 ................................................... 138
Women & The Vote ................................................................... 152
The Rise And Fall Of The Moa ................................................ 165
The Massacres At Wairau And Kaipara ................................... 187
What To Expect In Wellington's Big One ............................... 201
Life In New Zealand – Part 3 ................................................... 214
The Story Of The South Island ................................................ 229
How Ngai Tahu Sold The South Island ................................... 243
The Cultural Impact Of Mr Selfridge ...................................... 281
Call Of The Wild ....................................................................... 291
The Tarawera Eruption ............................................................. 309
Climate Change 150 Years Ago ................................................ 317
Educating Pita ........................................................................... 323
Life In New Zealand – Part 4 ................................................... 335
All That Glitters: The Goldrush ............................................... 341
Land Of Hope And Dreams ...................................................... 352

## Introduction

Several years ago, while researching old historical files for my book *The Great Divide*, it became apparent that New Zealand's recently digitised document archives were a treasure trove for historians and writers.

Once upon a time, it was impossible to study old documents without visiting the National Library or Alexander Turnbull Library in Wellington, or manually browsing print copies or microfiche of old newspapers at central city libraries.

The common thread in all that old-style research (which virtually every other New Zealand history book was created from) is that the documents were not text-searchable; you could not punch a keyword into a computer and quickly put documents in context by accessing every document simultaneously on a given subject.

Instead, the old research methods were very much a game of join the dots, a linear journey following a singular document trail.

Digitisation has changed all that. Now, New Zealanders can access their history not only from the comfort of their own homes, but if they know how to efficiently carry out document searches they can cover huge swathes of territory in one hit. As an example, whilst writing Our Stories I managed, at one point, to have more than 150 archival documents open on my computer simultaneously as I chased down every possible lead on one of the stories inside.

What you are about to read will entertain, enthral and inform you. This book not only casts new light on colonial life and Maori/Pakeha relations in the early days, but it actually takes you back in time to see New Zealand through the eyes and words of our first European settlers.

*Our Stories* is not an 'exhaustive' view of our past; there have been millions of news stories published over the years and these are just some of them. However, the stories I have selected for this volume offer an 'I was there' perspective on some major events in our history that traditional history books, often relying on formal reports rather than news coverage, don't have.

There are also some major lessons in here: Cantabrians will discover the city's major quakes were not at all unusual and that the cathedral has been damaged a number of times in the past – incidents long forgotten and so leading to a sense of complacency.

Readers will experience first hand the impacts on early settlements of tsunami as large as the Japanese one – witnesses reporting the disappearance of homes and bridges as the water poured in.

There are so many fascinating stories in this book that you'll discover for yourself.

One thing to note. The work by the government to digitise the newspaper reports used a conversion process called optical character recognition. It causes many typographical errors. We think we caught them all, but if you spot an obvious spelling mistake or typo (as opposed to a historically different way of spelling something, because we have retained the authentic spelling), drop us an email to the address on the Publisher's page at the front.

Enjoy the book, and enjoy the narrative of a country forged in the blood, sweat, tears and laughter of Maori and Pakeha alike.

This is New Zealand. These are our stories.

Chapter 1

# Young Auckland: A Portrait In Words

*The story of Auckland is the story of New Zealand in microcosm. Although arguably New Zealand's prime urban real estate, nestled on the shores of two harbours and providing a gateway north and south, its very desirability made it a place of bloodshed in ancient times, frequently abandoned as each Maori tribe that captured it found they couldn't hold it. The city became a kind of no-man's land, the scene of a Maori Mexican stand off.*

*The last great tribes to hold Auckland under their own muscle were Ngati Whatua and Ngati Paoa, but they got cleaned out by a musket-fuelled Ngapuhi raiding army of several thousand men in 1821 as historian Paul Moon has written:*

*"Nowhere was the slaughter more concentrated than in the area alongside the Tamaki River estuary that today houses the suburbs of St Heliers, Glen Innes, Panmure and Mt Wellington, then home of the Ngati Paoa: two attacks in 1821 effectively wiped out or captured almost all Ngati Paoa. The death toll has been estimated at between 1000 and 3000 and the feasting on the dead went on for days."* [1]

*Thus, when the first Europeans meandered into lush Auckland, they were welcomed with open arms by the few Ngati Whatua and Ngati Paoa who remained: anyone who could act as a barrier against Ngapuhi aggression, especially as the Ngapuhi were close to Pakeha, was a good thing for the region.*

---

1  The Treaty and Its Times, by Paul Moon and Peter Biggs, 2004, p47

*Paora Tuhaere, who became Ngati Whatua's paramount chief, recognised the future of his people was intertwined forever with encouraging Pakeha to settle at Auckland, and Ngati Whatua became one of the most accommodating and progressive tribes in developing good relations with the British (which made their ill-treatment over Bastion Point by later governments all the more distasteful).*

*The first immigrants to Auckland from the British Isles came on 'the first fleet': two sailing ships from Scotland named the Jane Gifford and the Duchess of Argyle. On board, the pioneer families of Auckland² – Scottish emigrants fleeing Glasgow and Paisley for a new promised land. Those vessels finally sailed into the Waitemata Harbour in October 1842, and there to greet them was a man nicknamed 'the father of Auckland', Dr John Logan-Campbell.*

*At the fiftieth anniversary of the fleet's arrival, in 1892, Logan-Campbell was still alive and waxing lyrical about the changes he'd seen in Auckland over a timespan roughly equivalent for modern readers to the time since Beatlemania broke out in the sixties:*

## Speech By John Logan-Campbell At 50th Reunion Of First Auckland Migrants, 1892[3]

We have assembled here to-night to celebrate the fiftieth anniversary of the arrival of the first immigrants who landed on the shores of the Waitemata in October, 1842, from the good ships the *Jane Gifford* and *Duchess of Argyle*. I have been asked to preside as being a pioneer of a still earlier date, and who witnessed the birth of Auckland in 1840.

It was my lot to be living on the little island of Motu Korea, now known

---

2  The Herald reports in 1892 that an honour-guard of surviving pioneers from the two ships included: *Jane Gifford*: – Messrs. J. McLellan, David Russell, Joseph Scott, Wm. Scott, Wishart, W. Oliver, Joseph Craig, W. Miller, Robert Scott, Trevarthen, W. Jamieson, Thomas Wylie, Wilson (Thames). *Mesdames* McLellan, Scott, Hill, Morrison, Griffiths, Hendry, Somervell, J. Carradus, McClusky, J. Culpan, Carmichael, Pulham, Kennedy, A. Gillan (Thames), Jamieson, Pollok, Caradus, Cooper. *Duchess of Argyle* – Messrs. Jas Wallace, Robert Laurie, W. L. Thorburn, H. Andrews, H. Gollan, Jas. Robertson, Thos. Finlay. W. Andrews, Ed. Clare, J. A. Wood, Jas. Clare, P. McNair, J. Caradus. *Mesdames* Donald, Jackson, J. Winks, A. Craig, Bell, T. Wylie, Robert Laurie, Scott, Lamb, Jas. Moore, Cameron, A. Pollock, Wishart, P. Robertson, Hannah, J. McEwin, Robert Lang, W. Hume, McBrierty.

3  Fifty Years Ago, New Zealand Herald, Volume XXIX, Issue 9006, 11 October 1892, Page 6 http://paperspast.natlib.govt.nz/cgi-bin/paperspast?a=d&d=NZH18921011.2.44

under the less euphonious name of Brown's Island, for some months previous to the Government arriving and founding the infant capital of New Zealand. I have, therefore, been an eye-witness to its birth, seen it arise from out the fern wilderness, and have lived to see the change which two-and fifty years have brought about.

How great those changes have been can only be realised by those who remember the fern-clad waste which then spread far and wide around the spot where we are now assembled, and which has since been converted into the well-paved and gas-lighted streets of this city.

How different indeed to the day when the pioneer settlers from the Clyde sailed into Auckland Harbour. Then, her shores boasted neither charming villa nor smiling farm homestead. Beautiful were her shores then, when robed in only Nature's vesture, and beautiful through all time her shores will ever be.

At that long ago date, high water tide rippled on the beach where now stands the Post Office. Some parts of Queen Street still presented patches of luxuriant flax swamps, and Shortland Crescent was the great thoroughfare. It was a thoroughfare winding along a narrow path through high fern and tea-tree away up a then very steep hill, passing the late site of St. Paul's Church, and leading away down the bay to the Government offices and dwellings of the officials.

When the two vessels arrived from the Clyde, Auckland was still in a very primitive state. We had not quite discarded the tents and raupo huts in which we first lived, and we were quite proud of the few scattered weatherboarded houses which began to mark out the lines of the streets.

As for the streets, these were literally in a state of nature, and that state of nature in wet weather was ankle deep at least in mud. Pedestrians in those days – and pedestrians we were all obliged to be – had to be very wary how they bent their steps, or they might come to grief. There was a well-known figure amongst us then – in point of age he was the father of the settlement, and had grown to be somewhat shaky in the knees. The poor old fellow every now and then did come to grief, and we had on these occasions to give him a helping hand to extricate him from the mud holes in which he got bogged. Hence, in course of time he became known amongst us by the appropriate soubriquet of "Old Stick in the Mud."

I can recall an incident, seeing a lady and her daughter who wanted to cross Shortland Crescent, standing critically scrutinising the treacherous-looking mud, where safest to make the venture. The old lady proved the bolder of the two, and made a dash at it – alas! when she got across she was minus a shoe! I cannot commend the young lady's conduct on seeing the plight of her respected parent, for she stood convulsed with laughter. It was all very well for her, for she was still on her own side of the street with both her shoes on!

As illustrating the vicissitudes of this life to which we are subject, I may tell you that worthy lady within a short period previously drove in her own carriage in Liverpool, her husband a merchant prince of that great city. Sudden and overwhelming losses overtook him, making it too painful to live in the scene of his earlier prosperity. Like a brave old man he took heart of grace, and faced a new life in a new land, and arriving amongst us, with an admirable resignation accepted the deprivations of those early days.

I doubt not that some of the grandchildren of my old friend, now long passed away, are listening to me tonight. They have every reason to hold his memory in proud remembrance.

I alluded to the loss of the shoe, as proving how much we required to mend our ways, and it so happened that it was the landing on our shores of the immigrants from the Clyde that first enabled us to begin. The simultaneous arrival of two ships' load of settlers of course glutted our limited capacity to employ labour, so we awoke to the first cry of the unemployed.

Then, as now, an appeal was made to the Government to find work; the appeal was responded to, and picks and shovels were served out from the Government store, and a road party was set to work.

I daresay you would like to know the value of a day's labour at that epoch. The motto of the working man of to-day of eight hours work, eight hours play, eight hours sleep, eight shillings a day, was then still far in the future – these were not eight shilling days; no, it was only the modest sum of half-a-crown [A crown was five shillings, or around 50 cents]. Times are indeed changed.

It was only lately that I read of a meeting of the unemployed at Christchurch. The spokesman indignantly upbraided the Government for only offering, as he put it, the miserable pittance of six shillings.

I see by my journal it was just a week after the arrival of the vessels, on the 17th of October, and I well remember the morning when the road party first commenced operations in Shortland Crescent, just opposite my firm's premises. What with levelling down the opposite side, which was away twenty feet up in the air, and levelling up the lower side, our premises got buried, so we had to put up a second storey and enter at the old roof level.

I am glad to say that it was for a very short time that our improvements were carried on at the two-and-sixpence a day rate. The new-comers soon found profitable employment at their respective handicrafts, and began to flourish. Of course, they had their struggles, their ups and downs in life, but they faced these like hard-headed Scotchmen which they were, and ultimately reaped their reward.

As a body they had little cause ever to regret they had left behind them "Caledonia stern and wild," and pitched their camp in this brighter and happier land, and they and their descendants have reaped a material prosperity which the old world would have failed to bring them.

That land – "land of the mountain and the flood" – dear as it is in old associations, has its sombre side: the sun shines but in fitful rays at fitful times, ever struggling to dispel the doom. Here we have a bright and beautiful sky, here we have a genial and inspiring climate which makes life an ever-existing pleasure.

Surely I may congratulate you, the children and children's children represented here tonight, even to the fourth generation, that your forefathers bade a last and long farewell to their native land, thus changing your destiny to this much brighter country, and that your lot has been cast in pleasanter places. The danger that lies in *your* path is that you may too easily acquire and indulge in those comforts and luxuries which lead to enervated lives and ultimately to deterioration of character.

Be but true to yourselves, and to the ancient traditions of the land of your forefathers, and a happy future is in store for you. How different are these days in which you live compared to those of half a century now hurried in the past, which we are commemorating. Many of us survivors may say that in those old bygone days we enjoyed a peaceful and quiet life that you in vain may seek.

The marvellous inventions of the telegraph and telephone, which almost annihilate time and space, have changed all things. We used to receive news from the mother country sometimes nearly a year old; now you have the news of the world given to you only twelve hours old, in the morning papers.

Methinks the race of life has become too keen – we are no longer content to say, "Sufficient unto the day is the evil thereof." We aim at discounting the future, we want to live to-morrow before to-morrow comes, and who shall say that we are any the happier?

Great indeed are the changes which we old identities have witnessed during the passing away of the last half-century – changes of a kind it is not likely it will ever be your lot to look upon. For we have seen a handful of the Saxon race land upon a savage shore, have seen that shore reclaimed from the wilderness, and slowly advance in civilisation until we have transplanted almost every institution from the mother country to the land of our adoption.

Indeed, without vain boast we may ask, "Where, for a young city of the same population as ours, can be seen what we can show in the advanced civilisation of the day?" Witness our Free Library – no mean building truly – our Elam Free School of Art, our Art Galleries, and the wonderful treasures there deposited; our Museum, this Choral Hall, and other kindred societies…The blind, deaf, and dumb cared for, places of worship of every denomination and last and most significant, and coming to what is more intimately associated with ourselves, look at the palatial structure of the Auckland Savings Bank, a monument of our industrial savings, and where lies half a million of money, the earnings of the working classes, a fruitful store against the proverbial rainy day, proving how generous has been to them their new mother country.

And here, close at hand, sits the manager of that institution, the son of a *Duchess of Argyle* colonist, born in Auckland. We have amongst us here tonight age venerable in the lengthened span of over 90 years. Let some young person – half a century old – just look forward to forty more years of life, and tell us what are the strange feelings such a prospect engenders.

I thought I had some claim to be considered somewhat of a venerable personage, but I feel dwarfed into a comparatively juvenile insignificance, and pale before the living record of five generations.

Truly, we live in a prolific and marvellous country whose kindly climate enables us to chronicle this night the fact that we can in our own day look upon the living representatives of five generations. You will have seen in this day's *Herald* the startling announcement that one lady in the ripeness of her years can count her six children, twenty-six grandchildren, forty-four great-grandchildren, and two great-great-grandchildren.

Why, one feels lost in a labyrinth of generations. After such a record who shall say we cannot hold our own in this direction? I think we may challenge the world. I can see an old friend who lauded from the *Duchess of Argyle*, and who, like myself, is now in the "sere and yellow leaf" of old age, and I can see his great-grandchild and many fellow great grandchildren, with young and happy faces, the world all before them – to us it is all in the past. And now that the snow of age has gathered on our heads, we may be well content to take our last long rest when the appointed day now soon at hand – shall come. The departed spirits of our old fellow-workers who have already joined the great majority, are beckoning us from the other side of the great river to follow.

Truly all that we have gone through since 1840 appears like a strange dream, but a dream which has the fascination of reality, for have we pilgrim fathers not lived through all the vicissitudes incident to the first settlement of a new colony, watched over its birth and foundation, stood by it during all its early struggles and varying fortunes, and taken our part in developing the resources of the land of our adoption? And we, whom it has pleased God to spare to this year of grace, are proud to compare our city of today with what it was in October, 1842.

We have lived to see the great fern wilderness reclaimed, to have seen the infant settlement unrobe itself of its first primitive garments of brushwood and breakwind huts and tents in which we were dwellers, and outliving its bush mask and wild appearance, enter on the path of progress. And we have our reward, that today we see that infant settlement, grown into a city, proudly advancing along the broadway of civilisation, a city yet destined to be one of the fairest in the world, and to whose shores will be attracted denizens from many and far distant lands.

*Logan-Campbell's reflections, in hindsight, illustrate just how far Auckland, and indeed the entire New Zealand nation, had come in just five short decades. But those intervening years had not been without danger.*

*Governor Hobson, soon after Waitangi, suffered a stroke and determined to establish Auckland as the capital of the new colony. Among those present at the birth of what would become New Zealand's largest city was a young missionary named Gideon Smales who found himself thrust into peril as Auckland faced its biggest threat in its short history:*

## The Maori Army Prepared To Defend Pakeha Auckland, 1845[4]
### Recollections Of An Old Missionary By The Rev. Gideon Smales

"As you are an old colonist, or a pioneer of old colonists and old identities, and as some of your contemporaries are giving us reminiscences of the past, cannot you tell something about Auckland?"

In answer to this appeal I jot down the following, which may fill up a corner in our history.

In 1840, whilst stationed at Hokianga, my first circuit was from Mangungu to Mangamuka, across Maungataniwa, through the valley of Oruru to Mangonui, and from thence along the coast to Whangaroa and the Bay of Islands, from which place I crossed the coast to Waihou, a branch of the upper part of the Hokianga and here, at his native village, I met my old friend Tamati Waka Nene, from whom I always received a warm "Haere mai! Haere mai!"

Here we generally collected his people together and held various educational and religious services. And in my shorter visitations from Mangungu to the nearer settlements, Waihou and Tamati Waka Nene had a fair share of my instructions.

I always regarded him as one of our best friends, and he always was more favourable to the pakeha and the Government than other chiefs of the district. Besides, he was the chief who turned the scale of influence when others opposed the Government at the signing of the Treaty of Waitangi, and whilst he was my pupil, although he might be considered as about 60 years of age, he was of a cheerful and happy disposition, with considerable tact and ability, but as docile as a child. He sat in the class with others of his tribe, industriously learning to read and write, and take in the religious, political, and social instruction I felt it my duty to teach.

After I had left that field of labour and found myself in 1845 at Aotea, pursuing my course to proclaim peace on earth and heaven's good will to men, I was aroused with the intelligence from Auckland that Heke had cut down the flagstaff, which was regarded as the emblem of our Government,

---

4  Auckland: Past, Present, And Future, New Zealand Herald, Volume XXIX, Issue 9058, 10 December 1892, Page 1
http://paperspast.natlib.govt.nz/cgi-bin/paperspast?a=d&d=NZH18921210.2.65.4

and sacked and burned Kororareka, and that he could muster 2000 men, with whom he intended to treat Auckland as he had done Kororareka.

The people of Auckland were aroused to the highest pitch of excitement, and commenced barricading the churches and throwing up earthworks for shelter, and there was great danger and dread that our infantile city would soon be laid waste and without inhabitants.

The next intelligence I had was that my old friend Tamati, with his usual chivalry, had come forward with his 300 men, and kept Heke and Kawiti fully occupied by frequent skirmishes until further help arrived from Sydney.

In the meantime, although a man of peace and whose work was to publish peace, a sense of the danger in which Auckland was placed induced me to call all my natives together at Aotea, and appeal to their loyalty and Christian feeling. My questions to the natives were much as follows –

"Are we to fall back to Heathenism? Are we to be governed by this Heke? Are your old enemies, the Ngapuhi's, again to ravage your country and destroy and kill you as they did your relatives in Hongi's time? Awake from your lethargy! Are your friends the pakehas in Auckland to be driven into the sea by Heke as he threatens? Is Governor Fitzroy to be supplanted by a Ngapuhi chief, and will you submit to be trampled under foot and your papapa (cranium) be made the drinking vessels and your matikata (fingers) the fish-hooks of the slaves of Ngapuhi?

"Arouse yourselves, and by all that is really and truly tapu on earth and all that is infinitely sacred above, come forward to the help of the Governor and Nene and defend the homes and families – the parents and children of your friends the pakehas in Auckland."

My appeal was so far successful that the natives came forward as a body, and exercised their influence with their friends and relatives, extending even into Waikato; and we mustered our people, and numbered the men of different tribes who were ready to come forward at the command of the Governor and march to Auckland to defend Auckland and its inhabitants, and, if necessity required it, to advance even into the enemy's country, and assist the [Government] troops and Nene and his warriors against the incursions of Heke and Kawiti.

After writing down the names of those who were prepared for this enterprise, it was found that there were no less than 700 warriors. And those I presented by letter to Governor Fitzroy as a contingent ready at any time when called upon to march forward to Auckland and receive his orders.

The efforts of Tamati Waka Nene had been, however, so far successful that the enemy had been kept in check, and it was hoped that further native help would not be required. But the arrangement had a good effect upon the mind of the Governor, for he felt his hands strengthened, and it helped to pacify the minds of the Europeans and, no doubt, intimidated those who were threatening to join those who were opposed to the Government.

I had a letter of thanks from Governor Fitzroy, who stated that should they not succeed in keeping back the enemy he would send for our contingent. Happily, Tamati Waka Nene mustered strong enough, and with the assistance of the troops who had come down from Sydney, to thwart Heke and Kawiti, and frustrate their evil designs. And now we are thankful that instead of a site of waste and desolation we have the pleasure of beholding a beautiful city.

We have indeed a great and goodly city, pleasant for situation, well adapted for health and utility, a city which in ages to come may command the whole of the Southern Pacific. The only fear is lest the people fall back into a state of weakness and enervation through excessive pleasure-seeking and gambling – or by setting labour before us as a burden and a curse, which always has been, and must continue to be, a physical, social, and political boon to every country and people.

We have a city worthy of a country flowing with milk and honey, and which, at any rate to the Briton, is the glory of all lands and there can be no doubt but that according to our individual and national industry, so will be our success and according to our courteousness. and charity (in its fullest sense), so will be our peace and happiness.

I cannot but say, may the blessing which maketh rich – in all beneficial riches – and addeth no sorrow thereto, rest on Auckland.

Note. There has been no native that I am aware of, to whom the colony has been more indebted as a defender, advisor, and friend of the pakeha and his Government than Tamati Wake Nene. The Government felt something of their indebtedness to him when they awarded him a pension of £100 per annum, which, though small, was an acknowledgment of his services and at his demise their sense of honour and gratitude inclined them to erect a monument to his memory at the Bay of Islands. He died in 1871, and must have been about 90 years of age.

*Smales was also able to shed some light on an ill-fated attempt to settle Waiheke Island in 1826:*[5]

The *Rosanna* was the first vessel that brought out regular immigrants for Now Zealand. They were sent out by an association of which Mr. Lambton, afterwards Lord Durham, was the head. This Association was formed in England in 1825.

The *Rosanna* brought fifty mechanics and other useful immigrants. Captain Herd had been sent as an advance agent for the company. It was said that he bought Waiheke and other islands in the Hauraki Gulf, and a piece of land at the Hokianga, called after him, "Herd's Point."

The *Rosanna* reached Waiheke towards the end of 1826. The passengers objected to the land, and some were intimidated by a war dance which the natives gave them as a welcome. Some went back to the Bay of Islands and Hokianga, and some returned with the ship to Sydney. I met some of them at the Hokianga in 1840, and I believe some of them afterwards settled in Auckland.

In 1840, the ship *Brilliant* was sent to the Manukau with immigrants, under the late Captain Symonds, who was drowned whilst crossing the Manukau harbour on an errand of mercy. He was taking medicine, it was stated, for the relief and support of Mrs. Hamlin, wife of the missionary who then resided on the south side of the Manukau.

Captain Symonds was an elder son of Sir William Symonds, who was at that time the head of Her Majesty's Docks, in England. Captain Symonds was a young man of considerable ability and great promise, and his loss was considered as a great loss to the colony. Karangahape[6], where the immigrants were located, was a busy place when I visited it in 1840, and some of the settlers were talking of it as likely to be a more important settlement than Auckland, which was then in a very primitive condition. Natives disputed the company's claim on the land, and the Colonial Government took them up, the Manukau Company ended, and the settlement gradually went down.

---

5   Episodes In The Life Of An Old Missionary, New Zealand Herald, Volume XXX, Issue 9379, 9 December 1893, Page 1
http://paperspast.natlib.govt.nz/cgi-bin/paperspast?a=d&d=NZH18931209.2.69.4
6   A bay at the northern entrance to the Manukau Harbour, close to what is now called Cornwallis. The 'Parish of Karangahape' now incorporates Piha and Karekare to the north

One of the features of New Zealand cities is that most of them are undergoing constant urban renewal. For some, like Christchurch and to an extent Wellington, change was forced by nature. But in Auckland, change happened often for the sake of change. In the early 1920s the city was undergoing more industrial and commercial expansion down towards its reclaimed wharf district, with the result the homesteads belonging to some of the city's founding fathers were being torn down:

## The City's Early Days, 1924[7]

A further stage in the removal of landmarks of early Auckland is being accomplished in the extensive levelling operations now being carried on by private enterprise at the foot of Hobson Street, on its eastern side, contemporaneously with the lowering by the City Corporation of the level of the western end of Swanson Street (formerly West Queen Street), between Albert and Hobson Streets.

The private works in progress consist of the cutting away, to the grade of Hobson Street, of the high-level block – opposite the old city power station, extending southward from the junction of Moore Street with Hobson Street, and just about where, a few years ago, stood a "Wonderland" that was the delight of Young Auckland.

It is, however, known that owners of adjoining allotments also contemplate a corresponding levelling scheme, and that the City Council will shortly undertake the lowering of the grade of Lower Federal Street (formerly Chapel Street). The net result, within at most a few months, will be the cutting away of the surface portion of the whole rectangular block bounded by Hobson, Moore, Federal, and Swanson Streets, and the conversion of what has till lately been a residential quarter, comprising houses that are a relic of Early Auckland, into an area, of warehouses.

### *Features of the Early Days*

Smales' Point was the generic name by which this neighbourhood was known to the early inhabitants. It is understood to commemorate the Rev. Gideon Smales, one of the early missionaries of the Auckland provincial district.

---

7  City's Early Days, New Zealand Herald, Volume LXI, Issue 18672, 31 March 1924, Page 9 http://paperspast.natlib.govt.nz/cgi-bin/paperspast?a=d&d=NZH19240331.2.2.76

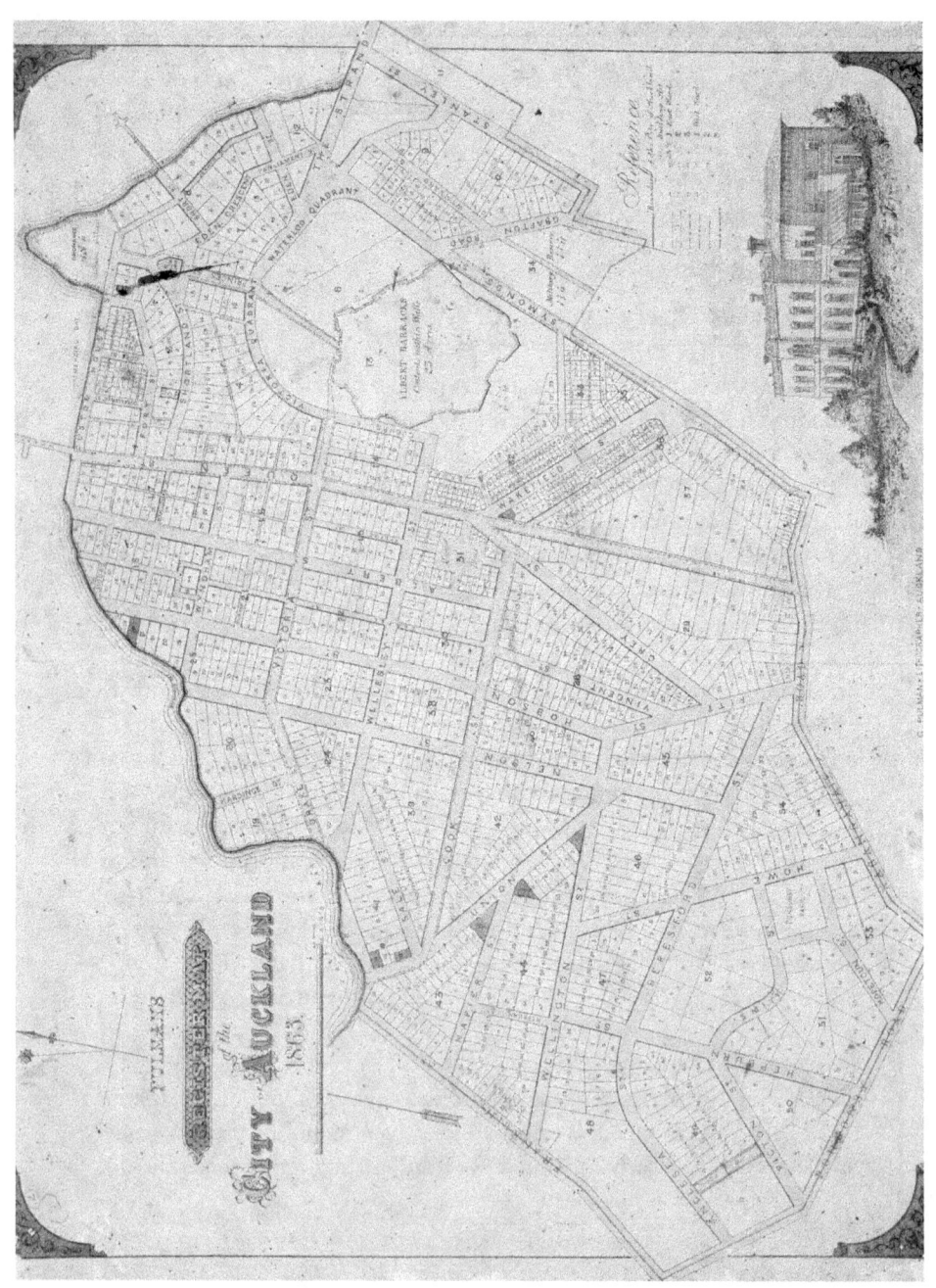

Smales' Point was the western bluff bounding Commercial Bay – the bay which originally came as far inland as the present site of the Victoria Arcade[8] – as Britomart Point overlooked its eastern side.

Between Queen Street and the foot of Nelson Street there was a high bluff, the outer end of which ran obliquely from a point in Queen Street opposite the end of Fort Street, across the present site of the Government Departmental Buildings, terminating in an almost square face, some 40 or 50 feet high, then turning inward at the foot of Hobson Street, and running somewhat sharply in to Brickfield Bay, at foot of Nelson Street, where, until their removal years ago to the further side of Freeman's Bay, stood the works of the Auckland Gas Company.

The bluff was capped by an almost level plateau, and just where the waterfront curved inward toward Brickfield Bay was a projection a little more prominent than the rest, the Smales' Point proper.

In years almost forgotten now except by the oldest inhabitants of the city, the waterfront portions of the bluff and plateau have been cut down, in the formation of the lower parts of Albert, Federal, and Hobson Streets, and the erection of the warehouses now standing on their main frontages. The present operations represent a further whittling away of the ancient surface, and encroachment upon the primeval hills.

## *On the Waterfront*

Across the harbour frontage of the bluff were the early shipbuilding yards of Auckland, those connected with the names of Duthie, Henderson and Spraggon, and Clare and Waymouth, for instance.

Here also, just to the west of Federal Street, was the 'bathing rock' from which Mr. H. Cooke, an early upholsterer of the city, dived into the Waitemata for the swim in which an attack by a shark cost him a serious injury – an incident well remembered by old settlers.

Not far distant, was the 'solid rock bath' – an excavation made by a local company, which was very popular with young and old. Close by was the strand on which the crews of the Maori war canoes, after their contentions in the Anniversary Day Regattas, were wont to set the beach trembling in the prancing of their hakas and war dances.

---

8   Demolished to make way for a BNZ centre in 1978, the Victoria Arcade was built in the 1880s and situated on the corner of Queen and Shortland Streets

Referring to the inlet of the harbour at the eastern side of the bluff, Mr. J. B Graham of Devonport remembers well when one of his brothers had a business place on the Western side of Queen Street, the back of which abutted upon a stream that ran in across what is now Customs Street West, and passed between the present site of the Government buildings and that of the Waitemata Hotel.

He remembers too, goods were brought by boat to the back of the warehouse; also when the tide water in the Ligar Canal backed up Queen Street to near the foot of Wyndham Street, and the boys of the city had a bathing pool in the canal above Shortland Street.

## *An Old Maori Village*

On one part of the bluff, between the present Star Hotel[9] and the foot of Hobson Street, there was, at the time of the arrival of the Auckland pioneers, a Maori kainga, known as Te Koranga; Here, according to tradition, about the 'teens' of the 19th century, lived the first European who settled on the shores of the Waitemata, named either Forsyth or Fordyce, who became a pakeha-Maori. The village is also said to have been visited by the Rev. Samuel Marsden, the pioneer Anglican missionary of the North, about 1820.

There also lived on the bluff for some time, just about the present position of the Star Hotel, Mr. C. O. Davis, notable in early history as 'a personage of influence' with the Maoris. There are citizens still alive who remember seeing, as visitors at Mr Davis's home, such celebrated chiefs as Te Wherowhero (Potatau) who became the first "Maori king," Rewi Maniapoto, Tamati Waka Nene[10]; Patuone, and, after his raiding days in the south had ended in capture, and deportation to the North, the blood-thirsty Te Rauparaha.

## *Original Residents Recalled*

The triangular block now standing between Moore Street and Customs Street is on what was originally the foreshore section of the north-west corner of the bluff. For a long period it belonged to a pioneer settler, Mr. Geo. Graham, the officer of the Royal Engineers who came to New Zealand as one of Governor Hobson's staff.

---

9   Situated in Albert Street and eventually demolished in the 1980s
10  One of the premier Ngapuhi chiefs who signed the Treaty at Waitangi

Mr J. B. Graham, now of Devonport, son of. Mr. Geo. Graham, at one time lived in a house erected on almost the edge of the bluff, about where one of Hutchinson Bros. warehouses now stands. This house, which was afterwards removed to Harding Street[11], and is still there, is about 60 years old.

Another ancient structure, at the corner of Moore Street and Federal Street, was the home of an early settler named Quigley, and is still standing; and Jock Finlay, a carpenter and builder of early celebrity, lived at the corner of Swanson Street and Federal Street, while Captain Pulham owned the residence at the opposite corner. Mr. Walter Combes and Mr. W. C. Daldy, both members of the mercantile firm of Combes and Daldy, and the Rev. Mr. Comrie, Presbyterian minister, also, lived for a long time in the same vicinity.

Adjoining the residence of Mr. J. B. Graham was another cottage, known from its prominent situation as "The Perch". This was in the early days occupied by Mr. W. F. Blake, and at a later stage by the Hon. John Sheehan, son of Mr. David Sheehan, an early licensed victualler, and himself a member of Parliament and Cabinet Minister in the Grey Administration.

Still standing on the block doomed to reconstruction are also several cottages dating from Early Auckland, in the front gardens of which flourish peach trees; and hedges in singular contrast with the busy commercial thoroughfares that hum within no great stone-throw from their fences.

*This then is the story of young Auckland, and through it the story of New Zealand itself, a land of eternal change, as we are about to discover...*

---

11  Now the site of the New Zealand Post Auckland Mail Centre

Chapter 2

## The Tsunami Menace

As we've just seen, Auckland urban renewal took place just for the sheer hell of it and in the name of commercial advancement. Further south, however, the forces of nature have played a big part in reshaping modern New Zealand.

This chapter could easily have been entitled "Why Buying Beachfront Is A Risk", and the answer to that question is not actually 'climate change'. Not only is New Zealand a highly geologically-active country with plenty of volcanic and seismic activity to generate tsunamis, the country's long coastline makes it a sitting duck for tidal waves emanating from Alaska or South America.

A lack of anything big since 1960 actually hitting New Zealand has bred complacency among people alive today, but a quick search of the record shows tsunami have hit New Zealand on numerous occasions, including three with waves of five metres or more since the Treaty of Waitangi.

This indicates the likelihood of something the size of the Japanese tsunami striking New Zealand beachfronts is relatively high.

The following news items record eyewitness reports of what today would be massive disasters resulting in wall to wall TV coverage. Of course, they happened in a time before broadcast news existed. These are the stories of New Zealanders caught up in large tsunamis. One of the largest to strike hit in 1868:[12]

---

12 The Press. Thursday, August 20, 1868. Press, Volume XIII, Issue 1715, 20 August 1868, Page 2
http://paperspast.natlib.govt.nz/cgi-bin/paperspast?a=d&d=CHP18680820.2.4

## Banks' Peninsula Tsunami

On Saturday morning last [15 August 1868] the inhabitants of the various bays of the Peninsula were aroused at an early hour by an extraordinary irruption of the sea, rolling with fearful force up the various bays and tidal rivers, carrying away bridges, fences and everything else obstructing its course. There was no apparent agitation of the ocean, the sea appeared perfectly calm, and the tide receded to an extraordinary distance.

The very rapid flow and ebb at very irregular intervals, varying from fifteen minutes to an hour, continued throughout the day, and were such as had never been witnessed here before. The highest rise occurred about the time of high water, and it was estimated at not less than twenty-five feet from the lowest to the highest level of the water during the time the phenomenon continued.

In Okain Bay at two miles distance from the sea [shore], the water rose over the top of the fences, completely inundating the lower portions of the locality. Very considerable damage has been done to both public and private property, and unfortunately many thousand feet of timber and posts and rails, &c., have been irrecoverably washed away.

In several cases the inhabitants had to leave their homes, and took refuge in the hills. In one or two cases the houses were destroyed or washed away. A very distinct shock of earthquake was felt during the forenoon on Monday.

## The Tidal Wave In Little Akaloa[13]

The tidal wave seems to have done considerable damage in Little Akaloa.

Mr H. A. Williams, who came up to Lyttelton on Tuesday last, states that he heard a noise to seaward as if it was blowing very hard, which commenced at two a.m., but took little notice of it till about half-past five, when the tide began gradually to rise much higher than usual, and at this time the water had risen over the rill of Mr Finlay's house, which is situated over 200 yards from ordinary high water mark.

The water then rushed in and out the creek at a terrific rate, gradually

---

13  Spelt 'Akaloa' in the original newspaper report, possibly reflecting a Ngai Tahu dialect similar to the pronunciation of 'Waihora' near Dunedin as 'Waihola'

increasing in height till about quarter to twelve, when it was at its highest. The water then receded and left the harbour dry halfway across. The ketch *Straggler*, belonging to Mr Pavitt, which had just been placed on the blocks for repairing, was repeatedly washed up and down the creek, having been carried over the corner of a paddock, where, if she had been left it would have been impossible to have launched her.

Mr McIntosh's house (a six or seven-roomed one), was lifted up bodily several inches, and considerable damage was done to the furniture.

Two bridges across the creek were washed away; one was carried up into a paddock, and the other was carried out to sea. A little craft called the *Gipsy* ran into Lavereaux bay and dropped anchor. No sooner was the anchor down than she was left high and dry.

The coast around Little Akaloa is strewn with timber of every description. Mr Samuel Graham, a resident in Little Akaloa, writes his father in Lyttelton to the effect that early in the morning he heard a rumbling noise, and ran out of the house to warn his brother-in-law next door, and the two families had barely time to escape from their houses. They were compelled to seek shelter with their more fortunate neighbours, from whom they experienced the utmost kindness and attention.

They did not return to their homes till Sunday morning. Mr Henry McIntosh has sustained damage to the extent of fully £100, in garden, fencing and timber.[14]

*In fact, the 25 foot (seven metre) tsunami that struck two miles inland on Banks Peninsula was part of a devastating series of waves that hit most of New Zealand that day. This report from the Chatham Islands:*

## Loss Of One Life[15]

DUNEDIN, AUGUST 27. The schooner *Rifleman* arrived at Port Chalmers this morning from the Chatham Islands, after a passage of six days, having left Waitangi on the morning of Friday, the 21st.

---

14   The Press. Thursday, August 20, 1868, Press, Volume XIII, Issue 1715, 20 August 1868, Page 2
http://paperspast.natlib.govt.nz/cgi-bin/paperspast?a=d&d=CHP18680820.2.4
15   Loss Of One Life, Wellington Independent, Volume XXIII, Issue 2729, 8 September 1868, Page 3
http://paperspast.natlib.govt.nz/cgi-bin/paperspast?a=d&d=WI18680908.2.7.1

She brings news of great disaster and loss to the inhabitants of the Chathams, who were suddenly awakened from their sleep by the water rushing into their dwellings, and were driven half-naked and trembling to the hills, while the receding waters carried away every relic of their property, and in one instance causing the loss of life. The following are the items as we received them.

Early on the morning of the 15th the Islands were visited with three immense earthquake waves, somewhat similar to those which visited the other islands of the colony on the same date, causing the almost total destruction of some of the settlements, and the loss of one life – a Maori.

At the settlement of Tupanga, which was situated on the northern side of the island, the phenomenon was felt with greatest force. The settlement was entirely destroyed, and not a vestige left to indicate where once stood the habitations of natives, the whole place being covered with sand and piles of seaweed.[16]

The inhabitants, who were principally Maoris, narrowly escaped with their lives. They were roused from their slumbers by the first wave, which came rushing into their houses. They immediately fled in alarm to the bush, or sought safety on higher ground but they had barely time to escape, before a second and larger wave came rolling after them, rapidly followed by a third, which completely destroyed and swept away the dwellings and everything they contained.

Captain Anderson's house, situated about four miles from Tupanga, was also swept away, the proprietor himself narrowly escaping with his wife and children. A Maori lost his life here while trying to save a boat – he was carried out to sea by the drawback, and drowned.

Further along the coast, facing south-westerly, Mr Hay, sheep farmer, lost his all. His house and other fixtures were carried to sea, leaving him without a shoe to his foot or a coat to cover his back.

At the settlement of Waitangi similar disasters occurred, and great loss was occasioned. Mr Beamish's accommodation house was wrenched from its piles, and a great quantity of Government stores and fencing were carried out to sea, together with some boats.

The beach presented a most disheartening spectacle after the phenomena

---

16  Other reports estimated the size of the tsunami when it struck the Chathams to have been 11 metres. See The Earthquake Wave. North Otago Times, Volume XI, Issue 342, 1 September 1868, Page 5

had passed away. There was household property of all descriptions strewing the sands, intermixed with bags of flour and other stores, the whole being festooned with seaweed. How the people escaped is considered miraculous.

On the eastern side of the island less damage was done, there being less to destroy. The only habitations destroyed were a few Maori huts. Some valuable boats belonging to the *Rifleman*, which was lying at Wangaroa at the time, fortunately escaped without accident, although in the same harbor[17] some huge spars were carried away, and deposited high and dry on a flat on the opposite side of the harbor.

*There is no indication in the Christchurch papers that the tidal wave had anything like a 25 ft (seven metre) impact in the city itself, on the northern side of Banks Peninsula, although Lyttelton Harbour was completely emptied by one of the surges. It is likely that the swampier parts of Christchurch had not yet been built on in any urbanised sense of the word, reducing the impact of the tsunami on locals. It would be a different matter today if a seven metre tidal wave thundered up the city beaches.*

*The source of the tsunami was a magnitude 9.0 quake at southern Peru (now known as Chile) a day earlier. New Zealand's vulnerability to a tsunami of that size is now obvious, and the speed of the surge rivalled that of a jet:*

## The Earthquake Wave[18]

The first wave reached New Zealand at 4 a.m. on the 15th August, having therefore travelled about 6,700 miles in 19 hours, or at the rate of 5.87 miles (10km) a minute. The three waves reached us at three-hour intervals, and must therefore each have been about 1,000 miles in breadth. The velocity at which waves travel over the ocean depends upon the depth of the water, and varies as the square root of the depth, so that the deeper the water the quicker the wave will travel.

---

17  In this book you will repeatedly find American spellings of words like harbour, rumour, colour and labour. These are the spellings used in New Zealand newspapers at the time. I have not corrected them to reflect modern usage.
18  The Earthquake Wave, Daily Southern Cross, Volume XXIV, Issue 350, 7 October 1868, Page 3 http://paperspast.natlib.govt.nz/cgi-bin/paperspast?a=d&d=DSC18681007.2.12

The wave raised by the earthquake at Lisbon[19] travelled to the Barbadoes at the rate of 7.8 miles a minute, while it went to London at very little more than two miles a minute. Professor Airey has shown that a fixed relation exists between the breadth of a wave, its velocity of progress, and the depth of the water on which it travels. The earthquake wave of December, 1854[20], was 217 miles in breadth, and travelled at the average rate of 6.1 miles per minute, from which Professor Rache concluded that the mean depth of the North Pacific was 2,365 fathoms, or 14,190 feet.

# Extraordinary Earthquake Wave In New Zealand[21]

On Saturday, Aug. 15, a most unusual phenomenon took place in this harbor, and also in other parts of the colony, as we learn by telegraphic despatches which we have received. We refer to the irregular tide which took place that day, and which created not only astonishment, but in some cases dread that a great disaster was about to happen.

On ordinary occasions, as is well known, the tide rises, under the influence of the moon, with the greatest regularity, to a height which can be previously ascertained with the utmost exactness. There are two kinds of waves – one the ordinary, ocean wave, occasioned by the wind, when the water does not move onward, and has only apparent lateral motion, in consequence of the rise and fall of the water in the same way as a field of corn, when the wind passes over it; the other the tidal wave, which ordinarily rises and falls twice a day with great regularity. That it does not always do so was shown on Saturday.

It is somewhat remarkable that the event was foretold during the whole of the week – a rumor was current in the town that there would be an unusual rise in the water on Saturday, attended with earthquakes. At every public-house bar the common expression was, "We're all going to be swamped on Saturday." Of course, generally, both spoken and heard in a half-incredulous manner but we have been unable to trace this rumor

---

19 Earthquake in Portugal, 1755
20 Earthquake in Japan, San Francisco hit by tsunami
21 Extraordinary Earthquake Wave In New Zealand, Wellington Independent, Volume XXIII, Issue 2729, 8 September 1868, Page 3
http://paperspast.natlib.govt.nz/cgi-bin/paperspast?a=d&d=WI18680908.2.5

to its source. We can only say that the prognostication proved correct.

On Saturday morning the water rose in an unusual manner, and consequently great excitement prevailed throughout the whole town. The first indication of the wave was about half-past eight o'clock in the morning, and from that hour up to noon, the tide kept bumping against the brickwork beside the watermen's gridiron sometimes rising above high water mark and then suddenly receding. Some people felt considerable alarm, for it was thought to be the precursor of something worse.

Those who are given to ill-boding were disappointed. The time for high water was three o'clock in the afternoon, so that, it would be dead low water at nine in the morning and the phenomenon was therefore more easily observed. There was a crowd of persons on the wharf all day. People who are very weatherwise prophesied that something was going to happen, and accordingly discovered in the result, the vindication of their opinion. The greatest observable difference in the tidal level was about eight feet.

At Te Aro the water almost came up to the public street, and floated a quantity of timber which lay a distance of twenty yards from the high water level. But a still more remarkable effect was caused at the mouth of the Ngahauranga river, where a bar of gravel has been thrown up to the height of two or three feet.

The reasons given for this extraordinary event are various, some say that it is the precursor of a great earthquake others that it has been occasioned by the recent earthquakes at St. Thomas. At all events, two slight shocks of earthquake wore felt here yesterday morning shortly after ten o'clock. It is supposed that the wave travelled westward, and some say that it had something to do with a solar eclipse which recently occurred in India. The following telegrams have been received from various ports:

Bluff. Tide higher last night than ever known. Between 8 and 9 this morning terrific rush of water. Tide very high. Large bodies of kelp washed in. Carried all the buoys up the harbor. 11 am Tide full, eighteen inches in twenty minutes.

Port Chalmers. Three buoys drifted. Large ships swung round twice in one tide.

Oamaru. Extraordinary change in sea level. Since daylight tide rising and falling about fifteen feet perpendicularly at intervals of fifteen minutes.

Lyttelton, 10 a.m. Heavy rush of water. It is also reported that the shipping has been much damaged. 10.30. Water up to flood level.

White's Bay, 11.30. Water up to Telegraph Office.

Nelson. There has been a heavy rush of water over Boulder Bank, water in harbor much troubled.
Picton. No disturbance.
Napier. Tide higher and lower in Iron Pot than ever known before.
Castle Point. No shocks. Tide higher last night than for ten years. 11.53. Tide up to high water mark

*Up until this time, New Zealanders had little experience of tsunami. No one knew, for example, that a massive comet had plummeted into the ocean south of Stewart Island in the mid 1400s, creating a 200 metre high mega-tsunami that inundated New Zealand dozens of miles inland on all coasts.*[22]

*Early historians noted already-disappearing Maori legends of a time when the lowlands were drowned by the sea:*[23]

"Ngatimamoe and Ngaitahu legends go back to Te Kahni Tipua, the period of the monster bird and ogre hand, a mythical race of giants who strode from mountain to mountain, and were succeeded by Te Rapuwai or Ngapahi, who left the shell heaps found all over the country, and in whose time the country at Invercargill was submerged, the great forests of Canterbury burned, and the moa was exterminated."

*With tsunami now entering the memory of modern Maori and European alike, people sought answers about this devastating phenomenon:*

## Dr. Hector On The Recent Earthquakes And Tidal Phenomena[24]

At the last meeting of the Wellington Philosophical Society, Dr Hector read the following paper, which, under existing circumstances, will be of great interest to our readers:

---

22  See The Great Divide by Ian Wishart, Howling At The Moon Publishing Ltd, 2012, p33
23  Hakopa Te Ata O Tu, Press, Volume XXXIX, Issue 5651, 29 October 1883, Page 3
http://paperspast.natlib.govt.nz/cgi-bin/paperspast?a=d&d=CHP18831029.2.23
24  Dr. Hector On The Recent Earthquakes And Tidal Phenomena.
Wellington Independent, Volume XXIII, Issue 2729, 8 September 1868, Page 3
http://paperspast.natlib.govt.nz/cgi-bin/paperspast?a=d&d=WI18680908.2.8

...Respecting the tidal disturbances, from careful consideration of the various accounts which have been received, it appears that they were experienced along the whole of the eastern coast of the islands, and also in Foveaux Straits and Cook's Straits, and that the irregularity of the usual flow and ebb of the tide was due to the influence of three distinct oceanic waves which reached the coast from eastward on the forenoon of Saturday, the 15th inst., at about the following periods: 1st between 3 to 4 a.m; 2nd between 7 to 8 a.m.; 3rd between 10 to 11 a.m. These waves were in each case followed by smaller waves, and the irregularities did not altogether cease for 48 hours after their first appearance.

The exact time at which the three great waves were observed, and also their distinguishing features, were modified at different points of observation by local peculiarities due to the outline of the land, the depth of the water, the exposure of the coast line to the direction in which the wave reached the shore, and lastly to the local time of tide. The intervals between the smaller oscillations appear to have been generally remarked at from fifteen to thirty minutes, and to have gradually declined in extent, and frequency until the next great wave supervened.

The earliest, notice of the wave which we have recorded beyond allusions to an extremely high tide the previous evening, was at Kaiapoi, where it was reported that at 3 a m. the tide had ebbed for two hours, a wave four feet in height rushed up the Waimakariri river, and swept the vessels which were lying at the wharf from their moorings. This was at a distance of four miles from the mouth of the river.

At Lyttelton and Pigeon Bay, the time reported was at least half an hour later, and for the other places no exact, time is reported for the occurrence of the first wave, while at several localities it appears to have escaped observation. From this time until 8 o'clock only lesser waves were remarked, but about that hour a great disturbance seems to have been observed at all the stations, being described at the Bluff as a terrific rush of water.

At Kaiapoi, sweeping up a line of breakers which would have been disastrous to the town had it not passed up the south branch and almost simultaneously at Nelson as having caused a reflux of the tide, at that time half-ebbed, so that it rose beyond the limits of high water mark, and flowed into the harbor over the Boulder Bank.

A third great rush of water appears to have been everywhere distinguished from the smaller oscillations which went on continuously, the time being variously stated from 10 to 12 o'clock, there being great irregularity in the hour reported. In this harbor, where I caused exact observations to be taken at frequent intervals, as might be expected from the wide expanse of water and the narrow entrance, these waves could not be so clearly distinguished as on more exposed parts of the coast, but there is a general agreement among all the observations taken at the different stations which leads to the above conclusions.

The altitude of each wave, as compared with its amplitude or breadth, has not been ascertained irrespective of the degree to which it was modified by the local form of the shore upon which it expended its energy, and this element is absolutely necessary for the purpose of determining the distance at which it originated.

Nevertheless, as compared with the ordinary effects of the tidal wave, we can form some conception of the gigantic force which must have influenced the ocean along the coast; when we find that the ebb and flow which these waves caused in most cases, appears to have exceeded the ordinary local rise and fall of the tide at the different localities. This leads me to expect that waves of such magnitude must have been observed at many points beyond this colony, such as the coast of Australia to the westward, and the Chatham Islands to the eastward; and that we shall receive information from these, and probably other localities, which will enable us to determine with tolerable exactness the focus from which they originated.

The following information appears to have escaped the notice of the journals in the colony; it is an extract from *Principles of Geology*, by Sir Chas. Lyell, 10th edition, 1868, vol. 2, p. 409. "Even in the present year (November 1807) a submarine volcano has burst out in the South Pacific, at a point 1200 geographical miles from New Zealand, and 1800 miles from Australia, between two of the most easterly islands of the Samoa or Navigator's Group, an archipelago where there had been no tradition of an eruption within the memory of man. The outburst was preceded by numerous shocks of earthquakes. Jets of mud and dense columns of volcanic sand and stones, rising 2000 feet, and the fearful crash of masses of rock hurled upwards and coming in collision with others which were falling, attested the great volume of ejected matter, which accumulated in the bed of the ocean, although there was no permanent protrusion of a new volcano above its level."

An earthquake shock which appears to have been felt throughout the colony a few minutes before 10 o'clock on Monday morning, the 17th inst, of a character very different from the local shocks to which we are accustomed in this place. From the appended record of telegraphic announcements, it appears to have occurred about three minutes earlier in the north-east at Napier than at Hokitika, on the West Coast of the Middle Island[25]. Napier is situated in Lat. 39d. 29m. S., long. 176d. 55m. E. Hokitika, in lat. 42d. 41m. S., long. 170d. 59m. E. This gives a horizontal distance of 402 miles but as we do not know whether the wave was travelling from the east or the north-east, it is impossible to infer its velocity.

*In the North Island, residents were equally anxious to know more about tsunami, and still could not get their heads around the incredible speed these waves travel at, much less the utter destruction they are capable of.*[26]

The destroying wave which mostly follows a violent shock of earthquake is caused – in my opinion – by the sudden upheaval of the shore, by which, in the first place, the sea is caused to recede from the, shore. On the land subsiding again; the sea instantly rushes back to its former level, and hence its terrific force.

The wonderful chain of mountains which begins at Cape Horn and ends at the Polar Sea, is studded with volcanoes throughout its whole length and they are the safety valves of that part of the world. When action ceases in one it often begins in another; sometimes a simultaneous eruption occurs in two mountains 300 miles apart and when action ceases in any part of the range, then people look out for the earthquake which is sure to happen after the safety valves have been shut up for some time.

The frightful results of these in the new world may be read in Humboldt's 'Cosmos' – cities swallowed up in a night, arid whole districts utterly desolated.

One of the most destructive was that of the year 1835, which destroyed the city of Conception.[27] When I visited the old ruins, many years ago,

---

25 The old name for the South Island
26 Tidal Waves, Wanganui Herald, Volume II, Issue 478, 12 December 1868, Page 2 http://paperspast.natlib.govt.nz/cgi-bin/paperspast?a=d&d=WH18681212.2.8
27 This shock measured 8.2. A subsequent 9.5 quake in the same general area in 1960 created a tidal wave of up to 25 metres in places which swept across the Pacific, drowning 61 in Hawaii and 199 in

a friend who had been present told me that though the whole town was laid in ruins, the shock only lasted a few seconds. The strongest buildings, as usual, suffered most. The cathedral, with walls four feet thick, was levelled with the ground.

Immediately after, a terrific wave, 25 feet high, rolled in, from seaward, over the doomed city and destroyed everything which the earthquake had shared; when it receded nothing but ruins remained, and all the inhabitants were left utterly destitute. Sixty villages were reported to have been destroyed, and the ships in the bay, which bad been riding at anchor, were left high and dry. The whole coast line was elevated about eight feet in one night.

The shock was felt over an area of 1000 miles, and two volcanoes, though 2700 miles apart, burst into action simultaneously. Strangers visiting the [Chilean] West Coast are all rather anxious than otherwise to feel a shock, and if they leave the country without having been so fortunate, they think they have "missed something", but the people of the country, who know too well from sad experience the terrible results which often follow, become more and more timid as they grow older. During an alarm all rush to the open street for safety, where most may be seen on their knees, and the air is rent with cries of "misericordia".

Earthquakes are most rude shocks to one's very strongest faith; for if there is one thing more than another which we believe utterly, it is the stability or solidity of this earth we live on. When one feels it for the first time violently heave and tremble under his very feet, and hears the long rumbling noise "in the hollow mine of earth" which usually accompanies the shock, the sudden uprooting of his old belief, the sense of a danger from which there is no escape, the consciousness of insecurity and of his own utter feebleness or nothingness, is so suddenly forced upon him, and in such a rough way, that it leaves an impression on the mind not easily forgotten.

*It took months to repair the tsunami damage on Banks Peninsula, and look how big the bridge was:* [28]

---

Japan. The wave struck New Zealand after only 12 hours and was around six metres in height. At Whitianga, the harbour emptied, exposing the wreck of the *HMS Buffalo* that sank in 1840. Sightseers rushed out across the drained seabed to get a first hand view of the old sailing ship, but were forced to flee for their lives as the sea surged back in to the bay, flooding central Whitianga township.

28   Latest Telegrams. Press, Volume XIV, Issue 1887, 3 May 1869, Page 2

Le Bon's Bay. – Our correspondent writes that the bridge across the river at Le Bon's Bay, which was washed away by the earthquake wave in August last, has been re-erected, and is now open for traffic.

The work of erection has been in progress during the last five months, and the bridge is the finest on the Peninsula. It is 126 feet long, and 12 feet in width, and contains about 15,000 feet of good sound totara and black pine timber. It has seven spans, and about 264 feet of approaches. The contractor, Mr D. Wright, of Le Bon's Bay, deserves credit for the excellent work which he has put into the bridge.

*There was no room for complacency on the New Zealand coastline, however, as this 1881 report reminds us:*

## An Earthquake Wave [29]

Wellington, June 28. A telegram received from Lyttelton states that the master of the steam tug *Titan*, which arrived from Pigeon Bay, reports experiencing an earthquake wave at the latter place at 11.40 this morning. It was ten feet high, and some injury was done to the steamers sponsons. The wave was not experienced at Lyttelton.

*Tsunamis and earthquakes, as even those in the 1860s had realised, go hand in hand. But no sooner had Christchurch and other cities finished licking their wounds from the big tsunamis, than Christchurch residents found out something their great-great-great grandkids had evidently forgotten: the garden city was prone to big earthquakes capable of bringing down buildings…*

---

http://paperspast.natlib.govt.nz/cgi-bin/paperspast?a=d&d=CHP18690503.2.14
29   An Earthquake Wave. Grey River Argus, Volume XXIV, Issue 4005, 30 June 1881, Page 2
http://paperspast.natlib.govt.nz/cgi-bin/paperspast?a=d&d=GRA18810630.2.11.9

Chapter 3

# Christchurch Hasn't Had Earthquakes: Yeah, Right

*Up until September 4, 2010, most people laughed at the idea of earthquakes in Christchurch. The most English of cities outside England itself, New Zealand's genteel southern settlement boasted hundreds of buildings constructed from brick or the sought-after nearby Oamaru stone. Some dated back almost to the birth of Christchurch itself.*

*When the 7.0 magnitude tremblor shook the city awake just after 4am on September 4, two things quickly rose to prominence: firstly, no one in the city was killed despite the large amount of falling masonry, and secondly, how no one had realised Christchurch was on a faultline.*

*Had the archived newspaper reports from two centuries ago been widely available at the time, light could have been shed on both of those discussion points. In regard to perceptions about Christchurch's vulnerability to earthquakes, there is ample evidence the modern complacency was the product of memory lapse – not only has the city experienced a number of damaging tremors since it was founded, it has also experienced big tidal waves as the previous chapter has shown.*

*Those waves struck in August 1868. Just a few months later, Christchurch experienced its biggest earthquake since its establishment just two decades earlier:*

## Earthquake, 1869[30]

A smart shock of earthquake, east to west, was felt in Christchurch at sixteen minutes past ten o'clock this morning. A smart shock was felt in Lyttelton about a quarter-past ten. It lasted 40 seconds. Mr Packard, at the railway station, thought the place was coming down.[31] He telegraphed to the Christchurch station, and was answered that the shock had been felt there.

*Seeking answers, Cantabrians turned to a vicar with knowledge of geology to explain what the city was experiencing:*

## Lecture, 1868[32]

A lecture on earthquakes was delivered in St. Paul's schoolroom, Papanui, by the Rev. L. Moore, on Thursday evening last. The room was densely crowded, and the remarks of the lecturer rendered easier of comprehension by a series of coloured diagrams, were listened to with the closest attention throughout.

The two principal causes operating to alter the surface of the earth – water and fire – were chiefly dwelt upon. The former was illustrated by the constant removal of matter to a lower level by rivers, and the latter by the unequal pressure exerted on the crust of the earth, whereby the surface was upheaved, causing subsidences, or finding vent through the craters of volcanoes.

From this the lecturer passed to a description of a submarine earthquake and earthquake wave, then touched upon the principal earthquakes and volcanoes recorded in history, and concluded by calling attention to St. Peter's statement that the world that now is, shall eventually be destroyed by fire, preparation for which the rev. lecturer solemnly urged on his audience.

---

30  Local and General, Star, Issue 234, 11 February 1869, Page 2
http://paperspast.natlib.govt.nz/cgi-bin/paperspast?a=d&d=TS18690211.2.10
31  In fact, the Christchurch Town Hall turned out to be so badly damaged it had to be demolished.
32  Local and General, Star, Issue 98, 5 September 1868, Page 2
http://paperspast.natlib.govt.nz/cgi-bin/paperspast?a=d&d=TS18680905.2.9

*One curiosity to emerge was date-related. The killer quake of 22 February 2011 appears to have had forerunners in the South Island:* [33]

Another Earthquake at Nelson. — *The Colonist* of the 21st instant says there was a rather smart shock of earthquake on Wednesday night, a few minutes before eleven o'clock. It lasted about ten seconds, and was very distinctly felt — the return movement being markedly perceptible.

It is a noteworthy fact, that in this month for several years, and almost at the same time of the month, earthquakes have occurred. On 21st February, 1864, on a Sunday evening, a smart shock took place; on 21st February, 1866, a similar but slighter movement was experienced, and on Wednesday last, 19th February, 1868, as sharp a shake occurred as that of 1864.

Hokitika, October 19, 9 a.m. At 12.12 this morning a very severe shock of an earthquake was felt here, which lasted about 50 seconds. There were no tidal, or ocean disturbances.

Very great alarm was felt in town. A large number of people rushed to the terraces, and remained there all night. The direction of the earthquake was from the north west to south east.

Nelson, Oct. 19, 12.5 p.m. A severe earthquake was felt in Nelson about fourteen minutes past midnight. It lasted about forty-five seconds, accompanied with loud subterranean rumblings.

The shock appeared partly vertical and partly horizontal. It has done some damage to chimneys. It appeared to come from the north-west to the south-east. It was felt up country keenly. Animals were alarmed.

Numerous smaller shocks succeeded, and continued throughout the night. They were of a varied character, some like a vertical stroke upwards. Tide is somewhat irregular. No such shock has been felt since 1855[34]. The chimney of the Government buildings was shaken and partly turned round. The day was close and sultry at times, with intervals of sudden cold. The night was close, and still masses of clouds towards N.E.; there were gusts of wind at intervals through the night.[35]

---

33  Local And General News, Wellington Independent, Volume XXII, Issue 2640, 25 February 1868, Page 3 http://paperspast.natlib.govt.nz/cgi-bin/paperspast?a=d&d=WI18680225.2.11
34  The Wellington quake
35  Latest Telegrams, Press, Volume XIII, Issue 1741, 20 October 1868, Page 2

*For the residents of Christchurch, however, earthquakes were to become a way of life in the 1800s – not big enough to kill, but large enough to remind Cantabrians they lived on shaky ground:*

## Another Earthquake In Christchurch, 1869[36]

Christchurch, Wednesday. A smart shock of earthquake was felt here this morning at five minutes to two o'clock. No further damage is reported.

*Then, there was Christchurch's first 'miracle' quake – the one that should have put the city on notice more than a century later. Just like the 4 September 2010 size 7.0 tremor that struck just after 4am and killed no one, so did this 1 September quake in 1888:*

## Great Destruction In Christchurch, 1888[37]

A very severe earthquake was felt at 4.10 this morning. Twenty-six feet was broken off the top of the Cathedral spire, and a few chimneys were thrown down.

The party [adjoining] wall of a house in Madras Street was shaken down. So far as known, no person was hurt.

There was great destruction of glass and crockery ware, especially in shop windows.

The direction was apparently northeast and southwest. The duration is estimated at fully a minute. Nothing so severe has been felt since a shock of 1869.

The earthquake caused great commotion here. People left their houses in numbers, but returned when they found the shaking had ceased.

A considerable crowd collected around the Cathedral, stones from the spire of which were scattered over the pavement for several yards. One piece narrowly missed a man named Ross, who was passing in the road-way at the time.

Some slates were knocked off the roof by the debris, but the building

---

36 Another Earthquake In Christchurch, Grey River Argus, Volume VII, Issue 530, 10 June 1869, Page 2 http://paperspast.natlib.govt.nz/cgi-bin/paperspast?a=d&d=GRA18690610.2.9
37 Cathedral Spire Damaged, Auckland Star, Volume XIX, Issue 206, 1 September 1888, Page 5 http://paperspast.natlib.govt.nz/cgi-bin/paperspast?a=d&d=AS18880901.2.32.1

otherwise is uninjured. It has been decided, however, not to hold service there tomorrow.

A small portion of the stonework on the Durham Street Wesleyan Church has been displaced, arid the services tomorrow will be held in the theatre instead of the church.

A quantity of plaster is down in the Normal School.

The chimneys fell at the East Christchurch School and a few private houses, particularly in Victoria Street. Generally, however, the damage is less than was expected. In the suburbs a few chimneys have fallen or been cracked.

No injury to life or limb is reported.

*That's how the Auckland Star reported it on the afternoon of 1 September, relying entirely on crisp telegraph reports tapped using the laborious Morse Code. On the scene in Christchurch itself, journalists at the local Christchurch Star were able to provide significantly more detail as the day wore on:*[38]

The violent earthquake shock, which so rudely roused everyone from sleep at a few minutes past four this morning, may possibly not be the severest on record in this part of New Zealand, but it has certainly been by far the most destructive since the Canterbury Pilgrims landed.

In the first place, what everyone feared would happen some day has actually happened, the spire of the Cathedral has come to grief. Its tapering, graceful outline, a landmark for every dweller on the plains within thirty miles, and a beacon for the mariner crossing Pegasus Bay, no longer cuts the sky.

Twenty-six feet of the cross and upper spire have given way, and the melancholy appearance of the wreck strikes every eye. Hanging by the iron bands built into the stonework, the cross and parts of the finial still remain aloft, the cynosure of all eyes in the crowd which constantly gathers and melts away in the square below. Fortunately, the rest of the building has suffered no serious damage. Even the lower part of the spire, as far as is known at present, is perfectly sound. The blocks of stone fell mostly towards Cathedral square, and spared the building, though bright white

---

38  A Severe Earthquake, Star, Issue 6332, 1 September 1888, Page 3
http://paperspast.natlib.govt.nz/cgi-bin/paperspast?a=d&d=TS18880901.2.16

spots on the grey masonry of the tower and ornaments show plainly where they struck in their descent, in some cases breaking off large splinters in their course.

One hole has been made in the high roof of the nave, but it is not large – the more noticeable damage occurring in the lower roof, which is broken through in several places. The falling stone, it is curious to note, struck clear of the memorial font to Captain Stanley, coming to the ground on either side of it, and spoiling nothing but a single arm of one of the tall gas-standards.

At the time of the shock a man named Ross, employed by Mr Brightling, was walking along the middle of the road through Cathedral square in front of the Cathedral. He states that the spire began to sway and the bells to ring almost with the commencement of the earthquake, and when the shock reached its climax, the upper part of the structure seemed to collapse, and came crashing to the ground.

One of the pieces of stone fell very near to Ross. Most of the stone struck the footpath, south-west of the tower, between the fence and the drinking fountain, about eight feet from the fence, and about on the spot where the small piece of stone which was detached from the spire by the earthquake of 1881, fell.

The mass of stone which came down this morning seems to have exploded like a bombshell, for fragments, some half as large as a man's body were strewn all over the footpath, and even on the road. The asphalt was smashed to pieces, for an irregularly shaped patch of nearly a yard in extent. A considerable portion of the debris fell into the Cathedral yard on the northern side of the tower.

A young man, whose name could not be ascertained, was also an eye-witness of the disaster to the steeple. He was on the footpath near the Godley Statue, and bolted, under the impression that the entire tower was coming down. Finding it did not fall, he returned, and was soon joined by others, anxious, like himself, to see the extent of the damage.

In a few minutes a crowd of considerable size was collected around the building. Many persons picked up the smaller pieces of the stone which were scattered about, to preserve as mementoes of the event. All devoted themselves 'to examining the tower' as well as they could in the dim light, and many expressed the opinion that it was considerably out of the perpendicular. When, however, the morning began to dawn, it was/

seen that the graceful shaft which has long been the architectural pride-of Christchurch was, although truncated, erect.

Mr Anderson, the steeplekeeper, went to the cathedral with the utmost promptness, and was inside it about ten minutes after the shock. He lighted the gas and found that there was only one place of leakage from one of the standards near the font. One of the branches of this had been broken off by a large splinter of wood, detached from a roof beam by the concussion of a blow on the roof by some of the falling masonry.

Having stopped the leak, he proceeded to make an examination of the building. He has had some experience of South America, par excellence the land of earthquakes, and knew what to look for. That was dust at the bottom of the walls inside. It seems that when a wall is injured by an earthquake, the shock dislodges certain particles of mortar, &c, which form tiny heaps and ridges on the ground.

Mr. Anderson's examination was satisfactory. Dust there was none. The walls were uninjured. Together with Mr A. Merton, and another gentleman, Mr Watkins, who joined him, he pursued his investigations.

He ascended the spire, to find that nothing was injured below the break. The cross, which, was hanging against the side of the steeple, he secured as well as he could with a rope. The four largest bells of the peal which had "been rung up," were "rung down" by the earthquake, and it was those which caused the clamorous peal which added so much to the startling effect of the shock.

During the morning the debris was cleared away, from around the base of the tower, and arrangements were made for lowering the cross from its insecure position. Barriers were erected across the footpath to prevent people approaching too near, and a constable placed as a sentry over them. The gates of the grounds were also fastened to prevent the public from intruding on what might be dangerous ground. It will be necessary to remove about six feet of the remaining stonework of the spire, as it has become loosened.

## *Comparisons*

We have said that the shock this morning was possibly not the severest that has been experienced here in Christchurch. A comparison of notes with people who remember the very alarming shake which occurred early on the morning of June 5, 1869, leads us to that conclusion.

One of the most vivid memories remaining in the minds of those who remember that phenomenon is the hideous fear that was exhibited by animals. The unearthly noise caused by the barking of dogs, the lowing of cattle, and expressions of fear on the part of other dumb creatures, can never be forgotten by one who heard it.

Nor is it easy to forget the waving of trees, the uncanny wave-like motion of the hedges, or the twisted and fractured chimneys that were to be seen in many quarters of the town. Still, the characteristic feature of the Cathedral City had not then been reared, and the damage done on this occasion, therefore, at once assumes a magnitude beyond that of former days.

*As with all earthquakes, and particularly in the days before telephones and radio allowed instant damage reports, it took time for the full extent of the damage to Christchurch and surrounding towns to become clear.*

*Christchurch by 1888 had thousands of residents, but nothing like the 300,000 or so who were impacted by the 21st century quakes. Nonetheless, some of the 1888 stories probably sound familiar to Cantabrians today:*

## Details Of The Damage Done, 1888[39]

12.20 p.m. The Normal School has suffered considerably. Two of its chimneys are thrown down, and all are more or less damaged. The South Wing of the building is also injured, and the ceilings of the upstairs class-rooms are split.

The shock was felt with great intensity at Amberley, north of Christchurch, and also at Lyttelton. At neither place was much damage done.

On the high bluffs on the Sumner-road, near Lyttelton, blocks of rock, ten tons in weight, gave way and went into the harbour with a great crash, carrying fences and other obstructions before them.

The steamer *Rotorua*, which arrived in Lyttelton this morning, felt the shock when off Kaikoura. Morton's block, a great pile of new buildings opposite the Bank of New Zealand, has sustained a considerable rifting.

The Young Men's Christian Association Building, in Cathedral Square,

---

39  Details Of The Damage Done, Evening Post, Volume XXXVI, Issue 54, 1 September 1888, Page 2 http://paperspast.natlib.govt.nz/cgi-bin/paperspast?a=d&d=EP18880901.2.38

shows evidence of having been considerably affected by the shock. The plaster is cracked in several places, especially in the corners of the stairwell. In the reading-room one side of the large square framed gasalier has fallen, and consequently is much damaged.

A rather narrow escape happened at the cottage of Mr. John Young, at Moa Place, off Madras Street North. His cottage adjoins the parapet wall attached to the house next door. At the time this wall was built, Mr. Young protested against it on the ground that it was not safe. However, the work was allowed by the Works Committee of the City Council.

About two feet of brickwork was knocked off the top of the wall last night by the earthquake, and stove in the roof of and completely wrecked a little room in Mr. Young's cottage. Some of the occupants [two young children] of the house [next door] were sleeping just on the other side of the wall at the time, so that if the debris had fallen only two feet, or perhaps even one foot further, a serious accident, if not loss-of-life, would most likely have ensued.

The shock was felt all over the Canterbury district, but was severest in Christchurch and the districts lying to the north of it. Another shock was felt in Christchurch at a few minutes to 11 this morning. 2.30 p.m.

## Alarming Earthquakes, 1888[40]

Large portions of Canterbury, Nelson, and the West Coast have just experienced the severest shock of earthquake or, more correctly, succession of shocks that have occurred in these districts since the commencement of the settlement of the Colony.

It seems that for three weeks previous strange rumbling noises had been heard by those residents of the Hanmer Plains, but these being attributed to wind or some similar cause no particular notice was taken of them. On Thursday evening the sounds were followed by others more alarming, resembling the report of single pieces of musketry fired in rapid succession. These were succeeded by shocks of earthquake about 10 o'clock in the evening. The noise continued to increase till Saturday morning when it was deafening, and shortly after 4 o'clock occurred the most violent

---

40  Alarming Earthquakes, Clutha Leader, Volume XV, Issue 738, 7 September 1888, Page 6
http://paperspast.natlib.govt.nz/cgi-bin/paperspast?a=d&cl=search&d=CL18880907.2.33

shock of earthquake which did a larger amount of damage.

A telegram received in Christchurch on Monday morning from Culverden, 25 miles south of Hanmer Plain reports that Glynroye Station buildings are completely wrecked, and that the men are living under canvas. Leslie Hills house is wrecked. Montrose escaped with only one or two chimneys smashed. Jollie Pass Hotel and Lahmet's, at Jack Pass, are intact and sustained no damage.

Atkinson's, Woodbank, a brick house, has collapsed, and Mr Atkinson and his family have have arrived safely at Culverden. Hopefield homestead is wrecked. The manager, wife and family have arrived at Culverden. The Ferry Hotel at Upper Waiau is damaged. The new Upper Waiau bridge is safe, but there are large landslips in the Hanmer cutting. Traffic, however, is not stopped.

There is great perturbation of the hot springs, but no damage is done to the buildings, etc., the chimneys were thrown down, and damage was done to the roof of the kitchen and conservatory. The chimneys of the overseer's cottage and men's huts were smashed. There has been considerable damage done in the Lower Amuri Ferry. The hotel close by the bridge is considerably dilapidated, but Mr Holmes (the proprietor) has not found it necessary to leave, and is setting about repairs.

At Leslie Hills, on the north side of the river, a large stone dwelling-house, built about 10 years ago, the property of Messrs A. and D. Rutherford, is a complete wreck. A recent addition in wood is considerably shaken, all the plastered walls having come down.

Up the Waiau Gorge, towards Glynroye and Hopefield, there are fissures from 6in to 12in wide. These small fissures soon closed up on account of the soil rolling into them through the constant shaking which has taken place. At the Hanmer Springs proper there has been no damage. The buildings there were uninjured. The only indication of an upheaval of the earth was the spilling of the water out of one of the natural basins.

While so little of the shock was felt there, houses 20 miles away were shattered to atoms, stone buildings have completely collapsed, and some wooden ones have been shifted many inches on their foundations. An illustration of the force of the shock is found in its effects on Mr Low's house. At his office at St. Helens there is an iron safe weighing 3cwt and standing about 3ft high. It stood against the wall, and during the occurrence it was thrown flat down on the floor to the north or north-west.

Mr Low's private house is of two storeys, and it suffered damage to the extent of about £150. A wardrobe in his daughter's bedroom was thrown down to the northward, and at the northern end of the house about 6ft of the centre of the wall was driven clean out. One chimney fell through the bedroom into the dining-room and kitchen, carrying the rafters along with it. Another fell north-east into the conservatory, and a third (the one in the schoolroom and bedroom above) fell northward. The washstands and dressing tables were thrown about in confusion, and during the time this was happening Miss Low's bed, in which she was lying, was lifted bodily towards the fireplace. When the dust cleared away a little she was able to see the stars shining through the hole made by the centre of the wall disappearing.

The Leslie Hills Station was shaken in and out in a most peculiar way. Mr Atkinson's place was shifted clean off its concrete foundations, and the occupants left at the earliest opportunity. Mr Atkinson got into Culverden about 10 minutes past 2 on Saturday morning. There were two large landslips at the approach of the Upper Waiau Ferry. They consisted of some 50 to 100 tons of earth, but have been so far cleared as to permit of traffic being carried on without intermission, and the coach is running as usual.

Between 4.20 and 4.30 on Saturday afternoon the coach had arrived at the Upper Waiau Ferry Hotel, and everybody was talking about the earthquake, when they were startled by another tremendous shock. This was the one which had brought the slips down in the cutting. It was preceded by a rumbling noise like the roar of a cannon, a noise that was almost appalling.

The tarred chimney in the hotel was driven upwards by the force, and at one time fully six inches of the untarred portion could be seen above the roof, which also moved very considerably. The chimney bobbed up and down a great many times. Simultaneous with this the coach horses bolted, and before anyone could move – all being intently engaged watching the dancing chimney – the animals had turned round and were dashing up the hill.

Mrs Holmes, the proprietress of the hotel, and others rushed out and witnessed what fortunately turned out to be only a trivial accident. During the progress of the coach party to the Ferry Hotel they heard loud boomings, and each was succeeded by a quiver of the earth. So accurate were these indications that immediately the noise was heard the driver would remark "Here's another," and the words would scarcely be out of his mouth before the vibrations were felt.

With all the damage to houses and buildings there is only one case of injury reported, the unfortunate man being one of those employed by Mr Atkinson, who has suffered as much, if not more, than anyone.

The earthquake was felt very severely in the Waiau and district. Four chimneys are down at Highfield, and about a dozen others in the township are damaged. A monument is overturned in the Waiau cemetery. Over 100 distinct shocks were felt since 4 a.m. on Saturday, and they continued on Sunday, but at longer intervals. At Hanmer Plains the shocks were accompanied by a heavy report. The shock at Jack's Pass Accommodation House on Saturday morning was most severe, and during the whole of Saturday the earth never seemed still, shock following shock in quick succession. Some rents in the earth have taken places on the Hanmer Plains and Upper Waiau, and gas is bubbling up in a number of places.

*It's not clear precisely where this September 1, 1888 quake was centred but one thing is certain – it was big enough to smash buildings in Christchurch and topple the Cathedral spire. Despite that, the passage of 132 years meant no one in Christchurch had living memory of the event and complacency had set in: "Christchurch doesn't get earthquakes".*

*Sadly, as we now know, it does.*

*As the aftershocks continued to roll in over weeks and months, toppling more chimneys and damaging more buildings, the media reported a now familiar Christchurch refrain: "The Hanmer Plains correspondent practically asks, 'Where is it going to stop at?'"* [41]

*At least one scientist called on the city to be better prepared next time by purchasing some seismic equipment.*

## Australian Papers: Wellington Destroyed, 1888 [42]

Some little damage is reported from the country districts, but none of great

---

41 Another Severe Earthquake, Auckland Star, Volume XIX, Issue 231, 1 October 1888, Page 8 http://paperspast.natlib.govt.nz/cgi-bin/paperspast?a=d&d=AS18881001.2.60
42 Severe Earthquake, Akaroa Mail and Banks Peninsula Advertiser, Volume XVI, Issue 1266, 4 September 1888, Page 2

importance, and though it was reported in Melbourne that Wellington was ruined, it appears that the shock was a light one causing no injury of any importance out of Canterbury.

Professor Hutton recommends instruments should be procured to record necessary data in connection with earthquakes. It appears those are inexpensive and automatic and can be understood easily by any reasonable person. This same gentleman thinks the Oamaru stone a mistake in the Cathedral spire as it is so porous it falls with its own weight. Brick chimneys stood in Oamaru when chimneys of this stone fail continually.

*Among those caught in the quake's turmoil, New Zealand's future prime minister Richard 'King Dick' Seddon:*[43]

News has reached here that the Christchurch coach had only gone two miles from the Bealey when a heavy slip was met. This was cleared away but others were encountered at the Otira. The whole road had slipped away leaving barely four foot of passage. It will take a week to clear a passage out of the side of the hill. The passengers, including Mr R. J. Seddon, procured horses at the accommodation house and came on to Kumara. Here they felt the eleven o'clock shock of yesterday while resting.

*In their official report to council on building damage, city engineers noted something their more modern counterparts had failed to pick up – building on the reclaimed swamp land had resulted in more damage:*[44]

"We consider that all brick buildings built on peat soil similar to this one are more likely to be damaged than those in other parts of the town."

*In Wellington, the afternoon paper editorialised on that morning's massive Christchurch quake, noting, like mayor Bob Parker did in 2010, that it was a miracle no one had been hurt:*

---

43  The Earthquake, Timaru Herald, Volume XLVIII, Issue 4327, 3 September 1888, Page 3
http://paperspast.natlib.govt.nz/cgi-bin/paperspast?a=d&d=THD18880903.2.22
44  Official Report On Public Buildings, Star, Issue 6333, 3 September 1888, Page 3
http://paperspast.natlib.govt.nz/cgi-bin/paperspast?a=d&d=TS18880903.2.25

## Christchurch Quake Miracle, 1888[45]

The upper portion of the Christchurch spire was deficient in elasticity, as compared with the base, and it seems, in consequence, to have snapped off under the shock.

It is most providential that no loss of life attended the unfortunate occurrence. Had the earthquake occurred during business hours, or on a Sunday during the hours of Divine worship, the consequences would have been much more deplorable. Cathedral-square is the busiest spot in Christchurch, the centre of the tramway system, the place from which busses start, and the site of a cab-stand. Had the spire fallen in the day time great loss of life must have occurred.

The last serious earthquake experienced in the Southern city was in 1868, when the Town Hall was so injured as to necessitate its being pulled down, and a stone church – a Wesleyan one, we think – also suffered some damage.

*Christchurch, obviously, had some shaky beginnings as a city, even if modern New Zealanders had forgotten that. Interestingly, though Christchurch's vulnerability to earthquakes continued to be demonstrated over the years, along with heightened awareness of the risk and the need for stronger buildings, as these next few items show:*

## Cathedral Damaged Again By Quake, 1894[46]

The Cathedral spire was injured by the recent earthquake. The damage, which is not serious and can easily be remedied, consists of a crack in the part thrown down by the heavy earthquake a few years ago, and since restored in firebrick.

---

45   Evening Post. Saturday, September 1, 1888. The Earthquake. Evening Post, Volume XXXVI, Issue 54, 1 September 1888, Page 2
http://paperspast.natlib.govt.nz/cgi-bin/paperspast?a=d&d=EP18880901.2.11
46   The Recent Earthquake At Christchurch, New Zealand Herald, Volume XXXI, Issue 9691, 11 December 1894, Page 5
http://paperspast.natlib.govt.nz/cgi-bin/paperspast?a=d&d=NZH18941211.2.29

*In 1929, Christchurch was hit with a tremor big enough to again raise concerns about the Cathedral once authorities began looking more closely for hidden damage:*

## Theatre Performance Rocks, 1929[47]

In Christchurch the damage done by the earthquake is very slight. From old chimneys bricks were dislodged and crockery was shaken from shelves, but instances of such minor damage are very few. The shock in the city was of only a few seconds' duration. There was a sensation in the Theatre Royal, where there was a crowded house. Fortunately the shock occurred during the interval, when the lights were up. In the gallery several women screamed, but those people who seemed inclined to rush for the doors were quietened by stern shouts of "sit down." There was no panic.

## Old Building Suffers, 1929[48]

An examination this morning disclosed the fact that the old Provincial Council Chambers, recently presented to Canterbury, had suffered severe damage as the result of the earthquake. The keystone of the north gable has broken, and has dropped half an inch. The north wall is in danger of falling.

## Damaged By Quake, 1929[49]

The Cathedral Chapter this afternoon was to receive a report from Mr. Hay, who was deputed by P. Graham and Sons, contractors, to examine the Cathedral for any traces of earthquake damage. Mr. Hay was not prepared to make a statement till he saw the chapter. There seems no likelihood that there is anything seriously the matter with the building,

---

47   Alarm In Christchurch, Auckland Star, Volume LX, Issue 59, 11 March 1929, Page 8
http://paperspast.natlib.govt.nz/cgi-bin/paperspast?a=d&d=AS19290311.2.84.3
48   Old Building Suffers, Evening Post, Volume CVII, Issue 57, 11 March 1929, Page 10
http://paperspast.natlib.govt.nz/cgi-bin/paperspast?a=d&d=EP19290311.2.75.13
49   Damaged By 'Quake, Auckland Star, Volume LX, Issue 62, 14 March 1929, Page 10
http://paperspast.natlib.govt.nz/cgi-bin/paperspast?a=d&d=AS19290314.2.98

which, according to Canon J. De B. Galwey, secretary to the chapter, should last another century or so without danger.

## And Yet Another 1929 Quake[50]

Green and Halm, Photo. Although there was no great damage in Christchurch as a result of Monday's earthquake, some minor losses were experienced. The photograph shows the roof and side of a house in Bealey Avenue, where one chimney fell, smashing the tiles, while a second chimney is seen to be in a precarious position.

*The second 1929 rumble also cracked open Christchurch City water reservoirs.[51] The point of all this is to show that within living memory – 81 years before the 2010 shock – Christchurch had again been damaged by earthquakes.*

*When Napier got slammed with its massive earthquake in 1931, it sent shivers down the spines of already shaky Cantabrians who'd lived through sixty years of damaging quakes by that time:*

---

50   Green and Halm, Photo. Evening Post, Volume CVII, Issue 142, 20 June 1929, Page 14
http://paperspast.natlib.govt.nz/cgi-bin/paperspast?a=d&d=EP19290620.2.107.2
51   Cracks In Reservoirs, Auckland Star, Volume LX, Issue 163, 12 July 1929, Page 10
http://paperspast.natlib.govt.nz/cgi-bin/paperspast?a=d&d=AS19290712.2.144

## Safety Of Buildings In Christchurch, 1931[52]

"There are many buildings in Christchurch which would suffer the same fate as those in Napier if subjected to a violent earthquake," was the statement contained in a report to the Canterbury Master Builders' Association in urging the inspection of public and semi-public buildings with a view to having them made as safe as possible against earthquake shocks.

The report further suggested that private owners of buildings should also give attention to the matter, as much could be done to reduce the risk of damage without excessive expense.

The general committee commended the instructions given by the Minister of Education in the circular letter to the authorities controlling school buildings, requesting an inspection of all brick schools. The committee was of opinion that this inspection might be carried out further, and applied to hospitals, churches, halls, banks and similar public and semi-public buildings.

*Christchurch scientists had become so savvy about earthquakes that one managed to predict a quake in advance, almost to within the hour!*

## The Earthquake, 1923[53]
*A Canterbury Prediction Timed To An Hour.*
*(By Telegraph. – Press Association.)*

CHRISTCHURCH, FRIDAY. An earthquake was recorded at Christchurch at 3.28 a.m. to-day, but the shock was only slight. No damage is reported. The earthquake was not altogether unexpected, as the Government meteorologist in Christchurch, Mr. F. H. Skey, states that calculations based on previous earthquakes showed that the shock would probably occur at midnight, on April 12, which was last night.

*All of which makes it hard to contrast the "we never get earthquakes" belief of the early 21st century, with the reality that older residents of Christchurch had*

---

52  Safety Of Buildings, Auckland Star, Volume LXII, Issue 61, 13 March 1931, Page 5
http://paperspast.natlib.govt.nz/cgi-bin/paperspast?a=d&d=AS19310313.2.39
53  The Earthquake, Auckland Star, Volume LIV, Issue 89, 14 April 1923, Page 11
http://paperspast.natlib.govt.nz/cgi-bin/paperspast?a=d&d=AS19230414.2.108

*lived with the gut-wrenching panic Cantabrians now 'know and love' – as recently as the late 1930s:*

## Unnecessary Alarm, 1937[54]

Causing apprehension out of all proportion to their magnitude, three small earthquake shocks rocked Christchurch citizens out of their sleep early this morning.

The tremors were small ones and were felt so distinctly only because of the nearness of the earthquake centre. That was situated at sea off Akaroa Harbour, 40 miles away from the Christchurch magnetic observatory.

*So what do we now know that we did not in 2010? In short, that Christchurch is built on a reclaimed swamp, which is why water bubbles up during earthquakes. That the city and its surrounding towns have been hit by both tsunami and earthquakes numerous times since European settlement, and that as far back as 1931 engineers were warning that old brick and Oamaru stone buildings in Christchurch were susceptible to crumbling in an earthquake.*

*We know that the Cathedral was damaged in 1881, 1888 and 1894 by earthquakes, and had a narrow escape in 1929.*

*We know that ten tonne boulders were in the habit of falling from the cliffs above Lyttelton during earthquakes, which raises the question of why town planners had not noted this when approving house and school construction adjacent to and above those cliffs.*

*They say those who forget the lessons of history are bound to repeat them.*

*Upheavals in Christchurch, however, were not the only thing capturing news headlines a hundred years ago, as we're about to find out.*

---

54  Unnecessary Alarm, Evening Post, Volume CXXIII, Issue 96, 24 April 1937, Page 11
http://paperspast.natlib.govt.nz/cgi-bin/paperspast?a=d&d=EP19370424.2.140

Chapter 4

# Life In New Zealand – Part 1

*One of the things you quickly discover, perusing the old newspapers, is how small the world was even then, perhaps more so than now.*

*The United States, Australia and New Zealand were all still young enough to share and maintain ties to Mother England. Events in New Zealand made the news in the USA, Australia and UK, and vice-versa, and there was a considerable movement of people between those countries.*

*In a book like this there are big and gripping stories, but also the minutiae of a daily life long ago sent to the graveyard of history. The small tales are just as fascinating as the larger ones, in terms of what they tell us about life back then:*

## The Inspector Of Nuisances, 1868[55]

The report of the Inspector of Nuisances was read. It states that he has been chiefly occupied during the past week in collecting the scavenging accounts for the June quarter and preparing for the next quarter's collection.

Notices are being served on persons whose gorse hedges overhang the footpaths.

The Inspector was instructed to use greater promptitude in collecting accounts.

---

55  Latest Telegrams, Press, Volume XIII, Issue 1741, 20 October 1868, Page 2
http://paperspast.natlib.govt.nz/cgi-bin/paperspast?a=d&d=CHP18681020.2.19

## The 1860s Version Of 'The G.C.' 1868[56]

Lecture. To-morrow evening an interesting lecture will be delivered in the Athenaum, by the Rev. J. Buller. The subject chosen is "My trip to Sydney and Melbourne, and the Session of the Wesleyan Conference. What I saw, heard, and thought." The admittance to the hall is 1s 6d, and the proceeds of the lecture will be devoted to the relief of a church fund.

## How To Survive On Seawater, 1871[57]

It ought not to be forgotten by anyone liable to shipwreck that thirst is quenched by soaking the clothing in salt water twice a day, or even oftener, and allowing them to dry upon the person. A noble and humane old sea captain, Kennedy, published this statement more than a hundred years ago yet it is very doubtful if two persons out of any company, taken promiscuously, are aware of so important a practical fact, to which the generous captain attributed the preservation of his own life and of six other persons.

If sea-water is drunk, the salty portions of it are absorbed into the blood and fire it with a new and more raging thirst, and a fierce delirium soon sets in. It would seem that the [wet clothes] system imbibes the water, but excludes all the other constituents. It is known that wading in common water quenches thirst with great rapidity. Persons while working in water seldom become thirsty.

And it is further interesting to know that however soaking wet the garments may become from rain, or otherwise, it is impossible for the person to take cold if the precaution is taken to keep off the feeling of chilliness until the clothing is perfectly dried or facility is afforded for a change but in changing the garments after a wetting, it is always safest and best, as an additional safeguard against taking cold, to drink a cup or two of some hot beverage before beginning to undress.

---

56  Local And General News, Wellington Independent, Volume XXII, Issue 2640, 25 February 1868, Page 3
http://paperspast.natlib.govt.nz/cgi-bin/paperspast?a=d&d=WI18680225.2.11
57  The Daily Southern Cross, Volume XXVII, Issue 4389, 8 September 1871, Page 2
http://paperspast.natlib.govt.nz/cgi-bin/paperspast?a=d&d=DSC18710908.2.11

## News In Brief, 1881[58]

There is now being exhibited in Paris a child of remarkably small size. She is four years of age, and only 15 inches (38cm) in height. She appears only a little taller than an ordinary quart bottle.

At Carabacel, near Nice, the remains of a human skeleton have been found at a depth of 110 ft, in a virgin soil, mixed with land and sea shells and alluvial deposit. As burial is not to be thought of, it has been concluded that the skeleton has been washed down from higher ground, although its position is thirty yards from the bottom of a valley. A photo of the find, along with a few of the bones, have been sent to M. Quatrepages, who states the skeleton belongs to the Quarternary period, has been brought down with other drift to form a calcareous stratum, and so is clearly a fossil. It belonged to the Cro-Magnon race.

The following extraordinary Adelaide telegram appears in the 'Argus': "A remarkable occurrence is reported to have taken place at Bungaree, near Clare. Two workmen named Russell and Godfrey quarrelled and had a stand-up fight, Russell knocked Godfrey down, and some companions induced the latter to pretend that he was dead, which he did, He was then covered over with a tarpaulin, and the parties to the deception told Russell that the man he had been fighting with was dead. Godfrey fell asleep under the tarpaulin, and the others retired to their tents, Russell in the middle of the night lit a number of candles and placed them round the tarpaulin, after which he began praying for the soul of the dead man. The prayers finished, he rolled up his swag and cleared out. He has not since been heard of."

## This Thing They Call The Electric Light, 1878[59]

The [Auckland] Queen Street wharf on Saturday night was densely crowded to witness the exhibition of the electric-light, which, at the request of the Mayor, Captain Canevro had kindly consented to show.

---

58 News In Brief, Tuapeka Times, Volume XIV, Issue 757, 27 July 1881, Page 5
http://paperspast.natlib.govt.nz/cgi-bin/paperspast?a=d&d=TT18810727.2.31
59 Untitled, Thames Advertiser, Volume XI, Issue 2879, 12 March 1878, Page 2
http://paperspast.natlib.govt.nz/cgi-bin/paperspast?a=d&cl=search&d=THA18780312.2.7

Punctually at eight o'clock, Government House and the shore at Official Bay was lit up by the bright white light, and then the lamp was turned round, sweeping in its course the whole foreshore and shipping.

Within the illuminated area a newspaper might be easily read a mile distant from the ship; and every object on the foreshore, the white cliffs, buildings, shipping, to the smallest rope in the rigging of a vessel became plainly distinguishable.

The light, as it streams from the lantern, is funnel-shaped – similar in fact to that thrown from a magic lantern – looking brighter perhaps on account of the surrounding darkness. The cliffs at Shelly Beach were distinctly lighted up, and when the lantern was turned on the North, the illumination could be observed at the Lake, a distance of four or five miles.

No boat could approach a ship using this light without being discovered, and whether for the detection of the movements of an enemy on sea or on shore, or for the purpose of tracing a dangerous coast line at night, the value of the light for naval purposes was strikingly demonstrated. – *Auckland Star*

## From The Wires: Cavewoman Found In Italy, 1878[60]

A sad affair has lately been brought to light in Italy. In a small cave near Odina a woman was found who had been imprisoned there thirty-three years.

In 1844 she became attached to an Austrian officer, but her father, a violent hater of the Austrians, who at that time were in possession of that part of Italy where he resided, refused his consent to a marriage.

The girl stated that she would then marry without his permission.

He dissimulated his anger, and during a walk, in which he accompanied her, he induced her to descend into the cave with him by means of a rope ladder, with a view of examining it. He was the first to ascend to the surface, and, withdrawing the ladder, left her.

She was regularly supplied with food and clothing. Even when her cruel father died she was not released, for her sister, whose hatred towards the Austrians was equally great, continued the imprisonment.

The unfortunate woman, on her liberation, had a complexion of a

---

60   Untitled, Thames Advertiser, Volume XI, Issue 2879, 12 March 1878, Page 2
http://paperspast.natlib.govt.nz/cgi-bin/paperspast?a=d&cl=search&d=THA18780312.2.7

death, like pallor, caused by the darkness in which she had so long lived, and her voice had departed, through constant cries for help during the early part of her sequestration; she could only speak in a hoarse whisper.

## From The Wires: Magazine Editor Kills For Story, 1878[61]

Two young gentlemen of Marseilles fought a duel with swords. One of them was mortally wounded.

M. Clovis Hugues, editor of the *Jeune Republique*, was married some little time ago, and the celebration of the marriage was merely civil.

M. Daymes, chief editor of a Bonapartist journal called the *Aigle*, criticised in his journal in very offensive terms the marriage, which was not consecrated by the Church. He went so far as to say that women married without the concurrence of the churches had no right to wear orange flowers, a symbol of maidenly chastity.

An ardent polemic between the *Aigle* and the *Jeune Republique* was the consequence of it, and it came so far that a duel was unavoidable.

It took place in a small wood in the environs of Marseilles on the Mediterranean shores. The two adversaries fenced at the commencement for a little while.

Daymes suddenly uttered a piercing cry, raised his arms to the air, and swooned in the arms of his witnesses. The sword of Hugues entered him above the right breast, and a flood of black blood was running from the gaping wound.

The wounded man was transported in a carriage which conducted him to his residence, but he died during the transit.

In presence of such a sad denouement, the courage fails me to give my opinion on the conduct of the unfortunate gentleman, who paid with his life the insult which he had given, what ought to be kept most sacred to a man of honour, the virtue of a woman.

The result of that unfortunate duel was that M. Clovis Hugues and his witnesses have hastened themselves to quit France. Proceedings have been taken against them, and they declared that they would present themselves before the assigned tribunal, but [only if] they would avoid preventive imprisonment.

---

61  ibid

## From The Wires: Hungry Rats Eat Sleeping Woman, 1889[62]

At Tuam, county Galway, Ellen Reddington, a servant, went to bed with grease on her arm, which attracted the rats, and being a heavy sleeper, she was not roused till she was terribly mutilated.

## The Invention Of The Cardboard Box, 1877[63]

An enterprising Chicagoan is about to make boxes directly from the pulp of the paper, thus saving much labour, waste and other expenses.

## A Lynchin' In Reverse, 1889[64]

American mail news states that Alfred Grizzard has been hanged by a mob of negro gamblers at Tiptonville. He won all the money which the negroes had, and they, enraged at their loss, took him into the woods and drew him up to timber, demanding that he should return the money. He refused, and they hung him. He was a noted gambler.

## Licked To Death By A Dog, 1889[65]

An extraordinary case of hydrophobia [rabies] has occurred at Chapeltown, near Sheffield. An ironmoulder named James Parkin died after several days' acute-suffering, but there is no evidence of his ever having been bitten by either a dog or a cat; and the doctor's opinion is that the malady was caused by a cut on deceased's face, sustained whilst shaving, being licked by a dog.

---

62   News In Brief, New Zealand Herald, Volume XXVI, Issue 9494, 12 October 1889, Page 1
http://paperspast.natlib.govt.nz/cgi-bin/paperspast?a=d&cl=search&d=NZH18891012.2.67.12
63   Taranaki Herald, Volume XXV, Issue 2610, 3 September 1877, Page 2
http://paperspast.natlib.govt.nz/cgi-bin/paperspast?a=d&cl=search&d=TH18770903.2.5
64   News In Brief, New Zealand Herald, Volume XXVI, Issue 9494, 12 October 1889, Page 1
http://paperspast.natlib.govt.nz/cgi-bin/paperspast?a=d&cl=search&d=NZH18891012.2.67.12
65   Ibid

## Eiffel Tower Made His Head Spin, 1889[66]

The enthusiasm of the people who ascend the Eiffel Tower is said to know no bounds, and they get their hats, cuffs, or pocket handkerchiefs stamped with the magic words, "Third Platform".

A workman engaged at the tower, wishing to see how the lift worked, put his head forward and was decapitated by the descending vehicle, the head falling upon a woman who was waiting below to ascend the tower.

## The Old Barn Door At 30 Paces Trick, 1877[67]

The Loafer in the *Canterbury Press* writes: Three friends of mine went out shooting, and not finding much game afoot, adjourned to an accommodation house for lunch. They agreed to put it down to [play a prank on] the landlord.

One of the sports, according to agreement beforehand, shortly retired awhile. During his absence his friends suggested to the host what a rare lark it would be to draw the shot from his gun and bet him £1 he couldn't hit a barn door fowl at thirty yards.

The host thought this would be a high old game, drew the charge, and on the return of the absent sport, lost no time in getting the wager on.

Then they all went outside, and the landlord choockled[68] about seventy fine fowls around some wheat he threw down to give, as he said with a jocund smile, the sport every chance.

Presently two barrels of a Purdy gun went off, and that back yard was a scene of carnage. Fowls were dead and dying all about and feathers darkened the air.

When the landlord had exhausted all the poetry of language he knew, or had ever heard, he paid a pound over, and wondered why it never struck him to make sure there were not double charges of shot in each barrel. I'm told the Boniface hasn't got hold of the right side of the joke yet.

---

66  Ibid
67  Through The Papers, Westport Times, Volume XI, Issue 1515, 4 September 1877, Page 3
http://paperspast.natlib.govt.nz/cgi-bin/paperspast?a=d&cl=search&d=WEST18770904.2.21
68  Yes, this was really a word in 1877

## The Invention Of Fibre-Optics And TV, 1877[69]

And now the telephone is outdone. A New York electrician claims to have invented what he calls an electroscope, by which friends thousands of miles apart – more or less – can see each other.

It is constructed, according to the inventor, upon the plan of the optic nerve, which radiates into almost infinite fibres as it approaches the eye, each fibre being sensitive to a certain light ray from the object whose image is formed upon the retina.

Copying this arrangement the inventor has a receiving box sensitively pierced by hundreds of the finest wires which run together and form a cable, Each wire answers to one of the nerve fibres of the eye, taking a point of light from the object in the receiving box, and transmitting over the cable to the other end, where the wires radiating into a box filled with gas or ether, the – nature of which is kept secret, upon which the transmitted rays of light are thrown, produce a phantom the exact counterpart of the object at the further end of the wire.

The inventor has not yet completed a working model, but he has abundant confidence in his theory.

## And You Thought Modern Weapons Were Powerful, 1892[70]

The following item will give us some idea of the power of modern big guns: A new Armstrong gun has just been tested in England. With a charge of 960lb of powder, it sent a cylindrical steel shot weighing 1,800lb through 20in steel armour, 5in of iron, 20ft of oak, 5ft granite, and 11ft of hard concrete. It could knock a hole through any ship in the world. It weighs 110 tons, is 43ft 9in long, and 5ft 6in thick at the base. But gunners cannot afford to miss the mark, for every shot costs nearly 1,000 dollars, and the monster cannot be fired more than seventy-five times before bursting.

---

69   Through The Papers, Westport Times, Volume XI, Issue 1515, 4 September 1877, Page 3
http://paperspast.natlib.govt.nz/cgi-bin/paperspast?a=d&cl=search&d=WEST18770904.2.21
70   Items. Oamaru Mail, Volume XVII, Issue 5280, 21 May 1892, Page 4
http://paperspast.natlib.govt.nz/cgi-bin/paperspast?a=d&cl=search&d=OAM18920521.2.32

## Child Labour, 1909[71]

In the course of an eloquent little speech at the Sydney Labor Council, Mrs Greville, delegate of the White Workers' Union, made some strong comments in regard to sweating in Sydney.

"My cheeks tingle with shame," she said, "when I recall that in this city there are young girls under 16 years of age working with a heavy iron all day long, pressing shirt-cuffs at one farthing a dozen. At that munificent remuneration they are scarcely able to earn what is now the minimum wage – four shillings a week."

Mrs Greville also stated that there were also girls who should be at school, working hard all day, sewing on buttons at 1d a dozen, and scarcely earning 4s a week. Competent shirt hands and collar hands were receiving not more than 20s a week from some of the shops which were obtaining from customers 6s 6d a shirt.

The lady speaker concluded: "Tom Hood's 'Song of the Shirt' is just as applicable to Sydney as it was to England. Bruns's historical reference in regard to Man's inhumanity to man pales into insignificance when compared with man's inhumanity to woman."

She concluded with an appeal to the council to help the white workers in the arduous task of organising.

## Progress In Native Civilization, 1846[72]

The anxiety and desire of the natives to acquire knowledge and practice of agricultural pursuits are daily becoming more universal, and numbers of them now travel a long distance from the interior, as well as from the eastern and western coasts, to seek employment on the farms in the vicinity of Auckland, and so to obtain practical information in husbandry, in order to cultivate their own lands.

They are apt to learn, and are soon initiated in field labour, to which they are much inclined. During the late harvest, their services have been

---

71   Marlborough Express, Volume XLIII, Issue 22, 27 January 1909, Page 2
http://paperspast.natlib.govt.nz/cgi-bin/paperspast?a=d&d=MEX19090127.2.7
72   Progress In Native Civilization, New Zealander, Volume 1, Issue 41, 14 March 1846, Page 3
http://paperspast.natlib.govt.nz/cgi-bin/paperspast?a=d&d=NZ18460314.2.11

of essential benefit to many farmers, and they have proved themselves to be excellent ploughmen, reapers, bullock drivers, &c.

In dealing and breaking up ground, they are laborious and clever, and they can trench ground as well as any European. As might be anticipated, some of the native districts have advanced more than others in the practice of European agriculture, producing crops of various grains, more especially wheat, for the purposes of food. But with the natives, as with the European Settlers, a productive harvest of wheat is comparatively no benefit to the resident population, unless there are mills on the spot to convert it into flour.

This very circumstance has much retarded the success of farmers in the neighbourhood of Auckland, where grain might be shipped to other ports, but such disadvantage would operate still more powerfully against the farmer in the interior, and indeed, in districts distant from the coast and without any roads to the capital, would prevent altogether the cultivation of wheat.

For some time past, wheat has been cultivated by the natives, residing in a valley called "Beecham Dale," at Aotea, and during the last two years, they have had, each year, about one hundred acres of wheat. At the harvest of last year, these industrious, intelligent natives, experienced their great want of means to convert their grain into flour, and perceived that unless the evil was remedied, before the next harvest, their cultivation of wheat was utterly unprofitable and useless.

The principal chiefs of the districts, and whose names are worthy of record, Paora, Muriwhenua, Hoari Kingi, Te Haratua, and Te Manihera, about nine months since, determined on the erection of a water mill, and aided by the advice of their pastor, the Rev. Gideon Smales, they have most completely accomplished their object and set a most praiseworthy example to their own countrymen.

The natives, themselves, excavated the ground, brought the stones from Kawhia, and cut them, felled the timber, &c, under the direction of a European mill-wright, Mr. Stewart McMullan, by whom the machinery and mill were erected, and to whom the natives paid the sum of Eighty Pounds sterling for his services.

The mill performs its work well, at the rate of two bushels per hour, and is considered the property in common of those chiefs and their natives, who assisted and contributed to its erection. This sensible, laudable act of the natives we mention, with the greatest pleasure.

This water corn mill, in the fertile districts of the Waikato and Waipa, amidst a numerous native population, cannot but operate most beneficially and we sincerely trust that it will stimulate them to pursue the peaceful occupation of husbandry, so as to secure for themselves wholesome nutritious food, as well as to induce further progress in the habits of social, civilised life.

## Local Gossip, 1894[73]

Jessie Ackerman, interviewed at Cape Town, told the irrepressible reporter that "the chief aim of the Australian girls is to play tennis and wait until someone proposes marriage".

Jimmy Poole, the well known book-maker, was taken to the Wellington Lunatic Asylum last Saturday evening week. It is said that the unfortunate fellow expended no less than £180 in one day in Wanganui last week, and then lost his reason.

Auckland is getting up its name as a home of novelists. Quite recently Mr Ward paralysed the world with 'Supplejack' (not half a bad yarn), and now Mr Wilfred Rathbone is to the fore with 'The Doom of the Spoiler: A Story of the Great Bank Robbery', shortly to be issued as a shilling-shocker of the most bloodcurdling description. Next, please.

During Darwin's last two years on earth his medical advisers recommended that he should "read nothing but absolute drivel." They ought to have sent the great thinker a file of *Auckland Herald*.

And so Lucky Hunt has made yet another pile at Coolgardie[74], so they say. Old Auckland identities will remember how Hunt made a fortune at the Thames, aye, and spent it right royally. He rode in his carriage-and-four in those days, lived on the fat of the land, and shouted champagne for all who would drink – until the fortune melted away, like snow in the sunshine.

And then A.W.H. prospected for another fortune. But it didn't come. Then Coolgardie broke out and Hunt was "amongst the earliest arrivals on the field".

---

73   Pars About People, Observer, Volume XV, Issue 824, 13 October 1894, Page 3
http://paperspast.natlib.govt.nz/cgi-bin/paperspast?a=d&d=TO18941013.2.5
74   A goldmine town north of Perth

Twas but the other day we read of him, a toil-worn, travel-stained digger, stopping at a tent door to beg a drink of water, penniless but sanguine. And now comes the news that he has struck it rich once more. Will he profit by the experiences of the past and bar shouting unlimited champagne for the crowd this time? Doubtful; your old hand digger doesn't understand how to save.

## Election Result Hinges On Carrier Pigeon, 1874[75]

Considering the thickness of the weather that night, our pigeons did good service in bringing in the returns from the polling places in the out-districts of Waitemata.

Before six o'clock we were able to publish all the returns with the exception of Helensville and Huia. With respect to the latter place we must acquit the bird detailed for the service from all blame, as the faithful messenger did indeed return with a despatch from our reporter, who had lost his way in the bush near the spot where the late lamented Rev D. Hamilton met his death.

Had the bird reached the Huia we doubt not that the return from that district would have been included in the number of those we were enabled to publish last night. The non-arrival of the pigeon from Helensville was no doubt due to the mist and darkness which rendered it impossible for a bird to see Auckland from such a distance and steer a clear course.

The pigeon came home early this morning and delivered its message in safety. The *Herald* and *Cross* to-day both have to acknowledge their indebtedness to our faithful carriers for returns which could not have been obtained last night in any other way. We give below the complete returns, which, it will be seen, place Mr Von der Heyde at the head of the poll by a majority of 50 votes.

---

75   The Waitemata Polling. – Our Pigeons, Auckland Star, Volume V, Issue 1393, 29 July 1874, Page 2
http://paperspast.natlib.govt.nz/cgi-bin/paperspast?a=d&cl=search&d=AS18740729.2.12

## Disappearance Of The Saddleback, 1921[76]

Although there are hundreds of thousands of acres of thickly-forested land in the Urewera Country, where human beings seldom go, the saddleback has completely disappeared from that district. The Maoris theory that it has been driven off by bees, which occupy holes and hollows in trees that were used by it for nests, is not acceptable. The bird's disappearance from the mainland is as deep a mystery as the extinction of the moa. Maoris know the saddleback as tieke, tiraweke, tirauweke, and purourou. Its ornithological name is Creadion carunculatus.

## The Last Moa, 1921[77]

Mr. A. Warburton, writing from Ngaruawahia, states that when he was a boy he wandered over the hills and mountains of Central Otago, and saw moa bones scattered on the surface of the ground from 1500 to 5000 feet above sea level.

The country had been occupied as a sheep run for about a-quarter of a century, and in those days the annual burn, unfortunately for the country, had been established as a custom.

When he lived at Cromwell he dug out of the sandy soil on low-lying ground, subject to flooding, some moa bones, which Dr. W. B. Benham, of Dunedin, stated were the largest he had heard of. Mr. Warburton secured the large bones of two legs, the toe bones, parts of the skull, and the tracheal rings of the windpipe. All were dug up with a walking-stick from a depth of a few inches.

He marked the place, intending to return the following day, and to obtain the remainder of the specimens, but a nor'-wester came up and blew a heap of sand over the place, and obliterated the marks.

"Those bones were only a few inches under the surface," he writes; "they were subject to heat and cold, to drying and wetting, and to the effects of the roots of plants and worms and insects. I cannot believe that they

---

76  Nature Notes, New Zealand Herald, Volume LVIII, Issue 17704, 12 February 1921, Page 1
http://paperspast.natlib.govt.nz/cgi-bin/paperspast?a=d&d=NZH19210212.2.123.8
77  Nature Notes, New Zealand Herald, Volume LVIII, Issue 17704, 12 February 1921, Page 1
http://paperspast.natlib.govt.nz/cgi-bin/paperspast?a=d&d=NZH19210212.2.123.8

could have remained in that state for a geological period."

He adds that Mr. B, Gilkison, solicitor, Dunedin, has in his possession a piece of moa bone with charred flesh attached to it. It was found on the surface of the ground near the Luggate, Upper Clutha Valley. Mr. Gilkison beat Mr. Warburton by a short time in becoming possessor of a moa's egg, found just outside of Cromwell.

Mr. Warburton concludes by stating that he read that whalers who frequented the Southern Sounds in the beginning of the past century actually saw a moa in Dusky Sound. The report was given wide circulation in newspapers of the time, but never was substantiated, and now is discredited, like the recent report that moas had been seen in the fastnesses of the North Island.

## Auckland Daze, 1891[78]

Dr. J. Giles, R.M., and Major Gascoigne, presided at the Police Court this morning. One inebriate, who was a first offender, was fined 5s, or 24 hours [in the clink] in default. Helena Wright for being drunk was fined 10s, or 48 hours. Kate Munro was fined 5s and costs for neglecting to keep the yard of her dwelling house clean. Mr G. Goldie, sanitary inspector, stated that the defendant had been previously warned before action was taken.

Six months for stealing an overcoat was the sentence passed on William Smith this morning at the Police Court. The accused was charged with having stolen an overcoat value 20s, the property of Arthur Farrar. He pleaded guilty. Sergeant-Major Pratt stated that the owner left his coat in his stable on the 10th August, and in the evening it had disappeared. Detective Hughes discovered that the coat had been pawned (at John Bunyan's in Grey Street), and he thereupon arrested the accused. Dr. Giles in passing sentence remarked that there was a bad record against the prisoner.

Patrick Dougherty, who was struck by the cow-catcher of the Kaipara train, was brought down to the Hospital yesterday afternoon by Constable O'Brien. It appears that he was lying on the embankment with his head on one rail. The cowcatcher struck him on the skull, which is fractured

---

[78] Auckland Star, Volume XXII, Issue 195, 18 August 1891, Page 4
paperspast.natlib.govt.nz/cgi-bin/paperspast?a=d&d=AS18910818.2.60

to the extent of about two inches. Dougherty remains unconscious but there is a chance that the injuries will not prove fatal.

The Auckland Free Public Library is to have a number of valuable additions made to it shortly. By the out-going mail yesterday an order was sent for close on 700 volumes of various kinds. When the order arrives it will make the additions to the Library this year 1,300 volumes, which exceeds all previous years in point of numbers. The Lending Library continues to be well supported. There are now 394 subscribers on the books, and fully 30 books are issued every day.

Riding a bicycle along a footpath is apt to get the offender into trouble, as it as an offence against the Police Offences Act. A youth named Arthur Firth appeared at the Police Court this morning, before Dr. Giles, R.M., and pleaded guilty to having ridden his bicycle along the footpath at Remuera.

He stated that the road was so muddy that he was forced to go on the path. Sergeant-Major Pratt stated that the younger man was noticed by Constable Rist of Newmarket. Under the circumstances the Bench inflicted a fine of 5s, and costs 7s.

*These were heady days in the young colony, what with gangs of hooligan teenagers rampaging all over the footpaths on their penny-farthings. Imagine what fun teenagers could have with the invention of a device allowing them to speak to their mates over a wire. Yes, New Zealand was about to get the telephone...*

## Chapter 5

# The Telephone Comes To NZ

*Today, we can make phone calls using watches on our wrists, and our phones have more computing power inside them than was available to the whole of the NASA team who put the first men on the moon.*

*The invention of the telegraph, linking cities instantly via Morse code, had already had a tremendous impact on the old messenger system involving ponyriders and ships. Wires were springing up all over New Zealand, humming to a million dots and dashes of code as communication flashed backward and forward.*

*While the telegraph was "revolutionary" – in the sense of using wires to communicate for the first time – subsequent development was evolutionary. Those racing to develop new forms of messaging were piggybacking on the new electric infrastructure. What this chapter will reveal is just how fast scientific ideas develop once the original concept becomes established. Although it would take decades for some of the ideas to become fully functional realities, you will see that within weeks of the "telephone" being released in the 1870s, the forerunners of radio, TV and smartphones were being conceived by people joining the dots of possibility.*

*The devices you take for granted today, owe their genesis to the ideas published in news reports contained within these pages. With the benefit of hindsight, you can now clearly see what your ancestors were fumbling for in the dark.*

*The very first mention of the word "telephone" in New Zealand appears in an 1874 news report (two years before Alexander Graham Bell won his pat-*

ent for the 'telephone'). In this first clipping, Bell doesn't even get a mention. Instead it's his arch-rival, Elisha Gray, who coined both the name and the initial technology to transmit sound:

## Music By Telegraph, 1874[79]

Elisha Gray, of Chicago, well known in the electric telegraph world, has succeeded, almost beyond his own anticipations, in perfecting an instrument which will convey sound by electricity over an unbroken circuit of extraordinary length – without the aid of automatic repeaters.

In the ordinary transmission of messages over telegraphic wires to points at long distances, a message is generally repeated by automatic working instruments about every 500 miles, in order to renew the current of electricity.

Mr. Gray has transmitted sounds which were distinctly audible at the receiving point, over an unbroken circuit of 2,400 miles. It is one of the greatest discoveries made since the early days of Morse.

Such noted electricians as George Prescott says it goes to prove what all electricians have long agreed upon: that we know little at present of the possibilities of the future of electric science.

The writer has heard music played on a small melodeon, or piano key-board transmitted through an unbroken circuit of 2,400 miles, and reproduced on a violin attached to the receiving end of the wire. Mr Gray played Hail Columbia, The Star Spangled Banner, God Save the Queen, Yankee Doodle, and other well-known airs, and they were unmistakably repeated, note for note, on the violin, which lay on a table near at hand. Even an accidental false note was immediately detected on the violin.

The apparatus, by means of which the feat is accomplished, has been named by Mr. Gray the "telephone", or an instrument for the purpose of transmitting sound to a distance. It consists of three general parts, the transmitting instrument, the conducting wire, and the apparatus for receiving the sound at that distant point. The transmitting apparatus consists of a key-board having a number of electro magnets corresponding with the number of the keys on the board, to which are attached vibrating

---

79  Music By Telegraph, Otago Daily Times , Issue 3929, 19 September 1874, Page 6 http://paperspast.natlib.govt.nz/cgi-bin/paperspast?a=d&d=ODT18740919.2.42

tongues on reeds, tuned to a musical scale. Any one of these tongues can be separately set in motion by depressing the key corresponding to it.

Thus a tune may be played by manipulating the keys in the same way as those of an ordinary piano or melodeon. The music, produced entirely by electricity, of these notes is so distinctly audible in the next room that, in spite of much talking, there is no difficulty in determining what the manipulator is playing.

*Between 1874 and 1876, fewer than two dozen references appear to the word "telephone" in New Zealand newspapers, but that all changed in late 1876 when international reports of Alexander Bell's invention exploded into public view:*

## The Newest Wonder, 1876[80]

Sir William Thompson, the President of the Physical Science section of the British Association, at Glasgow last month, told an attentive and admiring audience how ...he heard "To be or not to be?" recited through the electric wire and how, scorning monosyllables, the electric articulation rose to higher heights, and gave audible passages taken at random from the New York newspapers, such as:

"The Senate has resolved to print a thousand extra copies... The Americans in London have resolved to celebrate the coming Fourth of July," and a number of other utterances.

"All this," Sir William continued, "my own ears heard spoken to me with unmistakable distinctness by the thin circular disc armature of just such another little electro-magnet as this which I hold in my hand. The words were shouted in a loud and clear voice by my colleague, Professor Watson, at the far end of the line, holding his mouth close to a stretched membrane carrying a little piece of soft iron, which was thus made to perform, in the neighbourhood of an electric magnet, a circuit with the line, motions proportional to the sonorific motions of the air."

*While a well known New Zealand radio ad currently ascribes scepticism*

---

80   Electric Telephone, Colonist, Volume XIX, Issue 2158, 25 November 1876, Page 5 paperspast.natlib.govt.nz/cgi-bin/paperspast?a=d&d=TC18761125.2.13.5

*about the usefulness of a telephone to a Western Union telegraph executive, the newspaper archives show the question was actually raised by the New York Times, in an article reprinted in New Zealand:*

## The Telephone: "Of What Use Is Such An Invention?" 1876[81]

Sir William Thomson, at the Glasgow meeting of the British Association for the Advancement of Science gave foreign notoriety to another of the Centennial exhibits that has attracted great attention from the judges of the group to which it belongs.

It is a curious device that might fairly find a place in the magic of Arabian tales. A membrane is stretched over the end of a short speaking trumpet. The membrane carries a small piece of metal which is, so to speak, the armature of a magnet. The magnet forms part of a telegraph circuit, through which a current is passing.

To send a message it is only needful to talk loudly into the trumpet. The message is received by a similar trumpet with membrane and armature at the other end of the line and that trumpet being placed to the ear, repeats the sound like an echo.

Dom Pedro was with the scientific people who tested this instrument on one occasion. So accurately did it reproduce sounds that each member of the party was in turn recognised by peculiarities in voice or accent. The final text was the reading of a paragraph from the news columns of the "Tribune."

Of what use is such an invention? Well, there may be occasions of State when it is necessary for officials who are far apart to talk with each other without the interference of an operator. Or some lover may wish to pop the question directly into the ear of a lady, and hear for himself her reply, though miles away; it is not for us to guess how courtships will be carried on in the twentieth century.

It is said that the human voice has been conveyed by this contrivance over a circuit of sixty miles. Music can be readily transmitted. Think of a recording telegraph.

---

81   Some Recent Inventions, North Otago Times, Volume XXVI, Issue 1515, 23 February 1877, Page 2 http://paperspast.natlib.govt.nz/cgi-bin/paperspast?a=d&d=NOT18770223.2.19

*Within weeks of that news report, however, the usefulness of the telephone had become all too apparent. One British company ditched its entire telegraph unit, choosing instead to plug phones into the telegraph wires at all its offices. Ever the man with his eye on the main chance, a lightbulb went off in Thomas Edison's head and the world's first Dictaphone was built.*

## The First Answering Machine, 1878[82]

Edison, the distinguished electrician and mechanic, recently exhibited in the office of this paper his talking telephone, which, when a crank was turned, inquired about the editor's health, announced that it was a telephone, and said "good night", the words being reproductions of the sounds of a human voice.

The remarkable feature of this speaking telephone is the simplicity of its mechanism. The vibrations of a metal diaphragm caused by the voice of a speaker are transferred to a strip of tinfoil, and there recorded by indentations. This indented strip is made to speak again, when it is passed under a metal point which follows the indentations and reproduces in a metal diaphragm the same vibrations which had originally made the record on the tinfoil.

It is this little machine which, if perfected in the future, is to put an end to all denials of what speakers in important cases may have said, and is to reproduce the tone as well as the language of orators years after they have passed away.

It has always been the misfortune of actors, singers, and orators that their great qualities lived after them only in memory or in the testimony of their contemporaries. But the speaking telephone, if all its possibilities are made actualities, may preserve the voices of great speakers and singers of our day for the enjoyment of audiences yet unborn, – *Scientific American*

*Commenting on this, an Otago Daily Times correspondent marvelled at the possibilities of recorded voices as well, coming so soon after the invention of the telephone itself:*

---

82 A Speaking Telephone, New Zealand Herald, Volume XV, Issue 5051, 24 January 1878, Page 3
http://paperspast.natlib.govt.nz/cgi-bin/paperspast?a=d&d=NZH18780124.2.27

## Recording Telephones[83]
*(From the Engineer)*

The world has scarcely been startled by the introduction of the telephone, when a new surprise is announced. We learn from the United States that Mr Edison, a gentleman well known for his scientific attainments, has devised a means by which the utterances of the telephone may be put on record, and it will thus become possible to reproduce years hence, not only the words but the very inflection and tone of voice of individuals long dead. This is surely the most remarkable thing yet performed by electrical science.

Think what use might be made of such an instrument in treasuring up the accents of a good orator, such as Mr Gladstone or the Bey. Henry Ward Beecher. The notes of a prima donna can be put on record, and it may yet be possible to compare the voice of Patti with that of a songstress now unborn.

It is confidently asserted that Mr Edison has achieved such success that he fails only in recording the finer inflections of the voice. A few weeks since the world would have pronounced the whole idea of such an invention as fit only for the brain of a writer of fairy tales, but after the telephone all things appear possible in telegraphy.

*One newspaper columnist envisaged a day when people could listen to anything they liked over the phone:*

## Ah, So You'd Be Wanting A Smartphone Then? 1878[84]

The telephone threatens the press, the pulpit and the alike with extinction. This extraordinary instrument transmits the sounds of the human voice as quickly as they are spoken to a distance of twenty miles from the speaker; and there appears nothing to prevent it from sending them a thousand miles.

---

83  Recording Telephones, Otago Daily Times, Issue 4974, 26 January 1878, Page 2
http://paperspast.natlib.govt.nz/cgi-bin/paperspast?a=d&d=ODT18780126.2.34
84  The Telephone, Westport Times, Volume XI, Issue 1508, 10 August 1877, Page 4
http://paperspast.natlib.govt.nz/cgi-bin/paperspast?a=d&cl=search&d=WEST18770810.2.30

The first experiments were carried on between Boston and Salem, towns eighteen miles apart and the operators were able to make themselves distinctly heard by hundreds assembled at either terminus.

This wonderful invention opens up a perfectly boundless field of speculation. If a voice can be transmitted twenty miles, and heard as soon as the words are spoken, people will only have to lay on telephones to their houses to be able to hear everything that is said aloud.

By telephonic communication with the Parliament Houses we will be able to do without Hansard. A telephone can be laid on in the drawing room from the Council for ladies, and in the study for gentlemen. One clergyman can preach to the whole of Melbourne, and if either preacher or listener is getting drowsy the pipe that conveys the sound can be turned off.

And, without the trouble of dressing and going out of doors one can have the sparkling dialogue from the last new play laid on at so much a thousand words. It will help to reconcile me to the ills of old age if I can live to see parliamentary, religious and dramatic telephones laid on all over my house.

*In the United States, officials at Providence, Rhode Island, had discovered they could get police officers armed with portable Morse code telegraph units to tap into the city's streetlight system at any lamppost and alert authorities to a fire or a crime.*

*The street lights were gas, but ignited using an electric spark transmitted over wires. The idea was that the ignition wires could also be used to carry communications, and police were issued with a Morse code key to get access to the wires. Literally within weeks of that discovery, however, they realised they could do the same with phones instead of telegraph units:*

## Every Lamppost Tells A Tale, 1877[85]

If a policeman wishes to give notice of a fire or a burglary he has only to go the nearest lamp post, apply his 'key', and by the use of the ordinary telegraphic signals the information is at once conveyed. But, through this key, the policeman can receive no message back, and cannot even know

---

85  The Wonders Of The Telephone, New Zealand Tablet, Volume V, Issue 236, 9 November 1877, Page 9 http://paperspast.natlib.govt.nz/cgi-bin/paperspast?a=d&cl=search&d=NZT18771109.2.14.2

that his information has been received at the point or points to which he designed to forward it. This can only be done through the use by him of a regular telegraph instrument, the connection of the wires with it in the regular way, and the knowledge of a trained operator.

Within the past ten days, however, experiments made at Providence with the wires of the pneumatic electric system of lighting and extinguishing the gas used for street lights in that city have demonstrated in the clearest and most convincing manner that the newly-discovered principle of the telephone may be applied to this system of electric work and communication with most extraordinary results.

By the use of the telephone in connection, with the perfectly insulated underground wires of the Providence lamp lighting system it has been discovered that the human voice can be employed with great advantage over the arbitrary telegraphic signals used for communicating intelligence from one part of the city to all other parts and that electrical instruments and skilled operators may be entirely dispensed with for instantaneous communication wherever the wires extend.

*The news wires record that Australian scientists were "experimenting" with telephones by August 1877, although none had yet been shown publicly. In New Zealand, likewise, the race was on to telephonise, and by early February 1878 the papers were full of reports of different localities plugging in telephones to test:*

## "Is That You, Mr Logan?" 1878[86]

The telephone experiment between Mosgiel and Dunedin to-day was successful for a distance of fourteen miles. Mr. Logan, the telegraph inspector, sang several songs at the Mosgiel end, and every word reached the Dunedin end distinctly. The telephone instruments are merely line wire.

---

86  Dunedin. 5th February, Evening Post, Volume XVI, Issue 46, 6 February 1878, Page 2
http://paperspast.natlib.govt.nz/cgi-bin/paperspast?a=d&d=EP18780206.2.12.3

## Dr Lemon's Excellent Adventure, 1878[87]

Wellington, February 9. About mid-day, Dr Lemon experimented, in the presence of his Excellency the Governor, on a telephone manufactured at Dunedin; There was joined up eighty six knots of cable and thirty miles of land line, and the musical scale, singing, speaking, and cooing were distinctly heard.

*Back in 1876 the New York Times had wondered aloud "What use is this invention?" By 1878, it provided a tongue-in-cheek answer, and nearly every major New Zealand newspaper ran the column concerned:*

## The Telephone Unmasked, 1878[88]

It is time that the atrocious nature of the telephone should be fully exposed, and its inventors, of whom there are any quantity, held up to public execration.

When this nefarious instrument was first introduced, it was pretended that its purpose was an innocent one. We were told that the telephone would enable a man in New York to hear what a man in Philadelphia might say, and though it was difficult to understand why anybody should ever want to listen to a Philadelphian's remarks which, notoriously, consist exclusively of allusions to the Centennial Exhibition and an alleged line of American steamships, there was nothing necessarily immoral in this possible use of the telephone.

Then it was claimed that, by means of the telephone, conversations could be carried on with other than Philadelphians, and that political speeches delivered in Washington could be heard in any city of the continent. As the President was at that time making speeches in Vermont instead of Washington, the public was not alarmed by this announcement, and it was not until the telephonic conspirators mentioned that the uproar of a brass band could be transmitted to any distance through the telephone that any general feeling of uneasiness was developed.

---

87   Dr Lemon Telephoning, West Coast Times , Issue 2765, 11 February 1878, Page 2
http://paperspast.natlib.govt.nz/cgi-bin/paperspast?a=d&d=WCT18780211.2.7.4
88   The Telephone Unmasked, Grey River Argus, Volume XXI, Issue 2966, 15 February 1878, Page 2
http://paperspast.natlib.govt.nz/cgi-bin/paperspast?a=d&d=GRA18780215.2.13

Nevertheless, the vast capabilities for mischief of the telephone, and the real purpose of its unprincipled inventors, have been studiously concealed, and it is only by accident that the greatness and imminence of the danger to which the public is exposed have suddenly been revealed.

Suspicion ought to have been awakened by the recent publication of the fact that if the lamp-posts of our city were to be connected by wires, every confidential remark made to a lamp-post by a belated democratic statesman could be reproduced by a telephone connected with any other lamppost.

It is true that this publication was ostensibly made in the interest of the police force, and it was recommended that patrolmen should use the lamp-post as means of communicating with police headquarters. It was evident, however, that the result would be to make every lamppost a spy upon midnight wayfarers.

Men who had trusted to friendly lampposts for years, and embraced them with the utmost confidence in their silence and discretion, would find themselves shamelessly betrayed, and their unsuspecting soliloquies literally reported to their indignant families; strange to say, this suggestive hint of the powers of the telephone attracted no attention, and has ere this been in all probability forgotten.

A series of incidents which has lately occurred in Providence has, however, clearly shown the frightful capabilities of the telephone... We can now comprehend the danger of the telephone. If any telephonic miscreant connects a telephone with one of the countless telegraphic wires that pass over the roofs of this city there will be an immediate end of all privacy. Whatever is said in the secrecy of the back piazza by youthful students of the satellites of Mars will be proclaimed by way of the house-top to the eavesdropping telephone operator.

No matter to what extent a man may close his doors and windows, and hermetically seal his keyholes and furnace registers with towels and blankets, whatever he may say, either to himself or a companion, will be overheard.

Absolute silence will be our only safety. Conversation will be carried on exclusively in writing, and courtship will be conducted by the use of a system of ingenious symbols. An invention which thus mentally makes silence the sole condition of safety cannot be too severely denounced, and while violence, even in self-defence, is always to be deprecated, there can be little doubt that the death of the inventors and manufacturers of the telephone would do much towards creating that feeling of confidence which financiers tell us must precede any revival in business.

*Edward Snowden had nothing on the foresight of the New York Times. By November 1877, the bustling city of New York had, wait for it, five telephones in operation.*[89] *By January 1878, Dunedin had phones as well.*

## Use Of The Telephone, 1878[90]

DUNEDIN, JAN. 29. Telephones are being used here by one or two business people to connect warehouses with offices.

*The rest, as they say, is history. Now you can even read this book on a phone, turning the page with a sweep of your finger…*

---

89   News By The Mail, Press, Volume XXVIII, Issue 3837, 8 November 1877, Page 3
http://paperspast.natlib.govt.nz/cgi-bin/paperspast?a=d&cl=search&d=CHP18771108.2.17
90   Use Of The Telephone, Grey River Argus, Volume 21, Issue 2952, 30 January 1878, Page 2
http://paperspast.natlib.govt.nz/cgi-bin/paperspast?a=d&d=GRA18780130.2.9.6

Chapter 6

# The Last Huia

One of the unique features of New Zealand is its birdlife. Developing in a land without large predators since the extinction of the crocodiles and other bigger reptiles, the birds found here are in many cases found nowhere else in the world.

Classic examples include the moa and the huia – both extinct. No confirmed European record exists of an actual encounter with a giant moa; if such happened, as a result of a shipwreck, it lived only in the memory of the beholder.

Of huia, on the other hand, there were plenty of encounters. Let's journey, then, back in time to the New Zealand that greeted early settlers in the 1840s. A country rampant with birdsong. One man to tell that story arrived in the Hokianga with a team of missionaries in 1839. A prodigious writer, he penned this article just days before his death from heart failure in Auckland. It was the last story he wrote:

## Some Of The Native Birds, 1894[91]
### By The Rev. Gideon Smales

In early times birds in all their varieties were vastly more numerous than at present, and much tamer. It was no unusual thing when I had a native

---

91  Episodes In The Life Of An Old Missionary, New Zealand Herald, Volume XXXI, Issue 9701, 22 December 1894, Page 1
http://paperspast.natlib.govt.nz/cgi-bin/paperspast?a=d&cl=search&d=NZH18941222.2.77.3

companion with me, in a journey, when in a thick forest, for him to take a small twig with two or three leaves, and twirl it between his hands whilst spread open before his lips, and at the same time he chirped attractively.

The small birds would fly into his hands, which he would quickly close, and he would take them sometimes almost as fast as he could convey them to one side. Our beautiful kukupa, or pigeon, with his fine figure, his bronze wings, and his rapid flight, in some districts was very numerous.

Along the creeks and rivers the different species of shag were also abundant, as well as the wild duck and the teal. In the south part of the North Island, and in the South Island, the beautifully-coloured and variegated putangitangi, or paradise duck, was plentiful.

On the sand flats in the harbours the natives used to go out by moonlight and take in flocks of kuaka, or curlew, in their large nets and I have seen in the season a large hangi (native oven) full of fat cooked kakas (brown parrots), one hundred and more at once, and as many or more tuis (parson birds).

But it is only within the last thirty or forty years, since the extensive spread of settlers, that native birds have become so signally diminished. We cannot but lament their diminution for to the traveller their presence was most cheering, and, as our lively companions in the bush, they were a source of interest and delight.

A sacred feeling comes over the traveller when surrounded with living trees in a dense forest. We forget our years when we look at the noble old trees that have stood the war of the elements for hundreds, if may be thousands, of years. And yet we are still interested with the feathered race, whose time is more limited.

The trees have a voice, and sometimes as they enunciate the voice of the wind, it is a very melancholy and weird one. But the birds have animal life, and they twitter and chatter to each other in their shaded bowers like a party of young ladies who have met together to celebrate the nuptials of some fortunate sister. How enlivening to view "the strange bright birds on their starry wings, which bear the rich hues of all glorious things".

My object is to write of the refreshing influence exercised on the mind by the comely presence and interesting movements of our bush companions amid the loneliness and the pressure upon the mind as well as the body, when travelling alone and sleeping at times under a breakwind, or the projections of the root of a tree.

For my travels at the time referred to were of that nature and were not only between Wellington and Porirua, but extended along the coast as far as Taranaki.

In what was then the thick bush between Wellington and Porirua, the forest was enlivened by the graceful flight of numerous huia, a bird through whose attractiveness our late Governor, Lord Onslow, was induced to give its name to his son, born in the country, and thus commemorate his interest in New Zealand.

The huia is adorned with a bright, black, velvet-like coat, enlivened by a green metallic gloss, having a rather long tail with a stripe of white across the end, and carrying a pair of rich orange-coloured wattles on the sides of the head, and the male bird having a long curved beak, with which he more especially does the work of digging through the bark and into the decayed wood of old trees, bringing out the large luscious worm, and thus relieving his mate from the duties of breadwinner, for which nature has so specially adapted him.

In his form and general appearance, though somewhat larger, he is very like the tui (or parson bird) and has been described as a lady-like bird. His paces are sometimes rather awkward he hops about from branch to branch, but does not always stop gracefully. My friend, Sir Walter Buller, in his great work on the ornithology of New Zealand, speaking of the huia, says, "It was most interesting to watch these graceful birds hopping from branch to branch, occasionally spreading the tail into a broad fan, displaying themselves in a variety of natural attitudes, and then meeting to caress each other with their ivory bills (instead of cherry ripe lips), uttering at the same time a low, affectionate twitter."

"The natives formerly greatly prized the skin of the huia, and when it could be obtained, it was regarded as a rare and valuable ornament, which was suspended from the lobe of the ear of a chief. The feathers too were used to ornament the skulls and preserved heads (mokomokai) of the great men that were brought before the public on great festive occasions, such as the hahunga.

It was also a bird of omen. Thus, should a married man be anticipating an addition to his family, and fall into a deep sleep and dream that he saw on the ground human skulls ornamented with feathers, and if that of the huia, his child would be a girl, and if that of the kotuku [white heron] it would be a boy.

One of my pretty friends which I frequently met in the bush near

Wellington, was the kotihe or stitch bird. The male especially is a richly-coloured bird. He has a velvety black head and wings variegated with black, white, and yellow and an ornamental tuft of white feathers on either cheek, which he occasionally erects. The back and tail are of a yellowish grey, and he has a bright yellow circle around the lower part of the neck and wings, beautifully variegated with grey and brown.

When alarmed or excited he erects the tail and raises the ear tufts. The female carries the tail generally erect. He may fairly be called a gay-looking bird with striking colours. He sips deeply into the calyx of the numerous flowers of this country which abound with nectar as well as honey. In shape and size he is like the English thrush, but far more ornamental, and was one of my admired friends in the bush. The stitchbird is now extinct in Now Zealand, except on the Little Barrier Island.

There was also another bird which the natives termed "tieke," and which the Europeans term "saddle-back". It is a singular and uncommon-looking bird, although not very fine in its figure. Though somewhat sombre in its appearance, its colours are striking; the principal of them is a glossy blue black, and this is contrasted by a clear and distinct brown or ferruginous colour which covers the back and extends over the wings like two saddleflaps. It is also ornamented with a pair of beautiful golden yellow (sometimes Vermillion) wattles, which are suspended from the angles of the mouth.

Dr. Buller has given us a short description of some of its habits, as follows: "Active in all its movements, it seldom remains more than a few seconds in one position, but darts through the branches or climbs the boles of the trees, performing the ascent by a succession of nimble hops, and often spirally. This is naturally a noisy bird, and, when excited or alarmed, becomes very clamorous, hurrying through the woods with cries of 'tiakerere', quickly repeated. At other times it has a scale of short flute notes, clear and musical; but the most remarkable exhibition of its vocal powers takes place during the breeding season, when the male performs to his mate in a soft strain of exquisite sweetness. This love song is heard only on a near approach, and it is at first difficult to believe that so clamorous a bird could be capable of such tender strains."

Before concluding my account of some of the pretty and interesting birds of New Zealand, I should not forget the two yearly visitors we have, one of which is from Australia and the other from the warmer islands of the Southern Pacific. They are both of the cuckoo species.

The latter, which is named by the natives koekoea, or kohoperoa, is rather a handsome bird. It is beautifully strewed and spotted with dark brown and rufous, tipped with white, and glossed with purple, being a little larger than the thrush, with a long, beautiful tail, which causes it to be distinguished as the "long-tailed cuckoo."

Its visits to New Zealand extend generally from about September to January. It is a singing bird, but it is only heard during the summer months, and mostly during the night. The other cuckoo, which is known by the natives as the pipiwharauroa, or shining cuckoo, may fairly be regarded as the most beautiful bird we have in New Zealand and whilst it is a native of Australia, it is also a native of New Zealand.

It sojourns here from September to January, generally leaving a young brood behind, or takes one with it, when it returns to Australia. Its golden-green and coppery brown and purple, with glistening and opaline shades, like shot silk, variously striped and variegated, render it a most beautiful bird and it is not only beautiful in colour, but it is a model of graceful shape.

Both the cuckoos are useful birds to the farmer, as they are insectivorous, and feed largely on the caterpillar and other insects. Both, too, seem to be gifted with a species of ventriloquism. Its song consists of eight or ten silvery notes, quickly repeated. The first of these appears to come from a considerable distance, and each successive one brings the voice nearer, till it issues from the spot where the performer actually stands perched, perhaps only a few yards off. It generally winds up with a confused strain of joyous notes, accompanied by a stretching and quivering of the wings, expressive, as it would seem, of the highest ecstasy.

There is one objectionable feature, however, in the habits of these beautiful cuckoos, and that is that they are parasitic in their breeding habits, and entrust to a stranger both the hatching and rearing of their young. The little grey warbler or the black tit are the usual victims, but they are also known to take similar advantages from other species. The young cuckoos are known actually to eject the rightful owners from their nests and they are found dead on the ground, while at the same time the foster-parents are incessantly on the wing, from morning till night, catering for the inordinate appetites of their charge, whoso piping cry only stimulates their activity of self-denial.

The Maori has a proverb which is applicable to both cuckoos. When a child is deserted by its parents, it is said to be "Te parahako o te koekoea" (the rejected of the koekoea.) When they first appear their cry is different to what it afterwards becomes. The Maoris say that at first the cuckoo calls "Kui kui te ora" (life is starvation). As the summer advances, and the sun becomes warm the song changes to "Whiti ora, whiti ora" (Life is bright). If it continues the former cry, it will be a cold summer; if it sings the latter it will be a warm season.

The above, then, are a few of the many beautiful and interesting birds that have especially taken my attention, and been objects of interest and pleasure during many hours, days, and years of my sojourn in this country. There are others that are specially remarkable for their harmonious songs, such as the tui, or parson bird, and the korimako or bell-bird, while others are remarkable for their size and character. Others are remarkable for their peculiar construction and habits, as the kiwi.

## 300 Huia Massacred In One Session, 1873[92]

The natives of Te Ore Ore (some twelve in number), have just returned from a huia shooting expedition, and they succeeded in bagging three hundred birds. The scene of slaughter was the bush in the vicinity of Alfredton.

Such wholesale slaughter of native game, especially the huia (a very rare and beautiful bird), should be put an end to. The natives place an extravagant value on this bird, the skins and tail feathers of which are highly prized by them, and especially the natives of Napier, where the huia is almost unknown.

## A Huia In The Garden, 1893[93]

The other day I was attracted by a peculiar and strange sound in my garden, and, on cautiously approaching the spot, saw a peculiar looking bird moving through the branches of the trees, with a motion very like a kaka, but in size a little larger.

---

92  Masterton, Wellington Independent, Volume XXVIII, Issue 3845, 1 July 1873, Page 3
http://paperspast.natlib.govt.nz/cgi-bin/paperspast?a=d&d=WI18730701.2.16
93  Whakamara, Hawera & Normanby Star, Volume XX, Issue 2372, 10 March 1893, Page 2
http://paperspast.natlib.govt.nz/cgi-bin/paperspast?a=d&d=HNS18930310.2.16

It had a black body with white speckled feathers in its tail, and a good deal of red about the head. Afterward, on describing the bird to a friend, he declared it to be a huia.

I am told that the huia is now getting very rare and consequently would command a high price from any of the New Zealand institutes.

## Watching The Huia, 1873[94]

But what interested me most of all was the manner in which the birds assisted each other in their search for food, because it appeared to explain the use, in the economy of nature, of the differently formed bills in the two sexes.

To divert the birds, I introduced a log of decayed wood infested with the huhu grub. They at once attacked it, carefully probing the softer parts with their bills, and then vigorously assailing them, scooping out the decayed wood till the larva or pupa was visible, when it was carefully drawn from its cell, treated in the way described above, and then swallowed.

The very different development of the mandibles in the two sexes enabled them to perform separate offices. The male always attacked the more decayed portions of the wood, chiselling out his prey after the manner of some woodpeckers, while the female probed with her long pliant bill the other cells, where the hardness of the surrounding parts resisted the chisel of her mate.

Sometimes I observed the male remove the decayed portion without being able to reach the grub, when the female would at once come to his aid, and accomplish with her long, slender bill what he had failed to do. I noticed, however, that the female duly appropriated to her own use the morsels thus obtained.

## Having Watched It, I Shot It, 1873[95]

We camped that night near the bed of a mountain rivulet, in a deep

---

94 New Zealand Birds, Otago Witness, Issue 1101, 4 January 1873, Page 8 (reprinting an extract of Buller's History of the Birds of New Zealand book)
http://paperspast.natlib.govt.nz/cgi-bin/paperspast?a=d&d=OW18730104.2.19
95 Ibid

wooded ravine, and soon after dawn we again heard the rich notes of a huia. Failing to allure him by an imitation of the call, although he frequently answered it, we crossed to the other side of the gully, and climbed the hill to a clump of tall rimu trees (Dacrydium cupressinum), where we found him.

He was perched on a high limb of a rimu, chiselling it with his powerful beak, and tearing off large pieces of bark, doubtless in search of insects and it was the falling of these fragments that guided us to the spot, and enabled us to find him.

This solitary bird, which proved when shot[96] to be an old male, had frequented this neighbourhood (as we were informed by the natives) for several years, his notes being familiar to the people who passed to and fro along the Otairi track leading to Taupo.

On asking a native how the huia contrived to extract the huhu from the decayed timber, he replied, "By digging with, his pickaxe," an expression which I found to be truthfully descriptive of the operation and on dissecting this specimen I found an extraordinary development of the requisite muscles. The skin was very tough, indicating probably extreme age.

The stomach contained numerous remains of coleopterous insects, of the kind usually found under the bark of trees, also one or two caterpillars. In the stomach of another I once discovered seeds of the hinau (Eloeocarpus dentatus) and the remains of a small earth grub. Dr Dieffenbach states that in the stomachs of his specimens he found hinau berries, together with dipterous and coleopterous insects.

*By the 1880s, settlers and politicians alike had come to realise the huia was becoming more and more scarce. It had only ever been found in the lower North Island forests – it had never, for example, been known in the Auckland region despite the settlement of that name. We know from archaeological studies that the bird once lived as far north as Cape Reinga and as far south as Wellington, but had been hunted to extinction in most of the North Island*

---

96  The 'if-it-moves-shoot-it' school of exploration possibly reached its zenith in explorer Charles Douglas' account of his encounter with the last breeding pair of either the giant Haast's Eagle, or its only slightly smaller cousin the Eyle's Harrier, in 1870: "The expanse of wing of this bird will scarcely be believed. I shot two on the Haast, one was 8ft 4in (2.54m) from tip to tip, the other was 6ft 9in (2.06m)". Story and source recounted at page 20 of *The Great Divide* by Ian Wishart, ISBN 9780 987657367

by Maori long before Europeans arrived. The availability of guns made the birds that remained easy pickings.

For Maori hunters to shoot 300 of these large birds (the same size as an English crow) in one hunt indicates how prolific they must have been. Walter Buller reports more than 600 huia were taken in a later 1883 Maori hunt. But their spectacular plumage made these birds the talk not just of the marae but of the fashionistas in London and Europe as well, putting a bounty on the huia that remained.

New Zealand's Governor, Lord Onslow, named his New Zealand born infant son "Huia", which in turn drew a lot of attention to the plight of the bird:

## The First British Royal Born With A Maori Name, 1891[97]

A Great Compliment to the Maoris The Vice-Regal Visit to Otaki. Enthusiastic Reception by the Ngatihuia Tribe. (Per United Press Association.) Wellington, September 14.

On Saturday the Earl and Countess of Onslow and their children and Sir Walter and Lady Buller visited Otaki, where the Ngatihuia tribe, to the number of upwards of 300, had assembled for the purpose of receiving in due Maori form the Governor's infant son Huia.

The natives welcomed His Excellency in the tribal meeting house, which was magnificently decorated for the occasion. Several chiefs, including Taipua, M.H.R[98]., delivered speeches. It was mentioned that other Governors had done kind things to the native race, but it had been reserved for Lord Onslow to pay this great compliment to the Maori people: that of giving to his son a Maori name.

They also asked the Governor to restrain pakehas from shooting the huia bird, so that when his boy grew up he might see the beautiful bird which bears his name.

In replying, Lord Onslow said that in the natural course of events he would have to take his boy home to England, but his parents would see that means were placed at his disposal and every encouragement offered to him after he arrived at years of discretion to re-visit the country where

---

97 Lord Onslow's Son Huia, Wanganui Herald, Volume XXV, Issue 7518, 14 September 1891, Page 2 http://paperspast.natlib.govt.nz/cgi-bin/paperspast?a=d&cl=search&d=WH18910914.2.9
98 Member of the House of Representatives. In modern terms, MP.

his father and mother had met with so much kindness, and where they had passed several years profitable in experience and interspersed with pleasant recollections.

Huia was then taken from the nurse's arms by the chieftainess and presented to the hereditary chief of the tribe, who solemnly rubbed noses with the boy in the presence of the tribe, the women joining in a plaintive lullaby composed expressly for the occasion.

All the chiefs next came forward and cast their offerings, consisting of beautiful flax mats, fancy baskets, greenstones, and carted boxes before the child. Among the presents was an ancient pendant, an heirloom in Te Rangihaeata's family.

The Countess made a short speech, thanking the natives for their cordial reception and assuring them that every one of the presents would be carefully treasured. The meeting dispersed with three cheers for Huia.[99]

## Endangered Species Tag Paints Bullseye On Huia, 1902[100]

TO THE EDITOR: Sir, In a late issue I noticed a local relating to the huia bird. The way this beautiful and harmless bird is being ruthlessly shot down for the sake of its few tail feathers is scandalous.

It seems to me that nowadays the Government has only to protect a bird and its days are numbered.

I know myself, and so would anyone else who chose to inquire, that there are scores of men (both native and European) who make a living by huia shooting.

---

99   For those who wonder what happened to the aristocrat with the Maori name, it's a fascinating but tragic story. Although given English names as well, Victor Herbert, it was Huia that the boy chose to go by. His godmother was no less a personage than the Empress herself – Queen Victoria. At the age of 14 he returned to New Zealand from England at Christmas 1904 and was welcomed again by the Ngatihuia and Ngati Raukawa people at Otaki who gave him the title 'Rangatira' of the tribe. There is no record in the archives that young Huia Onslow ever made the acquaintance of the bird he was named after. Returning to the UK, Huia was sent to study at Cambridge, specialising in biochemistry. While on holiday in the Swiss Alps he dived into a mountain lake, smashing his head on a rock, and was left paralysed. Even so, he completed his degree and became a promising young scientist, until becoming as extinct as his namesake, upon his death in 1922 aged 31.

100   The Huia Bird, New Zealand Herald, Volume XXXIX, Issue 11641, 16 April 1902, Page 6 http://paperspast.natlib.govt.nz/cgi-bin/paperspast?a=d&d=NZH19020416.2.72.1

For the reason of this scandal we have to look in high places: First, Lord Onslow chose to call one of his children "Huia". That was the start, and drew public attention to the bird. Then the Duke of Cornwall and York further settled the doom of the poor huia by wearing a feather in his chapeau.[101]

The one who, however, has done more to popularise the wearing of the huia, and to whom in a few years we will be able to look to as the author (perhaps unintentionally) of its total extinction, is the Hon. James Carroll.

He it was who first set the fashion, and he it was who first distributed them round to his friends. Many a score feathers I have seen given to the wearer by the Hon. James. He had a fair amount to say in Parliament re the Maori Curio Bill; perhaps he might enlighten us next session as to where he procures his unlimited supply of huias.

I am, etc, Thos. J. Haworth

## The Huia, 1909[102]

Writing in the *Dominion* in regard to the huia bird, Mr. W. W. Smith, of New Plymouth, says: – "As there are many mercenary collectors travelling about the Dominion in search of the last living specimens procurable of the huia and other rare species of native birds, it is of the utmost importance for those who know, to preserve silence as to their present habitats until a sufficient number have been captured and securely placed on the insular bird sanctuaries.

Impatience for the honour attached to such very important work should be rigidly suppressed until it is successfully accomplished. The increasing great demand for huia feathers has been, and is, the chief cause of the rapid disappearance of this unique and beautiful native bird.

I have previously suggested, and again do so, that the Government should rigidly suppress the sale of huia and all native bird feathers, in order to prevent such nefarious traffic. We know that 95 or more percent

---

101  The Duke of York was the future King George V, who was given the feather for his hat during a visit to Rotorua in 1901, sparking a fashion rage in Europe when he returned. The price of feathers reached up to five pound each, making a single huia worth £60 per skin.

102  The Huia, New Zealand Herald, Volume XLVI, Issue 13977, 5 February 1909, Page 6 http://paperspast.natlib.govt.nz/cgi-bin/paperspast?a=d&d=NZH19090205.2.7

of feathers sold by dealers as those of the huia are spurious, and are chiefly 'faked' turkey feathers.

I think it is monstrous that such nefarious dealings and practices should be tolerated in the Dominion. If effectively suppressed, the demand for these charming birds would almost cease, which would enable them to live on in their beautiful forest haunts at least a few years longer.

*By the time the letter above was published in 1909, what would later be called the last 'confirmed' sighting of a huia had taken place two years earlier in 1907. In fact, travellers and workers in isolated bush areas as far north as the Urewera and as far south as Eastbourne outside Wellington reported sightings in the 1920s and even as late as the 1960s. No huia have been seen since.*

*The last breeding pair captured alive, in 1893, were destined to be transferred to an offshore bird sanctuary but, in a bitterly ironic twist, Sir Walter Buller pulled rank and purloined the pair to use as a gift for Lord Rothschild of the banking dynasty back in England, along with the last breeding pair of Laughing Owls.*

*New Zealand conservation officials mounted a number of final search efforts for live breeding pairs to transfer to Little Barrier and Kapiti islands in the early 1900s, but they came to nothing:*

## Hunting For Huias, 1908[103]

Wellington, Friday. "Gone like the huia," will soon be as expressive of extinction as the Maori proverb that has reference to the moa.

Mr. A. Hamilton, curator of the Dominion Museum, has been huia-hunting with three expert natives for several days, in what used to be a favourable spot, and the party has not seen a single huia.

Huia-hunting requires special skill. The fowler goes out in the early, misty morning and takes up a position on one of the ridges between the low gullies, which the huias used to haunt. Then he imitates the peculiar whistle of the bird,[104] and if there are any huias in the neighbourhood,

---

103  Hunting For Huias, New Zealand Herald, Volume XLV, Issue 13907, 14 November 1908, Page 7 http://paperspast.natlib.govt.nz/cgi-bin/paperspast?a=d&d=NZH19081114.2.40
104  If you'd like to know what a huia sounded like, you can hear a recording of a fowler calling in a huia at this link: http://www.teara.govt.nz/en/speech/13672/rewi-maniapoto-with-huia-feathers

they will come to him, when he endeavours to snare them in a noose.

Mr. Hamilton's fowling ground was practically the basin of the Mangatera, a tributary of the Upper Rangitikei, draining the lower slopes of the Ruahine Mountains. As a result of his experience, he reports that apparently the huias have been entirely exterminated in a very short period in an area where they were comparatively plentiful.

The weather conditions were favourable, and Mr. Hamilton has succeeded in calling huias in the past for as long a distance as a mile. He is more than ever convinced of the difficulty of obtaining specimens, but has not yet given up all hope.

Two expert Maoris have been left behind to continue the hunt for another week. The huia was always a strictly local bird, and Mr. Hamilton knows only two other spots where there is any hope of finding it.

## Another Fruitless Search, 1909[105]

The pretty native bird, the huia, has become almost exterminated. Living specimens are now very rarely seen, and it is feared that there will be great difficulty in preventing the total disappearance of a bird which Maoris and interested Europeans prize so highly.

Mr. A. Hamilton, director of the Dominion Museum, has just returned to Wellington from a further fruitless search of the Moawhango country. Speaking of his mission to a reporter, Mr. Hamilton said: –

"Huias never occurred in the South Island, but only north of a line drawn across the middle of the North Island from New Plymouth to Hawke's Bay. They have never been seen in the Auckland district; in fact, it is only within the memory of man, so far as we know, that they were found outside the true Wairarapa district.

"Originally the district in which the huia was found was the South Wairarapa, at the Tararuas, and the South Wellington district. Then, as civilisation came, and the country was cleared, the birds went northwards to the Ruahines and Puketois, but they have been exterminated from the Puketois for some time.

"The huia is an intensely interesting bird, male and female being so

---

105  Hunting The Huia, New Zealand Herald, Volume XLVI, Issue 14015, 22 March 1909, Page 6 http://paperspast.natlib.govt.nz/cgi-bin/paperspast?a=d&d=NZH19090322.2.65

different in character, and is of all the more interest because it is so much associated with the Maori chiefs. I am in hope that the Government will not give up the search, because it will be a great reproach to us if we allow such a beautiful native bird to become entirely exterminated.

"There is just a probability that a few birds may be still in existence in the Lower Wairarapa or in the rough scrub country between Palliser Bay and the lighthouse."

*With the last suspected sighting in the remote, misty Urewera ranges in the 1960s it is possible, just possible, that somewhere a breeding population of huia still exist. Perhaps the only hope of resurrecting this creature to the surface of the earth again lies in future advancements in cloning – there are stuffed specimens of huia all over the world.*

Chapter 7

# Ancient Peoples, Ancient Pathways

*One of the most controversial debates in New Zealand is the question of whether other cultures ever discovered this country.*

*The official position is no, they didn't. Nonetheless, the evidence tantalisingly suggests our well-paid historians have got it wrong.*

*Even the Maori legends collected by the first historians talk of other visitors and other people who lived here:*

## Arrival Of The Pakeha Foretold In Ancient Dream, 1882[106]

On the first day of the Native gathering at Reweti, [the Maori King] Tawhiao, in conversing with some of the Europeans present on the ancient history of New Zealand, alluded to some native legends with which the general public are not likely to be familiar.

Pointing to two of his chiefs from Kawhia – Hone Wetere and Pikia – he said they are the descendants of an ancestor named Tirewa, a seer who many generations ago from a dream predicted the advent of the Europeans, by proclaiming that a race yet unknown to the Maoris would come to New Zealand in ships, would wear many-coloured garments, and ride upon animals larger than dogs. That prophecy had been fulfilled.

---

106  News of the Week, Otago Witness, Issue 1578, 11 February 1882, Page 8
http://paperspast.natlib.govt.nz/cgi-bin/paperspast?a=d&d=OW18820211.2.18

Tawhiao also mentioned as a singular coincidence that one of his ancestors, before European settlement, while walking in the bush near where are now situate the Taupiri coal-mines, met a fairy, Patupaiarehe, who in a song told him that the name of this land was Tirani – the Niu Tireni or New Zealand of today.

He also gave an interesting account of the various methods of divination practised by the tohungas or priests for ascertaining whether peace or war would ensue between two tribes, or whether a certain warrior would die in battle or have a natural death. The methods referred to somewhat resembled those employed by the Roman augurs. His own future had been partially revealed by the art of divination, and – among other things – disclosed that Tawhiao will never die by drowning. His body may, however, be eaten by a fish.

The ground of this belief is that one of his ancestors was capsized in a canoe out of sight of land, and immediately a whale rose, upon whose back he at once scrambled, and it took him straight to Kawhia Harbour, where he landed in safety, he being an excellent swimmer. Tawhiao concluded by remarking, archly, that these legends, though implicitly believed in the olden time, did not seem to have so great a hold upon the mind of the people in the present day.

## Taranaki To Auckland, The Ancient Road, 1890[107]

THE WHITE CLIFFS: We found that frontier post, once numerously garrisoned, occupied by one mounted constable only. It was here that the Rev. Mr. Whitely and his unfortunate companions were massacred by the Hauhaus, and one of our companions was a member of the party who recovered the bodies, and he saddened our hearts and intensified the melancholy recollections in his own bosom by such broken ejaculations as, "Here we picked up poor so and so there another was found cruelly mutilated."

With heavy packs we left this post on a beautiful morning in January, and tramped along the beach past the ribs of an ancient wreck, over

---

107 **Through North Taranaki And Southern Auckland**, New Zealand Herald, Volume XXVII, Issue 8270, 31 May 1890, Page 1
http://paperspast.natlib.govt.nz/cgi-bin/paperspast?a=d&d=NZH18900531.2.55.6

heavy sand at times, and rough rocks occasionally, until a three mile spell brought us to the tunnel which has been opened into the cliff and through a narrow neck of land which separates the beach from a gully running parallel to the same, up which a good track has been made which leads to the narrow strip of open fern and grass upland, which separates the cliffs from the bush hills. And very narrow it is, never perhaps a mile wide, at times scarcely a quarter of that distance.

The sun was broiling hot above us, and the ground from the heat painful to the foot beneath, whilst our swags appeared to get heavier as the day wore on. The track was intersected by numerous gullies, and the hills beyond are, though apparently of gentle slope facing the sea, precipitous and rugged further inland. More than one of the party have vivid recollections of the deep papa rock-bound gullies, separated from each other by razorbacked spurs, which are the leading features of the country.

At Tongaporutu we were fortunate enough to find a canoe, and crossed the river successfully... There are probably more legends connected with the Tainui canoe than any other of the vessels which are traditionally reported to have brought the Maoris to this country.

Later on we were informed that a portion of this old waka was to be seen at Kawhia, turned into stone, and partially buried in the sand, whilst amongst other things told by Mr. White on the subject is the fact, from which an instructive moral may be drawn, that the immigrant natives failed in dragging the canoe overland, from Waitemata to Manukau, because the chieftainess of Tainui had loved "not wisely but too well" her bonded slave. In vain the stalwart natives toiled and tugged, sung their most persuasive song, and invoked their choicest gods, the canoe was safely anchored to land by the weight of the iniquity of its mistress, who revealed her guilt to them in song, and thus explained the matter satisfactorily to the toilers when she overtook them midway between the two seas.

The day after our arrival at Mokau, the natives held a meeting for the distribution of some money they had received from flaxmillers, for the purchase of the raw material. Many speeches were made, and it was finally decided that certain Europeans should receive notice to stop cutting, in consequence of the money having been paid to the wrong natives, and that application should be made to the Native Lands Court for allocation of interests and subdivision of the block.

This latter appears to be the only way in which the constant friction between native owners and European purchasers of flax can be remedied. The same disputes are rife further north, and this uncertainty as to ownership is dexterously used by the natives to sell to more than one European, and repudiate any agreement should a better offer be made to them.

On leaving Mokau we walked over a fair track to Berry and Newman's flaxmill at Awakino, some four miles distant. There were a large number of hands employed, European and native. The proprietors have a store for the supply of the necessaries of life to the employees. Most of those who spread the flax to dry and turn the same when necessary are native women.

The cook at the mill generously gave us tea and bread and butter. There were only three of us, our two friends having been delayed at Mokau for a time, and after crossing the Awakino in a canoe we tramped along a good beach for seven miles, passing the last frontier settler's place, Mr. C. Newsham's, without calling.

The climb up the cliff from beach to tableland was high and steep, not to say precipitous and dangerous. The whole distance from Awakino to Marokopa is a series of ascents from and descents to the beach, over cliffs one or two hundred feet high.

In some places a precarious assistance is afforded by flax or other vegetation, but in others there is nothing whatever to hold on to, and the material under foot is a shifting rubble, which slides away at every step. Once started on a slide, nothing could stop the unfortunate traveller, who would be dashed to pieces on the hard solid rock which skirts the base of the cliffs in which these rubbly slips generally terminate.

The ancient native track is ill-defined and unreliable, in consequence of landslips having made portions impracticable, and a detour necessary, and so little difference is observable between old and new paths, true and false, and all these are so much like pig and cattle tracks, with which the country abounds, that a guide, or unlimited time and patience amidst these devious ways, is a necessity. We were fortunate in Mr Phelps [the part-Maori guide], who was unerring in his choice of road.

There are also along the whole route numerous points of rocky bluff, which have to be passed at certain times of the tide; some are negotiable only at dead low water, some can be got round at half tide, whilst others again are never clear of breakers, and the hill has again to be climbed.

On the uplands the track is by no means level, gullies intercept the path at right angles every few hundred yards, necessitating the descent of a hill for the only apparent purpose of climbing up the other side.

The marine scenery is very grand, seen from the vantage ground of the point of a bluff dropping sheer down into the sea, or whose precipitous descent terminates in a hard stratified rock, lapped by the foamy waves. The laminated surface of this rock imparts to it an appearance of softness, which is added to by the feathery spume of the waves, whose advance it checks, but this is only when "distance lends enchantment to the view," for a closer inspection reveals the cruel hardness, which would crush to atoms anybody falling from a height upon it.

*The coastline leading up the western North Island is some of the most desolate and beautiful known to mankind, subject to a savage pummelling from the Tasman sea. Not only were you in constant danger of falling off the cliffs as you traversed the old coast tracks, but woe betide any ship that came to close.*

## A Mysterious Wreck, 1940[108]

Buried in the sand at the mouth of the Toreparu River between Raglan and Kawhia is an ancient wreck, believed to be that of an Oriental ship which may have gone ashore in days even previous to Tasman.

The wreck was first discovered about 60 years ago, but only three times since has it been exposed through the action of the river washing away the sand. It appears to be built wholly of teak and is of very solid construction. A massive bolt of solid brass, three feet long, taken from the wreck, has been lent to the Dominion Museum, the Director of which, Dr. W. R. B. Oliver, has recently returned to Wellington after a trip to Kawhia.

When this bolt was taken, with others, from the wreck many years ago, there was also removed a bronze plaque covered with Oriental hieroglyphs, but this became lost in transit to Auckland for expert examination.[109]

---

108 News Of The Day, Evening Post, Volume CXXIX, Issue 8, 10 January 1940, Page 6
http://paperspast.natlib.govt.nz/cgi-bin/paperspast?a=d&d=EP19400110.2.23
109 Historian Michael King claimed to have sent a piece of this wreck for testing:
"In my professional lifetime this phantom ship has been cited as evidence for Phoenician, Roman, Egyptian, Viking, Tamil, Portuguese and Spanish discoveries of New Zealand. It should be no surprise that Menzies has recruited it as proof of a Chinese discovery. The reason that this marvellously elastic piece of evidence fulfils all these expectations is that nobody can produce the wreck itself, which allegedly keeps appearing and disappearing in the sand dunes; nor, even, photographs or drawings of it. In 1969, deter-

There is a possible connection between this mystery wreck and the Tamil bell now in the Dominion Museum. This bell, obtained by the missionary Colenso from some North Auckland Maoris, has inscribed round the rim in Tamil "Mohoyeddin Buks – His Ship's Bell."

The Maoris, who used it for stewing sweet potatoes in, willingly exchanged the bell for a real cooking pot, and said that they had found the bell among the roots of a fallen forest tree. Probably a section of the bolt will be sent to England for expert examination, as an analysis of the alloy of which it is made might furnish some clue as to the origin of the vessel.

## Fragments Of A Wreck, 1872[110]

I have now lying before me certain fragments of a large piece of wreck, which, has come ashore at the mouth of Toreparu Creek, three or four miles north of the heads of Aotea Harbour.

They consist of wooden screws, of which the woodwork is full, and a piece of what I take to be felt (suggested by a gentleman of a morbid turn of mind to be a mass of human hair). The screws are made of a very, close-grained black wood, like puriri in appearance but much softer.

I am not aware that screws are used in the British mercantile marine, so I suppose the vessel to have been either a man-of-war or one of foreign build. I have not yet been able to visit the wreck myself, but I shall do so before my next.

---

mined to subject earlier claims to some kind of test, I sent a piece of the Ruapuke wreck recovered by a local farming family to the Forest Research Institute in Rotorua. The fragment was two ancient pieces of wood, which I was assured was teak, held together by two brass nails. The verdict was disappointingly sober. The wood was totara, and the institute established that, as an artifact, the fragment was little more than 100 years old. The Ruapuke wreck, in other words, was the remains of a vessel built in New Zealand in the nineteenth century." Michael King was dismissive, as you can see of this "phantom ship". However, pieces of the wreck of HMS Orpheus, destroyed on the bar of the Manukau Harbour to the north, later washed up at Ruapuke Beach near the Toreparu River, so it is not even certain that the wreckage King was testing came from the "oriental" vessel in question. The debate remains unsettled as the wreck has never been seen again. King's scepticism also needs to be tempered with the knowledge that King had no access to the newspaper reports and eyewitness accounts you are now reading.

110   Aotea: Inspection Of The School, Daily Southern Cross, Volume XXVIII, Issue 4740, 2 November 1872, Page 3

http://paperspast.natlib.govt.nz/cgi-bin/paperspast?a=d&cl=search&d=DSC18721102.2.16

## The Wreck Near Hokitika, 1888[111]

TO THE EDITOR. Sir, – ln a letter signed "Fox's" to-day, describing the wreck at Hokitika, he says the vessel was screwed together with wooden screws.

On the beach, embedded in the sand above high water mark, at the mouth of the Toreparu River, on the north side of Aotea harbour, is a wreck of a similar description. Is there any connection between the two? – am, &c., 150 Queen Street. T. B. Hill.

## The Mohoyd Buk Wreck, 1939[112]

An article, by John Watson appeared in the "Weekly News" of 18/8/37, quoting Mr. Peter Liddell, of Aotea, who gave him all known details of the "Mohoyd Buk."

First revealed in 1877, when the sands of Ruapuke Beach, near Raglan, were shifted by a heavy storm, it was reburied soon after, but reappeared in 1893 and again in 1909. This wreck was of a wooden ship constructed of teak, the planks being joined with wooden screws and heavy bronze bolts.

The deck was composed of five layers of 2in planking, each layer lying at an angle to the next and fastened with wood, copper, and iron bolts. With this hull is associated the "Tattooed Rocks," a few miles inland, and also the remains of some old stone drainage works supposed to be pre-pakeha and of non-Maori origin.

## The Appearance Of The Wreck, 1893[113]
### Maori Rock Carvings At Karioi

About five miles from Raglan, just under Mr. Savage's farm, on the coast line, Karioi, are some curious rock carvings, or tattooing formations.

---

111  The Wreck Near Hokitika, New Zealand Herald, Volume XXV, Issue 9047, 7 May 1888, Page 3
http://paperspast.natlib.govt.nz/cgi-bin/paperspast?a=d&d=NZH18880507.2.8.2
112  Postscripts, Evening Post, Volume CXXVIII, Issue 143, 14 December 1939, Page 12
http://paperspast.natlib.govt.nz/cgi-bin/paperspast?a=d&cl=search&d=EP19391214.2.63
113  Through Waikato, New Zealand Herald, Volume XXX, Issue 9217, 3 June 1893, Page 1
http://paperspast.natlib.govt.nz/cgi-bin/paperspast?a=d&cl=search&d=NZH18930603.2.77.5

The Maoris know nothing about them, not even in the shape of tradition, and as the Maoris have shown no proclivity for rock-carving, and have nothing of the kind elsewhere in existence they are necessarily shrouded in mystery.

The rock carvings are five in number, and some investigators conjecture that they were boundary stones in the olden times between different tribes. Mr. Cheeseman, curator of the Auckland Museum, has photographs of these curious rock carvings in the Museum.

The carvings assume all the spiral formations characteristic of Maori carving, so that there is no reason to doubt that they are the handiwork, at some time or other, of the Maori race. Mr. Cheeseman contemplates, during the ensuing summer, visiting the Waingaro Hot Springs, and a cave six miles distant, said to contain some fossilised remains. I trust that he will find time to visit Raglan, and elucidate if possible the mystery shrouding the foreign wreck near Aotea, and the Maori rock carvings at Karioi.

There is a fine beach leading to the latter spot, and it is a favourite resort of picnic parties.

## A Mystery Of The Sea, 1893[114]

There is lying buried in the sand, 18 miles from Raglan, in a bay near the native settlement of Makaka, not far from Aotea harbour, the hull of a vessel, apparently of ancient date and foreign build, of the existence of which natives and Europeans were wholly ignorant until the wreck was accidentally discovered.[115]

The discovery was made under the following circumstances: – in 1875[116] Mr. T. B. Hill, of Raglan, and Mr. R. J. O'Sullivan, Inspector of Schools, were bathing on the Ruapuke beach, at Aotea, when the latter looking up at the mouth of Mr. Hill's boundary river, the Toreparu, which empties itself into the sea a little to the north of Aotea harbour, remarked with surprise, "There's the wreck of a vessel up there!" On Mr Hill looking in

---

114 Through Waikato, New Zealand Herald, Volume XXX, Issue 9217, 3 June 1893, Page 1 http://paperspast.natlib.govt.nz/cgi-bin/paperspast?a=d&cl=search&d=NZH18930603.2.77.5
115 This is significant because Maori had good oral tradition regarding other shipwrecks, but no memory within their tribe of this one. Under Maori lore, finders of shipwrecks had scavenging rights.
116 Actually, 1872 as can be seen from the earlier article written by the Inspector of Schools

the direction indicated by Mr. O'Sullivan, he found that such was the case.

They at once dressed, mounted their horses, and on getting to the place jumped on to the wreck of what they considered the deck of a vessel, sloping upwards to the stern, the other portion being embedded in the sand.

The vessel seemed to have come in stern foremost. On getting the late Mrs. Charlton to come down and see the wreck, she at once saw that the course of the river had been altered. The sand had fallen down and changed the course of the river into the old channel in which it was known to have flowed in the olden times, thus accidentally exposing and revealing the wreck.

The portion of the wreck exposed was five thicknesses of two-inch timber, a sort of pine, bolted together with copper bolts and lignum vitas screws as numerous as they could be utilised.

Mr. Hill cut off a piece of wood with an inscription carved upon it in a foreign language, which he handed to the late Mr. Henry Falwasser, at the time correspondent for the Southern Cross, and believed to be portion of the name of the vessel.

On seeing a photo of a part of a ship's bell which is at the Auckland Museum, and referred to in the Transactions of the New Zealand Institute, he thinks the name is the Mohoyd Buk, and as far as his memory serves him is the same as the inscription on the wreck.

For years past the wreck has been covered up with sand, and the recent February gales again partially exposed it, but in Mr. Hill's opinion not the same portion as seen in 1875. Captain Austen, of the S.S. Glenelg, is of opinion that it is the side only of a large vessel which has drifted over from the Australian coast, and settled up soon after being stranded. Others think that it is the remains of a vessel built in Java or Japan, and constructed with bolts from the wrecks of other vessels, as the bolts are not uniform.

Owing to the late flood the portion exposed will be soon left dry again, as the river has changed its course once more, so that anyone will be able to dig around and satisfy their curiosity, or mayhap settle the mystery.

The strangest part of the business is that the Maoris should know nothing about the existence of the wreck, though a large Maori settlement has always been on the point just over it. In the month of October, 1892, Mr. Samuel Harding, C.E., of Mount Eden, was over in the Raglan district, and he paid a visit to the wreck, making some notes, as also a sketch of the locality and of the portion of the vessel exposed, and in the course of conversation he gave me the following particulars.

The wreck, which had been partly exposed 17 years ago, was again visible in the sands on the beach near the southern boundary of the farm of Mr. W. Thomson, J. P., Ruapuke, and a few miles north of the headland known as Albatross Point, near the entrance to Aotea Harbour.

At the locality of the wreck there is a magnificent sandy beach extending for three miles, and the stream flowing out that escapes to the sea is lost in seasons of drought when the scouring force is at the minimum, both wind and sea choke the entrance, obliterating the watercourse and causing its position to be altered until some heavy fresh reopens or causes it to force a new channel. This accounts for the wreck being buried for so many years in the sand, but again being visible.

Mr. Harding says he had no means of knowing how much of the wreck was covered with sand. The superficial area was 55 to 60 square feet, the surface flat, and composed of planks generally nine inches, with a few six inches wide. This deck, or whatever it might be, was composed of five planks in depth, each plank nominally two inches thick, giving a total of 10 inches in thickness. The timber was like inferior pine, with many knots, but though discoloured and somewhat "dosed," in a fair state of preservation.

But the construction was remarkable, each layer of planking being at an angle of 45 degrees from the last layer, the top and bottom planks were therefore parallel with each other. These planks were bound together by hard wooden screws, a little under 11 inches in thickness. The thread on two of the screws, the only ones available for examination, did not seem as if formed with a screw-plate, or mechanical contrivance. There were angular projections on the timber as if cut with a knife, but not sufficiently rough to impede screwing home. There were sixteen iron bolts.

Mr. Harding could not ascertain if the ends had been in the screw-plate; they were of the same thickness as the wooden screws. There were also a few spikes like the six inch spike we are accustomed to. They were driven at irregular distances, and might have been used for subsequent repairs. There were therefore 83 screws and bolts, holding together an area of about 60 square feet of deck, or whatever it might have been, constructed and designed in the strongest manner.

Mr. Harding says as the stream at the bend where the wreck is is only ankle deep, a few boards on edge so as to direct the current on the wreck, as suggested by Mr. Cheeseman, would lay bare the timber work, and so inexpensive a mode would be worth trying. A few fascines made from the adjacent scrub and jammed down would be equally as efficacious.

*The 'Tamil Bell' of legend was discovered being used as cooking pot by Northland Ngapuhi in 1836 by explorer and missionary William Colenso. There is no explanation as to how it came to that location, beyond the local tribe's recollection they had found it in the roots of a tree, although it should be noted the Ngapuhi had raided deep into the Waikato in the early 1800s and could easily have carried off the bell as 'plunder'.*

*Of one thing we can be more certain: had the bell simply been lost at sea, there was almost no hope of Maori finding it and dredging it up. The bell must have made landfall, either in a shipwreck, or a visit, or as a traded item by the crew of another ship.*

*That one of the co-discoverers of the Ruapuke shipwreck remembers similar 'hieroglyphics' on the plate recovered from that vessel increases the likelihood of a link; after all, had the letters on the inscriptions been in the Roman alphabet used by all European explorers, the school inspector would have recognised the European origin of the language. He did not. The Tamil characters on the side of the bell would qualify as 'hieroglyphics'.*

*Later suggestions that the ship name could be remembered as "Mohoyd Buk" would appear to be memory corruptions – mainly because the language was unintelligible to Europeans and Maori alike:*

## The Tamil Bell, 1901[117]
**By Jessie Mackay**

Forty or fifty years ago students of Maori history were puzzling over the mystery of the Tamil Bell, a mystery never solved, alas, or likely to be. The fullest account of it extant is probably that of Mr J T. Thomson, of Otago, in an able treatise on the "Whence of the Maori," published among the early "Transactions of the New Zealand Institute."

This debatable relic was discovered by the Rev. W. Colenso in the interior

---

117  The Tamill Bell, Star, Issue 7032, 23 February 1901, Page 6
http://paperspast.natlib.govt.nz/cgi-bin/paperspast?a=d&d=TS19010223.2.90

of the North Island. The Maoris could give no account of it, nor did Mr Colenso display it in public till the Exhibition, of 1862.

Mr Thomson, a learned Oriental scholar, was permitted to photograph the bell and its inscription. On sending copies of this photograph to India, he was assured that it "was" a genuine piece of Tamil work: Learned Tamil writers from Ceylon and Penang agreed that the inscription was "Mohoyideen Buks," ship's bell. But the grammar, they said, was wrong, and the letters differed considerably from modern Tamil characters.

Mr Thomson, while unable to refer it to any definite date, considered this showed the antiquity of the bell arguing that it was most unlikely that such a piece of excellent workmanship should be disfigured by writing which was incorrect at the time, and pointing out as an example how English has altered since Chaucer.

Thomson adduced the bell as a proof of communication at some early time, between South India and New Zealand, and offered two suggestions regarding its arrival. In the first place it might have been brought from Tongatapu by the first Maori immigrants. This would support his own theory of Maori origin, which counted them as descendants of the Barata, an active Negroid race of South India, daring navigators of early times, who have left traces of extensive migration down the Straits by Singapore.

Mr Thompson discounted the Malayan theory of origin formerly so widely held, as he considered the time of Malayan dominion of the Straits too late to have had much influence on the Polynesian migrations. In the second place, he temperately allowed that the bell might have been captured from some Indian vessel by Europeans some time during the last three or four centuries, and that these Europeans were afterwards cast away on New Zealand shores.

Indeed, there exists an apparently authentic Maori tradition of one such wreck before Captain Cook's time. This last suggestion is all but confirmed by later researches, which place the Maori migrations immeasurably before the approximate date accepted thirty years ago, which put the first Maori landing in New Zealand at only about fifty years before the discovery of America.

Mr Percy Smith, indeed, thinks it probable that the bell was bartered or given to the Maoris by Europeans after the time of Captain Cook, and even within the nineteenth century. He also emphasises the fact that no racial affinity exists between the Maoris and the Tamils, although their ancestors were probably neighbours in South India at some period. That period must, however, have been so remote that he questions whether the Tamils possessed any writing system at the time of the Polynesian migrations. Thus the Tamil Bell is shorn of its first glamour; but it must always remain a tantalising and suggestive incident in early New Zealand history.

## Mystery Of Pacific, 1931[118]

Recent reference in the "Star" to the probable discovery of New Zealand during the sixteenth century by Spanish and Portuguese explorers indicates that there is a fascinating field for research in the early exploration of the Pacific.

---

118 Mystery Of Pacific, Auckland Star, Volume LXII, Issue 181, 3 August 1931, Page 6
http://paperspast.natlib.govt.nz/cgi-bin/paperspast?a=d&d=AS19310803.2.57

From the Maoris and various South Sea tribes we have gained a fairly full account of the activities of Polynesian voyagers, but there is evidence to show that a great deal of exploration was done by early seafarers from Asia, Africa and Europe.

The discovery among the Maoris of the Tamil bell, dating from about the ninth century, indicates the possibility of a visit to New Zealand by Indian explorers. Then there was the recent finding in North Auckland of a carved lintel of Malayan workmanship. In the June issue of the South African weekly "The Outspan," Commander J. E. Capstickdale mentions that in 491 A.D. a monk named Hwai Shan, from Samarkand (near Tibet), sailed round the north of Japan, through the Aleutian Islands, and down to South California, returning safely. It seems probable then that civilised navigators from Asia early explored the Pacific.

Long before the birth of Christ, Egyptian and Phoenician sailors explored the Indian Ocean and the Malay Archipelago. Indeed, the Phoenicians, according to Professor G. Elliot Smith, explored Polynesia in 700 B.C., and he believes that a party settled somewhere in the South Seas. Could it have been at Easter Island? Though the Egyptians do not seem to have come so far east it is interesting to note that in the reign of King Necho they circumnavigated Africa from east to west, taking three years to do it.

No explanation has yet been given the mysterious people, white-skinned and red-haired, who, according to Maori legend, lived in the forests of New Zealand. They were said to be the original owners of the land, older than any other tribe.

From them the Maoris learnt many of the arts of weaving, and on misty days the sound of their singing and flute-playing could be heard among the forest-clad ranges. In his book "Te Ika a Maui" the Rev. R. Taylor records the tale that though a shy folk they were frequently seen; they wore white garments and carried their infants as Europeans do! Then there is the legend that by some mystic power they could not be harmed. Some of them seemed to be half flesh, half stone. Could they have worn some form of armour? If they were a lost Aryan race it might be so, these people seem to have been far further advanced in the arts than the Maori. One thing is certain, the study of man's history in the Pacific has only just begun.

## Tamil Bell And Spanish Morion, 1935[119]

Public prominence has been given to some riches of worldwide interest since the authorities of the Dominion Museum have prepared to leave their long outgrown quarters for the new National Art Gallery and Museum building. Some treasured trophies have been locked away in scattered storerooms for want of display space. Two items have as racy an interest as any in southern climes.

The finding of a ship's bell, and the accumulated evidence as to its origin have made New Zealand a more interesting country in the eyes not only of those who have enjoyed romantic stories from the "Iliad" to "Treasure Island," but also of ethnologists, historians and archaeologists.

Well named the Antipodes, New Zealand, according to available records, was not discovered by Europeans until the seventeenth century, when Abel Tasman visited its shores. James Cook's voyages stimulated a deep interest among American and British whalers, whose expeditions are recorded in the latter part of the eighteenth century. Whalers established temporary stations at various points on the coast, but it was not until the 'thirties of last century that anything in the nature of permanent settlement was entered upon.

In 1836 the Rev. William Colenso, F.L.S., discovered a relic truly startling in its import. Whilst exploring the interior, which hitherto had been unvisited by any but Maoris, he came upon a village in the Whangarei district, and saw the natives using as a cooking utensil a remarkable bell-shaped vessel.

The fact that the natives were essentially neolithic and were not known to possess any metal tools or utensils aroused his curiosity, and he examined closely the pot, of which they appeared very proud. Perhaps no more incongruous discovery could have been made.

His many inquiries of members of the tribe were all answered to the same effect – that the bell had been discovered many years before when a large tree had been blown down, and the roots had left the relic exposed to view.

---

119 Storied Trophies, Auckland Star, Volume LXVI, Issue 290, 7 December 1935, Page 11
http://paperspast.natlib.govt.nz/cgi-bin/paperspast?a=d&d=AS19351207.2.84

## *Recognised by Tamils*

The bell did not appear complete, since the lip had been broken off uniformly round the lower band, fortunately, however, leaving intact an inscription, in characters which subsequently proved to be Tamil, or South Indian.

Mr. Colenso's happy manner in dealing with the natives resulted in his acquisition of the bell as a gift. Mr. J. T. Thomson, who studied so early as the 'sixties the question of "Whence the Maori?" records in the Transactions of the New Zealand Institute of 1872 that he first saw the bell in the New Zealand Exhibition of 1862.

"I must confess I looked upon the Tamil bell with feelings amounting almost to enthusiasm," wrote Mr. Thomson. "So much so that I had the same photographed and copies forwarded to various parts of India."

The Klings or Tamils immediately recognised the photograph as exhibiting the upper part of a ship's bell such as is still in use by them down to the present day. Translations of the inscription were returned from Ceylon and also from Penang by favour of two friends of Mr. Thomson. Both translations were: "Mohoyiden Buks Ships Bell."

The Tamil writers of Penang gave what they termed the modern characters of 21 letters for comparison with the script of 23 letters on the bell. The forms of several letters differ greatly, the modern Tamil script being inclined and the ancient – more upright – characters having no punctuation.

## *A Migration Mystery*

Marco Polo, the thirteenth century explorer, had something to say about Madagascar and the traffic to and from that island from South India. Further, it is generally known that the natives of Malabar and Coromandel from time immemorial were skilful navigators whose voyages, besides extending west to Madagascar, were also undertaken easterly as far as Java, Bali and Ternati.

It is supposed that there was a great expansion of South Indian navigation long prior to the advent of Europeans in these South Pacific seas and even indeed to the Indian Ocean.

More of imagination than of fact must I span the gap between the known limits of South Indian voyages to Malaya and the appearance of the Tamil bell in far away New Zealand. Whether the bell was brought to New Zealand from "Tongataboo" by the first Maori migrants as a trophy of some sea fight in Northern waters, or whether a Tamil ship reached the shores of New Zealand, must remain a matter of pure conjecture in the absence of further evidence.

There is, of course, the less dramatic possibility that the Tamil bell may have been used by a ship of English, Dutch, Portuguese or Spanish origin following the capture of some South Indian trader.

The degree of interest in the Tamil bell depends to a certain extent upon its age. To have reached its final destination in New Zealand, the bell must be deemed to have been in existence for at least 150 years prior to 1836, when Mr. Colenso found it. The evidence of the Ceylon and Penang authorities as to the antiquity of the characters would suggest far greater age. The Bishop of Dornakel, South India, examined the bell in the Dominion Museum in 1923 and observed that, in his opinion, it was not an artifact of great antiquity, inasmuch as the name "Mohoyiden" is a Mahometan name. Antiquity, according to the bishop, may have meant Biblical antiquity.

### *Did a Galleon Visit Port Nicholson?*

The Tamil bell is not alone, however, as evidence of early unchronicled voyages to New Zealand. A Spanish helmet, or morion, as worn by soldiers of the time of Balboa and Cortez, was dredged from Wellington harbour several years ago – another Museum exhibit whose history is unknown. Its presence in Wellington harbour evidences nothing more than that a Spanish ship may have found the narrow/entrance on a rocky coast to a wide and sheltered haven which Tasman never approached, which Cook avoided because of a rising storm and which today is the port of New Zealand's capital city.

This possible solution can be only a matter of conjecture as the helmet may have been lost overboard from a much more recent arrival. Nevertheless these two items – the Tamil bell and the old Spanish helmet – are among the most interesting of a rich collection of exhibits in the Dominion Museum.

## A Curious Find, 1919[120]

Amid the highly-learned matter of which the March number of the Journal

---

120   A Curious Find, Evening Post, Volume XCVII, Issue 92, 21 April 1919, Page 2
http://paperspast.natlib.govt.nz/cgi-bin/paperspast?a=d&d=EP19190421.2.21

of Science and Technology is made up is a report of the discovery of a figurine at Mauku, Auckland.[121]

Mr Elsdon Best deals with the subject, around which a romance could be written. The little figure is made of steatite. It was picked up in unploughed land, uninhabited until twenty years ago; but Maoris occupied the lands in pre-European days.

Here, embedded in the clay, the little figure was found. It looks like a portrait of an ancient Chinese personage of distinction. Steatite and soapstone are identical. How did it get where it was found, and how long has it lain in the clay?[122]

It is placed by Mr. Best with the mysterious Tamil bell found on the West Coast. The dress of the figure is that of a pre-Manchu Chinese, which, in some respects, survives in the Korean national costume of to-day. Possibly some great junk out of the China Seas wandered down into these waters, and was never able to return, finally going to pieces on the coast in a westerly blast. The wrecked vessel would fall into the hands of the Maoris had they survived the seas; and of the wreckage that came ashore they would divide it among them.

The figure is not like the soapstone images now made by Chinese, mostly for the tourist and sailor trade.

*The mystery of whether New Zealand was visited by the Chinese, Spanish or Portuguese remains unsolved, and the wreck at the mouth of the Toreparu stream north of Aotea Harbour likewise remains unexcavated. So far no credible explanation exists for the discovery of a pre-Manchu Chinese figurine found in clay (not topsoil). The position of most of the government-funded historians however is "nothing to see here, move on".*

---

121  Close to Pukekohe, and about 70km as the crow flies from the Ruapuke wreck. Both archaeological sites are within Waikato tribal boundaries.
122  When historian Michael King repeatedly asserts "there is not a shred of evidence" of other cultures visiting New Zealand, he either does so in ignorance of the evidence, or he wilfully ignored it. The debate is covered in more detail in the book *The Great Divide*

Chapter 8

# New Zealand's Forgotten Dinosaurs

*If you grew up in New Zealand as a baby-boomer or Gen-Xer, you'd have been taught that New Zealand had no dinosaurs. Geologically we appeared to be a young country, and no one had ever found anything remotely resembling a dinosaur.*

*That myth was shot down with the work of amateur palaeontologist Joan Wiffen, who began uncovering fossils in the 1970s and 80s.*

*However, imagine the news headlines if something much bigger than a toe-bone or a tooth was recovered by scientists...*

## Huge Land Lizard Discovered Near Inglewood, 1896[123]

New Plymouth, 28th November. The fossil remains of what is believed to be a huge land lizard have been discovered near Purangi, inland from Inglewood.

It is estimated to be from 30 to 40 feet long, and in perfect preservation, the scale and fossilised skin being visible to the naked eye.

An officer of the Survey Department leaves on Monday to inspect with a view of securing the remains.

---

123 Interesting Fossil Remains, Evening Post, Volume LII, Issue 162, 30 November 1896, Page 5
http://paperspast.natlib.govt.nz/cgi-bin/paperspast?a=d&d=EP18961130.2.47

## Monster Fossil Found At Purangi, 1896[124]

An interesting discovery of fossil remains has recently been made in the bed of a creek running into the Waitara River in the neighbourhood of Purangi.

Mr Hertzog, who was out collecting shells and fossils for the New Plymouth museum, was crossing the creek when he observed the fossilised remains of a huge saurian monster embedded in a part of the bank which the water had cut away.

The head was exposed to view, and was in every respect like the head of the conventional dragon. In length the fossilised saurian was from 30 to 40 feet.

It is considered that the remains are those of a huge land lizard, which should throw some additional light on the geological formation of the country.

Mr Hertzog brought a part of one of the legs into the Land Office. This fragment is now in the possession of Mr Clarke, the chief draughtsman. The scales and fossilised skin can be plainly seen with the naked eye.

An officer of the Department will leave on Monday to inspect the place with a view of obtaining the remains, part of which is embedded in the papa rock.

This is the only specimen ever found in the North Island, and probably New Zealand.

## Photographs Of Dinosaur, 1896[125]

Photographs have been obtained of the fossil remains of the huge saurian discovered at Purangi, Taranaki, last week.

The *Hawera Star* says it is improbable that the Survey Department will go to the expense of digging the remains out of the cliff in which they are embedded.

---

124  Mammoth Fossil Remains At Purangi, Taranaki Herald, Volume XLV, Issue 10780, 28 November 1896, Page 2
http://paperspast.natlib.govt.nz/cgi-bin/paperspast?a=d&d=TH18961128.2.10
125  FOSSIL REMAINS, Star, Issue 5743, 10 December 1896, Page 2
http://paperspast.natlib.govt.nz/cgi-bin/paperspast?a=d&d=TS18961210.2.21.4

# NEW ZEALAND'S FORGOTTEN DINOSAURS

This is the only known photo of Taranaki's fossil 'land lizard'. Taken by survey official W H Skinner, the picture shows a man, believed to be Hertzog who first discovered the beast, posing beside the fossilised skull of the creature in the bank of a creek at Purangi. The Government decided not to excavate because of the remote location, and the fossil may remain there to this day if souvenir hunters have not disturbed it. PHOTO: Weekly Graphic & Ladies Journal, 13 February 1897

## Excavation Of Dinosaur Now Unlikely, 1896[126]

Mr W. H. Skinner returned on Wednesday from Purangi, where he had gone to inspect the fossil remains of the huge saurian that were discovered by Mr Hertzog. Mr Skinner obtained photographs of the head of the fossil. It is improbable that the department will go to the expense of digging the remains out of the cliff.

## Maori Reckon Dragon Is Taniwha, 1896[127]

With regard to the fossil remains of a saurian monster found at Purangi, the Crown Lands Commissioner is awaiting a reply from Wellington to Mr W. H. Skinner's report, before taking any steps to remove the remains. The Maoris, it is said, have a tradition that a monster, which they called Parahia, formerly existed in that district, to which it was customary to make an offering of the first fruits of the season, but whether Mr Hertzog's discovery has any connection with the traditional Parahia is uncertain.

## Dragon Guards Preservation Inlet Grotto, 1896[128]

The prehistoric saurian discovered in Taranaki has (writes a correspondent of the *Southland Times*), so far as I can gather from the particulars furnished, its contemporary in a fossilisation at Preservation Inlet.

It is embedded in the sedimentary rock or boulder clay (I would not be sure which) forming a cliff to the sea at the head of a cave or marine grotto on the Cuttle Cove side of the inlet. Its outlines are in many respects distinct head, eyes, fangs and feelers all well defined. Its measurements cannot be less than 20ft by, I should say, 18in at the fullest part of rotundity.

*A search of the New Zealand newspaper archives has failed to turn up any*

---

126  The General Election, Taranaki Herald, Volume XLV, Issue 10785, 4 December 1896, Page 2
http://paperspast.natlib.govt.nz/cgi-bin/paperspast?a=d&d=TH18961204.2.5
127  News Items, Colonist, Volume XL, Issue 8751, 30 December 1896, Page 3
http://paperspast.natlib.govt.nz/cgi-bin/paperspast?a=d&d=TC18961230.2.13
128  An Interesting-Fossil, Star, Issue 5740, 7 December 1896, Page 3
http://paperspast.natlib.govt.nz/cgi-bin/paperspast?a=d&d=TS18961207.2.41.3

*further articles on the 40 foot long "land lizard" with the head like "a dragon" and fossilised skin, so one can only assume it remains in the rocky bank of a creek entering the Waitara River near Purangi, now well hidden in the shrubbery and bush, awaiting someone with the time to dig through old New Plymouth museum records from 1896 in the hope of pinning down an exact location. If an intact skeleton of that magnitude was found in New Zealand the person who re-discovered it would enter the history books.*

## Miniature Elephant Fossil Found, 1898[129]

An exchange says that Mr Nathan, road inspector, made a curious find of fossil at Whangamomona the other day. The fossil was in the papa rock, and was in shape something like a pig or a miniature elephant. It measured about two feet in length by one foot in height, and was complete with the exception of the nose, which was broken off. The fossil has been offered to Sir James Hector.

## Giant Reptile Discovered Near Greymouth, 1887[130]
*By Telegraph [United Press Association] Greymouth, This Day:*

In Hungerford and Mackay's quarry, on the north side of the river at Cobden, a blast disclosed a large portion of a skeleton apparently of the saurian family. There are seven points of the vertebra, and a number of ribs.

Another portion of the stone containing the fossil was thrown over the tip-head before being noticed, but this will be recovered. The fossil weighs several hundredweight, and is about 4 feet-long by 2 feet. It has been given to the School of Mines.

The specimen, which was underlying a mountain of hydraulic limestone, appears to be that of some kind of reptile.

In 1940, miners excavated another massive skeleton, this time what they believed was a whale:

---

129  A Curious Find, Star, Issue 6489, 16 May 1898, Page 2
http://paperspast.natlib.govt.nz/cgi-bin/paperspast?a=d&d=TS18980516.2.29.4
130  A Fossil Saurian, Evening Post, Volume XXXIII, Issue 78, 2 April 1887, Page 2
http://paperspast.natlib.govt.nz/cgi-bin/paperspast?a=d&d=EP18870402.2.32

## Fossil Monster[131]
### Greymouth Discovery, Prehistoric Relic

The complete fossil remains of some prehistoric monster were discovered in a limestone quarry at Cobden, near Greymouth, last week. In the Greymouth Harbour Board's limestone quarry a 1000-ton block of stone was split by a powder charge, and this revealed the skeleton of what is believed to be the remains of some prehistoric animal of considerable dimensions.

Although the blast destroyed some of the fossil, it was still possible for even a layman to follow the outline of the fossilised skeleton, but it is not considered to bear marked resemblance to any present-day animal. The backbone and ribs are clearly traceable in the limestone, and are somewhat like those of a whale, but they are surmounted by other fossilised bone which appears to indicate that the animal, when alive, had shoulders and limbs.

It is believed possible that the fossil is that of either a prehistoric whale or some land animal of an early period in the world's history. The block of which contained the fossil was brought down from one of the top benches of the quarry by a blast about five months ago, and until a few days ago had remained intact. It was the largest single block ever obtained in the quarry and was composed of limestone.

The fossil was embedded almost in the centre, covering about 12 feet, which gives some indication of the size of the animal.

The fossilised backbone is between six and nine inches thick and the ribs are about two or three inches broad. The rock containing the greater portion of the fossil is being kept in the quarry and should provide scientists with interesting data on the period when the limestone of the coastal ranges on the West Coast was formed, and on the type of animals then in the Southern Hemisphere.

Dr. W. R. B. Oliver, of the Dominion Museum, expressed the opinion yesterday [not having seen the creature] that the remains were most probably those of a whale. The rock where they were found belonged to the tertiary age. In the Northern Hemisphere remains of whales of the

---

131 Fossil Monster, Evening Post, Volume CXXX, Issue 8, 9 July 1940, Page 5
http://paperspast.natlib.govt.nz/cgi-bin/paperspast?a=d&d=EP19400709.2.7

tertiary period were comparatively common among fossils, but in New Zealand very few had been found.

The Dominion Museum had one nearly completed fossil skeleton, and a few other smaller remains had been found and described by geologists. Whether it will be possible to acquire the new find for the Dominion Museum remains to be seen, but steps are already being taken to see what can be done in this direction.

## Crocodile Found At Oamaru, 1862[132]

TO THE EDITOR OF THE DAILY TIMES: Sir – You will probably be desirous of having the earliest intelligence of a remarkable discovery of fossil remains in this district, made in the course of excavating blocks of stone for the New Post Office in your city.

The limestone stratum is, as you are probably aware, nearly horizontal, and in course of splitting off one of the blocks, of large dimensions, the skeleton of an animal was laid bare.

The vertebrae are well marked, as also the ribs and what appears to be a tail, about 4ft long, and appearing to consist of 5 joints; the head is not so complete, but it is in a good state of preservation, and is about the size and very nearly the shape of that of an alligator or crocodile.

The block has been carefully preserved, and will be sent by the first steamer to Dr Hector, to whom a more minute description and drawing have been sent by this mail by Mr Campbell, on whose property it was found.

I am, &c, Charles Vail Symonds, Oamaru, 26th April, 1862.

## New Zealand's Oldest Tree[133]
*Tree 50,000,000 Years Old*

A discovery of considerable scientific interest was recently made by Mr R. C. Read on his property in the Tuapeka Flat district Otago.

The find is a portion of a small fossilised tree which Mr Read discovered

---

132 Discovery Of Fossil Remains At Oamaru, Otago Daily Times, Issue 1049, 1 May 1865, Page 4
http://paperspast.natlib.govt.nz/cgi-bin/paperspast?a=d&d=ODT18650501.2.7
133 Tree 50,000,000 Years Old, Bay of Plenty Beacon, Volume 9, Issue 1, 28 August 1945, Page 7
http://paperspast.natlib.govt.nz/cgi-bin/paperspast?a=d&d=BPB19450828.2.38

in some rock formation and which he handed to the Otago Museum where it is now on display. The specimen was referred to the geology department of the Otago University which has reported that the quartzite deposit in which the wood was fossilised dates to the beginning of the Tertiary period and is therefore about 50 million years old.

When found the fossil was believed to be contemporary with the schists which underlie the quartzite but inspection shows it to be of the period mentioned, while the schists are vastly more ancient. For all that, the fossil probably holds the record for age of timber in Dunedin at the present time.

## A Beast To Rival Four Tigers, 1873[134]

With respect to some gigantic fossil remains of New Zealand saurians which have been added to the collections in the Colonial Museum at Wellington, the *Independent* says:

"Probably some of our readers recollect seeing a few months back upon the wharf several huge grey boulders, showing here and there fossil imprints. These were found at Amuri, and sent to Dr Hector, under whose directions they are giving up bone by bone the remains which they have enshrouded for ages.

"The process of extricating these tell-tales of a past existence from their stony covering is an exceedingly delicate task, and one that would appear to require a special aptitude. With mallet and chisel, often not bigger than a bradawl, the workman patiently chips away, day after day, to once more bring into light the stray bones and articulations embedded in the stone.

"Some of these specimens of extinct life are remarkably perfect. Others are so huge that the beholder, reasoning *expede Herculem*, must involuntarily exclaim, 'And there were giants in those days.'

"Several complete portions of these anatomical skeletons have been chiselled out, placed in their proper position by Dr Hector, and afterwards mounted ready for view and several more fossil remains of distinct varieties are still to be chiselled out; all of them, no doubt, to form the subject of future learned and interesting papers for the 'Transactions of the New Zealand Institute.'

---

134   Fossil Imprints, Otago Witness , Issue 1128, 12 July 1873, Page 3
http://paperspast.natlib.govt.nz/cgi-bin/paperspast?a=d&d=OW18730712.2.9

"Many of the recent acquisitions by the Museum possess deep scientific interest while there are others which arouse it even in the most uncultivated minds. Amongst this class of specimens may be ranked that of a gigantic seal's skull, picked up near Hokitika. As its strength of tusk and body is computed to have been equal to that of four full-grown tigers, it must have been a truly formidable foe to the fishes of that period."

## The Nelson Caveman, 1916[135]
*Lecture By J. Taylor*

A lecture was given last night in All Saints' Schoolroom by Mr Joseph Taylor, on "My Discovery of Prehistoric Remains at Maruia – in Relation to the Antiquity of Man." The Rev. J. A. Rogers, BA., presided.

The lecturer commenced by endorsing the saying that '"the proper study of mankind is man". He described a find of remains which he had made in the Maruia Valley, and endeavoured to place them as to their geologic age, and their relation to the question of man's age on the earth.

Various fossil fragments were exhibited and explained, the general conclusion being that the fragments belonged either to the true genus 'homo' or else to one of man's earliest anatomical ancestors. There was very strong evidence, the lecturer said, to prove that this was really another of Darwin's missing links, especially as regards those fossil fragments which resembled the cast of a skull and of a section of a limb, with other bone-shaped parts of the human anatomy.

## New Zealand's Plesiosaurs, 1937[136]
*By A. W. B. Powell*

New Zealand is noted for possessing the only surviving link with the great reptiles of the geological past. Although insignificant in size when compared with the monsters of the past nevertheless our tuatara can claim this unique lineage. Strangely enough our fossil beds have not yet revealed

---

135  Prehistoric Remains, Colonist, Volume LVII, Issue 14227, 28 October 1916, Page 7
http://paperspast.natlib.govt.nz/cgi-bin/paperspast?a=d&d=TC19161028.2.32
136  Reptilian Monsters Of A Geologic Past, Auckland Star, Volume LXVIII, Issue 240, 9 October 1937, Page 11
http://paperspast.natlib.govt.nz/cgi-bin/paperspast?a=d&d=AS19371009.2.220

to us ancestral relatives of our tuatara or of any other land-dwelling reptile of this ancient stock. In the case of the marine saurians and related groups, however, New Zealand had its species as has been clearly demonstrated by local geologists.

The first notice of the occurrence in New Zealand strata of representatives of reptilian fauna characteristic of the "age of great reptiles," known as the Mesozoic or "Middle Period" of geological time, was made in 1861, when the great Professor Owen read a paper in London on a collection of fossil reptilian remains which had been discovered by the late Mr. T. H. Cockburn Hood. These fossil remains were obtained by Mr. Hood in a ravine on one of the tributaries of the Waipara River, at the northern extremity of the Canterbury Plains. These remains consisted of vertebra, ribs and several other kinds of bones belonging to a new species which Professor Owen named Plesiosaurus australis.

### *Our Only True Saurian Skull*

No further discovery of saurian remains was made till after the occurrence of a great flood, in 1868, when Mr. Hood again obtained a large collection and shipped it to England, unfortunately, by the ship Mataoka, which was lost on the homeward voyage.

Dr. Haast, however, communicated a short account of the collection to the Philosophical Institute of Canterbury, and states that he "made drawings and took measurements of all the more important specimens, so that, in case the collection should not reach its destination, the information at least will not be altogether lost to the scientific world."

This foresight was most fortunate, for notwithstanding the great number and variety of the remains since found, that collection appears to have contained the only skull fragment with jaws and teeth, of a true saurian that has yet been found in New Zealand.

In 1868 the late Dr. Haast made a detailed survey of the Waipara district and obtained a large series of saurian remains which are now preserved in the Canterbury Museum. The next big find of saurian remains was made in 1869 when the late Mr. John Buchanan, of the Geological Survey Department, made a survey of the cretaceous rocks of the Amuri district, about 50 miles to the north of the Waipara.

During the next two years further collections were made resulting in the accumulation of several tons of blocks of cement-stone containing fossil bones. After over three months of careful work in clearing the specimens from the hard rock in which they were embedded, the gratifying result was an array of bones representing 43 individual reptiles, mostly of gigantic size, all of aquatic habits, and belonging to 13 distinct species. Six distinct species of Plesiosaurus were found in the Waipara and Amur, beds, the largest of these representing creatures, in life, 10ft or more in length.

Also, examples of related kinds, Polycotylus and Mauisaurus were found, the latter being a new genus which seems to have been confined to New Zealand. A single vertebral section of an Ichthyosaurus from Mount Potts, Canterbury, shows that still another group of these great extinct reptiles once lived in these seas, and finally there were two distinct kinds of Mosasaurs or giant "sea serpents".

The plesiosaur was an animal with a long, slender neck surmounted by a comparatively small head, but with powerful jaws, armed with formidable teeth. It also had a tapering tail, but the main feature of the monster was four powerful paddles, which no doubt enabled it to pursue its prey with great speed; fishes, squids and cuttlefish probably forming the bulk of its diet.

The largest of the plesiosaurs attained a length of forty feet and had swimming paddles seven feet in length. A curious feature, as revealed by study of the vertebrae, is that the long neck was inflexible, almost rigid, being capable of lateral movements only. Apparently the plesiosaurs did not produce their young alive, but, perhaps, like existing turtles, laid their eggs on sandy beaches or amongst the smooth rocks along the margin of the sea.

### *An Extinction Mystery*

The plesiosaurs, along with the vast array of giant reptiles of the Mesozoic period, became extinct with the close of this "age of reptiles" as completely as if they had never existed. So far remains of these reptiles have been found in New Zealand rocks only in North Canterbury, Marlborough, Moeraki and Batley, on the Kaipara.

Mesozoic rocks, however, mostly unfossiliferous, are widely distributed in New Zealand and occur abundantly around Auckland. Practically the whole of Waiheke Island, the "Noises," and half of Motutapu Island are formed of rock known as "greywacke," and belong to the Jurassic period of the Mesozoic age, but so far practically no trace of a fossil has been found in them.

Who can explain just why these once abundant creatures suddenly became extinct with the close of the Mesozoic period, yet the even older order to which our living tuatara belongs goes right back to the far distant Permian period.

Despite the search for dinosaurs, for a long time New Zealand was home to the largest animal ever found by humans:

## Giant Whale Discovered, 1908[137]

Subscriptions for the purchase of the skeleton of the Okarito whale for the Canterbury Museum continue to come slowly. Some £110 of the £200 required from the public is now in hand.

Mr. E. R. Waite, the curator of the museum, is in no doubt in regard to the place the Okarito whale occupies amongst the world's giant mammals, and he points out that the skeleton will be a notable addition to the splendid collection in the museum. It represents absolutely the largest beast that has been known to exist in present or former times.

The whale in life was about 87ft. long. There is no authentic account of a larger whale having been seen. The great reptile which was unearthed at Wyoming, in the United States, and which has been named Diplodocus Carnegii, was only about 80ft. long, and even the mastodons and the colossal dinosaurs of the secondary epoch could not bear comparison with the cetacean that was cast ashore some months ago off the coast of Southern Westland.

*It's not just massive whales and old dinosaurs roaming around the coastal areas of southern Westland. As we're about discover, other exotic creatures may be roaming the Fiordland bush...*

---

137  Local And General, Dominion, Volume 2, Issue 312, 26 September 1908, Page 4
http://paperspast.natlib.govt.nz/cgi-bin/paperspast?a=d&d=DOM19080926.2.11

Chapter 9

# Untamed Country: The Story Of The Elusive Moose

*In sharp contrast to the extensively populated North Island with its huge tribes, when explorers and early settlers arrived in the South Island – then known as 'Middle Island' – they found the island almost empty.*

*From sea to shining sea spread a land of almost impassable snow-capped peaks and massive glacier-filled valleys, rising above fertile lowlands covered in grasses and native bush.*

*The countryside, particularly around the lower fiords, reminded explorers of Canada.*

*It is little wonder that Governor Hobson declared sovereignty over the South Island by virtue of "discovery", because the sheer scale of just how empty the South Island actually was leaps from the pages of accounts like this one from 1844:*

## Empty Heartland[138]

Having seen most of the Australian colonies, and acquired a little experience at some expense, I see no occupation which affords so good a prospect of rapid return upon the money invested as sheep-grazing in this country,

---

[138] Remarks On The Middle Island Of New Zealand, by Dr. MONRO, of NELSON. [From the Nelson Examiner.] New Zealand Spectator and Cook's Strait Guardian, Volume I, Issue 3, 26 October 1844, Page 3
http://paperspast.natlib.govt.nz/cgi-bin/paperspast?a=d&d=NZSCSG18441026.2.15

wherever pasture is sufficiently abundant and there is a great extent of grass land between Banks' Peninsula and the Bluff.

This district of country possesses also a great advantage in this, that there are almost no natives. On the great plain to the south of the Peninsula there are not, we were told, more than thirty or forty altogether. Otago and its neighbourhood and Robuki are their head-quarters, and there their numbers are very inconsiderable. In the fine district behind Molyneux Bay, there are only four men. To the southward, along the coast, there are hardly any. So that settlers in this part of the country have nothing to fear from claims to land or annoying attempts at extortion.

On the west coast of the Middle Island, commonly called by the whalers "the West Side," we heard a good deal both from the whites and the natives. All accounts agreed that it is of a most rugged and inaccessible character. Mountains towering to an immense height rise, it is said, almost perpendicularly from the water, while their sides, rent and shattered, for deep sounds and arms of the sea affording the most perfect shelter. It would seem that no part of the coast of New Zealand is so inaccurately delineated on the charts as this. Instead of the tolerably uniform line with which it is drawn at present, I believe it will be found, when surveyed, to present an outline somewhat like that of the west coast of Norway. The small portion of it which has been surveyed, viz., Dusky Bay, will afford an illustration of this.

Numerous harbours, known only to the sealers, and named by them, were mentioned to us. We were told that harbours for boats could be found every five or six miles. There are still upon this coast a few seals, the pursuit of which gives occupation to one or two boats' crews. In former times they were very abundant, and yielded a very handsome profit. The sealers do not go further north in general, than Jackson's Bay, or a harbour called Harness, which is still further to the north. Beyond this, there is said to be a narrow belt of low land between the mountains and the shore, which consists of open beaches without shelter. There is no level land of any extent on the west side. The climate is said to be mild, with much rain. In answer to our enquiries about the natives there, we were told that at one time there had been a considerable number, and that they were remarkable for their ferocity. At present their total number is about six. The greenstone, so much prized by the Maories, and also it was hoped by the Chinese, is found in various places on the west coast. It has principally hitherto been worked in a place called Barn Bay. A block of it, weighing several tons, lay on the beach here, in breaking up which Captain Anglin and some of his crew were so much injured. But the mineral must be abundant, for I was shown several rounded pebbles of it picked up on the beach, where they are sufficiently common. There are two kinds of greenstone, that which is commonly seen, and which is named the ponamoo, and another sort more glassy and transparent named tuggewai. The ponamoo is exceedingly hard, and has an irregular fracture. The tuggewai is much softer, of a more transparent green, and divides easily into plates. It can be scratched with a penknife, and thin plates can thus be raised. The greenstone prized by the Chinese is undoubtedly the same mineral, slightly different in colour. It has a transparency and brilliancy which I have never ytt seen in the New Zealand stone. Ornaments made of the Chinese greenstone look almost like a stained glass, or some parts of them are nearly colourless, while others are clouded with beautiful transparent grass-greens and whites. The mineral of these shades of colour is exceedingly valuable in China worth its weight in gold. It is by no means unlikely that the mineral having the requisite shade may yet be found in New Zealand. Where there is a large extent of greenstone, it is rather indeed probable that very considerable varieties in its tint will be met with. The kiwi, called by the sealers the emu, is met with in great abundance on the west side. It is a common article of food with them, being caught with the assistauce of dogs. It seems likely that there are two species of kiwi, one much larger than the other.

*Within sixty years, however, regular travellers were no longer seeing so many kiwi and other native birds, or in fact any at all. This report is written by cabinet minister Thomas Mackenzie in regards to a visit to Fiordland:*

## Exploration In Western Otago, 1907[139]
Br *Thomas Mackenzie, M.H.R.*

### Bird Life
This has sadly changed since my former ramble. We neither saw nor heard the kiwi or kakapo, whereas 10 or 11 years ago we could hardly sleep with their

---

139  Exploration In Western Otago. Otago Daily Times , Issue 13829, 16 February 1907, Page 14

calls. The saddle back, Jack bird, blue crow, native thrush, golden-headed canary and blue mountain duck have all gone – or at least we did not see a single specimen, although I saw two flocks of the other variety of canaries.

Lake Ada, when I was there last, was covered with waterfowl – now, not over a dozen were to be seen. At one place, and one place only, did the bush seem full of life, and that was at Glade House. There the stately paradise ducks would settle on the lawn near the river, the wood pigeon would feed on the low shrubs. The kakas disported and gambolled on the rata trees, wekas came around stealthily. Paraquets, tuis, and mokis were well represented. But why all this delightful assembly of our native charmers? The reply simply is that there was a. gentleman protecting them there – Mr Garvey. He will allow neither gun nor dog on any pretence whatever to be taken there, and our bird-life is in consequence preserved.

The birds in the Clinton Valley were shot out by the roadmen when the track was formed. In the Eglinton two robins took possession of our camp. It was like meeting dear old friends to see them, and watch all their pretty and confiding ways. In the early morning, too, we had a grand song from the cock bird – a song full of glee. Such a song I have not heard for years, and to hear which I would go many a long mile.

Now, just a word about our native birds. We need not here enter into the economic reasons for introducing the natural enemy. It has, however, been fairly well demonstrated that the weasel and ferret, alone and unaided, will not exterminate all our species. On the other hand, it is equally certain that the natural enemy, aided by our Cockney unsportsmanlike pot-hunters, will seal the doom of nearly every bird in the forest. That being so, the clear duty of every lover of our land is to insist on passing an Act that will absolutely protect our native birds.

Do not all of us know men who glory in shooting down everything they can see, and in many instances killing more than they can carry away? It is not the backwoods settler who, when food runs short and he requires to take a bird or two, is exterminating the game. It is these city men who delight in going where birds are protected, and who shoot the poor things almost sitting on the gun, that are doing the work of destruction.

Whilst I recommend the protection of our native birds, I recognise that sport is required for our visitors and ourselves. Millions of acres have been declared a national park, in the promotion of which I was prominently concerned. The country is not, on the whole, adapted for sheep or cattle raising, although there is ample feed. The country should be stocked with deer, chamois, moose, and kindred game, and the lakes and rivers with fish of various kinds. The Upper Eglinton and Lake Gunn are as yet unstocked.

It may not, at this point, be out of place to refer to the progress the moose are making that were liberated behind George Sound some two years ago.[140] It was by no means the best place to choose for them, but in this, as in many other cases, influence was used to override experience, and George Sound was fixed on.

When the Hinemoa was in George Sound, having some little lime at my disposal, I went inland. We had not proceeded far before traces of the game were seen quite fresh. They are evidently breeding, because I got the trace of mother and young. The hoof marks were 4in by 3in and 2in by 1.5in. Many of the trees were newly barked. Their favourite food is the panax colonsoi and p. arhoreum, or native fig, a tree about 1oin in diameter, which was barked clean all round up to 8ft high. Other favourites were the stink wood, coprosma foetidissima, astelia, plagianthus (ribbon wood), fuchsia, kamahi (weinmannia silvicola), maples. Black pine and birch, and even the totara, were scratched. Young fern trees, too, had some fronds eaten off. With the exception of the panax and fuchsia, the other plants of which they browsed were all young.

Had I had time to follow, I think that possibly I might have got a glimpse of the moose. I have given the names of the plants fully, as it may be useful for future liberations.

The tourists' map shows a track connecting George Sound with Middle Fiord, Te Anau, and Hut and Boat at the George Sound end. For the information of venturesome travellers, I should here mention that the hut is a desolate ruin and the boat a wreck, whilst the bridge over the river is in fragments. I think the Tourist Department would do well to leave things there as they are, so that the moose may be safe from disturbance until they get fairly established.

## *Fire is destroying our countryside*
The time has quite arrived for the Government to take up a much stronger

---

140 Mackenzie was confused. The animals released in George Sound were American Elk, the only free range Elk herd in the Southern hemisphere. Four moose had been released near Hokitika in 1900, but it would be 1910 before moose were set loose in Fiordland.

attitude on the question of fires. Eighteen years ago, my earnest desire was to have some comprehensive method adopted, but my suggestions were utterly unheeded.

Since then we have seen much of our finest forest destroyed, and even those who do their best to preserve bush, whether for beauty or for use, very often see the whole of it destroyed by the thoughtlessness of others. On coming down the Greenstone Valley the disastrous effects of recent fires were seen. The forest for two miles on each side of the river was destroyed, and that about Lake Rere greatly injured.

For all that, we saw fires being lighted in the Caples Valley. No doubt the runholders feel they must make the best of things. Fires can have but one result finally, and we already realise the disastrous effects, not only in what it has done in much of the pastoral country of Otago, but also in other provinces.

If firing is to be permitted, it must be done subject to certain regulations. The finest grasses are gradually becoming exterminated, and in many cases where formerly there was good feed we see nothing but bare arid clay and rocks. This indiscriminate burning of native grasses is now beginning to be most seriously felt.

*Within sixty years, then, Fiordland's fringes had been stripped of native bird life where previously kakapo and kiwi were so prolific that travellers struggled to sleep above the nighttime calls.*

*The causes of this were, according to Thomas Mackenzie MP in 1907, city shooters slaughtering birds so tame you could almost pick them up with your hands, and a farming policy of clearing land by fire.*

*To divert the shooters, Mackenzie applauded the 1905 release of "moose" in Fiordland's George Sound, as a future game animal. Although the beasts were in fact elk gifted by US President Teddy Roosevelt, not moose, the principle was similar, and in 1910 a herd of moose obtained from Canada were in fact released at Dusky Sound. The question on everyone's minds: would they survive and breed?*

## Acclimatising Moose, 1912[141]
### Evidences Of Success

There is reason to believe that the moose which were liberated in the West Coast fiord district some years ago are thriving and breeding. A member of the mining party which visited Dusky Sound last week told a *Southland Times* reporter that at Supper Cove they found the clearest traces of the moose on a track running down to the coast. Members of the party saw fresh marks, of the cloven hoofs of the moose, which could not have been more than ten days old, and among the larger impressions smaller replicas were distinctly visible, showing that at least one calf was with the older beasts.

This is the latest evidence supplied of the success of the attempt made to acclimatise the moose in New Zealand, and sportsmen will be keenly interested to learn that the animals seem to be doing well in their new home.

*For a decade, there was no sign that the moose still existed:*

## Moose In Dusky Sound, Official To Investigate, 1921[142]

Several moose brought to New Zealand by the Government were released in Dusky Sound in the Fiordland National Park about 10 years ago. Since then no reliable reports have been received regarding the animals.

Visitors to the park have reported on several occasions that they have seen the tracks of large deer, and one party asserted that they had actually seen animals that they believed to be moose, but they might have mistaken wapiti for moose, especially as the animals were seen at a long distance.

An effort to ascertain definitely whether or not the moose have established themselves in the fiord country is to be made shortly by a representative of the Government, who will make a search for the animals in the rough country around Dusky Sound. If the deer have become acclimatised they can scarcely escape observation.

---

141 Acclimatising Moose, New Zealand Herald, Volume XLIX, Issue 15166, 4 December 1912, Page 8 http://paperspast.natlib.govt.nz/cgi-bin/paperspast?a=d&d=NZH19121204.2.91
142 Imported Game, New Zealand Herald, Volume LVIII, Issue 17692, 29 January 1921, Page 8 http://paperspast.natlib.govt.nz/cgi-bin/paperspast?a=d&d=NZH19210129.2.94

TOP: The "classic" Fiordland moose shot, taken by Max Curtis in 1952/53. BOTTOM: This 1995 remote automated camera shot deep in the Fiordland bush appears to prove there are moose. PHOTO: Ken Tustin, "A (Nearly) Complete History Of The Moose In NZ", p173

The wapiti, or American elk, was established in George Sound well north of Dusky Sound some years ago. The late Mr. Roosevelt, when he was President of the United States in 1905, presented 10 wapiti to the New Zealand Government, and these animals were released on the shores of George Sound. They have increased in numbers since, and appear to have settled in their new home.

A very successful venture in acclimatisation has been the establishment of the European chamois in the Southern Alps. The late Emperor of Austria presented chamois to the New Zealand Government on two occasions, and the animals were placed on the slopes of Mount Cook. They have found the snow slopes, glaciers and mountain meadows quite to their taste, and have increased in numbers very rapidly in recent years.

*The first hard evidence of surviving moose came almost two years to the day after that report, and when it came it came with bells on – not just moose but the presumed extinct takahe as well.*

## Moose In Southland: Ranger Gets Photographs, 1923[143]
*The Rare Notornis Seen*

INVERCARGILL, 26TH JANUARY. The Southland Acclimatisation Society received a telegram yesterday from Ranger C. J. Evans that he had secured photographs of moose, also a bird believed to be a notornis [takahe].

Mr. Evans is at present engaged investigating the acclimatisation of moose in the country surrounding Doubtful Sound. The moose were liberated on 24th February, 1910, and were imported from Western Canada.

This is the first concrete evidence that the moose have become acclimatised, though traces have been seen previously.

These are the only moose in the Southern Hemisphere. Should the second portion of the telegram be correct, it will prove that the notornis is not extinct. Only four specimens of the bird have ever been found, three of these being in the Fiord district. The last capture was made about 25 years ago.

Mr. Evans is in the hinterland of the Sounds district, and the message has apparently been sent overland with tourists.

---

143 Moose In Southland, Evening Post, Volume CV, Issue 23, 27 January 1923, Page 7
http://paperspast.natlib.govt.nz/cgi-bin/paperspast?a=d&d=EP19230127.2.41

*From a question of 'do moose exist?', suddenly local experts were making some amazing guesses are being made about moose and elk populations.*

## Wapiti Deer And Moose Thriving In Fiord Country, 1923 [144]

INVERCARGILL, 3RD MAY. The first Wapiti deer secured in the Southern Hemisphere was shot on the West Coast Sounds by V. Donald (Masterton), and L. Murrell (Manapouri). The best of three obtained was a fifteen-pointer, the spread of the antlers being 53 inches, length 49 inches, and beam 6 inches. The weight of the head was 27lb (12kg).

The hunters also saw a moose cow in Supper Cove, and in other places saw plenty of traces of these animals. They estimated that there are now 118 moose and 2345 Wapiti in the fiord country, the figures being based on the breeding habits of the animals. The original herd was eighteen Wapiti, presented by the late Mr. Theodore Roosevelt, and liberated in George Sound in 1908.

Reports by fishermen and others indicated that the animals are doing well, but Mr. Donald's is the first comprehensive report. Mr. Donald considers the fiord country to be the finest hunting ground in the world, because of the abundance of virgin feed necessary for deer and moose.

*By the summer of early 1924, hunting licences were being issued for the mighty North American fauna in Fiordland, although no one was precisely sure how many animals there actually were.*

## Moose And Wapiti: Good Season Predicted, 1924 [145]
### *Increase In The Herds*

According to statements made in Invercargill by Mr. L. Murrell, who, in his capacity as manager of the Doubtful Sound Track, has gained an extensive knowledge of the Fiord country, those who have been fortunate enough to secure the moose and wapiti licenses issued for the season which opens next month, should enjoy some good sport.

---

144  Wapiti Deer And Moose, Evening Post, Volume CV, Issue 105, 4 May 1923, Page 11
http://paperspast.natlib.govt.nz/cgi-bin/paperspast?a=d&d=EP19230504.2.123
145  Moose And Wapiti, New Zealand Herald, Volume LXI, Issue 18645, 28 February 1924, Page 11
http://paperspast.natlib.govt.nz/cgi-bin/paperspast?a=d&d=NZH19240228.2.126

Wapiti were very plentiful, stated Mr. Murrell, especially in the country round about Caswell and George Sounds and Lake Alice. Last year the herd was estimated at 2000, and he was of the opinion that that had been a conservative estimate.

The conditions were entirely different for moose, which did not increase so rapidly. As the virgin food became less the wapiti would spread all over the coast, and within the next 15 or 20 years would be located from Milford to Doubtful Sound.

Moose also appeared to be fairly numerous, and he had seen many traces of them in and around Supper Cove. There was every reason to believe that the herd was increasing.

Within a few years the Fiord country should develop into "one of the finest sporting grounds in the world", and if the holders of licenses for the coming season were successful, it would probably lead to an increased number of licenses being issued in future seasons.

*The problem with moose is that very few people had actually seen one, the creatures being extremely 'emoosive'. Unless, of course, you happened to be in the wrong place at the right time, miles away from where any self-respecting moose should have been.*

## Moose Sighted, Wandered From Haunts, 1932[146]
### *Animals Increasing*

INVERCARGILL, 29TH MARCH. Three young men, when looking for cattle on the edge of the bush on Mr. Lionel Galt's property at Papatotara, near Tuatapere, were astonished to see what at first they thought an exceptionally large deer with peculiar antlers coming toward them across an open swamp.

The animal on closer view proved to be a moose, which had evidently wandered a long way from its usual haunts. The animal made for the bush, and has not been seen since, but Ranger Smith, who was in the vicinity next day, was quite convinced that the animal was a moose from the description given, and also from hoof marks he examined. These were 6 inches long and 4 inches wide.

---

146   Moose Sighted, Evening Post, Volume CXIII, Issue 75, 30 March 1932, Page 4
http://paperspast.natlib.govt.nz/cgi-bin/paperspast?a=d&d=EP19320330.2.22

In July 2010 a night vision camera set up by Ken Tustin snapped what appears to be a juvenile moose just before dawn in Fiordland. Young moose look more like horses at that stage of development. A photo of an Alaskan juvenile moose in daylight [inset] is provided for comparison.

It is stated that the moose was about 40 miles from where the herd is believed to be. It was in 1910 that the Southland Acclimatisation Society released moose in the fiord country. The animals came from the northeastern coast of America, and from reports received from time to time by the society it was evident that they were finding their new habitat quite congenial.

A big increase in the number of tracks seen was reported, and at times the animals themselves were observed. The distinction of securing the first moose head ever obtained in New Zealand, and possibly in the southern hemisphere, was gained by Mr. E. J. Herrick, of Hastings, who in 1929, in company with Mr. J. Muir, of Hawea Flat, spent five weeks at the head of Dusky Sound.

*Moose were again photographed in 1953 and, it would appear, in 1995 as well. Moose tracker Ken Tustin has published a book on his own hunt for these creatures, "A (Nearly) Complete History Of The Moose In New Zealand", but is yet to claim the $100,000 reward for irrefutable proof in the great wild moose chase. If you're looking for moose traces, the trick is to look quite high up in the trees:*

## Moose Murder Trees At Eleven Feet, 1930[147]

It may perhaps be news to some that even the remote country in the Sounds district shelters large herds of deer, and that there also the inevitable destruction takes place, as the following extracts, taken from letters written by Mr. E. J. Herrick, of Hastings, will show. I may mention that Mr. Herrick is a well-known stalker, who has visited Dusky Sound on more than one occasion, and that his letters to me were quite unsolicited, and the information therein was given quite voluntarily. Mr. Herrick enclosed in his letter some leaves of the pokaka, a large forest tree, and writes: "The enclosed twig is from a tree that has been killed in very large numbers by ring-barking caused by the eating of the moose. I have a photograph of one of those trees ring-barked up to a height of eleven feet by measurement, and I have seen the barking higher still.

"The moose are very fond of these trees, literally hundreds of them have been killed through this barking. This eating of the bark must not be mistaken for the rubbing of their horns – the results of the two actions are entirely different. In this eating business, one never sees a scrap of bark broken or left on the ground; but in the rubbing the ground is strewn with shavings and bark."

*It has been assumed that moose have gone the way of the huia and the moa, but trackers continue to report signs that somewhere, deep in the fiords, moose still live to this day.*

---

147 Forest Damage, Evening Post, Volume CIX, Issue 132, 7 June 1930, Page 15
http://paperspast.natlib.govt.nz/cgi-bin/paperspast?a=d&d=EP19300607.2.126

Chapter 10

# Life In New Zealand – Part 2

## The Criminal Fraternity, 1871[148]

The Supreme Court resumed sitting yesterday morning. Two charges were disposed of, both of which were for entering dwellings and carrying away property. Turner and Graham were each sentenced to three years' penal servitude, for entering a dwelling at Parnell and stealing a quantity of clothing. Previous convictions had been recorded against them. Thomas Cain, for robbery at the premises of Mr. George Boyd in Fort Street, was found guilty and sentenced to 15 months' imprisonment with hard labour. The Court rose at 6 o'clock.

Of the 20 prisoners whose names are entered on the calendar of the present criminal sitting, 13 are described as being married, and seven single; 18 could read and write, two could neither write nor read. Ten are of the Church of England faith, eight are Roman Catholics, one Church of Scotland and one Hebrew. Two have been previously convicted once, one twice and two three times. One prisoner has been in the colony 31 years and the majority of them over 10 years. There are only two who have been less than five years. Eight are English, six Irish, two Scotch, one American, one Pole, two natives of the colony. Two are set down as

---

148   The Daily Southern Cross, Volume XXVII, Issue 4389, 8 September 1871, Page 2
http://paperspast.natlib.govt.nz/cgi-bin/paperspast?a=d&d=DSC18710908.2.11

storekeepers, two settlers, two miners, two sailors, two clerks, one broker, one sailmaker, one surveyor, seven labourers. On the whole none are described as possessing a superior education.

His Worship the Mayor and Mr L. D. Nathan were the presiding magistrates at the Police Court yesterday morning. A few drunkards wore disposed of, and three men fined for behaving in a disorderly manner in Wellington Street.

A little boy was brought up by his master, charged with having absconded from his apprenticeship. Both wished to have the indenture cancelled, which the magistrates could not do. The boy's parents were living in Fiji. The boy complained of having received ill-usage from his master, when it was suggested that if the master chose to withdraw the present charge, and permit the boy to bring a charge of ill-usage against him and if he would plead guilty to it, then the magistrates had power to cancel the indenture. This course was agreed upon. The charge was withdrawn, the boy discharged, and an information laid against the master and the case will come on for hearing to-day.

The Coroner's Jury at Queenstown found Waldmann guilty of arson in having set fire to his store in Ballarat Street in that town on January 23rd and he has also been committed for trial by the Justices at the local Court on the charge of attempting to set fire to his house on the Terrace.[149]

At the City Police Court on Monday Robert Findley was charged with having attempted to commit suicide by hanging himself in his workshop in Macfoggan street on Thursday last, and evidence having been taken, accused was committed to take trial at the next sessions of the Supreme Court, bail being allowed in his own recognisance of £200, and sureties of £100 each.

To show the extent to which larrikinism has attained in Melbourne, the *Argus* publishes the statistics of the Police office for a year, showing 1097 arrests for assault, and 2044 for insulting behaviour in Melbourne and suburbs. And, it adds, if our sceptical friends are still not convinced as to the serious character of the ruffianism which prevails in this community, perhaps the notes, taken from the records of the police hospital from January, 1881, to the present time will prove more demonstrative.

---

149 News of the Week, Otago Witness , Issue 1578, 11 February 1882, Page 8
http://paperspast.natlib.govt.nz/cgi-bin/paperspast?a=d&d=OW18820211.2.18

These notes comprise a list of 23 members of the force admitted to the hospital suffering from injuries at the hands of roughs. In three cases the men were incapacitated from duty, and have been superannuated. Seven constables, admitted since Christmas, now remain in the hospital. If more facts were wanted (continues the *Argus*), we could point to one constable (O'Grady), who some two years ago was overpowered by larrikins, and whose leg they stretched over the water-channel in Little Bourke Street, and whilst a number held him down one fellow deliberately jumped on the limb until he broke it, or to scores of policemen who bear scars representing wounds inflicted by stones, sling shot, and the knifemarks which can never be effaced.[150]

## Above And Beyond, 1935[151]

After entering the Waikato River from the Hamilton Bridge yesterday afternoon, a young woman was drowned and a constable who attempted to rescue her also lost his life. The victims were: Miss Daisy Hislop, aged about 23, employed as a domestic at 12 Radnor Street, Hamilton; Constable Charles Hayward Williams, aged 31, of Hamilton, and formerly of Auckland.

Miss Hislop, wearing a fur coat, was noticed by Mr. C. A. Clark, a carpenter, aged, 27, standing on the bridge footpath about half-way across the bridge. She was looking down at the river, over 80ft below. Mr. Clark, who was working on the bridge, turned away, and a moment later he saw the woman floating downstream.

Racing to the western bank, Mr. Clark removed most of his clothing, picked up a lifebelt and jumped in to rescue the woman. He swam out and caught hold of her. She was conscious, but made no attempt to help herself. With a gallant effort, Mr. Clark managed to bring her within a yard of the bank, but a rip current made it difficult for him to retain his hold.

The bank at this point rose 20ft sheer out of the water, and there was nothing for Mr. Clark to grasp. He battled hard to prevent himself and the

---

150   News of the Week, Otago Witness , Issue 1578, 11 February 1882, Page 8
http://paperspast.natlib.govt.nz/cgi-bin/paperspast?a=d&d=OW18820211.2.18
151   Rescue Fails, Auckland Star, Volume LXVI, Issue 191, 14 August 1935, Page 9
http://paperspast.natlib.govt.nz/cgi-bin/paperspast?a=d&d=AS19350814.2.88.1

woman from being swept down the river, but finally he became exhausted and was forced to let the woman go.

Near London Street he was pulled out of the river by several men holding a rope. The woman floated rapidly down the river, and her groans could be heard in the distance. People on the banks who could see the woman swimming in midstream shouted to her to make for the bank, but she did not heed them. Then Constable Williams, who had been on duty in Victoria Street, arrived. He took off his tunic and helmet and plunged in below London Street.

Quickly he swam out to midstream and caught hold of the woman, who again made no effort to help herself. Strenuous and valiant efforts were made by the constable to push the woman downstream towards the western bank. He kept going for several chains, but then became exhausted. "Come quickly, I am done," he called out.

Although wearied by his previous gallant effort, and considerably out of breath through running for half a mile along the rough river bank, Mr. Clark again dived into the river. He swam for a, chain and a half, but when he reached Constable Williams he realised that the strain on him had been too great, and he was forced to make for the bank again. With the greatest difficulty he was pulled out exhausted.

Strenuous efforts to reach the shore were made by Constable Williams. He battled hard against treacherous currents, but was soon in difficulties. At this stage Mr. E. G. W. Thorpe, child welfare officer at Hamilton, and Mr. W. Murphy entered the water opposite Gwynne Street, three-quarters of a mile below the railway bridge. People on the bank shouted that both the constable and the woman had disappeared.

A police launch and two rowing boats started to search the river, and dragging operations were begun. Search was also made from the banks on either side of the river. No trace of the young woman or the gallant constable who attempted to rescue her could be found. The police commenced a search for the bodies this morning. Rescue efforts were also made by Mr. O. Hall, of the State Fire Office, who jumped in but had to return to the bank.

Constable Williams joined the police force in Auckland in 1932, and was transferred to Hamilton in November, 1933. He served in Auckland with both the detective and uniform branches, and was a well-known and popular young officer. He served in the New Zealand Division of the Royal Navy, and later in the merchant marine before joining the police force.

He was an exceptionally powerful swimmer. For four years before joining the force in Auckland he was a member of the Samoan Constabulary. He was a member of the Marist Football Club and was single.

The body of the young woman was recovered by the police early this afternoon, near the spot where she was last seen. An inquest for identification will be held later this afternoon.

"This is an unfortunate affair which was the result of extreme devotion to duty leading to the loss of a valuable life," commented the Coroner, Mr F. W. Platts, at an inquest today into the circumstances of the death of Constable Charles Hayward Williams, aged 31. The evidence showed that the constable lost his life in the Waikato River on August 13 while attempting to rescue Daisy Hislop from drowning after a fall from the railway bridge.

A verdict was returned that the constable was drowned, in attempting to rescue Miss Hislop. The inquest into the death of Daisy Hislop, aged 23, was also concluded before Mr. Platts. The evidence showed that the deceased jumped from the railway bridge into the river.

"We have it in evidence that the deceased had a quarrel with a young man with whom she was keeping company, about his going to a party without her, also trouble about an engagement ring," stated the Coroner. "The unfortunate girl was despondent at the time and the verdict will be that she committed suicide by drowning while temporarily insane.[152]

## The Public Servant Who Turned Down A Pay Rise, 1871[153]

"Atticus" writes as follows in the *Melbourne Leader*: "I should like to know the name of the Taranaki sergeant of police who, when it was proposed to increase his salary, declined upon the ground that he already got as much as he was worth.

"Is the happy valley of Rasselas found at last, and does it exist in New Zealand? The birth, parentage and education of this prodigy deserve to be written in letters of gold. Could he be induced, at any cost, to transfer his valuable services to Victoria? His example would be cheap at any price unless

---

152   Double Drowning, Evening Post, Volume CXX, Issue 83, 4 October 1935, Page 11
http://paperspast.natlib.govt.nz/cgi-bin/paperspast?a=d&cl=search&d=EP19351004.2.111
153   The Daily Southern Cross, Volume XXVII, Issue 4389, 8 September 1871, Page 2
http://paperspast.natlib.govt.nz/cgi-bin/paperspast?a=d&d=DSC18710908.2.11

indeed his life were bullied out of him for his 'unprofessional and ungentlemanly conduct in proving false to the traditions of the class of officialdom.'

## Snow In Auckland, 1883[154]

Snow has been seen as far north as Mahurangi. The natives there were astonished.

## Fall Of Snow In Auckland, 1883[155]

Auckland, This day.
There was snow on the ranges at Pukekohe and Drury yesterday for the first time in the memory of the oldest inhabitant. Cattle have died of exposure.

## Snow In Auckland District, 1941[156]

Snow fell in high-lying parts of the Auckland Province at the weekend, blocking traffic routes in several areas. In the city temperatures dropped sharply with a change to southerly winds on Saturday morning, the lowest temperature registered being 43 degrees (6C) and the highest 56 degrees (13C). Travellers on the 3 o'clock express from Wellington were greeted by a heavy snowfall in the National Park area, the drift at Waiouru at one stage completely covering the permanent way.

## Maori MPs Behave Better Than Rest, 1889[157]

*Chambers' Journal* for July contains an article on "Maoris in Parliament" by a New Zealander, the closing passage of which is as follows: "This sketch would be incomplete were I not to say that the general conduct of the Native members has been exemplary, and in some respects a pattern to

---

154   Snow In Auckland, Grey River Argus, Volume XXX, Issue 4681, 27 August 1883, Page 2
155   Fall Of Snow In Auckland, Daily Telegraph , Issue 3779, 25 August 1883, Page 3
156   Snow In Auckland District Evening Post, Volume CXXXI, Issue 152, 30 June 1941, Page 9
157   Waikato Times, Volume XXXIII, Issue 2684, 24 September 1889, Page 2
http://paperspast.natlib.govt.nz/cgi-bin/paperspast?a=d&d=WT18890924.2.12

their European colleagues. No unseemly interruption of a speaker is ever heard coming from a Maori member, nor has it ever been suggested to my knowledge that a good dinner at Bellamy's was unfavourable to oratory in the case of a Maori legislator, whatever scandals in that respect may be circulated about his white-skinned confreres. To this may be added that no Maori has ever been known to vote against payment of the full honorarium to members; but then he has never been guilty of the hypocrisy of pretending to be in favour of a reduction while fervently hoping it will not be carried, and voting for the motion for retrenchment after making quite sure that there is no chance of its being adopted."

## Lawyers The Same Everywhere, 1889[158]

A Patea Maori was relating his experience of the law and its peculiarities the other day. He said:

"My lawyer came to me and said he could get me some land I claimed by Maori title from an ancestor, and which the pakeha knew was in dispute. I told him all about it, and he said 'It is a very good case you ought to win.' I thought that was all right, so I said, 'Go on quick, and get me my land.' He said, 'Very good.'

"By and by he came to me and said he wanted one of my pigs to pay expenses, and I caught the pig and gave it him. Very soon he came for another pig, and I had it caught for him. In a few weeks he had taken all my nine pigs, but he had given me no land. I said nothing, but I did not like this. In about a fortnight he came and took away my horse. Then I said to him 'I have had enough law. If I let you go on, you will eat up the land too. You have taken all my pigs and my horse that is enough – enough law for me and enough pay for you!'"

## Accident And Emergency, 1889[159]

Two more of the Tauwhare natives have caught the fever, and the young

---

158  Waikato Times, Volume XXXIII, Issue 2684, 24 September 1889, Page 2
http://paperspast.natlib.govt.nz/cgi-bin/paperspast?a=d&d=WT18890924.2.12
159  Waikato Times, Volume XXXIII, Issue 2684, 24 September 1889, Page 2
http://paperspast.natlib.govt.nz/cgi-bin/paperspast?a=d&d=WT18890924.2.12

girl, whom we last week reported as ill, has succumbed to it.

Two natives came into Cambridge on Saturday to fetch the material for her coffin; they both imbibed more than they ought, and one Wiremtu Matawhiri was thrown out of the cart, and was badly cut about the head, Dr. Cushney having to stitch the gash up. He is now progressing favourably.

## Chinese Maidens Sold At Profit In Victoria, 1865[160]

The *Bendigo Advertiser* is responsible for the following paragraph, which if it be true, brings out a new phase of Chinese life in the colonies.

Recently a Chinaman brought from the flowery land his wife accompanied by her maid-servant – two very fair specimens of the almond-eyed, small-footed feminine beauties of that country. The maid-servant having been purchased in China, the Chinese husband thought on the arrival of the two ladies, that he might fairly, as well as justly, dispense with the maid's services, and accordingly he put her up to auction and, if our information is truthful he realised £120 for what he had paid only about £10 in China.

The happy purchaser, on receiving delivery of his property, added the marriage rites of the Chinese joss-house to his legal rites and took home his newly-bought bride. We hear that the lucky speculator, and others of his countrymen, intend having further consignments of such tender goods from China.

## The First Genuine West-Coaster, 1865[161]

The *West Coast Times* chronicled the first birth which had taken place at Hokitika, as "Mrs T. McCarthy, late of Picton, of a daughter." The honor of giving birth to the first child born of European parents on the West Coast is disputed, and is claimed by a Mrs Smith, who was confined a week previously.

---

160  Local And General News, Wellington Independent, Volume XX, Issue 2221, 20 June 1865, Page 3 http://paperspast.natlib.govt.nz/cgi-bin/paperspast?a=d&d=WI18650620.2.17
161  Local And General News, Wellington Independent, Volume XX, Issue 2221, 20 June 1865, Page 3 http://paperspast.natlib.govt.nz/cgi-bin/paperspast?a=d&d=WI18650620.2.17

## Land Wars Confiscation Minimal, Says Herald, 1865[162]

"We understand," says the *New Zealand Herald*, that the quantity of land to be given to Te Oriori, as an acknowledgment of his submission, is 500 acres. It is situated at Tamahere, between Hamilton and Cambridge, and it does not encroach upon any military settlement in fact, it has not yet been surveyed. Twenty thousand acres at Whangape, opposite Rangiriri, and on the proper left bank of the river, are to be set apart for rebels who have surrendered and taken the oath of allegiance, but it will, of course, be confined to those to whom the confiscated block [originally] belonged. William Thompson has lost but little land by confiscation, and Rewi loses none, it is said.

It is understood that there was a sort of joint proprietorship, between these men, and that the proclamation expiring on the 4th of June next has been mainly instrumental in bringing at least one of them to a sense of the danger of delay."

## Enormous Sheep[163]

The *Southern Cross* says Mr Dudley, butcher, Queen Street, recently had in his shop a four-year-old sheep of aldermanic proportions, which shows the extraordinary size to which these animals, by good management, may be brought in this province.

It is a cross between the Leicester and Lincoln breeds, was bred and led by H. Hayr, Esq., on the rich pastures of Mount Albert.

It weighed, when alive, 106 lbs (48kg), and now 60 lbs, and has somewhere about four inches of fat over its ribs. We are informed that amongst the flock from which this sheep was taken are several others of equal or nearly equal size."

---

162 Local And General News, Wellington Independent, Volume XX, Issue 2221, 20 June 1865, Page 3
http://paperspast.natlib.govt.nz/cgi-bin/paperspast?a=d&d=WI18650620.2.17
163 Local And General News, Wellington Independent, Volume XX, Issue 2221, 20 June 1865, Page 3
http://paperspast.natlib.govt.nz/cgi-bin/paperspast?a=d&d=WI18650620.2.17

## Pakeha Will Be 'Great Source Of Riches': A Maori Death Notice, 1865[164]

From the *Canterbury Press* of the 15th, we republish the following notice respecting the death of Priscilla Panepane, a native woman of rank among the tribe residing at Kaiapoi:

Kaiapoi, 29 Mei, 1865. E hoa ma, kia roko Koutou, kua mate a Pirihira Panepane, he wahine rakatira no roto i te hapu i a Tuahuriri, no roto i a Tuteahuka, no roto i a Maru. Na, e hoa ma, kia roko Koutou ki tana kupu poroporoki i penei i kona ra e koro ma, e kui ma, e tama ma, e hine ma, i kona ra ri te ao, kia atawhai hoki i te ao nei ki to tatou taonga nui ko te pakeha. Ka mutu tana poroporoki."

[translation.] Kaiapoi, May 29, 1865. Let all our friends be informed that Priscilla Panepane is dead. She was a woman of rank of the family of Tuahuriri, which is related to Tuteahuka and descended from Maru. Hear, friends, her last words, which were these 'Farewell all you: ye mothers, ye brothers, ye sisters. I leave you in the world; be ye obliging towards our great source of riches, the white people.' Thus ended her words."

## Mother England's Final Public Hanging, 1868[165]

The *London Times* of May 26 observes that yesterday witnessed the last of those hideous spectacles familiar enough to the hard eyes of our predecessors, but more and more repulsive to the taste of these days.

We have only to think of the horror with which we all now instinctively regard the barbarous punishments inflicted late down in our history, and we may conceive what posterity will think of capital executions before a motley crowd of vulgar and often brutal spectators.

It so happens, however, that the accompaniment of publicity was in Barrett's case specially appropriate for the crime, which was absolutely unparalleled for its openness, and for its more than warlike hostility and recklessness.

---

164 Local And General News, Wellington Independent, Volume XX, Issue 2221, 20 June 1865, Page 3 http://paperspast.natlib.govt.nz/cgi-bin/paperspast?a=d&d=WI18650620.2.17
165 The Press. Thursday, August 20, 1868, Press, Volume XIII, Issue 1715, 20 August 1868, Page 2 http://paperspast.natlib.govt.nz/cgi-bin/paperspast?a=d&d=CHP18680820.2.4

# Beware Big-Spending Politicians, 1870[166]

The news from England shows that New Zealand is, at least, likely to derive one benefit from the war which is now devastating Europe. It will, perforce, be saved from running into ruinous speculation.

The echoes of the guns of Weissenberg have sufficed to blow all Mr. Vogel's fine schemes into thin air, and while France and Prussia are fighting, New Zealand will have time to recover its senses, and calmly and critically examine what the dazzling visions conjured up by Mr. Vogel really are when subjected to the test of common sense.

When the temporary insanity, incited by the delusive brilliancy of the financial scheme, shall have passed, people will feel inclined to be grateful that they have been saved, in spite of themselves, from the commission of irretrievable folly.

Had it not been for the war in Europe, it is very probable that Mr. Vogel would have been able to have involved the Colony in engagements from which it could never extricate itself in a debt which it could never pay, and in works which, once commenced, would have to be carried on at any sacrifice.

Money was plentiful at home [England], and Colonial securities were in favor as an investment. New Zealand's demand for a large loan would probably have been freely responded to, and the money once in the Colonial Treasury it would have been rapidly squandered.

The prospect of a large Governmental expenditure is at all times an alluring one to a great many people; and to those who possess no stake in the country, and are simply desirous of making the most they can here, and going somewhere else to spend their gains, it is an exceedingly good thing.

We doubt, however, that it is equally beneficial to those who have a stake in the country, who have made it their home, and intend it to be their children's home. Little of the Government expenditure is likely to find its way into, or to remain in, their pockets, and the facts of the Government borrowing large sums of foreign capital does not necessarily imply that the actual amount of foreign capital in the Colony is increased.

At the present moment a very large amount of foreign capital is employed

---

166   Evening Post, Volume VI, Issue 203, 10 October 1870, Page 2
http://paperspast.natlib.govt.nz/cgi-bin/paperspast?a=d&d=EP18701010.2.5

in developing the resources of this Colony. A competent authority has estimated the amount of British capital invested here as being between twelve and thirteen millions, and the withdrawal of any large proportion of this sum would most seriously affect the industrial pursuits of the Colony, and greatly cripple all classes of the community.

No government expenditure in the shape of public works made out of borrowed money could compensate for a withdrawal of any large proportion of the foreign capital now privately inverted here and yet such a withdrawal would be the almost inevitable result of the negotiation of any large Government loan.

Those who have money invested in the Colony would at once ask themselves how the interest on the new loan was to be met. They would see that the revenue of the Colony was, at the present time, absolutely insufficient to meet the ordinary expenditure. They would look at the items of the revenue, and would find that the Customs revenue would admit of no further expansion, that the only method of increasing the revenue was by means of a property or income tax and as this tax would fall principally, or at least largely, on them, they would, with all convenient haste, withdraw their investments.

In fact the more we borrowed the poorer we might very probably become. It is impossible either to feel any confidence in the administrative ability or the honesty of the present Government. Their past administration has been distinguished by reckless expenditure in defiance of all the dictates of prudence and common sense. With a decreasing revenue they have largely increased the departmental expenses, and have in small matters shown a want of prudent foresight, which should not encourage anyone in the desire to entrust them with the carrying out of larger matters.

## Old Soldiers Owe Their Limbs To NZ Wars Medical Breakthrough, 1868[167]
### *Gunshot Fractures and Amputation*

The following paragraph from the *British Medical Journal* discloses an interesting and important fact in surgery: several of the men who were

---

[167] Local And General News, Wellington Independent, Volume XXII, Issue 2640, 25 February 1868, Page 3 http://paperspast.natlib.govt.nz/cgi-bin/paperspast?a=d&d=WI18680225.2.11

wounded in the New Zealand campaign seem to have brought home arms and legs which (according to the standard rules of military surgery) they ought to have left behind them.

Out of six cases of gunshot fracture of the femur at various parts treated in the New Zealand war, five recovered without amputation, four of them with very useful legs; one man, wounded through both legs, died.

The surgeons were moved to disregard the peremptory injunctions of military text-books, to give the sufferers such chance of recovery as may be obtained by amputation, "by the excellent condition of the men, and the facilities for treating them in well organised field hospitals without the necessity of premature removal."

They were rewarded for their intelligent boldness by a success unprecedented in military surgery, but which, under circumstances similar to those in the New Zealand campaign, may be usefully borne in mind.

Of ten cases, also, of gunshot fracture of the humerus, eight united solidly and well, and in one case only was amputation had recourse to; here the amputation was primary. Guided by the experience of the above cases, says Inspector-General Mouat, V.C, C.B., it would be fair to expect, when 80 per cent of gunshot fractures of the humerus recover without difficulty, that amputation of the arms in such cases might be delayed for secondary operation, if, after all, found to be necessary.

It may be objected to this that the description of firearms used by the insurgent Maories against our men threw bullets less destructive than the bullets of rifled muskets now in ordinary use for military purposes. It is, however, a doubtful point whether such is or is not the case; doubtful how far preconceived theory of the superior penetrating power of a conical bullet over that of a round one has influenced public belief in the matter

## Electric Light Not Enough, We Want Steam-Powered Homes!, 1882[168]

The Americans are not satisfied with the electric light, which is now distributed through portions of New York streets like gas, but (says the *Scientific American*) the next steps of social and domestic organisation

---

168   News of the Week, Otago Witness , Issue 1578, 11 February 1882, Page 8
http://paperspast.natlib.govt.nz/cgi-bin/paperspast?a=d&d=OW18820211.2.18

promise to be the distribution of motive power with our illuminant, and the displacement of our heaters and cooking-stoves by steam conveyed through the streets in pipes, making it possible to banish fire absolutely from our dwelling offices, and factories, either for warming or lighting, for cooking or for mechanical operations, heat, light, and motive power being generated in and supplied from huge central stations.

## Oamaru's First Public Building, 1882[169]

Oamaru is to have a courthouse which, according to the *Times*, will be the first public building ever erected in Oamaru, all previous places of public business being but huts. The new building will be one of the handsomest in the town, and is to have a frontage of 80ft to Thames Street.

## Slave-Trading In The Colonies, 1868[170]

A great deal of excitement has been caused in Queensland by the discovery that a man named Tancred, who had been employed by a firm to escort a party of South Sea Islanders to Comet Downs, had sold a Kanaka boy to a blacksmith named Macpherson for £2.

It seems that the lad was a runaway servant, and joined Tancred's party. On the way Macpherson met Tancred, and after some chaffering about terms handed over the boy to him, receiving £2 cash.

Tancred was subsequently fined by the Rockhampton Bench for his little transaction in "the color trade."

---

169 News of the Week, Otago Witness, Issue 1578, 11 February 1882, Page 8
http://paperspast.natlib.govt.nz/cgi-bin/paperspast?a=d&d=OW18820211.2.18
170 Local And General News, Wellington Independent, Volume XXII, Issue 2640, 25 February 1868, Page 3
http://paperspast.natlib.govt.nz/cgi-bin/paperspast?a=d&d=WI18680225.2.11

Chapter 11

# Women & The Vote

*If you open up any New Zealand school history textbook, it will proudly declare that New Zealand was the first country in the world to give women the vote, back in 1893.*

*If only that were true.*

*Magnificent as the efforts of Kate Sheppard and the other suffragettes were, they were not the exclusive pioneers of a worldwide movement, no matter how much the claim has been romanticised and enhanced by proud kiwis, documentary-makers and politicians.*

*Instead, Sheppard and co were standing on the shoulders of giants – women in other countries who had already won full or partial rights to vote and whose efforts the New Zealanders appropriated.*

*Whereabouts? I hear you ask. Well, an American state gave women the vote back in 1869, and the story of how successful that was made the New Zealand papers before 1893:*

## Women Suffrage Interview, 1892[171]

**KATE FIELD**[172]: Is woman suffrage a success in Wyoming?

---

171  Women Suffrage, Clutha Leader, Volume XVIII, Issue 931, 20 May 1892, Page 3
http://paperspast.natlib.govt.nz/cgi-bin/paperspast?a=d&d=CL18920520.2.7
172  Long before the modern feminist movement took shape, Kate Field was an established American

Chief Justice of Wyoming: Decidedly. When I came here in 1880 I was prejudiced against it. The first woman I saw vote was a half-breed Cherokee Indian, without the ghost of an idea of the responsibility of her act. On inquiry I learned that she was a much better 'man' than her husband.

The next woman was a native of Massachusetts, who came to the polls with her blue-eyed boy. She bore the name of the Concord sage and philosopher, and then I thought of what Emerson had said, that if all the vices were represented on the list of voters surely some of the virtues should be.

**FIELD:** Do you think women appreciate the importance of voting more than men?

**CJ:** On the whole, yes and they are more unselfish. It brings the home element into politics, and serves as a check to the 'bummer' element. Women will not support candidates who are known to be drunken or immoral. Hence both parties are compelled to nominate men of clean private and public record.

**FIELD:** You paint a cheerful state of things, Mr Chief Justice: Eastern opponents declare that, by the introduction of the woman element into politics, confusion will be confounded, as disreputable women will vote and good women will not.

**CJ:** This is a slander as far as Wyoming is concerned, where there are more respectable women in proportion to the population than elsewhere. Our polls are alike for both sexes, and no woman ever was insulted at the ballot-box. Saloons are closed, and the utmost courtesy is paid to women voters.

**FIELD:** Are political meetings frequented by women?

**CJ:** Yes, and it sometimes happens that husbands and wives vote differently, yet no more discord ensues than where male members of a family disagree.

**FIELD:** Is woman suffrage a party question?

**CJ:** No. The clause incorporating equal suffrage was passed in convention with one dissenting voice. Republicans and Democrats met on common ground.

**FIELD:** Was there ever an attempt made to abolish woman suffrage once upon a time?

**CJ:** Yes, the measure passed both Houses, but was vetoed by Governor

---

journalist and commentator who could command big speaking fees across America in the late 1800s

Campbell in 1871 since then no retrograde movement has been advocated.

**FIELD:** Is any discrimination shown to the salaries of public school teachers on account of sex?

**CJ:** None, whatever. Our school system is fine, and our State University at Laramie is well maintained. According to the census of 1880, Wyoming had the smallest percentage of illiteracy of any State in the Union, and I hope that the last census will tell an equally flattering tale.

**MISS FIELD ADDS:** "Thus ended my interview with Wyoming's Chief Justice. Later in the day I met a number of Cheyenne's leading men and women at the residence of Senator and Mrs Warren. Not a man but assured me he approved of woman suffrage, but seemed to take pride in the privilege accorded by an enlightened public opinion."

*So, far from New Zealand being the first place in the world to give women the vote, it turns out we were beaten to the draw by a bunch of American cowboys in 1869 – a full twenty-four years before New Zealand got around to it. What makes it even more galling is they were boasting about equal pay rates in the public sector for women as well!*

*Even the polygamist state of Utah beat New Zealand to the punch by two decades, giving the full vote in 1870, although women ironically lost the right to vote in 1887 as a punishment from the state legislature because they kept voting in favour of polygamy rather than against it.*

*OK, you say, maybe we weren't the first 'place', maybe we were the first 'country' to do so. Or maybe we weren't. It turns out Sweden introduced the vote for taxpaying women in the mid 1700s, formalising it nationally in 1862 although it was restricted to one vote per household, which meant married women effectively did not vote. True full suffrage came after New Zealand so although Sweden was ahead on points they didn't go all the way.*

*For all of the issues regarding sex abuse on Pitcairn Island, the women descended from the Bounty mutineers had been voting since 1838 and continued the tradition when they resettled on Norfolk Island in 1856.*

*Likewise, the newly independent former French Pacific colony of "Franceville" gave women full voting rights in 1889 – four years earlier than New Zealand, thus becoming the first country to formally give women 'the vote'. Franceville's place in history was eclipsed, however, when the territory was re-annexed by France several years later, renamed the New Hebrides, and its voters came back under the control of French law.*

*If you want to be really pedantic, New Zealand was not even a sovereign country in 1893, merely a self-governing British colony. It was actually similar in status to Wyoming or Utah or, for that matter, the Isle of Man where women who owned property (and thus paid tax) were given the full vote back in 1881.*

*No matter how you slice and dice it, New Zealand's claim to have been the first country to enfranchise women is rapidly falling into the 'legend in your own lunchtime' category.*

*In New Zealand in the 1880s, however, public debate over women's rights was raging and while the full story of our journey to suffrage is covered in more detail in other history books, nonetheless the flavour of the debate is captured well here:*

## Woman's Rights, 1884[173]

(TO THE EDITOR OF THE EXPRESS) Dear Mr Editor, – I was enjoying your excellent paper the other night as I always do (I think people who are getting a little older generally like a newspaper) when I came to a letter signed 'Sophia Tompkyns', on a subject which always roughs me up the wrong way.

That subject is Woman's Rights, coupled with Universal Suffrage. Of course I don't know Mrs Sophia Tompkyns personally, but I should like to tell her that when she talks about mothers leaving their babies at home, while they attend meetings and vote in Parliament, she is speaking very plainly of neglecting her rightful duties.

Just think of the poor little dears screaming themselves black in their sweet little faces while their mothers are interfering with other people's business! No, no, my dear Sophia, you have rights, and plenty, but they are 'the rights to soothe, and cheer, and bliss, with woman's own true tenderness,' and you will not maintain them by going into Parliament or meddling with votes.

Then I saw last night that another young woman had written upholding Sophia, and talking about "tyrannical husbands," etc. Now, I should have been positively ashamed to confess that grandfather ever was a tyrant. My dear Mr Editor, don't you think that it is the fault of the wives if husbands are tyrannical?

---

173   Woman's Rights, Marlborough Express, Volume XX, Issue 230, 30 September 1884, Page 2
http://paperspast.natlib.govt.nz/cgi-bin/paperspast?a=d&d=MEX18840930.2.26

I wouldn't give much for a woman's tact if she can't 'coax' and 'wheedle' all the tyranny out of a man in six months. I used to be a great horse woman when I was young, and I always think that men are exactly like very tender mouthed horses; with a light hand you can do anything with them, but touch the curb heavily, and they rear directly – you must not even let them feel you have a hand on the bridle.

I should advise Sophia and Seraphina to rule their homes and their children well before they think of ruling nations, and I should like to see myself leaving one of *my* grandchildren at home whilst I went to a voting meeting, much less Tom or John, or William, or Jane, or Kate, or Lucy, or any of the others when they were little. The very idea made me so angry that I shook my specs off with indignation.

Believe me dear Mr Editor,
Yours faithfully,
Granny
September 28 1884

*And on the other hand:*

# Woman Suffrage, 1890[174]

TO THE EDITOR: Sir, In the weekly issue of the *Southland Times* of the 5th September, appears an article headed "Woman Suffrage," a well written letter, concise, to the point.

To attack a problem we must begin by clearly defining its position, which the writer on the above subject has very clearly done. The brilliant array of names she quotes of men at Home who are in favor of giving women the power to vote, constitute a very respectable representation of the world, in intellect at any rate, which is the point in question.

The Isle of Man is quoted as a proof, that the method of giving equal political rights to women as with men, has been in operation for the past nine years, and the Governor, Sir Henry Holt, testified that the results had been good; also in the states of Wyoming and Washington in America they were equally satisfactory.

---

174  Woman Suffrage, Bruce Herald, Volume XXI, Issue 2211, 21 October 1890, Page 3
http://paperspast.natlib.govt.nz/cgi-bin/paperspast?a=d&d=BH18901021.2.13.1

Such writers, who think the granting of the franchise to women as a prodigiously foolish project, seem to overlook the part women will take in bringing on the much needed reform in religion. It is quite possible that eight-tenths of the religious instruction is imparted to the children by the mothers, more praise to them, but who at present get their views in theology from the minister, but the more enlightened woman of the future will clearly see for herself what is historical and founded on facts and teach accordingly, and then the reform will be taking giant strides, and like the pent-up waters of a dam escaping, sweep away forever what is nothing more than trading on the imbecility of their hearers.

Saint Gregory Nazianzen in the early days was of the opinion that words are sufficient to deceive the vulgar who admire the more the less they understand, and followed the instructions of the pious Bishop Eusebius who declared, in the thirty-first chapter of the twelfth book of his Evangelical Preparation 'that it may be lawful and fitting to use falsehood as a medicine for the benefit of those who want to be deceived'.

The digiously foolish project writer's experience must be taken from not a fair average in Mr Trollope's domestic manners of the Americans, amusing sketches from life of the kind of women George Eliot[175] detested.

George Eliot writes, "I hate the sound of women's voices – they're always either a buzz or a squeak."

She had no doubt in her mind's eye the gossiping small-intellect woman; the true womanly women, with the religious element well in hand, are the great purifiers of the world, and would certainly help considerably in getting better men returned to Parliament. We sadly want, at the present time, good and capable men, less log-rolling and working only when influence can bring pressure to bear upon them.

A proper and useful representative requires no pressure if he is satisfied with the equity of the case, whatever it may be, and does his best in the matter. The other man is guided in these matters in quite a different manner and will do nothing for you however just and reasonable your request may be, unless you are some person of influence and he sees his bread and butter in danger, then he yokes to, but only in a half-hearted manner.

The people of New Zealand should rise to a man and insist upon a less

---

175  George Eliot was the pen-name of one of the Victorian era's leading female novelists – Mary Ann Cross – who died in 1880.

expensive system of Government. Something on the Swiss or American method would be more in accordance with our means and heavy liabilities. When women hold the position they are entitled to and are fast approaching, witness their latest achievements, viz., Miss Fawcett and Miss Ramsay, and when they honor the public through the Press on subjects of importance and general interest, they will demand, and should receive due courtesy, which I certainly think the following devoid of.

From the pulpit we expect to hear the truth, and from the Press surely a good example might be set in courtesy. "Not even a Person," the writer on above "Woman Suffrage" of Sept. 5th., might for all we know be a woman, one might be proud to know, and she sees what is written [by the editor] below attached to her letter as if she was some child or doll in intellect: "Our correspondent should not trouble her wise little head wondering what horrid man wrote the leader she objects to. That is a question of mere curiosity, a waste of pains, and of our valuable space, a due proportion of which she is always welcome to for the discussion of any question she thinks herself fit to tackle. But let us have something more cogent than a few negations, an array of authorities who after all do not constitute 'the world', and an assertion or two."

Such a method of discussing a great question is no doubt very womanish, but accomplishes little in the way of elucidating the matter. The result of a little unprejudiced thinking on all the points involved in the proposal might be highly beneficial, might even convert the editor. – I am, &c, SCRUTATOR

Seaward Bush,
October 1.

*It is worth remembering that not even all men had the vote back in Britain at this time:*

## MP Demands Suffrage For Men, 1881[176]

The programme of the Democratic Federation, the new political party forming in England, and a leading member of which is Mr Joseph Cowen,

---

176   News In Brief, Tuapeka Times, Volume XIV, Issue 757, 27 July 1881, Page 5
http://paperspast.natlib.govt.nz/cgi-bin/paperspast?a=d&d=TT18810727.2.31

M.P. for Newcastle, embraces manhood suffrage for all parliamentary and municipal elections, triennial Parliaments, equal electoral districts, payment of members election expenses to come out of the rates.

In addition to discussing this programme, a conference that was to meet in London on June 8 was to be asked to consider the following subjects: Adult suffrage; nationalisation of the land; abolition of the House of Lords; bribery at elections to be made an act of felony; legislative independence for Ireland.

*We often presume, in the 21st century, that the nineteenth century was akin to the Dark Ages, yet the ancient newspapers disclose attitudes and trends – even then – well familiar to us in 'modern' times:*

## The Influence Of Spinsters, 1892[177]

A favourite topic of discussion just now in feminine circles is the women who do not marry, and among men there is a certain amount of curiosity as to why they do not wed.

It seems to be conceded that there is a growing disinclination on the part of women to commit themselves to wedlock, and this seems to have been the inspiration of a recent article by Mrs. E. Lynn Linton on the "Revolt against Matrimony," in the *Forum*, and of Mrs. Kate Gannet Well's paper in the *North American Review*, entitled "Why more girls do not marry."

A hundred years ago marriage and motherhood were regarded as the crown and consummation of female life, and the girls of every household were trained solely with the view to becoming qualified heads of homes in which they should be installed by the marriage service.

It is only of late years, since what is known as the higher education has come into vogue and our modern civilisation has absorbed women into so many pursuits, that the disinclination to matrimony has arisen and the "superior woman" of the day found herself looking down with contempt on the work of sweeping the domestic hearthstone and rocking the cradle.

The college graduate, highly educated, capable of earning a salary and making a place for herself in the world, is a new factor in femininity, and

---

[177] The Influence Of Spinsters, New Zealand Herald, Volume XXIX, Issue 8968, 27 August 1892, Page 2 http://paperspast.natlib.govt.nz/cgi-bin/paperspast?a=d&cl=search&d=NZH18920827.2.53.13

she finds herself refined up to a point where she is unwilling to sink her identity in that of a man and play second fiddle in his household. In the opinion of one of the writers whom we have spoken, "woman has heretofore commended herself to man by reason of her simpleness and silliness," and now that these have outgrown their sweet simplicity, the ordinary man has ceased to admire them or fears their power in the household of which he is the recognised head.

If it is true that there is a growing disinclination on the part of women to marry, it is still doubtful whether the world is to be the gainer by the change. True, there are too many unfit and hasty marriages, and the tie is made a cloak for vulgar passion whose satiety finds refuge in divorce but, in spite of all this, marriage remains the divinest institution of the world.

With the rapid growth of the world's population under the peace and sunshine of modern civilisation, what is needed is not so much large households of children, but better, healthier children. These are to be the fruit of wedlock, honoured and honourable, and the mother's care, love and example are still to be the grandest pictures that life can paint. To the end of time the hand that rocks the cradle is to shape the destinies of the nations.

Meantime, the unmarried woman is to have her own place and her work. The rewards of genius, of philanthropy, of money, of scholarship and art are all within her reach, and it may be that in the field of politics, as well as professional life, she will achieve, fame and fortune. But that her influence will equal that of the woman who finds in wedded life and motherhood the field for all that is best and purest in woman's nature, no thoughtful man will admit.

It is a pitiful thing on the part of woman or man to despise matrimony and so to deliberately cut themselves off from life's purest joys and prepare for themselves that worst of all fates – a homeless old age. Theories are all very fine on paper, but when it comes down to practice the girl who is willing to marry will carry the suffrage of masculine hearts, and her influence will outweigh that of a hundred blue-stockings and spectacled female foes of wedlock.

## Editorial, Tuesday, August 18, 1891[178]

It is evident the factious opposition of Mr Fish and a few other obstructionists to the woman franchise question is having the effect of putting their opponents upon their mettle.

The chief advocates of the measure, at a caucus held yesterday, expressed themselves resolved not to permit the majority to be coerced by the stonewalling tactics of a noisy minority.

The Premier ...acknowledged the justice of their demand, and promised that a special sitting of the House for Monday should be moved for to discuss the female franchise question, which is to be brought down in a separate Bill.

Apart from the merits of the subject, the obstructive conduct of Mr Fish has given a prominence to it which it had not before assumed, and at Wellington woman suffrage is being forced to the front and rapidly becoming the burning question of the hour.

The tactics of Mr Fish and his party are neither likely to secure their immediate object nor to raise those members in the estimation of the more intelligent portion of their constituents. If sound and cogent reasons can be advanced against woman suffrage, they will no doubt have all due weight given to them both in the House and out of it. It is quite another thing, however, when a senatorial windbag persistently obstructs a measure of public policy involving important issues, apparently from no other than the most sordid motives.

The contemptible nature of the procedure becomes still more glaring when, instead of advancing something like rational arguments, Mr Fish spends two hours in ranting and gesticulating, taking up the time of the House with what ...demonstrates chiefly the utter ignorance of the honourable gentleman of the subject be is treating.

It is characteristic of the tribe of Fish that they can only deal with the subject of female suffrage either as something particularly funny and affording an excellent opportunity for evolving senseless jokes and threadbare criticisms, or else as a measure to be used by designing individuals and societies, each with some special axe to grind.

Mr Blake, for instance, predicted the House would make itself the laugh-

---

178 Auckland Star, Volume XXII, Issue 195, 18 August 1891, Page 4
http://paperspast.natlib.govt.nz/cgi-bin/paperspast?a=d&d=AS18910818.2.60

ingstock of the world by advocating female franchise. In the opinion of this 'intelligent' member, the whole question is evidently a screaming joke, which will appear so comical when the world hears of it that old Cosmos will split his sides with laughing. It is really sickening at this time of day that the patience of the House should be taxed with listening to such drivel.

Messrs Fish and Blake are probably unaware that what to them is such a rich joke forms a subject that has been strenuously advocated by some of the most eminent political economists of the age, and that the measure has already, in one instance at least, passed beyond the experimental stage. Among great authorities who have supported woman suffrage may be mentioned, the names of Beaconsfield, Salisbury, Sir John Macdonald, Herbert Spencer, and Charles Kingsley, while Mr Gladstone has declared that a number of circumstances rendered it inconsistent "to grant men the extended suffrage and to exclude women."

In the territory of Wyoming women had been admitted to Government offices, and when Wyoming was admitted by Congress as a State in the Republic, although the recognition of woman suffrage had not been embodied in American law, Congress made an exception in the case of Wyoming, and on the ground of the success with which the principle had been carried out there, it was embodied in the laws of the State. The question of further extending the principle has made such headway of late years that it is proposed to amend the Constitution of the United States that the franchise may be extended to women in every State of the Union.

Whether this be ultimately accomplished or not, the question of female suffrage is regarded by sensible men in all English-speaking communities as within the range of practical politics, arid it is left to the Fish and Blake mental calibre to find in it food for that mirth which is not inaptly described as "the crackling of thorns under a pot."

It is noticeable in reading the discussions on extending the franchise to women, that both in our own Parliament and the recent debate on the question in the New South Wales Assembly, it seems to be assumed by some members that the measure is designed exclusively to serve the purposes of men, while any direct interest a woman may have in recording her vote from the standpoint of her own sex is studiously ignored. Mr Fish was positive only a very few women desired the franchise, while Mr Blake, with characteristic 'elegance' predicted that franchise to women would "mean a continual row from year's end to year's end."

The unfolding of a petition seventy yards long, signed by nearly 8,000 women, was a good object lesson for the loquacious Fish, and we should be glad to see the most voluble old washerwoman who would keep up more "row" than the screaming Blake. That both politicians and organisations are already counting on women's votes in support of their pet hobbies, we have every reason to believe.

The Temperance Societies, for example, make no secret of their belief that women's franchise will turn the scale of victory in their favour. The Bible in Schools party hint not obscurely that their ranks will receive an accession of strength. Some secularists imagine the influence exerted by priests over women in the confessional will be used to secure the special objects aimed at by the Catholic Church with regard to grants for educational purposes.

There may be a fragment of truth in all this, but equally doleful predictions as to the way in which the masses would be led by the nose if the one-man-one-vote principle were recognised have from time to time been urged by the opponents of that measure.

If we can educate the lowest class of men to properly exercise a vote, undoubtedly we can also do so with even the lowest class of women. Strenuous, efforts may possibly be made by designing leaders and politicians a block female vote for their own purposes, but although in some instances more, likely to be influenced by sentiment than the sterner sex, we have no doubt that with the extension of the privilege will come a sense of responsibility, and as women naturally will take an increased interest in political questions, we very much doubt whether they will be found so pliable as political, agitators suppose.

Women are gifted with a keen insight which often stands them in good stead when their logic is faulty, and they will soon begin to compute the value of their votes on the well-being of their own sex. This aspect of the case is constantly lost sight of by politicians of the Fish type. They cling to the old notion that woman is to be the mere plaything of man. They are likely to be rather roughly awakened from their dream; The world has not yet afforded many instances where women have had an opportunity of making their individuality felt in politics. An Elizabeth of England and a Catherine of Russia have proved that given the chance, there is no lack of female political personality.

When female suffrage is the law of the land, as very soon it will be, it will dawn upon the minds of some Parliamentary Rip Van Winkles that women have a distinct personality, that if they work for their bread they will demand equitable conditions: that they will not, at the same time, have equal voting powers and [yet] unequal measures meted out to them in Factory and Shop Bills, and that they have not received votes merely to secure monopolies to any class of men without a thought to the claims of their own sex.

It must be remembered the nation is half made up of women, and one object of the Female Franchise Bill is to remove what in the eyes of enlightened men is a glaring injustice. The only wonder is not that woman suffrage is now in the air, but that in an enlightened age the present anomalous system has been so long suffered to exist.

## Respect For Working Women, 1892[179]

On the arrival of Dr. Kate Mitchell of London, in Chicago, the lady physicians of that city honoured her by a public reception. The number of lady students in Switzerland is continuously increasing. Out of 701 students at the Zurich University, no less than 120 are ladies.

*Interesting to see then how far the emancipation of women had come, even in the late 1800s.*

---

179  The Ladies' Column, Bush Advocate, Volume VII, Issue 644, 2 July 1892, Page 6
http://paperspast.natlib.govt.nz/cgi-bin/paperspast?a=d&cl=search&d=BA18920702.2.41

Chapter 12

# The Rise And Fall Of The Moa

*Few topics excite the imagination more than the possibility of meeting up with some long-forgotten creature out in the wild.*

*In New Zealand's case, rumoured sightings of the presumably extinct moa speckle the news headlines from time to time, usually the result of a cunning hoax.*

*But what if, somewhere deep in Fiordland or off the beaten tracks of the national parks, moa still existed, unseen by humans?*

*The common assumption by scientists is that the giant moa were long gone by the time Europeans arrived in New Zealand, hunted to death by Maori. You are about to see those assumptions – both of them – challenged by the evidence:*

## The Last Moa?, 1861[180]

About three weeks ago, while Mr. Brunner, chief surveyor of the province, and Mr. Maling, of the survey department, accompanied by a native, were engaged in surveying on the ranges between the Riwaka and Takaka valleys, they observed one morning, on going to their work, the footprints of what appeared to be a large bird, whose tracks they followed for a short

---

180  Monthly Summary Of Events, Nelson Examiner and New Zealand Chronicle, Volume XX, Issue 50, 12 June 1861, Page 2
http://paperspast.natlib.govt.nz/cgi-bin/paperspast?a=d&cl=search&d=NENZC18610612.2.8

distance, but lost them at length among rocks and scrub.

The size of the footprints, which were well defined wherever the ground was soft, was fourteen inches in length, with a spread of eleven inches at the points of the three toes. The footprints were about thirty inches apart.

On examining the bones of the foot of a moa in the Museum, we find the toe to measure, without integuments[181], eight inches and a-half, and these evidently from part of a skeleton of a very large bird; the length of the impression of the toe of the bird in question was ten inches.

The native who was in company with Messrs. Brunner and Maling was utterly at a loss to conjecture what bird could have made such a footprint, as he had never seen anything of the kind before. On a subsequent morning similar marks were again seen, and as a proof that they had been made during the night, it was observed that some of them covered the footprints of those the party made the preceding evening.

The size of these footprints, and the great stride of the supposed bird, has led to a belief that a solitary moa may yet be in existence. The district is full of limestone caves of the same character as those in which such a quantity of moa bones were found about two years ago in the neighbouring district of Aorere.

We believe it is the intention of the Government to take steps to ascertain the character of this gigantic bird, whether moa or not, which keeps watch in these solitudes, and the search cannot but possess great interest for all students of natural history.

*The sighting is credible and extremely significant for two reasons. Firstly, the witnesses are two senior civil servants and skilled observers, being government surveyors. Secondly, the nature of pioneering survey work took men into areas where humans generally had not been. The Maori population of the entire South Island was only a few thousand, meaning there was plenty of opportunity for admittedly rare moa to go about their business unmolested by hunters.*

*Additionally, the release of pigs into the South Island bush provided much easier food for Maori to hunt than a mythical large bird, which would have also taken the pressure off any remnant moa population.*

*We don't know how long moa lived, but if they are anything like parrots it could be a century or more in the right circumstances. With a lack of predation*

---

181  Gristle and skin

*from hunters (who no longer thought they existed), there were few creatures left who could have threatened a moa once it had grown beyond the size of a turkey.*

*Interestingly, the world's largest bird, the Elephant Bird of Madagascar, went extinct not because it was hunted as an adult, but because humans raided their nests for the massive eggs. It is possible the last moa disappeared from New Zealand not by being speared, but by the introduction of rats and pigs capable of eating its eggs. This would leave the adult population alive but effectively childless, dying out in their old age.*

*One man who spent a lot of time considering the extinction was the Royal Society's Captain Hutton:*

## The Rise And Fall Of The Moa, 1896[182]
### By Captain Hutton, F.R.S.

Before New Zealand was trod by the foot of man it was more extensively covered by forest than now, and both forest and open country were inhabited by numerous birds very different from those of neighbouring countries. Birds may be said to have been the dominant race of the islands, for there were no mammals except two small bats.

Some five or six hundred years ago the Maori came and brought with him the art of making fire, with which he burnt down the forest, and the art of bird-snaring, with which he played havoc among the birds, assisted to some extent by his companions the dog and the rat. The Maori was followed by the more energetic Pakeha, who not only burnt everything dry enough to burn, but introduced the cat, the ferret and the weasel. To crown all there came the skin-monger, who dubs himself "naturalist."

Cats, ferrets, and weasels may have their good points, but what can be said for the skinmonger? Tempted by high prices offered by collectors he deliberately set to work to destroy all that is left of our beautiful and unique fauna, and, unless the existing laws are stringently enforced, most of our remaining native birds will become things of the past.

But it was the Maori, not the skinmonger, who exterminated the stately moa, and I am afraid he did it to supply his inner man; a low motive, but one which we can respect.

---

182  The Rise And Fall Of The Moa, Press, Volume LIII, Issue 9563, 2 November 1896, Page 5
http://paperspast.natlib.govt.nz/cgi-bin/paperspast?a=d&cl=search&d=CHP18961102.2.26

How numerous and how varied must the moas have been when the Maori first came. Innumerable bones have been found scattered over the ground, as well as in the sand-hills on the coast, and in the swamps and caves among the hills.

Great heavy birds were the moas, but remains of birds almost as great and heavy have been found in Madagascar, in Patagonia, and round the margins of Lake Callabonna, in South Australia. However, in none of these places are bird-bones anything like so numerous as in New Zealand; both in thickness of leg and in abundance of individuals the moa bears the palm[183].

The commoner kinds of moas were comparatively small birds, from 3ft to 5ft high, and it seems probable that the giants of the race which attained a height of about 12ft, had all died out before the advent of man.[184] At any rate there is no record of any bones of Dinornis maximus or of Dinornis gigantius having been found among the remains of Maori feasts.

About twenty-six different species of moa[185] have lived in New Zealand since the close of the tertiary era, and it is very remarkable that fourteen of these are found only in the South Island, and ten only in the North Island, while not more than two species occurred in both. This shows that the two islands were separated by Cook Strait during the whole of the time for if such had not been the case the various kinds of moas would have intermingled.

Confirmatory evidence of this long isolation is found in the different kiwis, wekas, crows, thrushes, robins, and other birds which are confined to one or other of the islands. Two extinct rails, or wood-hens, have been found in the Chatham Islands, but they are different from the rails found in New Zealand. No bones of the moa or kiwi have been found there, both these birds being confined exclusively to the two main islands of New Zealand; the so-called moa bones in Australia belonging to extinct emus and not to moas.

But the moa, although the most remarkable, is not the only extinct bird of New Zealand. There is the great eagle (Harpagornis), larger than

---

183 takes the honours
184 See story above for evidence contradicting that belief
185 After much reassessment of bones and genetics, the number of moa species categorised today has been whittled down to less than a dozen different varieties.

the condor of the Andes, but with shorter wings; the great wood-hen (Aptornis), the size of a turkey; a large coot (Fulica); the large swamp-hen (Notornis[186]); and the flightless goose (Cnemiornis), related to the Cape Barren goose of Australia, but larger and with shorter wings!

It is not supposed that either the Pakeha or the Maori is responsible for the extermination of these birds. Their remains are found in swamps mixed with those of the moa and of some still living species, such as the kiwi, but without any trace of human implements or relics of dog or rat such as we should expect to find if these deposits had been formed after man inhabited the islands.

There is, however, one point to notice. While bones of the moa are found in great quantities, those of the other birds are much fewer in number; so much so that the skeleton is not completely known in any one of them except the moa. In this there is, nothing remarkable, the remarkable thing is the enormous quantity of moas, not the rarity of other birds. To try to explain it let us just glance at their past history.

The, early ancestors of the moas had, no doubt, slender legs, like other birds, and could run well, and if we went further back still we should find their progenitors to be flying birds of ordinary size. This we judge to be the case because the moas have large air-cavities in their bones like flying birds, and because the kiwi, the cassowary, and the emu – all undoubtedly, descended with them from the same stock – have rudimentary wings formed on the same pattern as those of flying birds, which can only be explained on the supposition that these wings, now rudimentary, were of use to their ancestors.

The progenitors of the moas, then, must have flown into New Zealand across some narrow strait which at that time separated it from northern Australia, leaving behind them their mammalian companions. The moas on landing found an earthly paradise – plenty of food, and no worries. There were no carnivorous mammals to destroy either them or their eggs, and, being vegetable feeders, armed with a stomach full of stones, they were able to digest anything. No wonder they multiplied; in a country so well watered and with such abundant and varied vegetation as New Zealand.

In other countries all animals are subject to the law of natural selection,

---

186  This is the takahe, which was not discovered alive until 1948, going to prove that remote populations of 'extinct' birds may survive

under which the weakest and stupidest succumb to their enemies, eaten up, while the less perfectly developed starve in a time of scarcity.

But in New Zealand, in those happy days, there were, for the moas, no enemies and no times of scarcity, and thus arose rapid increase in their descendants, varying in an unconstrained manner, but much to the detriment of the individual. Strong, thick legs were useful for scratching up roots, and wings were not required to enable them to escape from their enemies, or to carry them from one feeding ground to another. Food was everywhere for those who could digest it, and digestion was a strong point with the moas – witness their gizzard stones.[187] No wonder then that they increased in numbers.

The other birds which lived with them had more fastidious tastes, and consequently they had no chance in the competition. The eagles liked animal food only, but were unable to kill the far stronger moa, and not having powerful wings, they probably had to depend on sick or dead animals for a supply of food. The wood-hens lived chiefly on berries and insects, which in the winter will always be scarce. The goose probably required succulent herbs, which were not common in New Zealand before the introduction of European annuals. It was, however, more numerous than the others. None could digest the roots and twigs with which the moas filled themselves, and consequently they all fell behind in the race. They remained comparatively few in numbers, while the moas spread over the whole face of the country, and even ascended the mountains to more than 5000 ft above the sea. It was the triumph of a good digestion.

As the moas were so numerous we might expect to find their remains occasionally as fossils, but only occasionally, for birds live and die in places where they cannot be buried, and their bones as well as their flesh decay

---

187  This is a debate central to New Zealand's current conservation policy. Some scientists believe there were huge numbers of moa in this country because they filled the niche occupied by deer, goats and other browsing animals in forests. Amateur conservationist Leonard Cockayne, widely regarded as the father of NZ forest conservation policy, wrongly believed however that moa were solely grassland feeders and that our forests had never been browsed. His views on keeping native forests "pristine" were based on a misunderstanding about just how moas kept the forests stripped of low shrubs, which allowed giants like kauri, totara and rimu to get enough sunlight while they were seedlings. Critics argue DoC's current policy of 'no browsing' is repeating Cockayne's fundamental error, and allowing shrubs to crowd out and strangle the ancient forest giants as they struggle to regenerate. NZ's current policy results in the regrowth of 'native bush' rather than 'native forest'.

and pass into dust. Something more, therefore, is necessary to account for the immense numbers of bones found packed in small patches in swamps – sometimes the remains of several hundreds of birds in one place – and in looking for an explanation we must carefully consider all the facts that have to he explained.

In the first place none of the swamps in the plains of Canterbury or Otago contain moa bones in masses. All the moa bone swamps are situated among low hills, as at Glenmark and Waimate in Canterbury, and Enfield, Waikouaiti and Hamilton's in Otago. In the second place these bone deposits are certainly very old. That at Glenmark was covered with from four to twelve feet of peat, that at Waimate with five feet of clay. At Hamilton's the bones, although nearer the surface, were found in the bed of an old pond or lake, and a neighbouring affluent of the Taieri river has since that date, cut down some twenty feet, thus leaving the bone deposit on the edge of a terrace. Below the deposit was a bed of clay about six feet thick, and below this again about thirty yards from the first was a second patch of bones larger than the first.

I mention these facts in order to clear the ground at once from the idea that Maoris or moa-hunters had anything to do with driving the birds into these places. They date back to a period long before man came to New Zealand. Other important facts in this connection are the large number of bones belonging to quite young birds mixed with those of the old ones, the absence of egg shells, and the abundance of gizzard-stones.[188]

Ordinary flying birds attain their full size within a year of hatching,

---

188  All of these factors just mentioned point to an event that Captain Hutton and the Royal Society knew nothing of back in 1896 – that New Zealand had been hit by a massive asteroid or comet, up to a kilometre across, in the early to mid 1400s, known as the Mahuika impact. The event was witnessed at night by aboriginal tribes in Australia and became part of their oral tradition. I discussed this and cited the evidence in my earlier book The Great Divide. A 20 km wide impact crater has been found in the seabed south of Stewart Island, and scientists estimate the impact caused a 'mega-tsunami' higher than 200 metres, which struck the whole New Zealand coastline, along with an absolutely massive series of earthquakes. The South Island bore the brunt of it. A wave that big would have punched its way right across lowland plains right into the foothills of the Southern Alps and Central Otago, which is precisely where huge numbers of dead moa are found in piles, left there by the receding tidal waves. This singular event would also explain why no eggs were found in the boneyards, if the impact happened outside the breeding season. You can blame the moa extinction on the asteroid, not humans. Sure, humans may have finished off the obvious remnants that they found, but the massive boneyards show the moa were largely wiped out by this event.

but the struthious birds – to which group the moas belonged – continue growing for two or three years, and consequently we should expect to find a larger proportion of immature birds among the moas than among ordinary birds. Still, the number of young in the swamps seems to be too great to be thus accounted for, their death ratio must have been greater than in the adults.

Now, let us see if a hypothesis can be framed which will account for these facts. The presence of gizzard-stones shows that the whole bird was buried and not isolated bones only. The remains occurring in patches, surrounded with peat or clay, shows that the deposits were not formed continuously, but intermittently, with intervals in which no birds found their way to that particular place. This would not be the case if the swamps had been traps for wandering moas, and it is not likely that they would get bogged in any quantity if they were not frightened by men or dogs. This is still more unlikely to have been the fate of flying birds like the eagle and kaka, or wading birds like the wood-hen and coot, or swimming birds like the goose. And, when we remember that these birds never got bogged on the plains we must, I think, agree that they were not trapped in this way among the hills either.

The bodies of these birds must, therefore, have come to the swamps after death and not when alive – in other words the birds died on the hills and their bodies were washed down into the valleys and deposited in ponds or lagoons, which afterwards became swamps. Also the deaths must have occurred at a time of the year when the females had no hard eggs in them, and the death rate must have been proportionally greater among the young than among the adult.

Nothing like this could take place now, and to account for it we must look back to a time when the climate of New Zealand differed from that of the present day. We go, therefore, back to the pleistocene period, when the eccentricity of the earth's orbit was greater than now; when long cold winters were followed by short, but very hot, summers. The autumn snows, we may well imagine, would bury hundreds of birds on the hills, and the vapid thaws in the summer would cause great floods, which would wash the dead bodies into lagoons, where they would be buried.

This process would go on only while the eccentricity of the orbit was high; as it decreased the climate would grow milder, the moas would no longer be caught by sudden falls of snow and the bones in the lagoons would be covered over with clay or peat without any bones in it. Such appears to me to be the only hypothesis which gives a reasonable explanation of the facts as we now know them.

No doubt the Maoris may have killed many moas by fire, but this was long after the formation of the bone deposits in the swamps. The bones of moas killed by Maoris lie on the surface. Sir James Hector says that in the early days he found, on a triangular piece of land alongside Lake Wakatipu, a place where a number of moas had been killed by fire. Stopped by the steep hills on one side and the deep lake on the other they had perished, no escape being possible. I think the fact that these birds allowed themselves to be burnt to death sooner than try to escape by swimming is an important addition to our knowledge of their habits.

What makes the ancient moa-bone deposits so remarkable is the sharp contrast they present to the collections found in the Maori kitchen-middens, for in the latter we find plenty of egg-shell, but few, if any, bones of young birds. Why should the Maoris eat the eggs and the old birds but not the young ones? The answer, I think, is that as the Maoris destroyed all the eggs, which were no doubt easy to find, there were no young birds to eat; and the moa became extinct from the supply of young failing. The date of these kitchen-middens is, therefore, very nearly the date of the extinction of the moa, and to this much debated question we must now pass.

Mr J. S. Polack was the first, 1838, to publish anything about the moa. He states that the Maoris of the East Cape district told him that they had a tradition that in times long past very large birds had existed in New Zealand in the South Island they were still to be found, and were accused of killing and devouring men. In 1839 the Rev. W. Colenso and the Rev. R. Taylor were told by Natives of Waiapu that one moa still lived in a cave on the mountain called Whakapurake, about eighty miles distant; it always stood upon one leg, and was guarded by two lizards, who kept watch while the moa slept. However, no one had seen it. In 1847 the Hon. W. Mantell ascertained for the first time, from the old kitchen-middens among the sandhills, that the ancient Maoris had killed and eaten moas near Wanganui, and from that time the Maori recollections of the moa appear to have improved year by year until, in 1866, Kawaua Paipai actually told Sir G. Grey that he had himself in his youth hunted it on the Waimate Plains, near Taranaki.

Indeed there are several people now who think that the Maoris have always had a very complete and correct knowledge of the appearance and habits of these birds. If these people are asked to explain how it is that Maori poems and legends hardly ever refer to the moa, they answer that the bird was so well known and so common that it was not thought worth while to mention it. The fact that many of the oldest Maoris have stated that they know nothing about it is left unexplained.

On the other hand, there are a few who follow the late Sir Julius von Haast in thinking that the ancestors of the Maoris never saw the moa at all, and that the people who exterminated and ate it belonged to another race distinguished under the name of Moa-hunters. Mr E. Tregear seems to go still further, and to deny the existence even of moa-hunters. The word moa, he thinks, has nothing to do with the bones we pakehas call by that name, but means merely the domesticated fowls kept by the ancestors of the Maoris previous to their colonisation of New Zealand and he explains the ancient Maori saying "Lost as the moa is lost" as referring to the loss of their poultry, presumably on the voyage to New Zealand.

But he has not explained the Maori legends of finding the moa on their arrival, and of its subsequent extinction by fire and earthquake. I think no one would care to uphold this view who had seen the fragments of the skeletons of moas scattered about at the site of an ancient Maori feast. Heads with a portion of the neck, or parts of legs with one of the bones broken across and separated from the rest of the body; all the bones of each fragment in their proper places as when thrown away, but now, owing to the decay of flesh and sinew, each bone quite detached from the others, so that, in collecting them, they have to be carefully held together.

Undoubtedly the early Maoris killed moas. That they also ate their eggs is proved by the quantity of broken eggshell often found in the neighbourhood of the old umus, or ovens, some of the fragments being burnt on the outer side only. It is quite true, as some have objected, that moa bones may have been used for fuel, and that a burnt moa bone does not necessarily imply a cooked moa bone. But with eggshell the case is different. It will not make a fire, and if thrown into one would be burnt on both sides. An egg shell burnt on the outside only means that the contents of the egg have been cooked.

The truth probably lies between the extreme views just mentioned. The Maori traditions, often condensed into phrases or even into single words, have received considerable confirmation by the discoveries made during the last twenty years, and prove sufficiently that the ancestors of the present Natives saw the birds alive, and were identical with the moa hunters. But the slightness of these traditions and the way they are mixed with fabulous stories are also a sufficient proof that many generations have passed away since the moa lived.

It is indeed highly improbable that birds so easily seen and killed, could have lasted long after the Maoris had become numerous and spread through the islands, and the date of their extinction depends upon the date of the arrival of the Maoris. On this point authorities differ, some allowing only eighteen generations, others twenty-eight, to have passed away since that time. This gives 360 or 560 years if we allow twenty for each generation, and 450 or 700 years if we allow twenty-five years.

Perhaps between 500 and 550 years is the best estimate we can make, and if we allow 100 to 150 years for the process of extermination, we arrive at the conclusion that it took place about four hundred years ago.[189] This is for the North Island; for the South Island the case is rather different, for it must have been colonised long after the North Island. The Hon. W. Mantell, who examined the kitchen middens with moa bones, near Oamaru in 1852, calls them the umus of the extinct tribe Waitaha, and no doubt his information was obtained from the Natives who accompanied him.

The Rev. J. W. Stack says that the present Maoris of Canterbury have an indistinct tradition that it was the tribe Te Rapuwai who formed the shell mounds so commonly found on the coast, and who exterminated the moa. He thinks it not improbable that Te Rapuwai and Waitaha were hapus of the same tribe, at any rate they were contemporaries, and formed the vanguard of the migration from the North Island.

These tribes were destroyed by the Ngatimamoe, who were in their turn destroyed by the ancestors of the present Nga-i-tahu. The Nga-i-tahu count ten or eleven generations since the occupation of the island, and Mr Stack allows one hundred years for the Ngatimamoe occupation, so we are led to the end of the sixteenth century as the time of the destruction of Te Rapuwai and Waitaha, and also of the extinction of the moa. I know of no evidence to contradict this. The finding of bones with skin

---

189  Again, working backwards from 1896, you get to the 1400s which is when we know the asteroid struck. Everything fits for New Zealand moa suffering their own 'dinosaur extinction asteroid'.

and tendons attached in sheltered places in the dry portion of Central Otago is easily explained, for in that climate dried animal tissues might be preserved for many centuries, like mummies in Peru, and it is very unlikely that the last moas inhabited just that place where their remains could be dried up and preserved.

We may therefore conclude that the last of the moas lived in the South Island not less than three hundred years ago. The date of their first coming to New Zealand is far more difficult to fix. As they came from the north it must have been at a time when New Zealand stretched towards New Caledonia and New Guinea, for it is not probable that they could have crossed a very broad arm of the sea. The last extension of New Zealand in this direction was probably in the beginning of the pliocene period, or towards the close of the miocene. But there was another and earlier extension of the land in the eocene period, and we must choose one or other of these. We have nothing to guide us beyond the fact that there were moas in New Zealand in the pliocene, and as we must allow a long time for their development from flying birds, it seems most probable that they arrived in the eocene period, but none of their remains have been found at so early a date.

## Chapter 13

# Clash Of Cultures: What The Missionaries Found

*If you look at high school history books these days, our children are taught a mythology about New Zealand's past that simply did not happen. The way the text books teach us, Maori were a wise and enlightened indigenous people living in harmony with the environment whose ancient ways were crushed by evil colonising missionaries and British traders.*

*The truth is a little more complex than the Smurf-like image presented in NCEA exams. Pre-European Maori were an intelligent and advanced people, but they were human like everyone else and subject to the same corruptions as everyone else. Their society was also very, very brutal.*

*The slave trade was a mainstay of society, and when slaves were not performing menial tasks they were often slaughtered and eaten when they outlived their usefulness. The concept of "utu" or revenge, ran so strong that if one person committed an offence, often his entire tribe were killed in punishment. With the stakes so high, war was frequent and peace between the tribes almost unknown.*

*Today, New Zealanders of all descriptions no longer face such threats when venturing outside their doors. Maori people today are the civilisational equals of every other Westerner on the planet; they are no closer to their savage ancestors than the modern Brit can be tarred with the brutality of their Celtish ancestors – the door closed on those periods of history a long time ago.*

*Nonetheless, there is something of immense value to be gained for all of us if we re-open some of the 'forbidden' stories – the ones you are not allowed to* teach in school — because they help all of us understand just how far we have come as a nation in the 200 years since the missionaries arrived.

## Keeping A Head For Business, 1893[190]
### By The Rev. Gideon Smales

"Honour to whom honour is due." All honour to the first missionaries who prepared the way for the colonization of New Zealand. The memory of such men as the Rev. Samuel J Marsden and the Rev. Samuel Leigh is worthy of all honour and praise.

Mr. Marsden, like Captain James Cook, was a native of Yorkshire. Young Marsden was brought up in connexion with the Wesleyans... Through the influence of the famous William Wilberforce[191], of Hull, he was recommended to a chaplaincy in New South Wales, and on the 28th of August, 1793, his vessel weighed anchor for that country. Here he became exceedingly useful, took great interest in the London Missionary Society, and every other good work. And it was during a two year visit to his native land that Mr. Marsden laid the foundation of the Church of England Mission to New Zealand.

On his return from England he sent Messrs. Hall and Kendall, with the New Zealand chief Ruatara, to commence the mission, and after their return to Sydney.

His first voyage to this country was with the brig *Active*, of 100 tons. She left Port Jackson [now known as Sydney], November 19, 1814, and entered the Bay of Islands on December 22, 1814, with Mr. Marsden, and Messrs. Kendall, Hall, and King, and Ruatara, and his uncle Hongi, two Tahitians, and four Europeans, and Captain Lydiard Nicholas.

At this period the reviews, magazines, and newspapers, as well as a good portion of the clergy of all denominations, expressed the opinion that, "If the heathen are to be won back to the rank and standing of civilized men, you must make them good mechanics, and then make them good Christians if you can."

---

190   Episodes In The Life Of An Old Missionary, New Zealand Herald, Volume XXX, Issue 9279, 9 December 1893, Page 1
http://paperspast.natlib.govt.nz/cgi-bin/paperspast?a=d&d=NZH18931209.2.69.4
191   Wilberforce was the man responsible for ending the Slave Trade in the British Empire

"Men must be rational and civilised," observed Dr. Lardner, "before they can be Christians. Knowledge has a happy tendency to enlarge the mind and to encourage generous sentiments."

"Barbarous nations," said the Bishop of Carlisle, "are unable to bear the truth, and vicious and immoral ones are incapable of bringing forth the fruits thereof. Christianity cannot immediately transform the minds of men, and totally change the general temper and complexion of any people."

These views being entertained and avowed by some of the highest authorities in the church and State, Mr. Marsden himself was induced, when in England, to embrace them, and selected New Zealand as the field in which their validity was to be tested.

Mr. Leigh, on the other hand, believed the calling of missionary societies to be a spiritual calling, and that the office of the missionary should be restricted to spiritual objects.[192] No deviation from this general principle could, in his opinion, be justified but by extraordinary circumstances.

As a fair illustration of the state of things in his time, the following is given respecting an experience of the Rev. S. Leigh, the earliest of the Wesleyan missionaries:

"On the second Sunday after his arrival, he went out in the afternoon to a village not far from the settlement. As he entered it, he was shocked to see twelve heads of men, neatly arranged on the right hand side of the path. They were beautifully tattooed, and presented a calm and placid aspect. This exhibition brought some of the most savage and atrocious developments of human nature under his own immediate observation. He felt, at the moment, that he had entered the region and shadow of death, 'and was treading on soil but recently moistened with the blood of man'.

"Mr. Leigh sent for the chief, and said to him, 'I did not expect to witness so revolting a spectacle in your village. Why have you placed those heads in such a situation?'

"He replied, with an air of contempt, 'Because I expected you to buy them!'

---

192   This difference of opinion explains why the early Christian missionaries led by Marsden failed to convert virtually a single Maori to Christianity, even though they were educating them in 'Christian' schools: Marsden's focus was in building skills. What he ended up with were highly educated warlords like Hongi Hika who then purchased guns and carried out genocidal raids against rival tribes. The later missionaries, who chose to 'convert' Maori, succeeded in changing the heart of a people, and that led directly to the Treaty of Waitangi. See The Great Divide for details of how this unfolded

" 'Buy them?' said Mr. Leigh, with considerable vehemence, 'I buy spars, pigs, and flax, but not the heads of men'.
"On returning through the same village in the evening he perceived that the heads had been removed. On meeting the chief he inquired why he had removed the heads. 'Because,' he observed, 'you did not like to see them, and wished that you might not see any more, but the captain of the next ship will, in all probability, purchase them'."

*After reporting back to England about this and other similar instances of murderous behaviour, Reverend Leigh won the debate over skills vs morals, and persuaded the Church Missionary Society to expend far more of its efforts on spreading the spiritual message of Christianity among Maori.*

*The Reverend Gideon Smales was one of the few outsiders ever to have witnessed a raising the bones of the dead ceremony on a marae in the early 1840s, and the recently rediscovered account of that ceremony gives a rare glimpse into ancient tribal life:*

## Raising The Bones Of The Dead, The Hahunga[193]

The mass assembled at the hahunga, or raising of the bones of the dead, was made up of all manner of physical and mental characteristics, displayed in all manner of dress and ornament. There were a goodly number of well-built men, tall of stature and broad of shoulder, whose muscular development bespoke great athletic power.

There were others, who were easily distinguished by dark and terrible features, whose very appearance was a complete index to their heredity and training in their little world of vice and diabolic rule. There were a fair proportion of old men who had borne their threescore years and ten, and several who seemed to have passed the time of their fourscore years and upwards.

Some were pointed out as old tohungas (priests); others as old toas (champions, warriors); and great interest seemed to be attached to the men whose minds were stored with legends and the love of genealogy

---

193  Episodes In The Life Of An Old Missionary, New Zealand Herald, Volume XXXI, Issue 9587, 11 August 1894, Page 1
http://paperspast.natlib.govt.nz/cgi-bin/paperspast?a=d&d=NZH18940811.2.60.3

and history of the country and its inhabitants the men whose elocution inflamed the multitude with the greatest success and swayed the minds of the people with their songs, proverbs, and maxims, and those in most cases were the tohungas, who ruled absolutely not by truth but by the deceptive incantation and oracle.

There were those pointed out who were skilled in tattooing, others in carving; some as builders of canoes; some as skilled in working out greenstone ornaments and some as experts in swimming, climbing, running, fencing, weaving dogskin and other mats, and some as cultivators of the land and as producers of food. And they were all looked up to with reference to the work of art and skill in which they were experts.

The women also seemed to take a prominent part in the great festival. Some of the old women appeared to have considerable deference paid to them, being the wives or widows of leading chiefs. There were also a few leading chieftesses through birth who took a prominent part in all the movements, but especially in the direction of the slaves and in the preparation and serving up of the food.

Several women, too, were pointed out as those skilled in weaving mats and in other acts of dexterity and labour. Some were known as even skilled in warfare, some with the paddle, some with cultivating food, some in native dances, and some in guiding and governing the slaves with tact and success.

Nearly all, both men and women, were tattooed, some more and some less fully. Many were also painted; some with only one side of the face painted black and some with red and some painted like the morning sky, streaked with crimson. Some were crested like the kotuku, with the great kotuku's feathers and some were decorated with the plumes of the huia, and the tui, and the toroa (albatross). Some carried an upoko tikitiki (high head) decorated with ornamental heru (combs carved in wood), and heru-paraoa (carved comb from the bones of the sperm whale).

There was a great and varied show of native garments, from the kahukiwi to the common pureke; and comparatively little European clothing, except where the natives had been connected with one of the mission stations, whence, the female was dressed in a calico or print roundabout, and the man with a shirt, and sometimes trousers and coat. Others, who had visited the pakeha Maori's store, had obtained a pair of trousers or a coat; and, being a novice to such like wear, one had clad himself in the trousers for a coat, and another had decided that a coat made a better nether garment than the trousers; and they thus, to the civilised eye, cut a most fantastic and grotesque appearance.

The plateau, where all collected together, was at the foot of a mountain of considerable height, which seemed to give a weird shade to the scene, and especially after the tohunga and his tapu (sacred) party had come down from thence with the tapued heads and bones of the celebrated characters over which this great feast was said to be held. They had under considerable ceremony of prayer and incantation been to the cave whore the sacred heads and bones were deposited. The tohunga had with sacred staff touched the sacred relics, offered his karakia (service-worship), and brought them down with some degree of solemn pageantry, with one of the tapued party marching in front with a leafy branch.

### *The Women Wailing*

Coming to the site then, imagine a score of old women, nearly naked, moving up to the front of the mokomokai (the enbalmed heads) of ten or a dozen of the leading celebrities of their tribe. These heads are skilfully arranged, sometimes in a straight line, sometimes in a semicircle, and so placed between some ornament of coloured cloth or Maori dress, that nothing but the face is seen staring you grimly face to face.

Some of these women who have come forward and formed themselves into a line, have no clothing, except a small garment around the loins. The upper part of the body is fully exposed, showed in long lines the cicatrized wounds of former lacerations. Each carried in her hands a piece or pieces of sharp obsidian (volcanic glass), or sharp cockle or mussell shells.

They commenced their tangi (cry) by swinging their arms and bending and twisting their bodies with the most hideous contortions, they broke out into a very agony of lamentation, and then uttered "a cry that shivered to the tingling stars."

They howled and yelled in the most doleful and dreadful manner possible, whilst they at the same time were cutting and gashing their faces, and breasts, and bodies most frightfully with the sharp instruments they held in their hands, until the blood streamed down the cheeks, and naked breasts, and bodies most copiously. Then came forward the old men, each leaning on a hani (a chief's staff), a taoroa (or long staff), or some other support, over which they bent and leaned; and they began in a low, monotonous tone, and tangied, or cried in the most pitiable manner, every now and again repeating the excellencies or famous deeds of the parties whose heads were confronting them.

## *The Preserved Heads*

It is difficult to calculate the effect upon the mind and heart even when a striking portrait is brought before us. To an affectionate and sensitive daughter, the sight of a mere portrait of a kind and loving mother, though she may have been separated by death for years, is likely so far to excite the sympathetic memory as to create a ready and copious flow of tears. To a valorous, enterprising, and patriotic warrior, the very sight of a portrait of a Wellington or a Nelson will excite the warlike spirit. Here are not merely the portraits or busts of the native celebrities, but the very heads of the men whose lives and conduct have been impressed upon their nature by a long course of years – the head, it may be, of the tohunga, or native priest, upon which they have fixed their eyes. They are looking into the very face of the man who had driven deep the uhi-a-mataora (the tatooing adze) into their limbs and over their faces, the cuts and gashes of the curiously-wrought moko (tatoo) whilst tapu, (sacredness) was indelibly impressed upon their minds by the prayers and incantations of the priest who was supposed to be under the direction and inspiration of his atua (god).

They are gazing upon the face of the man who, according to their estimation and belief, has had the power by his prayers and incantations to influence the very gods themselves. And then again their spirits are aroused, and their feelings excited by the stiff, stern-looking face of the celebrated toa or brave, whose skill and courage has enabled him to stand out single-handed as the deliverer of his people. The very head and face of the man, who like David of old, has stood out from the ranks, and listened to the threats and curses of the champion Goliath of the enemy's tribe: and who, by his expertness, skill, or athletic force has not only bravely stood the insults and challenges thrown against himself and his tribe, but has been able to stand out in single combat and conquer his antagonist.

These, then, are the scenes which the people naturally bring before them in connection with the very sight of these grim visages of death. The mourners, the speakers and others are kept gazing on the faces of the men; who have been regarded as their great examples of courage, of skill, of daring enterprise and their deliverers from wretched slavery and cruel death. They are looking into the faces of those who have led them to victory and triumph – of those with whom they gloated over the bodies of their conquered victims – of whom they have heard wonderful tales and remarkable deliverances. After feasting their eyes, and almost exhausting their bottles of tears with tangi-ing, and dessicating their throats with their howling, and working themselves up to the highest pitch of excitement, the mourners sat down or retired.

## *An Orator*

Then it was that a middle-aged man rather suddenly arose who was to be the leading speaker on the occasion. He was tall and well built, one of nature's noblemen. He was fully tattooed, and had a large head of curled black hair, he had a pohoi, that is, a tuft or bunch of albatross down, suspended from his right ear, and a mako, or shark's tooth, suspended from the left ear; he had a highly-ornamented topuni, or dogskin, mat over his shoulders, reaching below his waist, and a maro, or girdle, round his loins; and he carried a hani, or chief's staff, beautifully carved, and highly ornamented with the russet feathers of the kaka (parrot) at the sharp end, in his right hand.

He walked forward into the centre of the arena with native dignity and conscious importance ...Confronting these heads which faced him in the grim visage of death, it may easily be imagined with what powerful emotion, and with what impassioned eloquence, he clenched his arguments for any enterprise of crafty diplomacy or determinate war.

He continued to work on their feelings with recollections of the past. He then raised them to the highest pitch by appealing to the multitude as the brothers and sisters, sons and daughters, friends and comrades, of the men whose heads were before them The excitement was immense, and the multitude appeared to throw themselves entirely into the will of the speaker. Trite maxims, pointed proverbs, and striking and startling figures, were poured forth most profusely, and these were followed by an exciting apostrophe to the mokomokai, or celebrated heads before them:

"O ye sons of the gods! Ye children of Tangaroa! Ye children of Tu! We again see your faces You have come from the Reinga. Yonder is the place, but here are your faces! Here are the eyes that looked at me, the head that spake to me with its tongue and listened to me with its ears. The head that held the brains, that thought for us, that prayed for us, that loved us! We love you for the gods were your friends, and they blessed us for you. You are the tohungas by whom we live! And you, the toas, were the sons of the mighty, who delivered us, and saved us when the enemy came like a mighty rushing wind to destroy us, and to consume us...Speak now to your children!"

And the speaker chanted an appropriate waiata, (song) in which the multitude united, and then sat down amid the greatest- excitement. Speaker after speaker then arose and delivered themselves with varied ability, but all with great earnestness, and almost uniformly ended with an appropriate waiata.

## *The Feast*

In the meantime a large body of women were all busily engaged in preparing the feast, and as the steam began to break forth from the numerous hangi's (native ovens), the sign of the food having been cooked, an intimation was given that the speaking must give way for the feasting.

The food was placed in lines and heaps over a large surface, when the tohunga went round with his staff in hand and called out with a loud voice, the names of the tribes and sub-tribes to whom the different sections or parts were apportioned, not forgetting, of course, the tohunga's share and indicated all by touching it with the point of his staff. The various portions were very soon on the spot appointed for each party and the intermission was brief before the various heaps were greatly reduced.

Kumaras and potatoes, taro and Indian corn, hue and para, sharks and stingray, pigs and birds, eels and schnapper, pupu and toheroa, paoa and pipi, were soon disposed of. And now all went on with a merry ring, and seemed to remind one of a large and gleesome picnic. The old people were garrulous and full of excitement the young people were warbling with the koanau or the putorino (musical flutes), and all seemed to be as lively and merry as a Mayfield Fair in London in olden times.

As the public speaking ended, and discussion finished during the day, the more hilarious portion of the assembly kept themselves awake during most of the night in all manner of sports and play – dancing, singing, wrestling, racing. This speechifying, and feasting, and gossiping, and merry-making was kept up for three days, and I have known occasions when it has been kept up for seven days.

*These, then, were the old ways, the tohunga-driven tribal customs that governed Maori society. It was a very different world to the one the settlers brought with them. That culture clash was about to come to a head, only three years after the Treaty of Waitangi was signed.*

*Smales, the author of the above, again found himself on the scene soon after one of New Zealand's most notorious massacres, and had to play a key role in quelling tension lest the country erupt into war. It is to that story, and how Maori and Pakeha subsequently forged a new way of putting the past to rest, that we now turn...*

## Chapter 14

# The Massacres At Wairau And Kaipara

*In 1843, New Zealand's race relations powderkeg looked set to blow. At the centre of it was a large Wellington tribe who'd recently carried out a devastating series of raids on tribes in the upper South Island and seized the territory of the vanquished. Enter some naïve Europeans and it was a recipe for trouble.*

The backstory to the Wairau tragedy was simple. Captain Arthur Wakefield, younger brother of Edward Wakefield, was attempting to enforce New Zealand Company title to a piece of land allegedly purchased under contract but not yet paid for, from Ngatitoa chief Te Rauparaha.

The land was at Wairau, near Nelson, part of the region now held by Ngatitoa.

There had been some preliminary legal skirmishes, with Te Rauparaha refusing to accept payment for the land and saying he no longer wished to sell it.

Testosterone got the better of Captain Wakefield who led a delegation of men from Nelson up to Wairau, armed with cutlasses and guns and deputised as special constables, with a warrant to arrest Te Rauparaha.

Around 50 British ended up facing 90 Ngatitoa, including some women and children, across a stream. Amid the tension a nervous British finger brushed a trigger too firmly, and a shot rang out. Immediately both sides started firing at each other, and in the confusion a bullet killed Te Rauparaha's daughter Rongo, married to a warrior named Te Rangihaeata.

Wakefield called a ceasefire, and Ngatitoa took him and 21 settlers captive. Te Rangihaeata demanded "utu" for his wife's death, and then exacted his revenge *by executing every British prisoner who had surrendered – 22 men in total. The Reverend Gideon Smales picks up his side of the story:*

## The Wairau Massacre Of 1843[194]

I had not been long in Wellington before the Government brig arrived there from Cloudy Bay with Mr. Tuckett, the chief surveyor, also two white men and one Maori wounded; and brought the alarming and painful intelligence of the collision between the natives and Captain Wakefield and the party who went with him to take Te Rauparaha and Rangihaeata prisoners, and seize the land at the Wairau.

This collision had been of the most dreadful character, ending as I foresaw, and which I warned both Captain Wakefield and Mr. Tuckett to avoid, as recorded in a former paper of mine. It was most pitiable and distressing to hear that nearly all the leading gentlemen of Nelson, as well as a great many other excellent men, had been either shot or tomahawked.

The people of Wellington were violently alarmed, and were apprehensive that the natives would come down upon Wellington, and they made their danger greater by their alarm and the cultivation of a strong agitation for revenge – as the natives termed it, utu (payment or compensation). And no sooner had the Government brig arrived than a considerable number of men were putting their arms in order, and even threatening the natives with their determination to have utu.

About 100 men, fully equipped for war, went on board of the Government brig with the intention of going to revenge the fate of those who had fallen at Wairau. It always appeared to me most providential that a gale set in which would not permit the vessel sailing. There she lay under the lee of the land during the Sabbath day; and by Monday or Tuesday, when the breeze had abated a little, and the time for departure had arrived, the courage of the armed men had cooled, down, and most of them landed again.

There is little doubt that if they had been permitted to sail in time to meet the natives before they crossed the straits for Porirua, and come into collision with them, but that the same or a similar fate would have

---

[194]  Episodes In The Life Of An Old Missionary, New Zealand Herald, Volume XXX, Issue 9223, 10 June 1893, Page 1
http://paperspast.natlib.govt.nz/cgi-bin/paperspast?a=d&d=NZH18930610.2.76.3

happened to them which happened to the unfortunate men whose fate they were going to revenge.

Instead of a war party proceeding it was finally arranged that a deputation from the Wellington magistrates, with Dr. Dorset, should proceed to learn further particulars and they sailed for Cloudy Bay on Wednesday, the 21st of June. On their arrival at Cloudy Bay they found that the Rev. S. Ironside had preceded them with two boats' companies of whalers, and they had discovered the bodies.

I have the copy of a letter before me written by the Rev. S. Ironside, which he sent me, which gives a summary of the affair at Wairau as he learnt it on the spot, which runs as follows:

"H. A. Thompson, Police Magistrate and Native Protector; Captain England; Mr. Richardson, Crown Prosecutor; Mr. Cotterell, Surveyor; Mr. Howard, company's storekeeper; Mr. Putchett, and about fifteen others, all of Nelson, have been killed. They were accompanied with about fifty men with muskets, cutlassses, etc.

"Te Rauparaha was served with a warrant and ordered on board the Government brig, but he refused to go. High words passed on both sides, and firing commenced, on which side first is disputed by both parties. The white people were beaten, and fled in all directions, and were killed, except about eighteen who have escaped.

"Captain Wakefield, Mr. Thompson, Mr. Cotterell, and others were taken prisoners; and, after all was over, were tomahawked as payment for Te Rongo, a chieftainess of rank, who had fallen. This was on Saturday, 17th instant (June, 1843).

"On Sunday evening I heard of it; could not get to the scene of action before Wednesday on account of a violent gale; found nineteen bodies of white people. In all there are more, but we could not find them in the bush. We made a large field grave where the massacre of the magistrate and, others took place, and put thirteen there, three in another grave, two in another, and one in another, where we found them.

The natives say they would not have killed the prisoners but for this chief woman. The mission natives were there, not, of course, expecting a fight; but they joined in it, and followed after the warriors. But when they saw the butchery of the prisoners commence they fled in all directions, and left the heathen.

The bodies found were all barbarously tomahawked about the head, beside shots wounds. The very recollection of the sight sickens me, every time I sleep the whole scene is before me, and I awake with a shudder."

It may easily be imagined the sensation such a thrilling record would create. I must say, in defence of the Christian natives, that I believe they simply fired in defence; and, as above stated, so soon as the heathen displayed their spirit they fled.

## *A Vivid Description*

Almost immediately after receiving this alarming intelligence I hastened to Porirua, so that I might stand in the gap which had been made by this terrible collision. On arriving at Porirua I found all the natives had crossed the straits [to Porirua]. Many of them were at our station at Takapuahi; and others were at the heads of Porirua, at a place called Taupo.

All seemed greatly excited; and, of course, they must relate all the circumstances connected with their collision with the pakehas at Wairau. At length, after I had heard several particulars from the Christian natives, Te Rangihaeata, who had been the leading actor in the dreadful scene, came forward, and in real Maori war costume, with abundance of paint, with his upoko tikitiki (high-decorated head), and a tomahawk in his hand.

He marched out in front of the assembled natives, and stood forth a veritable picture of man in his barbarous and heathenish state. He at once threw his whole soul into what he was about to relate. No tragedian – neither a Irving, nor a Kean, nor any other – could over depict the horror and the force of passion exhibited by that fierce, wild, untutored, ungoverned savage.

He spoke as he felt, and his feelings were inflamed with the recollections of his past experience of the most dreadful orgies of murder and cannibalism.

Ho seemed to have a vision before him of the darkest and most horrible character. The most vivid pictures had been phonographed on the mysterious convolutions of his cerebral globe and they spoke as not coming from the mechanism of a lifeless cylinder[195], but, as they were in reality, from an excited and wildly vivacious brain.

It seemed as though the spectres of the departed, whose lives he had

---

195  In this paragraph, written in 1893, Smales is analogising the oratory with a phonograph recording on the old drum cylinders that preceded the invention of the gramophone.

taken and many of whose bodies he had eaten, had, as a vast legion, taken possession of him. He ran, he jumped, he raved, and his body was thrown into the most violent contortions. He writhed; he grinned with a sardonic grin; he pukanaed – that is, he violently forced his eyeballs beyond their sockets, and forced his tongue beyond his mouth and below his chin, and again his lips curled, and he snorted, and sneezed, and tossed his head.

He displayed the utmost contempt and derision for the men he had so recently murdered. "They came," said he, "with their irons, clanking them before my face, thinking they could put them on my hands and the hands of 'Para' (Te Rauparaha), and when they found they could not do that they then thought they would settle us by shooting us. But where is all their boast? They have got what they deserved.

"Here is the book from which Thompson (the magistrate) thought he would condemn us!"

And he held up "The Magistrate's Guide," all marked with blood.

"This is his guide, and this is his blood. Here is the book, and look at the blood. This is Thompson's book, and this is his blood! Ah! Ah! The kuware (the fool), did he think he could take us?

"I cut his head off, and I kicked it about the ground like a pumpkin" (Mr. Thompson was a gentleman about middle age, and bald.) Using the action to the word, with his wild stare and his defiant and scornful look, and putting himself in the attitude, and kicking something along the ground, imagining he was kicking about the head of poor Thompson, he exclaimed to me, "Me kore – kua penei hoki koe me Tamehana!" "Had it not been" (for some reason or other which he would not name or could not account for) "yours would have been the fate of Thompson!"

And he kept up his violence, for he had just come red-handed from the heat and excitement of the massacre of the men at the Wairau. It was stated that it was Rangihaeata, the butcher of Te Rauparaha, who tomahawked, with his own tomahawk and by his own hands, all those who were massacred after the fight of Wairau.

Again and again Rangihaeata reverted to the scenes of that day. It appeared that neither the cries of pity and compassion nor the moans and dreadful shrieks of the dying victims had the least effect in softening his savage nature, but rather hardened his heart, and aroused his spirit of cruelty, revenge, and savagery, for in various ways he endeavoured to imitate and burlesque the agonies and shrieks of the dying.

Alas, alas for fallen, depraved human nature! And alas for the many of our noble, adventurous, and valorous men who have fallen beneath the weapons of our barbarous predecessors.

I let Te Rangihaeata exhaust himself in the relation of his bloodthirsty exploit, for it would have been dangerous to interrupt him in his violent harangue, and I then begged of him the book, "The Magistrate's Guide," with the brand of poor Thompson's blood on it. And, after a few days' delay, he conceded my request; and I took it to my friend Major Richmond, who was then the chief Government official in Wellington.

He expressed himself as greatly indebted to me for my labours amongst the natives, and was most anxious that I should assist the Government in every possible way. He was thankful that I had taken him the book. He desired that I should endeavour to recover Captain Wakefield's cutter, which the natives had taken after the massacre and brought across the straits to Porirua, and anything else which they might have taken from the murdered men.

As the Europeans generally had become considerably excited and unsettled, and were living in continued dread of the natives coming down upon Wellington and destroying it, as they said, root and branch, I was particularly desired to keep up a perfect acquaintance with the feelings and movements of the natives, and give him every information, so that they should not be taken unawares.

My time for some months was greatly occupied in travelling backwards and forwards between Porirua and Wellington. Whilst sojourning at either place I was employed in conciliating and quieting the pakeha on the one hand and the Maori on the other. I was continually reminded whilst speaking to the natives that they were a body of men who, only a short time back, had fought their way from Kawhia to Wellington and Wairarapa, besides their raids further South, killing and eating the people as they proceeded, offering hecatombs of holocausts to their war-god, Tu, the Destroyer, and leaving desolation and ruin and weeping and wailing behind them.

It was no easy task at times to hold back the hounds of war, who were thirsting for blood, within the leashes of peace and propriety. At this period one person who had been living in a very loose way amongst the natives, and noted by them as a very immoral man, was reported to me as a man whom they had reason to think was endeavouring to poison them, or watching an opportunity to shoot some of them, in retaliation for parties fallen at the

Wairau; and they would have taken summary retribution upon him, but before they had time to carry out their design one of the natives informed me, and I used my influence to have him removed to Wellington.

I saw that it was bettor that he should be banished than that we should have another murder. He, however, cultivated a bitter feeling against the natives and the missionaries and perhaps never fully understood that his ostracism was, at least, his temporal salvation.

*Discretion being the better part of valour, Smales' cautious diplomacy won the day. So too did the wider work of the missionaries: within just 17 years of the Wairau massacre and the traditional Maori tikanga that justified killing 22 people for the death of one, Te Rauparaha's son, Tamihana Te Rauparaha, was steering his tribe towards a new future, far away from what he called the 'old' ways. The occasion was a massive hui at Kohimarama in Auckland in 1860 to review progress since Waitangi, and to discuss the tino-rangatiratanga movement of the Maori King.*

## The Kohimarama Hui, 1860[196]

"The customs of former days have been abandoned, and will, in future, be trampled under our feet. We are now following a new path, and a right one. It is this which causes the heart to rejoice. The fathers have disappeared. We are their children, who now meet to discuss questions; therefore, I say, let us not be inactive in this Council.

"I am grieved about this new thing. I mean this new name – the Maori King. Its tendency is to cause division and ill feeling between the Maories and the Europeans. Its tendency is to lower both Pakehas and Maories. I say let this movement be suppressed...and let the Pakehas and the Maories live together as brethren.

"Let the Queen be Queen for both England and New Zealand, It was not without good ground that the title of Queen of England and of New Zealand was assumed.

"I say, let our views be clear. Let it not be supposed the Pakehas wish to enslave (oppress) the Maories. It is not so. The Pakeha wishes to raise the

---

196  All Kohimarama conference speeches cited in this book are available online at http://www.nzetc.org/tm/scholarly/tei-BIM504Kohi-t1-g1-t1-body1-d2.html

Maori. I am therefore very much grieved on account of this movement.

"Our old Maori customs are at the bottom of it, and it has been set up to attract our younger brothers. What has changed our clothing, and caused the dog-skin mat to be laid aside? This new name will lead to our debasement; therefore, I say, let it be suppressed.

"Let this King be put down. We are becoming divided amongst ourselves by means of this King. It therefore appears to me we shall be of this opinion, Chiefs of the Conference, that we must support the Governor, and that we should avail ourselves of advantages offered to us and thus share in the superiority of the Pakehas.

"Let us abandon Maori customs. Look at the superior condition of the Pakeha! This is not slavery. Let this title of King be put down. Even though the King's flag has been hoisted at our place Otaki it shall be cast down, it shall never be allowed to stand. It is calculated to produce ill-will and division, and if the Maori is separated from the Pakeha, he (the Maori) will find himself wrong. The Queen's shall be our only flag. We will hold our lands under the protection of the Queen.

"What you say, Hetaraka, about educating the Maories in the schools – that the boys and girls may learn Pakeha customs – is correct…Schools are good. It is right that the children should be instructed in what is good. It was the law of Christianity that put an end to our cannibal practices. It is right that when murder is committed by a Maori or a Pakeha he should be tried by the English law and hanged for his crime; and that minor offences should be treated with a summons."

*To modern readers – pakeha and Maori – who've been taught the 'Smurf' version of ancient Maori life in high school it may seem hard to understand why Tamihana Te Rauparaha, paramount chief of Ngatitoa, was so strong in rebuking traditional Maori customs; our distance from the events, as they say, lends enchantment.*

*The chiefs gathered at Kohimarama, however, were much closer to their former lives than students of Maori culture today will ever be; they well remembered what they had left behind by accepting British law and customs:*

"When the Gospel was preached in this Island," noted Kaipara chief Arama Karaka, "I asked my father, 'What is this?' He said, 'It is a Pakeha'.
'What does he say?'

'He preaches that we should believe on Christ, who was crucified that all men throughout the whole world might live...Then I embraced it (Christianity) and rested upon it. I said, This will put down all evil. I said, its laws are good laws, for they teach that all men should love one another and give up cannibalism.

That which binds the Ngatiwhatua is the law of God and of the Queen. The laws of God are for the enlightenment of my heart, and those of the Queen are clothing for my body. The old men pass away, but I shall continue to speak the same language. You have heard what binds us; I refuse to acknowledge the Maori mana, or Maori government (chieftainship). I have seen its evils. It was the law of the Queen which showed me what is good for men – love and kindness."

*Perhaps it should not come as a surprise that the Maori rebel movement tried to resurrect the old ways as a defiant point of difference to the Western culture most Maori were embracing.*

## Hau-Hau Cannibal Feasts, 1868[197]

We have received further intelligence from the rebel district. One of the women of Tito Kowaru's hapu visited the wife of a settler near Wairoa, and has given an account of this cannibal tribe.

The horrible cruelties perpetrated by the New Zealanders in former times on their prisoners have again been indulged in to satiate their inveterate hatred and revenge towards the Pakeha.

The wounded who were left behind in the retreat from Raururu were dragged into the pah, subjected to insult and torture, and eventually burned to death, their bodies afterwards cut in pieces and eagerly devoured even by the women and children.

Any of the men who were not fortunate enough to obtain a piece of human flesh were hooted by their wives and abused as cowards.

*This then, was the choice facing Maori in the 1860s: go forward or go backward. The vast majority chose to forget the bloodthirsty reign of the tohunga*

---

197  Hau-Hau Cannibal Feasts, North Otago Times, Volume XI, Issue 359, 30 October 1868, Page 3 http://paperspast.natlib.govt.nz/cgi-bin/paperspast?a=d&d=NOT18681030.2.7

*era in favour of the new culture. Fewer and fewer Maori chose to acquire facial moko for example – for that generation the moko was strongly associated with Maori spiritualism and blood sacrifice to ancient gods, and that was something they had put behind them forever. Even so, changes in attitude did not happen overnight.*

*Arama Karaka's words at Kohimarama about the supremacy of the rule of law over tribal custom came to be tested sooner than anyone expected. The details of the crime that follow are tragic, yet Ngati Whatua's method of handling it stands in stark contrast to the events of the Wairau massacre and, as officials later noted, brought honour on Ngati Whatua and its iwi at Kaipara, Helensville, just northwest of Auckland.*

## The Kaukapakapa Murders, 1863[198]

The presiding Magistrate (Mr. Heaphy[199]) and jury proceeded to view the bodies, which presented a fearful appearance. Florinda Thompson, being sworn, stated –

I am the daughter of John Reed Thompson and the deceased Matilda Ann Thompson. I live here at my father's farm, "Violet Hill," Kaukapakapa[200]. I am 20 years of age.

On Monday last, 21st December, about 2 o'clock, a Maori man called Ruarangi, whom I have known for nearly three years, came to this house. This native lives at Tamati Davis's place, the Kawau, at Kaipara. He has the name "Ruarangi" tattooed on his arm. I should know him again.

He sat down in the kitchen beside the fire. We gave him as much beef and pork and bread as he could eat. My sister Olivia (deceased) asked him in Maori what he came for. He replied "Taihoa – by and by I will tell you."

There were no men about the house save Ruarangi. After dinner, having to get the cows in, we wanted the Maori away from the place; I told him to leave, for we wanted to go away too. This was about two hours after he first came. My mother, my sister and myself then left the house,

---

198  The Kaipara Murders, Taranaki Herald, Volume XII, Issue 596, 2 January 1864, Page 3 http://paperspast.natlib.govt.nz/cgi-bin/paperspast?a=d&cl=search&d=TH18640102.2.10
199  Major Charles Heaphy, of Heaphy Track fame
200  The Violet Hill farm is on Peak Road opposite the Chatham Road intersection and now owned by a local farming company

and the Maori went some distance past the stockyard. Having found the cows, we returned, and Ruarangi met us at the stockyard. He then called us in and bought 20 pounds sugar. My mother gave him the sugar, he offered a £1 note in payment, but we told him to pay father, whom he would meet at the mill.

Ruarangi then went away from the house for about half an hour. He then came back and wanted to take only half the sugar, but said to my mother – "Never mind about the weight, but give me 3s. 6d-worth more sugar."

This was in the back kitchen. I was standing with the baby in my arms close to my mother. When she turned round to get the sugar he wanted out of a box on the table, Ruarangi then, with an axe he had in his hand, struck my mother a blow on the back of the head or neck and she fell down dead. I retreated into a corner with the baby and my sister.

Ruarangi followed us and shook the axe over us. He said he would kill all the pakeha wahines (white women) and all the white people about the place except McLeod, who was ka pai, good to them. Ruarangi was not under the influence of drink, nor did he look like a person deranged. He had always been a peaceable Maori, and was peaceably behaved until he struck my mother.

No altercation whatever took place between him and my mother, or any of us. He did not appear angry when we asked him to go away. When he was shaking the axe over my head, I called to my sisters to run to Mr. Penney's, a neighbour. My sisters were at the stockyard milking the cows.

I called to him, "For God's sake, why did you not kill me and spare my mother?" He ran out with the axe to attack my sisters. I immediately shut and barred the back door, and looked for a carving knife, having determined to attack him with it or to defend myself. He came back from pursuing my sisters, and struck the closed door close to me with the axe. [The mark on the door examined – a deep cut in the wood, with blood spattered around it.]

When Ruarangi desisted striking the door I looked out and saw him running after my sister, Hannah Matilda, who is between 11 and 12 years of age. I also saw him running his best in pursuit of my sister Olivia, whom I have not seen since. She was 14 years old.

Ruarangi then returned towards the house, and I ran to escape towards a creek near Mr. Penney's house; Ruarangi pursued me. I was carrying the baby. At Mr. Penney's I did not find any one. After a time I came back towards our house to look for my sisters. I saw the Maori at the house.

I then ran into the bush and heard the crashing of twigs, the noise was such as to lead me to know that more than one person was in pursuit of me. I crossed several gullies. Where the fern was high I had to use my hands to divide it, and then carried the child by its clothes in my teeth.

I ran past the "Peak" hill to Smith's bush, – about five miles off – and gave the alarm; Tom Smith and Andrew Brown came to me.

Hannah Matilda Thompson, understanding the nature of an oath, and being sworn, states: I am the daughter of John Thompson. I am between 11 and 12 years of age. I remember last Monday, at about two in the afternoon, a Maori man, who told us his name was Ruarangi, came to our house and asked for some sugar.

He partook of some beef, pork, and home-made bread with us. We went out for the cows and he also went out quite pleasantly with us. My sister Olivia went to a further hill for some cows of hers. My sister Olivia and I having brought home our cows, we proceeded to milk them, and whilst so engaged we heard screams in the direction of the house; we were about 60 yards from the house.

I heard the screams, and then the screams ceased; I knew that somebody was killed in the house. I ran down the hill to the 5th bridge; I waited there for Olivia, who was coming towards me pursued by Ruarangi, who had something like a stick in his hands.

She was nearer to me than to the Maori, and she put her hands over her head and screamed out. She ran in the fern with the Maori after her, having something in his hand. My sister never spoke again. I then allowed the Maori to approach toward me, he stepped across the body of my sister to do so. I ran and called out, as if to Mr. Penney, and the Maori stopped. Presently Mr. Penney's dogs came up, the Maori ceased to pursue me. I have seen the corpse of my sister Olivia.

I got to Mr. Penney who proposed coming over to shoot the native, and asked if there were others. I told Mr. Penney that Ruarangi had said there were to be plenty more natives. Mr. Penney found that his revolver would not go off. We looked out, and saw several Maoris, whether they were men or women I cannot tell; it was getting dark then.

*The inquest jury considered the evidence of a number of witnesses in piecing together what had led to the attack, and found that:*

Mr. Penney had seen Ruarangi in the middle of the day, near Mr. Thompson's house, with a spear in his hand. It appears to be the general impression at the Kaukapakapa, that the man Ruarangi had lost some friend at the Waikato, and that the murders were committed partly in utu (payment), and partly in order to raise a war at the North, and so create a diversion in favour of the Waikatos.

The magistrate expressed to Miss Thompson the high sense the jury and all had of the courageous manner in which she had acted in saving herself and her sister.

The Maoris, true to their promise, assembled yesterday to the number of 300, held a runanga, and were quite ready and willing that the alleged murderer, whoever he might be, should be picked out from amongst them.

*In fact, no less a personage than Ngati Whatua's paramount chief, Paora (Paul) Tuhaere, took charge, arriving at the Helensville marae from Orakei with the government delegation. The husband and father of the murder victims, John Thompson (in sharp contrast to Te Rangihaeata's actions in the Wairau Massacre) was not permitted to get close to the alleged offender.*

## The Arrest Of Ruarangi[201]

It was feared that he might very naturally be tempted to take the law into is hands. After some little persuasion he was induced to remain upon the rising ground close by, with his younger daughter, and with some of the police and other persons who were present.

Mr Fox and the Commissioner, with the elder daughter Florinda and Paul the chief, accompanied by the interpreter and two of the police, then went down upon the beach alongside to where the Maoris were seated. The natives, however, demurred at the immediate presence of Europeans, desiring that no white person should be allowed to accompany the girl along the ranks, lest she should be prompted by them on arriving opposite the accused.

After some consultation this proposal was agreed to, the Orakei chief Paul undertaking to lead her by the hand along the line of natives who were grouped upon the beach, and Mr. Fox and the police remaining at a short distance.

---

201   The Kaipara Tragedy, Lyttelton Times, Volume XXI, Issue 1180, 7 January 1864, Page 5
http://paperspast.natlib.govt.nz/cgi-bin/paperspast?a=d&cl=search&d=LT18640107.2.24

They had passed about one-third of the line when they came opposite to a group of about ten or twelve young men all of the same stature, dress, and cast of features, and all, as did the rest of the natives, holding their heads somewhat bent down, when turning sharply round with an ejaculation of "There he is!" Florinda Thompson sprang towards the group, pointing at Ruarangi with her parasol.

All eyes were turned upon him, and the Commissioner, who with his two men had been gradually approaching nearer to this spot, at once closed in.

Ruarangi appeared unmoved, and made no attempt to escape. It was then explained that, he would have to be taken to Auckland and examined in the Resident Magistrate's Court, and if found guilty, committed to prison for trial of his life.

Several chiefs got up and spoke of the heinous nature of the crime, and urged the advisability of surrendering him up. The question was then put to the assembly by an aged chief, and it was resolved to surrender him.

Mr. Naughton then advanced to the accused and arrested him in the name of the Queen, leading him a few paces from the rest. The natives then expressed a lively wish to be allowed to embrace the prisoner before he was taken from them, and one and all, young and old, took their farewell.

This occupied fully an hour, Mr. Fox improving the occasion by delivering an address to the natives, which was interpreted by Mr. Monro, and in which he alluded to the friendliness which the tribe had always shown towards the Europeans, and the surprise which the latter felt on hearing of the commission of such crime, assuring them that he believed that the crime had been not one of the tribe, but of an individual, and praised them for having kept faith with the Government in giving the murderer up for trial. He also informed them that the tribe would not be held responsible for the act of Ruarangi.

Mr. Naughton then marched his prisoner away handcuffed, and taking a boat, arrived in Auckland and lodged him in the gaol by eleven o'clock on the same night.

*Ruarangi was duly executed by hanging for the murder of Matilda Thompson and her 14 year old daughter Olivia. New Zealand's justice system was beginning to work. The developing question was whether it could work for Maori in land disputes...*

Chapter 15

# What To Expect In Wellington's Big One

We've seen what can happen to a city like Christchurch in an earthquake, but the elephant in the room is Wellington. New Zealand's capital city sits astride the notorious Alpine Fault – a similar sort of beast to California's San Andreas fissure.

The Alpine Fault has a history of generating shocks up to magnitude 8.0, and whacked Marlborough and Wellington with a 7.5 rumbler in 1848 that destroyed much of the eight year old Wellington settlement.

Of course, there's no one alive today who's experienced a direct hit on Wellington of that size, and therefore most of us have no real idea what might happen to the city where houses cling to the hillsides like rock limpets.

Which is why the old newspaper reports about big quakes in Wellington are worth reading, because these quakes were direct big hits, complete with tsunami and liquefaction and land lifting out of the ocean.

Wellington was a lot smaller back when these tremors smashed it, so we don't have much information on how homes perching on mountainsides might cope. Nonetheless, the stories do give us priceless detail on just how Wellington rocked.

What is perhaps surprising, given what Wellington city planners obviously knew back in the day, is how many quake-vulnerable buildings were given approval for construction after two previous major rebuilds of the city...

# Earthquake At Wellington, 1855[202]

We have received the painful intelligence that the city of Wellington and its neighbourhood has again been visited with a most severe earthquake and we find that the shocks which have been experienced in Nelson during the present week, like the shocks of October, 1848, have been but the half-spent wave which first rose somewhere on the shores of the southern extremity of Cook's Straits, but the exact locality of which we have yet to learn.

To the arrival last night of H M. Sloop *Pandora*, we owe the receipt of this intelligence and Captain Drury, with a kindness we can scarcely sufficiently acknowledge, has placed at our disposal a copy of his journal, which narrates the whole calamity as it passed under his eye. To this document, which we publish in its entire form, we may safely refer for the history of the most dire calamity which has ever befallen New Zealand since it has been a British colony but while on the one hand we may turn to it to learn the full extent of the disaster, as far as known when the *Pandora* left Wellington early on Thursday morning, it will also be most valuable for the purpose of showing the real extent of the mischief done, and thus prevent our readers from being misled by stories already in circulation, which magnify the calamity, great as it has been.

## *Extract from Commander Drury's Remark Book*

COOK'S STRAITS, JANUARY 25, 1855: The Anniversary of the Wellington settlement was most auspiciously celebrated – a brighter or a calmer day never beamed on the harbour. The boot races, and every description of sports on shore, went off with much good humour and eclat, and the only drawback was want of wind for the sailing boats.

In the evening, a light N.W. wind sprang up, which increased gradually during the night and at 8, on the morning of the 23rd, it blew violently. The sports, however, continued, and the race-course drew nearly the whole population of Wellington; but a drenching rain at noon checked the further progress of joviality, which was to be repeated on the morrow.

At 11 minutes past 9 o'clock, p.m., the gale still blowing strong, we felt suddenly an uncommon and disagreeable grinding, as if the ship was

---

[202] Earthquake At Wellington. ("From the Nelson Examiner, February 28) Daily Southern Cross, Volume XII, Issue 801, 2 March 1855, Page 4
http://paperspast.natlib.govt.nz/cgi-bin/paperspast?a=d&d=DSC18550302.2.13.2

grating over a rough bottom. It continued with severity for more than a minute – the ship slewed broadside to the wind – we were then in 6 fathoms, so there was little doubt but it was an earthquake.

Lights were seen running to and fro in all parts of the town, and evidences of consternation combined with a loud crash. Lieutenant Jones and myself immediately landed. We found the tide alternately ebbing and flowing. The first scene before us on landing was the Government offices, entirely destroyed, the upper story (the falling of which had caused the crash we heard) lying on the ground; the stair-case, the Council Chamber, the papers and documents in heterogeneous confusion; an adjoining chemist's shop, whose simples and compounds admixing, had a decided bias to peppermint, while the doorway of the public house was a confusion of broken bottles.

The sentinel in charge of the Government building, who had just been thrown backwards and forwards, was now walking in front of the wreck with perfect sangfroid, no doubt crying "All's well" to the hour.

It is not my intention to narrate more than the general effects and disasters of this severe shock and firstly we have to be thankful to God, that amidst the general wreck of property but one life has been sacrificed, and not more than four others seriously wounded, up to the time of our departure. This would appear astonishing to a person viewing the wreck of the houses, the mass of brickwork from the falling of the chimneys, the dislodgment of furniture, the fissures in the earth, the extraordinary rise of tide, the entire destruction of some tenements, the collapse of others, the universal sacrifice of property, and the natural terror and despair among the inhabitants, all tending to far greater personal disaster than fortunately I have to narrate.

And here I would especially dwell upon the benefit of the warning of 1848 to the inhabitants, which, under Providence, by causing them to occupy wooden houses, has been the salvation of many lives and the hour, too, was favourable to the escape of adults, who seized the children from beneath the tottering chimneys, themselves not having generally retired to bed.

Few, if any, since 1848, have been rash enough to build a "brick" house; the chimneys had generally been secured as well as possible by iron braces, &c. The most substantial two-storied house – Baron Alsdorff's hotel – of lath and plaster, buried its owner in the partial ruins.

Government House, had it been occupied, must have destroyed its inmates, for every room was a pile of brick-work, the chandeliers, &c,

utterly destroyed. The guard had a wonderful escape from the guard room, and the gun at the flagstaff turned over.

I have already mentioned the entire destruction of the Council Chamber, the upper storey being completely severed from the lower; the treasury strong box, and the papers and documents apparently in irretrievable confusion.

The elegant and substantial new building, the Union Bank, is, in its front, a perfect ruin, and I hear the damage within is not much less. Opposite this building, on the road, a considerable opening emitted slimy mud[203], and the main street was overflown by inundation.

The most substantially built wooden houses of one story, with the exception of the chimneys, are mainly standing. Those of less substantial calibre (and I am sorry to say there are many) are in a state of collapse. There is a universal destruction of crockery, bottles, &c, and a pitiful loss of valuable ornaments, clocks, &c. Several stores are unapproachable, until neighbouring dangers are removed.

The principal shock occurred at 9h. 11 min., p.m and it was by far the most severe. During the night scarcely half an hour elapsed without a lesser shock, more or less violent, accompanied by a deep hollow sound but all these subsequent ones were of much shorter duration and the first having levelled every portion of brick work in the lower part of the town, there was less to fear, but the inhabitants generally fled to the open ground, and the following day the streets and gardens were the scene of an involuntary picnic.

From what we noticed, it appeared the elemental wave proceeded from W.N.W. to E.S.E., that its actual effect upon terra firma was slight, and that the fissures were generally where the road was made, although the mud emitted from the crack at Te Aro must be considered as subterraneous deposit, from what depth not easily decided.

From close observations on the barometer, I have no reason to believe that the effect before or after the principal shock was evident (it ranged from 29.90 to 30.00), nor that the calm preceding, or the gale attending, the earthquake, had any connexion with the subterraneous convulsions.

We witnessed, during the 48 hours following, every variety of wind and weather, yet with repeated shocks; but although I would disconnect the atmospheric influence with the earthquakes, we had every reason

---

203   Liquefaction will obviously be a problem in any future big Wellington quake

to believe the latter had immediate local influence on the atmosphere, producing violent gusts after the shocks. If it is a fact that an action, or firing, will produce a local calm by the disturbance of the atmosphere, the phenomenon here may be more easily accounted for.

But a more interesting and extraordinary phenomenon occurred (I say extraordinary, because no person appears to have observed it in the earthquake of 1848) for eight hours subsequent to the first and great shock, the tide approached and receded from the shore every twenty minutes, rising from eight to ten feet, and receding four feet lower than at spring tides. One ship, I heard, was aground at her anchorage four times. The ordinary tide seemed quite at a discount, for the following day (24th) it scarcely rose at all.

The general effects of the earthquake were evidently felt more upon the lower parts of the town; at the Hutt most severely. The bridge there was destroyed, and the houses much damaged. I am also informed the Porirua is sunk in some places.

Recurring to our landing after the first shock, Lieutenant Jones and myself went into several houses. The panic was certainly great, and many accepted the offer to go on board – the houses we were in swinging to and fro, and the ground in a constant tremulous motion. It was sufficient to unnerve the stoutest hearts but after a delay of three or four hours (in which we were visiting other parts of the town), on returning to the parties who had accepted an asylum on board, we found one and all had determined to abide on shore – indeed they were getting accustomed to it.

The wives would not desert the husbands, and the husbands would not desert the town. We returned to the ship at 2am., the tide having at that time having receded about four feet lower than at ordinary spring tides.

On the 24th the shocks continued but at greater intervals as the day advanced, but the tremulous motion was continuous. The scene on the streets was novel – some people standing at their thresholds, groups upon mats, clear of the houses, or in tents in their gardens. Those who had suffered less than their neighbours were assiduous in rendering assistance. What a different scene would have occurred in the fatherland.

With shops exposed and every temptation to plunder, there seemed to be neither fear nor thought of robbery, but a generous and manly feeling to lessen each other's burdens pervaded all classes, from the Superintendent to the lowest mechanic, from the Colonel to every soldier of the 65th regiment; nor can I forget to mention the ready asylum offered by the merchant vessels in the harbour to the houseless and more nervous inhabitants.

On the 25th, at oh.55min., a.m., there was a very sharp but comparatively short shock. Having ascertained we could be of no farther assistance, we weighed for Nelson, and in crossing Cook's Straits, we felt one shock in 26 fathoms, at noon, off Sinclair's Head (exactly the same feeling as when at anchor), and a slighter shock in 80 fathoms, off Queen Charlotte's Sound.

In these events there is much to be thankful for in the absence of fire: had it been winter, the universal falling of chimneys would have assuredly fired the wooden houses; had the first shock been an hour later, many lives would probably have been lost, as the populace would have been in bed.

Much fear is entertained for the soldiers at Wanganui barracks. I trust we shall find that Nelson has suffered as lightly as on former occasions.

*Commander Drury's report remarked that the tsunami accompanying the 1855 quake was unprecedented – there hadn't been one in 1848 he thought. In fact, there had, as you can see from the 1848 newspaper coverage:*

# Earthquake At Wellington, 1848[204]
*From the Wellington Spectator, Oct. 18.*

Within the last few days this settlement has experienced a severe and terrible visitation of Providence. From Monday morning last up to this morning (Wednesday), a succession of earthquakes more or less violent have occurred, which have occasioned a great destruction of property, and produced a very general feeling of alarm.

In relating the occurrence of the last few days, we shall best discharge our duty by giving a plain statement of facts, and thus counteract the circulation of incorrect and exaggerated reports. Before describing the effects of these convulsions of nature however, it may be necessary to say a few words on the previous state of the weather.

During Monday the 9th instant, there was a strong south-easter, accompanied by very heavy rain, and though towards the middle of the week there intervened a few days of fine calm weather, on Saturday last another

---

204  Earthquake At Wellington, Nelson Examiner and New Zealand Chronicle, Volume VII, Issue 347, 28 October 1848
http://paperspast.natlib.govt.nz/cgi-bin/paperspast?a=d&d=NENZC18481028.2.6

south-easter occurred of equal violence with the former one, which continued the two following days, accompanied also by very heavy rain, so much so, that the quantity of rain which has fallen during the last week amounted to ten inches, or more than three times the quantity of the whole of the previous month.

At about twenty minutes to two o'clock on Monday morning, a most severe shock of an earthquake was experienced, which lasted for the space of nearly a minute the direction of the shock appeared to be north and south, the motion was horizontal and undulatory until towards the conclusion, when it seemed to have an upheaving or vertical motion this was followed at an interval of half an hour by another shock not so intense as the first, and during the subsequent nineteen minutes a succession of severe shocks occurred with lesser ones at intervals in fact during the whole of this period, the ground appeared to be in a state of oscillation. Nearly the whole of the night the south-easter prevailed, so that this fury of the wind added its force to the destructive agencies at work.

When it was daylight it was found that several of the brick buildings at Te Aro, and in other parts of the town, had been seriously injured by the first shock, which had caused the greatest amount of damage; among the buildings which had suffered most was the Wesleyan Chapel. This building was of brick, and cemented; the north elevation consisted of four pilasters, with a central doorway, and a large window on either side the pilasters were surmounted by an entablature and pediment, the weight of which acted as a lever in bending forwards the wall when in motion from the earthquake, separating it from the roof and causing it to overhang so much as to render it necessary to be immediately taken down.

The greater part of the chimneys in different parts of the town were also either thrown down, or so much cracked and twisted, as to render it necessary to take them down. The damage was almost entirely occasioned by the first shock, which was the most severe that had been experienced in this settlement.

The ships in the harbour equally felt its influence; the sensation experienced on board *H.M. Fly* is described to have been as though the vessel had suddenly grounded. The shock was felt most in the fore part of the ship, and all the men ran up on deck.

During Monday, a succession of smart shocks occurred, one at a quarter to six in the morning, another at twelve, and another about half- past three, p.m.; during the night some lighter shocks were felt, and on the following morning a severe shock at about half-past seven, while during the whole of this time a continuous tremulous motion of the earth was distinctly perceptible.

On Monday the wind moderated, and during the afternoon and night, and on Tuesday, it became perfectly calm. On the afternoon of that day (yesterday) at twenty minutes to four, a severe shock occurred, followed in quick succession by another of about half a minute's duration – this last was as severe as that on Monday morning, but more destructive in its effect, the motion appearing to be more vertical.[205] This completed the damage occasioned by the former shocks, very few brick buildings escaping its destructive effects.

The buildings rocked to and fro in a fearful manner. All the brick stores at the head of the Bay were more or less damaged, the walls being either thrown down altogether, or rent in different directions, and thrust out from the perpendicular. All those buildings that had been injured by the former shocks were quite destroyed, while those which had previously escaped were now reduced to the same ruin.

Among the latter is the colonial hospital, which has only been recently completed, and which was so injured as to render it necessary immediately to remove the patients, who were taken to Government House, where they will be accommodated for the present. The walls of the gaol also, and of a large building at Thorndon, used as a barrack for soldiers, are so much cracked as to be no longer habitable. Nearly all the chimneys which had previously escaped were now either thrown down, or more or less twisted and injured.

The walls of the Wesleyan chapel were split in every direction, so as completely to destroy the building. A man who was employed in nailing up some boards against the end of the roof, which was open by pulling down the pediment, was in imminent danger of being thrown to the ground; he was, however, providentially enabled to preserve his hold until the shock was over, when a ladder was placed against the building, by means of which he descended from his perilous situation.

We regret to have to add to this destruction of property loss of life.

---

205  This is similar to the Christchurch quake, it was the vertical movement from a tremor under the city that caused the immense G-forces

Barrack Sergeant Lovell and his two children, who were passing down Farish Street from the Government store at the time, were buried by a mass of falling wall, one of the children, a girl of eight years, was killed on the spot, the other, a boy about four years old, received so many severe injuries that he died about eleven o'clock last night. Sergeant Lovell himself was also very much bruised, his left leg being very much injured. Two severe shocks were experienced in the night, one at a quarter to eight o'clock, the other at twenty minutes to one this morning, with several slighter shocks at intervals, that last was at ten minutes to two this afternoon. Nearly all the shocks were immediately preceded by a hollow rumbling noise.

This morning the tide rose to an unusual height, overflowing part of Larnbton Quay, and all those sections at the head of the bay fronting the water and immediately adjoining the swamp.

During Monday and Tuesday night a long streak of pale light was observed by several persons, it appeared to be settled, at a very great distance, and in a northerly direction.

The effects of the earthquake appear to have been most violent at Te Aro and Thorndon, and on brick buildings of two stories. With the exception of the chimneys, the buildings along Lambton Quay have not suffered so severely; those also which are on more elevated ground appear to have escaped with less injury, and several brick buildings of only one story in height have been either but slightly damaged, or are quite sound, while all the wooden buildings are perfectly uninjured.

The preceding account has only reference to the town of Wellington, but we understand that the earthquake was as severely felt at the Hutt and Porirua, nearly all the chimmeys being throw down at the Hutt, while the stone barracks recently erected at Porirua have been so shaken as to be quite uninhabitable.

We cannot conclude this hasty and imperfect sketch without acknowledging in this visitation the finger of God. Mighty is the Lord's doing, and is marvellous in our eyes. It is a calamity against which no prudence could guard, and to which, as Christians, we must submit with becoming resignation, having deep cause for thankfulness that amidst this destruction of property, whether occurring, as at first, in the dead of the night, or yet later, in the face of day, it has not been attended with greater loss of life.

ABOVE : Queen Street, Auckland in the early 1900s. BELOW: Princes Street, Auckland, 1913

ABOVE : Queen Street, Auckland, 1920s. BELOW: Auckland's former wharf area, Quay Street in the 1920s

ABOVE : Wellington, 1905. BELOW: Lambton Quay, Wellington's old waterfront until the 1855 quake raised the land. Seen here in 1919

ABOVE : Courtenay Place, Wellington, 1930, looking down towards the Embassy Theatre.
BELOW: Queenstown during the 1878 floods.

Chapter 16

# Life In New Zealand – Part 3

## The Man Who Never Left His Bed, 1907[206]

George Thompson, the Lurgan man who stayed in bed for 29 years, getting up only because his mother became ill, and had no one to attend to him, has now gone to the other extreme. He declares he will never go to bed any more. The sight of the green fields and the busy world during a brief walk he took has changed the current of his ideas, and now, at the age of 42, he is determined to make amends for the years misspent in bed.

## Telephone Allows Villagers To Hear Home Invasion, 1907[207]

Fifteen women in Wayne, County Ohio, United States, living in lonely farmhouses, listened on 25th February aver the telephone to the screams of another woman, who was attacked by a robber.

The house of Mrs Stech was entered by a thief, and the woman, who was alone, rushed at once to the telephone to call for help. The line was a

---

206  Local And General News, Nelson Evening Mail, Volume XLII, 14 May 1907, Page 2
http://paperspast.natlib.govt.nz/cgi-bin/paperspast?a=d&cl=search&d=NEM19070514.2.12
207  Local And General News, Nelson Evening Mail, Volume XLII, 14 May 1907, Page 2
http://paperspast.natlib.govt.nz/cgi-bin/paperspast?a=d&cl=search&d=NEM19070514.2.12

"party" one, in which the same circuit is shared by a number of subscribers, and there were fifteen farmhouses on the circuit. One ring summons all the subscribers on the circuit, and when the bell rang simultaneously in all the farmhouses in the neighbourhood the women hastened to answer the call. They were just in time to hear Mrs Stech's agonised call for help, the thief's oaths, and the sounds of a desperate struggle.

They summoned their husbands from the fields; and the men armed themselves hastily and hurried to Mrs Stech's house. They found the woman lying on the floor bound and unconscious, and the house ransacked. After reviving the woman, the men started in pursuit of the robber, declaring that if they caught him they would lynch him.

## Inspector Plod Treating Big Ears As Suspect, 1898[208]

An English writer who for more than 15 years has been a student of criminal anthropology says large voluminous ears are the most characteristic mark of the criminal mind.

## Childish Pranks Costs Foot, 1896[209]

A Wellington boy, who kicked with his bare feet at a passing cyclist, had his toe caught by the chain and torn out, necessitating the amputation of the foot.

## Mother Saves Child From Cow, 1896[210]

A child which was playing in a paddock at Havelock the other evening, was rushed by a cow. The mother, Mrs Simmonds, ran to the rescue, and succeeded in diverting the cow's attention to herself. The animal knocked her down, broke her wrist, and gored her severely about the arms and body, but her plucky action saved the child.

---

208　Scotland, Otago Daily Times , Issue 11305, 24 December 1898, Page 3
http://paperspast.natlib.govt.nz/cgi-bin/paperspast?a=d&cl=search&d=ODT18981224.2.30
209　Local and General, Ashburton Guardian, Volume XVII, Issue 4075, 23 December 1896, Page 2
http://paperspast.natlib.govt.nz/cgi-bin/paperspast?a=d&cl=search&d=AG18961223.2.6
210　Ibid

## NZ's Oldest Maori Voter, 1896[211]

It is never too late to vote. Amongst the Maoris who voted at Wanganui on Saturday was a woman whose age was variously estimated at from 100 to 120 years.

A Dunedin lady is reported to have received such a careful instruction from her husband as to the candidates for whom she should vote, that the dutiful woman brought back – in her handbag – her ballot-paper, which [instead of depositing] she had carefully preserved to prove to her spouse that she had voted straight!

## From The Wires, The Old Whiskey Bottle Trick, 1897[212]

An American paper vouches for the accuracy of this story. Two tramps went into a saloon at East Oakland, California, the other day, and handing a demijohn over the counter, asked the proprietor to fill it with "good whiskey".

The saloon keeper obliged them, and was tendered a dollar in return. He at once refused it, as it was debased. The tramps had no more money, and, there being no alternative, the saloon man emptied the whiskey back into the cask, and the tramps left with their demijohn.

A few minutes later the tramps went into a vacant lot and carefully broke the demijohn. From the pieces they delicately lifted out a bath sponge, which was thoroughly soaked with whiskey.

## Entire Schools Of Fish Found In Stone, 1897[213]

For a score of years geologists have known of the existence of immense beds of shale in Wyoming, which occasionally have yielded fine specimens of fossil shell fish, but it is only recently that similar beds have been discovered in Colorado.

---

211  Daily Circulation. 1680. Thursday, December 24, 1896, Oamaru Mail, Volume XXI, Issue 6776, 25 December 1896, Page 2
http://paperspast.natlib.govt.nz/cgi-bin/paperspast?a=d&cl=search&d=OAM18961225.2.15
212  Miscellaneous, Clutha Leader, Volume XXIII, Issue 1177, 22 January 1897, Page 7
http://paperspast.natlib.govt.nz/cgi-bin/paperspast?a=d&cl=search&d=CL18970122.2.44
213  Ibid

These beds of petrified fish, containing millions on millions of individual specimens, cover hundreds of square miles in the northwestern parts of the State. They extend a distance of 100 miles in the direction of Green River, and shelve out for 100 miles more towards the interior of the State. In some cases these beds – almost a solid mass of perfectly fossilised fish – are from 150 to 200 feet in thickness.

One of the greatest puzzles regarding the find is the fact that they are about 8000 ft above sea-level.

## Finders Keepers Letter Forces Old Woman To Marry, 1897[214]

Of all the strange love stories, we have never (says Home Chat) heard a more quaint and original one than this.

Mdlle. Adelaide de Brigesse, a poetess, wrote a letter when she was a young girl in the form of a sonnet, promising her hand to the finder. She secreted it in a secret drawer in an old bureau, and then forgot all about her work.

Years after, the poetess having reached the mature age of seventy, the bureau was bought by a romantic old colonel in the army. He found the love letter, and considered himself duly engaged to the writer. The poetess determined to be faithful to her promise, made when she was only seventeen, and their marriage has just taken place.

## Speights Woman Found In South Island, 1897[215]

At a recent prayer meeting, at which a prominent banker was present, a laughable incident took place: The minister, turning to the gentlemen present, asked – "Dear brethren, did any of you ever know or hear of a perfect man?"

The divine paused a few moments, then repeated the question, and, receiving no answer, turned to the females present, and asked, "Dear sisters, did any of you ever hear of a perfect woman?"

He repeated the question a second time, when a tall, lean, patient female

---

214  Ibid
215  Miscellaneous, Clutha Leader, Volume XXIII, Issue 1177, 22 January 1897, Page 7
http://paperspast.natlib.govt.nz/cgi-bin/paperspast?a=d&cl=search&d=CL18970122.2.44

arose and looked the minister straight in the face. For a moment he was incredulous, but, recovering his sang froid, he asked, "Did you ever hear of a perfect woman, sister?" He did not wait long for an answer.

"I did, but only one. It was my husband's first wife."

## Queen Victoria's 'Outwit, Outlast, Outplay' Moment, 1897[216]

Queen Victoria has outlived all the members of the Privy Council who were alive in 1837. All the Peers who held their titles in 1837, except the Earl of Darnley, who was ten, and Earl Nelson, who was fourteen in that year. All the members who sat in the House of Commons on her accession to the Throne, except Mr Gladstone, Mr Charles Villiers, the present Duke of Northumberland, the Earl of Mexborough, and the Earl of Mansfield, and Mr John Temple, Leader.

Her Majesty has seen 11 Lord Chancellors, 10 Prime Ministers, six Speakers of the House of Commons, at least three Bishops of every See and five or six of many Sees, five Archbishops of Canterbury, and six Archbishops of York, and five Commanders in-Chief.

She has seen five Dukes of Norfolk succeed each other as Earls Marshal, and has outlived every Duke and Duchess and every Marquis and Marchioness who bore that rank in 1837. She has outlived every member of the Jockey Club and every Master of Foxhounds that flourished in 1837. She has seen 17 Presidents of the United States, 10 Viceroys of Canada, 15 Viceroys of India, and France successively ruled by one King, one Emperor, and six Presidents of a Republic.

## Female Ingenuity Gains Rental Accomodation, 1919[217]

"Have yon any children?" inquired the landlord of a woman who was seeking tenancy of his house (reports the *Hawera Star*). Snappily, idle woman replied, "I don't see what that has to do with you," and then, in a rather mournful tone, "but if you particularly want to know, I have four – in the cemetery."

---

216   Ibid
217   Untitled, Dominion, Volume 13, Issue 61, 5 December 1919, Page 6
http://paperspast.natlib.govt.nz/cgi-bin/paperspast?a=d&d=DOM19191205.2.32

The deal was at once concluded. Then the woman retrieved four children from the cemetery where she had left them to read about the virtues of dead landlords pending the result of her negotiations with a live one.

The distressed man consulted his solicitor, but was not given much hope of getting an order of ejectment, and the woman, it is understood, defends her finesse, holding Mint: 'everything is fair in love and war' – and in house-hunting nowadays.

## Big Families Back In The Day, 1919[218]

Berlin official returns of births during July record the case of a woman who gave birth to her 21st child, which is while two women had each their 16th child. Seventeen women gave birth to twins.

## Big News Day In Oamaru: A Politician Drove Past, 1896[219]

The Hon. John MacKenzie passed through Oamaru by the express train from the north last evening on his way to his home at Shag Point.

## Sharks Infest Napier Beach, 1896[220]

During the summer months, says the *Hawke's Bay Herald*, the bay is swarming with sharks, and when there is no breaker to speak of on the beach, they venture very close, because the water is deep to within a few feet of the shore.

On Tuesday last when the *Te Anau* was at the breakwater wharf, a shark, judged to be from 12 to 15 feet in length, disported itself along the pier close to the boat steps, where a number of people have been in the habit of bathing, and the Harbor Board diver also relates some thrilling experiences of those monsters while attending to the blasting of the Auckland Rock.

The captain of the fishing trawler *Toroa* states that in all his experience he never saw such a sight as he witnessed during last week when hauling in

---

218  Ibid
219  Daily Circulation. 1680. Thursday, December 24, 1896, Oamaru Mail, Volume XXI, Issue 6776, 25 December 1896, Page 2
http://paperspast.natlib.govt.nz/cgi-bin/paperspast?a=d&d=OAM18961225.2.17
220  Ibid

the net. Hundreds of sharks were round the vessel, and he expected a rush from them. The rush would have been disastrous to him, but by feeding them with spare fish he had onboard he saved his nets and his haul of fish.

## The Penalty For Swearing, 1908[221]

In the Magistrate's Court this morning, before Mr H. S. Fitzherbert, S.M., a case in which a Maori named Puno was charged with having used obscene language in a public place was called on.

Puno failed to appear, and His Worship therefore issued a warrant for his arrest.

## When Lightning Comes Down The Chimney, 1908[222]

The *Western Star*, Riverton, reports a remarkable instance of the danger of lightning. At ten o'clock one morning about a fortnight ago, a thunderstorm broke over Otaitai Bush, and a settler there had a startling experience.

He and his wife were sitting at the fireplace when the lightning struck the chimney, carrying away a number of bricks. In its downward course it knocked a kettle off the hook and continued its way out by the door. Then it followed a steel wire, which was connected to some twenty-five or thirty macrocarpa trees.

All the trees were damaged, one being cut clean off 20ft from the ground.

At the farther end of the fence two horses were feeding from a box containing chaff. This was smashed to atoms, and one of the horses received a shock and fell.

The settler himself was rendered helpless for a few moments.

## Ballerinas Tackle Lion, 1908[223]

A lion broke loose at the electrical exhibition at Marseilles on June 22,

---

221 Untitled, Taranaki Herald, Volume LIV, Issue 13723, 12 August 1908, Page 4
http://paperspast.natlib.govt.nz/cgi-bin/paperspast?a=d&d=TH19080812.2.23
222 Ibid
223 Ibid

and made his way on the stage of the theatre, where a ballet was being rehearsed. The panic among the ladies of the ballet when the lion suddenly appeared in their midst was intense. Three of the ladies, however, were possessed of more courage than the rest, and, snatching off their shoes, they beat the greatly astonished beast into submission.

When the lion-tamer arrived the lion welcomed him with evident joy, and allowed himself to be led back to his cage in the most docile fashion. He seemed as glad to get away from the ballet girls as they were to be rid of him.

## Yank Tanks Imported By The Dozen, 1919[224]

The consignments of American motorcars imported into the Dominion seem to grow larger with each vessel that reaches port. On Thursday the Leitrim arrived at Auckland from New York with about 300 motor-cars for New Zealand.

Of this number 71 cars, including five motor lorries, are for Auckland. She has brought 28 motor-cycles and several cases of tyres and motor-car repair parts for this port; in addition to these heavy consignments for the Dominion the vessel is also carrying 300 cars of various makes for Australia.

## Governor Grey Calls For Men To Have Voting Rights, 1878[225]

GREYMOUTH: Sir George Grey addressed the largest meeting ever held here. He advocated manhood suffrage[226], equal electoral districts, triennial Parliaments, taxation on lands improved through public works, and reform in the administration of Crown lands. A unanimous vote of confidence in Sir George Grey was passed.

---

224 Local And General, Dominion, Volume 13, Issue 51, 24 November 1919, Page 6
http://paperspast.natlib.govt.nz/cgi-bin/paperspast?a=d&d=DOM19191124.2.27
225 New Zealand Telegrams, Taranaki Herald, Volume XXVI, Issue 2757, 27 February 1878, Page 2
http://paperspast.natlib.govt.nz/cgi-bin/paperspast?a=d&d=TH18780227.2.9.3
226 The term "manhood suffrage" is the concept of one man one vote. At this time voting was restricted to landowners (the logic being that they were the ones paying taxes) in the same way that city council votes were for a long time restricted to those registered as ratepayers.

## Inquest At Timaru, 1878[227]

At an adjourned inquest on the body of a female child of Margaret Wilson, the jury returned a verdict of acquittal. The accused was of weak intellect, and showed it throughout the inquest.

She did not appear to realise her predicament till the close of the evidence, when the Coroner explained it to her.

## Coins Deflect Fatal Bullet On Southerner Express, 1878[228]

Mr Jabez Heaseman, the guard on the Southern Railway, had a narrow escape from death on Saturday evening.

Cate Butler and his step-brother, Thos. Williams, were travelling between Timaru and Christchurch when, near Dunsandel, Butler became excited, asserting that he had been robbed.

His step-brother sent for the guard, and told him that Butler was deranged, and that he had a loaded revolver in a bag between his knees. At this time Butler had his right hand in the bag and looked very excited.

Heaseman asked Butler to let him take the bag into the luggage van, when Butler immediately pulled the revolver out and shot at Heaseman. The latter felt a smart blow on the left side but nothing more. He seized Butler, and with the aid of the passengers took the revolver away and bound him.

Subsequently Heaseman found that the bullet had struck him on the left side, but having a purse full of copper and silver coins in his waistcoat pocket, the bullet was turned aside by them, and Heaseman was saved from almost certain death. All the chambers of the 'revolver were loaded.

Butler until lately has been farming at One-Tree Point, Invercargill. A short time ago he appeared queer in the head, and his step-brother had him examined by Dr. Hannan, Invercargill, who recommended his removal to the Dunedin Lunatic Asylum. The step-brother started to take him there but on reaching Dunedin, Butler said he would go to Canterbury, also that there were lots of bad men and devils about him and he would buy a revolver to keep them off. This his brother allowed him to do.

---

227 New Zealand Telegrams, Taranaki Herald, Volume XXVI, Issue 2757, 27 February 1878, Page 2 http://paperspast.natlib.govt.nz/cgi-bin/paperspast?a=d&d=TH18780227.2.9.3
228 Ibid

Butler was brought up at the Resident Magistrate's Court on Monday, and remanded for medical examination.

## The Dread Convict Sullivan, 1868[229]

Not a little excitement was caused in town on Saturday afternoon, by the circulation of a report that the convict Sullivan of Maungatapu notoriety had been brought up from Nelson by the steamship *Phoebe*.

As the vessel neared the wharf, a strong body of police under Mr Inspector Atchison were seen to assemble on the T alongside of which she would bring up, and no sooner was she moored than they went on board, and without hurry or confusion conducted an individual ashore.

Such an unusual number of constables surrounding one person naturally attracted some attention, but it was not till near the shore end of the wharf that someone recognised in the carefully guarded captive the wretch Sullivan.

Cries of "Sullivan," "Sullivan," resounded on all sides, and a general rush at once was made, but Mr Atchison waved back the crowd and the police stepped briskly forward and pushed their captive into a covered car, which at once drove off at a rapid pace to the gaol amidst the groans and hisses of the bystanders.

Sullivan, who was attired in every day garb and not handcuffed, appeared very desirous of eluding observation, and as the groans and hootings reached his ears, trembled like an aspen and showed other signs of alarm.

Too much credit cannot be given to Mr Atchison for the care he employed in keeping the convict's arrival a secret, as, had it not been for his judgment and the firm decided action of Sergeant Monaghan and the constables, we are convinced that the reception New Zealand's greatest criminal would have met, would have been too warm to be strictly agreeable.

It is no doubt pleasant for a man to make his name a household word in the ears of his fellow-men, but it is the reverse of pleasing to feel convinced of a notoriety so abominable as to ensure public execration. Sullivan evidently greatly dreaded some forcible demonstration of popular indignation, for he cowered and shivered like a whipped dog as he was

---

229  Local And General News. Wellington Independent, Volume XXII, Issue 2640, 25 February 1868, Page 3

being conducted to gaol. Yesterday the miscreant was removed to the station house, and will, to-day, be taken in the *Phoebe* to Dunedin.

## One-Legged Man Runs Himself Over, 1869[230]

A fatal accident happened in Molesworth Street, on the morning of the 15th ult., by which a man named Jas. Muson met his death. He was a one-legged man, and accidentally fell before the wheel of his cart, which passed over him. He died within an hour, and leaves a wife and six children.

## First English Birds In NZ, 1863[231]

A successful attempt has been made to bring out some of our national songsters from the groves of old England. We have seen, with feelings of pleasure, some half-dozen sky larks and a pair of thrushes, and the sight of their speckled breasts reminded us of old familiar friends.

The favourite singing station of the thrush is the top of a poplar tree. These are flourishing with us, and we hope, that ere long, we shall have the unspeakable gratification of hearing both thrush and lark in full song.

## Christchurch Knows How To Spend Money[232]

### *Cathedrals*

It is most refreshing to read of the way they do things at Canterbury. If they contemplate a wharf it is a hundred thousand pounder; if they want a new loan nothing short of half a million will suffice; or if they want a Cathedral they don't talk about spending four or five thousand pounds upon it, but forty or fifty.

Just now an appeal is put forth for the requisite funds to build the nave of the proposed Cathedral at Christchurch, twenty thousand pound being the amount required for this portion alone. At present they have only £1800

---

230   Local Memoranda, Wellington Independent, Volume XXIV, Issue 2835, 13 May 1869, Page 6 http://paperspast.natlib.govt.nz/cgi-bin/paperspast?a=d&d=WI18690513.2.33
231   Canterbury, Nelson Examiner and New Zealand Chronicle, Volume XXII, Issue 54, 20 June 1863, Page 3
232   Local Intelligence, Wellington Independent, Volume XVII, Issue 1813, 6 January 1863, Page 3 http://paperspast.natlib.govt.nz/cgi-bin/paperspast?a=d&d=WI18630106.2.7

towards it, £1,000 of which is a contribution from the Government, and £700 from England, but the subscription list, now to be handed round, will, it is confidently anticipated, justify a speedy commencement of the building already designed by one of the most eminent ecclesiastical architects in England. The prospectus thus details the objects contemplated by a Cathedral, beyond those of an ordinary church:

"The purposes of a Cathedral are manifold. Amongst these are, that it is
1. A perpetual and conspicuous witness to the presence and majesty of the most Holy Trinity.
2. The church of the diocese, where the Bishop's cathedral or chair is placed, and therefore representing a branch of the great Christian society in its complete organization of bishop, clergy, and people.
3. A central place of worship for the diocese and for strangers, where all the seats are free for ever and where none may feel that they are intruding on parochial rights. As the central church of the diocese, it represents the unity, and as open to all strangers, the universality of the Christian church.
4. A sacred edifice, adapted in size and dignity for the performance of specially Episcopal functions, such as that of ordination, and for the assembling together of large numbers of the people on occasions of more than ordinary solemnity.
5. A sanctuary, where prayer may be daily offered, and the highest office of our religion weekly celebrated, that so the fire of devotion may be rekindled from day to day, the incense of prayer and praise never cease to be offered up in the name and on behalf of the diocese at large, and while the inhabitants of the city and neighbourhood may reap the fruit of these blessings continually, the sojourner of a day or of a week may thankfully embrace the occasional opportunities, which nothing but this constant circle of holy services could with certainty provide.

# Women Becoming Too Fashion-Conscious, 1863[233]

We hope not. – The rage for dress which now animates the whole female sex, and which tends to so much extravagance, debt and discomfort, is continually seeking new modes in which to expend itself.

---

233  Ibid

The following is the latest from France. A recent letter from Biaritz gave an account of a ball at the imperial villa. "The toilets of the ladies," it is said, "were richer than ever. Hair-powder seems to be coming into vogue again, for many of the ladies used it on this occasion."

## These Days You'd Be Shot And Tasered, In That Order, 1863[234]

Constable Michael Monahan brought up John Fuller and his wife, Mary Anne Fuller, on a charge of being drunk and disorderly. C. B. Borlase, Esq., appeared for the prisoners.

It appeared, from the evidence adduced, that the male and female prisoners were using obscene language in the public street, and that when Constable Monahan, aided by Constable Ard, apprehended them, they violently resisted, dragged off Monahan's cap, and tore Ard's tunic and trowsers.

The Resident Magistrate said that as they had already been forty-eight hours in confinement, he should only order that the price of the policemen's wardrobe be made good, and adjourned the case until such time as a tailor could determine the amount of damage done.

## NZ To Split Into Two Countries, 1865[235]

While the question of separation is being agitated, it may not be uninteresting to notice the struggle that is now rife in Victoria and New South Wales. It is patent that, however imposing the subject of separation may seem in theory, the practical working of the question is one of extreme difficulty, and will ultimately lead to a collision of interests, jealousy, perhaps bloodshed.

To evade a rupture between the two governments, a confederation such as is taking place in Canada, is pointed out by men of eminent talents and large colonial experience as the only solution of the difficulty on an equitable footing.

---

234  The Evening Post. Monday, February 20, 1865, Evening Post , Issue 11, 20 February 1865, Page 2 http://paperspast.natlib.govt.nz/cgi-bin/paperspast?a=d&d=EP18650220.2.6
235  The Evening Post. Monday, February 20, 1865, Evening Post , Issue 11, 20 February 1865, Page 2 http://paperspast.natlib.govt.nz/cgi-bin/paperspast?a=d&d=EP18650220.2.6

If that is to be the emetic given to our sister colonies, after having gone through all the turmoil, anxiety, and trouble of separation, we must be excessively blind who insist in trying to raise similar obstacles to the progress of New Zealand, and who, in spite of the evident consequences that must accrue by dividing these islands into two or more governments, are sowing the seeds of future broils, party feeling, perhaps even of a civil war, and only to satisfy petty jealousy and disappointed ambition.

As regards our position to the Southern Island, it is somewhat similar to that of Victoria and New South Wales: their boundary is a river, whilst ours is a narrow strait; the same question which they find so difficult of solution, namely, taxation, would in our case prove a stumbling block of no mean order to separation.

The mode of raising a revenue in the two islands would, through force of circumstances, be diametrically opposed to each other. The Middle Island, probably wishing to adopt direct taxation, would open her ports to free trade; the Northern one, on the other hand, precluded from taxing native land by Imperial Legislature, would be under the necessity of, as at present, making the natives pay their proportion by indirect taxation to the support of Government.

One of the consequences would be that the former, enjoying the benefits of direct taxation and free trade, would try to force her trade and commerce upon us free of taxes – smuggling would ensue, there would be a constant effort made to evade the law, and duties involving upon the island a large expenditure for revenue service. Independent of this great obstacle to peaceful government, there would arise interminable disputes at every turn.

"Unity is strength" a "bundle of sticks", and the instability of "a house divided against itself", are trite, well worn, but very true proverbs. We might as well expect the Siamese twins to live and possess the same unity of feelings if their connecting link were severed.

If separated politically, the position of New Zealand would decrease, financial confidence would be destroyed, while here, as a colony, we are looked upon with respect, as holding a fair position in the commercial world – divided, we should be pointed out as doubtful, and as making a retrograde movement in our youth.

We do not hold with those who confidently assert that the public have heard enough on the question, inferring that they attach little or no importance to the matter; it is a subject of vital interest, and one that requires free ventilation, as, by being fully discussed now, it may show the rising generation, who, doubtless in of time, will reagitate the movement, the evil result that must inevitably follow should the interest of the islands be divided.

Party feeling is strong enough at present. Witness the attempt of some of the Otago members to oust from their Provincial Council gentlemen not agreeing with the question, and who have the moral courage to vindicate the cause of union, foreseeing the disastrous consequences of separation to the onward progress of the colony.

Chapter 17

# The Story Of The South Island

*The story of New Zealand is essentially the story of two big islands. Up until the 1880s, the South Island was known as "Middle Island" – as you may already have guessed from previous chapters.*

*The warmer North Island was heavily populated, but the cold South was almost deserted when Governor Hobson declared sovereignty over it by virtue of discovery, rather than Treaty.*

*Yet the South Island is home to one of the largest Treaty of Waitangi claims, so clearly someone lived there. The most useful aspect of writing a book based on old reports is that they are unfiltered by modern historians working, in many cases, to a political agenda. Back in the 1800s, European writers did not feel threatened by Maori aspirations, and Maori did not want New Zealand to be governed in "partnership" – no matter what your Treaty studies lecturer tells you today, the partnership meme is a modern interpretation, not an accurate historical one.*

*That means there was no 'culture wars' clash like we have today, and in turn that means the old newspaper reports are untainted by the partnership agenda and its baggage. Instead, pakeha and Maori historians in the 1800s were doing their best to document the histories without fear or favour.*

*This, then, is the history of the South Island, in their words.*

## How The West Coast Was Won, 1896[236]
### By Thomas Mackenzie

On the authority of a publication issued by the Government two years ago, I said that Captain Cook's party called Acheron Passage "Nobody Knows What," and that he did not go all the way through it. But since then, on consulting Captain Cook's and Captain Vancouver's own works, I find that they both sailed through it, and that Captain Cook gave the name "Nobody Knows What" to what is now known as the entrance to Broughton Arm. When Vancouver came along 18 years afterwards (1791) he sent his lieutenant (Mr Broughton) to explore this passage, and altered the name to "Somebody Knows What."

Captain Vancouver himself explored the opposite, arm, which now bears his name. The point separating these two arms, bears the name of Lieutenant Broughton's vessel, the Chatham, the opposite headland being called Discovery Point, after Captain Vancouver's sloop of war.

I do not know whether all travellers like to know the reason why certain names are attached to the leading geographical features of our southern land, but I am always deeply interested to know. The works of the earlier explorers containing the necessary information are yearly becoming more difficult to consult, and the early pioneers who possessed the unrecorded history of 50 and 60 years ago have nearly all passed away.

As I have had the advantage of reading some books and talking with a few pioneers, I am sure no apology is necessary for me to justify the extension of the narrative to include these facts.

My last week's notes closed as we had finished fixing our camp just below the first rapids. Captain Cook was stepped by the same impediment. He entered that river on Tuesday, April 20, 1773. In his diary he thus describes the place:

"I proceeded up the river, shooting wild ducks, of which there were great numbers, as we went along, now and then hearing the natives in the woods. At length, two appeared on the banks of the river – a man and a woman and the latter kept waving something white in her hand as a sign of friendship.

---

[236] West Coast Exploration, Otago Daily Times, Issue 10631, 28 March 1896, Page 2
http://paperspast.natlib.govt.nz/cgi-bin/paperspast?a=d&cl=search&d=ODT18960328.2.7

"Mr Cooper (one of Cook's officers) being near them, I called to him to land, as I wanted to take advantage of the tide to get as high up as possible, which did not much exceed half a mile when I was stopped by the strength of the stream and great stones which lay in the bed of the river."

Few boats since Captain Cook's have breasted the waters of that river, and every feature and surrounding excepting the presence of the Maori is still the same. Even the bird life, which is usually the first to disappear alter the approach of man, has altered but little. Captain Cook's association with this place gave the locality an interesting fascination for me.

Before an interview with the Indians (as Cook called the natives) was arranged, various ceremonies had to be observed, such as having a piece of grass held out to him, the chief taking the other end. Salutation then followed, and perfect friendship was established by the chief taking his mat off his back and placing it on Cook's shoulders.

Cook's first meeting actually occurred at Indian Island, lower down the sound. His first interview was with a chief and his two wives, the women doing the most of the talk, especially the younger, which occasioned one of the seamen to say "women did not want [lack] tongue in any part of the world," and Captain Cook remarks "that her volubility of tongue exceeded everything he ever met with."

Before leaving she entertained them with a sprightly dance. It is clear that there must be something in the climate of New Zealand which inspires the women, otherwise Maoriland would not have been the first British country to grant the franchise to her daughters.

The natives paid but little attention to the various articles presented to them by Captain Cook except the hatchets and spike nails – these they valued, most highly, and would not part with them or lay them down anywhere, even for an instant; They were most shy about coming on board the ship, and Captain Cook had to use the strongest inducement to entice them there. As a last resort he ordered the bagpipes to be played and the big drum. The natives had, however, not been educated sufficiently to appreciate the beauty of the pipes, and therefore they preferred the drum, thus clearly showing that they were a degenerate race!

After coming aboard they spied into everything, but would not eat any food. They were anxious to see where Cook slept, and were much struck with the number and strength of the decks. Works of art they looked at with a bewildered gaze.

Before coming on board they struck the ship with a green branch, and muttered a prayer and threw the branch away. Cook remarks that the customs of the Dusky Bay natives were different in some respects from those of the natives in other parts of New Zealand, and he expressed surprise at a few natives living there away from all the other inhabitants of the country.

This leads me to give a sketch of what I believe is the history of the natives of that part of the South Island. I think it is of great importance to any young country to instil into the minds of the people the history and traditions of those races who have possessed the land in former times.

The history of the Maori is one that will well bear telling. They were a noble race, who have performed deeds of valour which may have been equalled, but never surpassed, in any part of the world. The typical ancient Maori chief was brave, truthful, courteous, and dignified. It was only after the influence of the worst type of whites was felt, that the race began to degenerate.

In order to give an account of the West Coast natives it is necessary to go back and briefly describe the history of the Maori occupation of the South Island. The first were the Waitaha, a noble, generous tribe descended from Waitaha, who came from Hawaiki in the Arawa canoe about the fourteenth or fifteenth century. A party of them left the east coast of the North Island and settled in the South, where they increased and multiplied and prospered exceedingly. They occupied the land undisturbed for 250 or 300 years. The great heaps of shells now found near the coast are attributed to them, and with the Waitaha is associated the extinction of the moa.

Many contend that the Maori and moa were not contemporary. Tregear, the author of the Maori Dictionary, maintains that they were not; but if to the Waitaha is attributed the formation of these shell heaps, I can from my own exploration and observation conclusively prove from specimens of bones which I possess that the Maori and moa lived at the same time. During my explorations in the Tautuku forest 10 years ago, our party discovered many old Maori camping places, with shell heaps of great extent covering acres, and having a depth of from 2ft to 4ft. In these shell heaps we discovered numbers of moa bones, which were all broken to get at the marrow; mixed with these bones and shells were human bones, native dog bones, seal, kakapo, and kiwi bones, &c.

Now regarding the antiquity of this midden or shall heap we had an excellent guide. On the top mould formed by many years of decay a totara forest has grown, with trees ranging from 2ft to 4ft in diameter. This proves the age of the shell heaps to be not less than 400 to 500 years. Before leaving this point it is not uninteresting to note the fact that kiwi and kakapo existed on the east coast in those days; also that the presence of dog bones clearly proves that native dogs were here before the days of Captain Cook.

The South Island was then known as "the land of the abundance of food," and the Waitaha being generous and hospitable used frequently to send presents to their friends in the north. They remained undisturbed until a tribe called the Ngatimamoe, who also lived on the east coast of the North Island, began to cast envious eyes on the south. They waged war on the Waitaha and finally conquered them, and treated the vanquished very cruelly, and made slaves of those whose lives they spared for a time.

The natives discovered by Cook on the West Coast were descended from these Ngatimamoe. They held the South Island, it is supposed, for about 100 years, and were in turn conquered by the Ngaitahu, a much worthier race, of which our [chiefs] Taiaroa and Topi, of Ruapuke, are members.

For a time after the Ngaitahu conquered the Ngatimamoe some intermarrying occurred. But the treacherous blood of the conquered race would out – "The women made bad wives, which finally caused ruptures, with disastrous results to the culprits." Mr Chapman tells a good story in his paper on *The Working of the Greenstone* which illustrates the opinion held by Ngaitahu natives of the Ngatimamoe:

"It is a subject of reproach to have pakeha or European blood, and a halfcaste lady once told me that being thus reproached by relations, she replied that that was necessary to neutralise the bad strain of Ngatimamoe blood in our veins."

After the Ngaitahu had practically vanquished the Ngatimamoe as a tribe, internal disturbances arose among themselves. White, in his *Ancient History of the Maori*, gives an incident which occurred at the Peninsula, and which is almost comic in its ghastliness, to serve as a specimen of the warfare in those times. A quarrel arose about a tohunga (wise man or priest) who taught history incorrectly. "It was he who told the younger Turakautahi chief that Tiki made man, whilst the fathers had always said it was Io. Tawera, another chief, adopted a novel method of preventing his teaching surviving him, or his spirit escaping and perverting the mind of any other tohunga. Having made an oven capable of containing the entire body, he carefully plugged the mouth, nose, ears, and rectum, and then cooked and ate the heretical teacher."

It would be very interesting at this point to follow the history of the occupation of the South Island by the Ngaitahu – the incident of the introduction of greenstone to that tribe by the woman Rau Reka, which Mr Stack thinks was about 1700 AD – the consequent wars in connection with greenstone – the attempted conquest in 1830 of the South Island by the Napoleon of the Maoris, Te Rauparaha – the great siege of Kaiapoi, its long and valorous defence – Captain Stewart's treacherous conduct with the brig Elizabeth – the capture of the chief of Kaiapoi, Tama-i-haranui, who slew with his own hand his daughter to save her from disgrace – his own transportation to Kapiti, where he was handed over to the wife of Pehi, and his tragic death – Te Rauparaha's subsequent conversion to Christianity, and the discontinuance of the southern conquest. But that must be passed over. My object in referring to the Maori history was to give an account of the West Coast Maoris, and I must keep to my text.

The complete conquest of the Ngatimamoe was planned by the chief Kaweriri (continued anger), he taking command. On crossing Waitaki the party divided, one proceeding inland and the other coastwise. They then drove the Ngatimamoe before them to Aparima, where at a gorge they were brought to bay, and after a most desperate fight, in which great courage was shown on both sides, they were defeated. Kaweriri was slain.

The Ngatimamoe then proceeded up the river, taking up a fortified position. They were still superior in number to their pursuers. Another desperate battle occurred, and the doomed tribe were once more defeated, after a desperate resistance, with great slaughter. White adds: "The few who escaped, fled into the forest towards the west across Lake Te Anau."

Some members of the scattered tribe were left and intermarried with the Ngaitahu, but a disturbance arising out of using the bone of a deceased chief for a fishhook caused a young Ngaitahu to be killed. Taikawa, a Ngaitahu chief, then addressed the Ngatimamoe, and said "You have done foolishly, for not one of you will be spared. You will be banished to the haunts of the moho (Notornis Mantelli or what is now called a 'takahe' rather than moho), and in the depth of the forest will be your only safety." This was carried out – they were all driven along the south-western coast.

Traces of these fugitives have been met with up to recent date. Some 50 years ago a Maori on his way to plunder a sealing station came across a Maori woman. Discerning she was a Ngatimamoe, he killed and devoured her on the spot. Mr Waite adds "In 1842 a sealing party while pulling up one of the sounds observed smoke issuing from the face of a cliff. Climbing to the place they found a cave evidently just deserted. It was apportioned across the middle, the inner part being used as a sleeping place, the outer for cooking. They found a handsome feather mat, a patu-paraoa (whalebone), some fishhooks, and some flax baskets in process of making."

They tried to capture the natives, but failed. They then stole the natives things. Mr White states "the mat was sent to Otaki and the patu-paraoa given to Rev. Mr Stack." Mr White concludes by observing: "It is just possible that a small remnant may still be secreted in the recesses of that inaccessible region." Regarding this latter remark, I do not think that one is left. The country which I have been exploring during my last two expeditions practically traverses the only piece of unexplored country of any extent. I did not find the slightest trace of recent occupation and I think that the last of the race has been for many years extinct.

Not a sign of the Maori was to be seen by the *Acheron* when Captain Stokes spent much time in his careful and exhaustive survey of the West Coast sounds in 1850.

I would like to mention that I am largely indebted to Mr White's works for much of the Maori history, also to Mr F. Chapman's papers delivered before the Otago Institute.

Further insight on the plight of the Ngaitahu emerges in an obituary marking the death of a celebrated Ngaitahu warrior.

## Hakopa, The Shark Rider, 1883[237]

In our notice of the death last month at the Kaiapoi pa of the Maori warrior Hakopa Te Ata O Tu, some allusion was made to his life during the stirring times of Te Rauparaha, and in the same connection might now be repeated shortly the history of the tribe to which he belonged, as well as the part he played in Te Rauparaha's invasion.

The history of the first Maoris in the South Island is dated back to

---

237 Hakopa Te Ata O Tu, Press, Volume XXXIX, Issue 5651, 29 October 1883, Page 3
http://paperspast.natlib.govt.nz/cgi-bin/paperspast?a=d&d=CHP18831029.2.23

1477[238], when the Wataha crossed Cook's Straits from the North Island, and this tribe, by the historians, is credited with holding possession till 1577, when they were conquered by the Ngatimamoe, who held the country till 1677, and then the Ngaitahu appear to have migrated hither from their residence in the Wellington province and along the sea coast.

The fairly reliable history of the latter tribe may be traced back about 200 years. Ngatimamoe and Ngaitahu legends go back to Te Kahni Tipua, the period of the monster bird and ogre hand, a mythical race of giants who strode from mountain to mountain, and were succeded by Te Rapuwai or Ngapahi, who left the shell heaps found all over the country, and in whose time the country at Invercargill was submerged,[239] the great forests of Canterbury burned, and the moa was exterminated.

The Ngatimamoe were fought out by the Ngaitahu, and the former took to the bush, in which the remnants of that tribe are said to have terminated their existence. The Ngaitahu held its own as a tribe till the invasion by Te Rauparaha in 1827, when that renowned chief created such terrible havoc here.

On some small pretext of an alleged offensive remark made by a Ngaitahu tribe respecting Te Rauparaha, the latter gathered a large force and proceeded to the South, conquering the Maoris of Nelson and the Kaikoura peninsula. In the latter instance the Ngaititoas, under Te Rauparaha, it is estimated, killed no less than a thousand men of the Ngaitahu tribe, the former being equipped with firearms, and also mistaken for a friendly party till close upon landing at the Kaikoura.

Subsequently, Te Rauparaha made up his mind to attack the Kaiapoi pah. On his way down he overtook and killed a large section of the Ngaitahu at the Omihi pah, on the Glenmark run, and then pushed forward with a part of his warriors for the Kaiapoi pah, then situate upon a piece of higher land than the rest of the country, and surrounded by a swamp.

The war party endeavored to represent their visit a friendly one, but in this were not successful, and the Ngaitahu, detecting the designs of their visitors, visited them with severe punishment, so that they retired,

---

238  Carbon dating of ancient oven sites near Dunedin has pushed human occupation possibly as far back as 900AD. See The Great Divide, p17
239  The asteroid strike around 1450AD with the 200m high tsunami that drowned the South Island and killed Maori and moa alike

to await the arrival of reinforcements. The invaders being strengthened by numbers some short time afterwards, marched on to the pah in such a manner as to be able to take it by surprise, as a number of the Ngaitahu warriors were away with Taiaroa (father of H. K. Taiaroa, M.H.R.), and numbers of the men were out on their cultivations.

The Ngaitahus were able to close the fortifications of the pah, and the invaders had to take it by siege. Meanwhile Taiaroa's party returned, and though at first mistaken for their enemies the Ngaitahu were by a clever manuoevre got within the entrenchments, and the pah was successfully held for some time, till Te Rauparaha's party had carried in a sap, and by piling up brushwood expected to smoke out the besieged.

The holders of the pah, finding the wind favourable, set fire to the brushwood, but as the wind changed while the fire lasted the smoke was blown on to the Ngaitahu, and the pallisading of the pah set fire to. In the midst of this a general massacre of the Ngaitahu took place.

One of the last to surrender his greenstone club, which had done terrific execution, was Hakopa, who is said to have fought like a very demon for his home and his people. Ultimately, as stated in the account of his death, he was taken prisoner and subsequently released.

The prowess of Hakopa was greatly admired, and his commanding figure and strength of arm and endurance caused him to be respected by his captors, and looked upon as an acquisition to their side in battles with other tribes. Two remarkable stories have been recently told to us of Hakopa, which have been presented to us by his son Simeon.

At Motungarara, one of the small islands near Kapiti, there had been a large catch of fish, which the Maoris were engaged in cleaning and splitting to dry for winter stores. The offal thrown into the sea attracted an immense shark (taniwha), which came close to shore. Six of the natives, with a harpoon lance with lines attached, waded out up to their waists to try and catch the shark, which, every time it came within reach, had the harpoon thrown at it without success.

Hakopa, seeing them all miss the shark, asked for the weapon, but they refused it saying, "Do you think you can kill this shark when all six of us have missed it?"

After some persuasion they gave him the harpoon, and the other six held to the line. Hakopa waded out and, cautiously watching his opportunity while the shark was gorging on the offal, he drove the spear into the fish.

The shark rolling over bent the harpoon, so that it formed a hook. The fish then made for sea at a terrific rate of speed, the force on the line throwing down the six men, who held the rope.

Hakopa, however, caught the line, and taking a turn with it round his arm the shark drew him away at high pressure speed. Hakopa, however, thought so long as he could breathe he would hold on, and when compelled to leave go would swim back to land. He found that the speed of the shark parted the water, and he was enabled to recover his breathing. He, therefore, was delighted with the ride he was having, so even, so smooth, and at such a railroad rate.

The people on shore began lamenting his decease, but some put off in canoes to pick him up. These having paddled about for a long time saw the shark on the surface, and directly behind it was Hakopa. As the men paddled up the shark started off again, and went round Ames (sic) Island, at the north end of Kapiti; then it came back among the islands, till it ran ashore in death agonies near the spot at which it was first struck.

When it came ashore Hakopa was in the water waiting for the fish to go on, and afraid lest it would turn, but on looking up he saw the wahines (women) cutting the shark open to get its liver, the oil from which is greatly prized by the native women.

The scene of a tale of Hakopa's heroism is laid between the Hurunui and Waikari. Hakopa and Simeon, his son (the narrator), were on the beach fishing, when a wild bull and two heifers came from the bush towards them. Hakopa hid Simeon under some drift wood, and he was about to follow suit when the bull came at him, and, in order to save his boy, to whom he was dearly attached, Hakopa conceived the idea of inducing the bull to follow him into the sea.

The animal chased him some distance along the beach, whereupon Hakopa took to the water, and the bull followed him. They swam out some distance, aud each time the bull turned for shore Hakopa came near enough to induce it to attack him, and so decoyed it some two miles away. He swam with it into some floating kelp, and managed to hamper its progress by throwing some of it over the horns of the animal, and then, by diving, came up on the other side of the bull, and swam away to his son, who had given him up for lost, and to regain his clothing, which he had hastily thrown aside on entering the water.

## The Canterbury Natives[240]

At a time when the Native Question occupies so large a share of public attention, a few particulars respecting our more immediate neighbours, the Maories of this province, may not he devoid of interest; especially as so little is known about them. We propose, therefore giving a short account of their past history and of their present condition and resources.

At no very remote period, this province and the country south of it was occupied by the Ngatimamoe a numerous tribe, now extinct. The present inhabitants are a remnant of the once powerful Ngaitahu, formerly resident on the southern shore of Cook's Strait.

When Hongi Hika returned from England in 1821 to the neighbourhood of the Bay of Islands, laden with muskets and powder, and ambitious of fame, he inaugurated a new and bloody era in Maori annals. The introduction of fire-arms led to an entire revolution in Maori warfare.

As Hongi for a time enjoyed a monopoly in these weapons, his name became the terror of the whole country. At the head of a thousand warriors he opened his first campaign in the Hauraki or Thames Gulf. Having more than decimated the warlike Ngatiwhatua, he marched southwards and ravaged the Lower Waikato country far and wide. Whole districts were depopulated, and large and powerful tribes driven from their ancestral possessions.

The Waikato pressed upon the Kawhia tribes, who in their turn, headed by Te Pehi and Te Rauparaha, and making common cause with the Ngatiawa, came down upon the Ngatiruanui; these again became involved with the neighbouring tribes. Thus war spread from tribe to tribe, till the whole North Island had become one scene of bloodshed and massacre.

From the commencement of Hongi's warlike career to the establishment of British rule about 20,000 lives were sacrificed. Report says that Hongi and his party, in returning home through the districts they had overrun, were compelled to live almost entirely on human flesh!

In 1824, this renowned Rauparaha, having obtained a large supply of arms and ammunition, crossed Cook's Strait and carried destruction among the Ngaitahu (or Ngatikuri, as they were then called). They too

---

240  The Canterbury Natives, Lyttelton Times, Volume XVI, Issue 920, 4 September 1861, Page 5
http://paperspast.natlib.govt.nz/cgi-bin/paperspast?a=d&d=LT18610904.2.17

had been provided with muskets by the Cook's Strait whalers, and now that they were driven from their own territories, they retreated upon the defenceless Ngatiruanui.

Physically a feeble people and having no firearms, the latter fell an easy prey to their invaders, who followed them up to their utter extermination and then took possession of their lands. Vengeance soon, however, overtook the victorious Ngaitahu. Te Rehi, principal chief of Ngatitoa, had been treacherously murdered and his body eaten, when on a friendly visit to the natives of Bank's Peninsula; to avenge his murder, Te Rauparaha, in 1830, chartered a European brig and came down here with a picked force.

Attacking the unsuspecting Ngaitahu on several points at once he completely routed them, killed about two thousand and carried home with him to Kapiti several hundred captives. A few years later, when the introduction of Christianity among the natives led to a general manumission of slaves, the liberated Ngaitahu returned to their shattered tribe. They have since remained unmolested, and now live dispersed in small parties over Bank's Peninsula and along the eastern and western coasts of this island.

They number collectively about 1000, some two-thirds of them being located in this province. The males are in excess of the females, but, as compared with the population of the north island, the percentage of children is large. Their principal settlement is Kaiapoi, the population of which fluctuates from 50 to 150. Their land reserves (all well selected) comprise upwards of 7000 acres of the best land in the province, including some 1500 acres of fine timber, and may be now valued, at the lowest as worth £50,000. They own upwards of 200 horses, 220 horned cattle, a few sheep, and 197 pigs, and have several hundred acres under cultivation. On the whole then, they are a comparatively wealthy class.

Compared with the northerners their characteristics may be thus summed up: – Physically, somewhat inferior to them; socially, rather in advance of them; morally, apparently below them. This last feature is not to be wondered at, for till recently no provision existed for their moral or religious education.

In each of their principal settlements there are several good weatherboarded bouses, and the number will soon be increased. A decided tendency to social progress is evinced in the general desire to have their reserves partitioned off and individualized. We are glad to learn that the General Government have undertaken the work for them, and that the valuable reserve at Kaiapoi is now being surveyed and sub-divided, with a view to the creation of individual tenures, and as a preliminary step to the issue of Crown grants.

We understand that the partition of the Kaiapoi reserve will secure to each proprietor a farm of fourteen acres, besides a share in the bush. One of the immediate advantages it promises is the opening again of the native bush trade, interrupted last year in consequence of difficulties created by the unlicensed occupation of the reserve by Europeans, and the unsatisfactory, undefined character of the right of the numerous Maori joint proprietors to give any secure title of occupancy to the sawyers and others. This, we believe, is the first attempt ever made by the New Zealand Government towards conferring upon the Maori an individual and clearly-defined title to his land.

It has not been without great difficulty that the Maories here have been induced to consent to a partition of their reserves. To Mr. Walter Buller, of the Native Department, is due the credit of removing the strong mistrusts and doubts they entertained on this question, long debated and often rejected by them. To bring them to a right understanding of the advantages each individual would secure to himself in the sole and undisputed possession of a piece of land, has required much care and management, and the greatest patience.

The plan upon which the sub-division is being made has been devised by Mr. Buller with method and sound judgment. Keeping in view the probable important position value, the Kaiapoi reserve will, from its proximity to a shipping port, acquire, at no distant date, special attention has been given to the shape of the blocks and the road reserves. These are now being laid off under the experienced direction of Mr. John C. Boys, specially detached for this service by the Provincial Government.

So long as seventeen years ago Mr. Clark, then chief protector of aborigines, recommended to the Government the plan here for the first time being put into execution. He advised and urged a general survey and registration throughout the North Island of all undisputed territory belonging to each tribe, thus defining so far tribal rights with a view either to the easy acquisition of land by the European or the Crown, or its future partition with clear title to individual members of the tribe. He thus proposed to pave the way to a settlement of the title, tribal or otherwise, over all disputed territory.

Mr. Clark's was a wise, humane, and far-sighted policy. Had it been steadily and pertinaciously – no matter how slowly – pursued from that day to this, the colony would never have heard of this miserable Taranaki war. The "garden of New Zealand" would still be enjoyed in plenty and happiness by those who made it. Teira and William King doubtless at this moment would be grubbing fern root and planting potatoes in all the quiet and obscurity from which military mismanagement and imbecility has suddenly upraised them to rank, even in England, as passing celebrities of the day.

That the experiment at Kaiapoi will prove completely successful with our own Maories we can entertain no doubt. But if the day be not already gone by, we look to its bearing other fruit. It ought to bring about in the North Island the adoption of Mr. Clark's policy as one to be systematically followed up till every disputed tribal title is settled. Then – when every native may become assured of the quiet enjoyment of the result of his own industry on his own plot of land – and not till then – may we entertain any firm belief in the possibility of civilising the Maori race.

This, then is the story of Ngai Tahu, formerly known as Ngati Kuri. By virtue of the game of musical chairs that was Maori society at the time, they just happened to be the last people standing in the lower South Island when the Government came looking to buy land.

The Waitangi Tribunal ruled that Ngai Tahu had been very hard done by:

"The Tribunal cannot avoid the conclusion that in acquiring from Ngāi Tahu 34.5 million acres, more than half the land mass of New Zealand, for £14,750 pounds, and leaving them with only 35,757 acres, the Crown acted unconscionably and in repeated breach of the Treaty of Waitaingi".

Let's read the historical accounts, and find out what really happened in the words of those who were actually involved.

Chapter 18

# How Ngai Tahu Sold The South Island

*To get an idea of the land rush, you first have to understand the complex situation the fledgling New Zealand Government found itself in. As this story from 1845 indicates, a comparatively large Maori population was capable of laying waste to young Auckland, yet in the "Middle" Island there were probably fewer than 1,500 people in the whole island.*

## Native Population, 1845[241]

The following is extracted from the *New Zealander*. We have compared it with the Return printed in the Minutes of Council from which it was copied, and corrected a few errors and omissions.

By persons well informed on the subject it is stated that the whole population of the Middle Island does not exceed 1500, and we are satisfied that the number in Cook's Straits is greatly over estimated in this return but it would be too much to expect accuracy in the Chief Protector in anything that related to the Southern Settlements.

During the last Session of the Legislative Council there was laid before that body a Return of the Native Population of New Zealand, and it may

---

241 Native Population. New Zealand Spectator and Cook's Strait Guardian, Volume II, Issue 54, 18 October 1845, Page 3
http://paperspast.natlib.govt.nz/cgi-bin/paperspast?a=d&d=NZSCSG18451018.2.9

not be uninteresting to consider it, in reference to the various settlements, and investigate how the several tribes are divided and situated.

The aggregate number, by this return of the Chief Protector, is 109,550, of which about 40,000 are, in their religion, proselytes of the Church missionaries; about 16,000 under the Wesleyans; about 5,000 are Roman Catholics; and the remainder are termed Pagans.

We have divided the Return into seven districts giving the principal locality or abiding place of each tribe, with the name of the head chiefs.

Consideration of this Return plainly indicates how completely surrounded the district of Auckland is by the Native population. On the East coast, there are 30,000; between that and the West coast, there are 10,500 and between the river Mokau and Manukau, there are 18,400 – exclusive of the Ngati Watua and Houraki tribes, amounting to 6000 more; making altogether nearly 70,000 Natives within three hundred mjles of Auckland, of which 50,000 are within three days march of Auckland. This most important fact should awaken the vigilance, as well as stimulate firmness and decision in the present crisis.

*In the shifting sands of tribal warfare, the right to sell land was dependent on whether you had the power to control the land on an ongoing basis. Thus, the hugely powerful Waikato tribe had sold the conquered land in Taranaki (formerly Ngatiawa/Ngatitoa territory) to the British because – although Waikato had not occupied the land in force, it had scared the former occupants away.*

*In the South Island, Ngatitoa had of course swept down and pushed Ngaitahu out of the northern part of the island, and attempted to exterminate them in Kaiapoi and Banks Peninsula.*

*Despite horrific defeats, Ngaitahu kept their fires burning on that land. Under Maori tikanga, might was right and they'd managed to hold their own, even though a large chunk of their people had been either slaughtered or enslaved.*

*The Government, when looking to buy land in the South Island, had dealt firstly with Te Rauparaha's brutal Ngatitoa tribe. It hadn't gone so well. One "it's in the bag" deal with Te Rauparaha turned into the Wairau Massacre; in another case, Ngatitoa convinced the Government that it owned Kaiapoi, and sold it to them.*

*This caused the first recorded complaint for land compensation by Ngai Tahu, who initially raised their concerns through a letter to the editor of a*

| Residence. | Tribe. | Chief. | Population. |
|---|---|---|---|
| Kaitaia. | Te Rarawa. | Nopera. | 4,000 |
| Bay of Islands. | Ngapuhi. | Nene. Pomare. | 12,000 |
| | | | 16,000 |

### WAITEMATA AND COROMANDEL HARBOUR.

| | | | |
|---|---|---|---|
| Auckland. | Ngatiwatua. | Kauwau. | 2,000 |
| Houraki. | Ngatimaru. | Taraia. | 4,000 |
| | | | 6,000 |

### EAST COAST.

| | | | |
|---|---|---|---|
| Tauranga. | Ngatiawa. | Tupaea. | 2,000 |
| Wakatane. Opotiki. | ,, | Hikaro. | 8,000 |
| East Cape. | Ngateporu. | Tekani. | 10,000 |
| Turanga. | Ngatikahunu. | Te Hapuku. | 10,000 |
| | | | 30,000 |

### WEST COAST AND WAIKATO.

| | | | |
|---|---|---|---|
| Waikato. | Waikato. | Te Werowero. | 18,400 |
| Taranaki. | Taranaki. | ,, | 2,000 |
| | | | 20,400 |

### INTERIOR.

| | | | |
|---|---|---|---|
| Rotorua. | Ngatiwakane. | Tohi Tongoroa. | 9,000 |
| Taupo. | Taupo. | Heuheu. | 1,500 |
| | | | 10,500 |

### NORTHERN SHORE OF COOK'S STRAITS.

| | | | |
|---|---|---|---|
| Ahuriri. | Ngatikahupunu. | —— | 5,000 |
| Waikanae. Port Nich. | Ngatiawa. | Reritawangawanga. | 3,950 |
| Waimate. | Ngatiruanui. | —— | 3,000 |
| Otaki. | Ngaterankawa. | Te Rauparaha. | 5,000 |
| Wanganui. | Wanganui. | Turoa. | 5,000 |
| | | | 21,950 |

### MIDDLE ISLAND.

| | | | |
|---|---|---|---|
| Cloudy Bay. | Ngatitoa. | Te Rauparaha. | 1,000 |
| Pelorus Riv. | Rangitane. | —— | 100 |
| Banks' Pen. | Ngaitahu. | Taiaroa. | 3,000 |
| Otakou. | —— | —— | 600 |
| | | | 4,700 |
| | | | 109,550 |

newspaper. *That paper's editorial commentary, and the letter itself, illustrate how Ngai Tahu were keen to see British justice done:*

## They Sold Land They Didn't Own, 1849[242]

SPECTATOR: We have received for publication the following letter relating to the purchase of Lands in the Middle Island, made by the Government from the Ngatitoa tribe in 1847. The letter, which we have accompanied with a faithful translation, is the genuine and unassisted production of the writer, a chief of the Ngaitahu tribe, who forcibly sets forth their claims to Kaiapoi and other districts included in the purchase, extending northward from Bank's Peninsula to Kaikoura.

In a rapid sketch he explains the origin of Te Rauparaha's wars with the tribes in the middle Island which were attended with such disastrous results to the latter, and shows that although they suffered many reverses, they eventually succeeded in maintaining their ground, and have held undisputed possession of these districts where they still remain.

He reproaches Puaha and the Ngatitoas for their insincerity, since, having become converts to Christianity they profess to hold their former customs in abhorrence, and yet they do not hesitate to profit by them when an occasion offers, by receiving payment for lands to which they assert a title by conquest which they cannot substantiate, and complains that the Government should have treated [negotiated] with them to the prejudice of the rightful owners of these districts who have not heen consulted in the purchase, and whose claims have been overlooked and disregarded and appeals through the *Press* to the Governor for justice.

We do not intend to enter into a discussion of these claims, since we desire to act impartially between the two parties, and shall be pleased to afford Puaha equal facilities for replying to these statements. But we think we way fairly refer to this letter as an indisputable proof of the advancing civilization of the natives. Formerly any dispute as to the title or possession of lands was invariably the prelude to violence, and the question was too often decided by the law of the strongest. Nearly all the difficulties that have arisen in the colonization of these islands may be traced to the same

---

242 New Zealand Spectator and Cook's Strait Guardian, Volume V, Issue 370, 17 February 1849, Page 2 http://paperspast.natlib.govt.nz/cgi-bin/paperspast?a=d&d=NZSCSG18490217.2.4

source. But in this instance we find the natives, believing their pretensions to be well founded, desirous of appealing to reason rather than to force, and of submitting their claims to the tribunal of public opinion.

We may also infer from this act the well-grounded confidence which the natives entertain in Sir George Grey's sense of justice, since they must be satisfied, in making this appeal that their claims will be fairly considered and decided upon by the Government.

But more than this, it evinces on their part a growing deference to the opinion of the pakeha, and a desire to excite in him an active interest in questions connected with the native race, it is thus [that] civilization will imperceptibly extend its influence among them, and the different barriers that separate the two races be gradually removed, until they disappear altogether.

By becoming daily more sensible of the advantages of a strong Government and of an impartial administration of justice, on every occasion when they consider themselves to be aggrieved, instead of resorting to violence or taking the law into their own hands, they will feel the more disposed to the established tribunals, or if the question, as in this case, be not of a nature to admit of such a reference, to follow the example of the pakeha and appeal to public opinion.

### *Te Aro, February 7, 1849.*

This is a protest concerning our matter, that the whites may understand the clandestine sale of our land by Ngatitoa: – Friend, Governor Grey, do you, and all the whites in every place, hear the truth of Te Rauparaha's connection with the lands in these parts.

Kawhia was his [original] land, it has passed into the hands of Waikato. He came to Kapiti and dwelt there. The tribes who owned these lands heard of this. The names of the sub tribes are innumerable, Ngatikahununu, Ngatiepa, Ngatiera, Ngatimoe, Ngaitumatakokiri, Ngatikuia, Rangitane, these are the tribes.

There were four tribes connected with these parts: Kapiti, Porirua, Port Nicholson, and Wairarapa. There were also three tribes belonging to Arapaoa on the other side. These tribes assembled to fight with Ngatitoa. The men of these parts were defeated at Waiorua. They renewed the fight, but all these tribes were always defeated and killed.

Those who survived this defeat fled to the bush, some to Wairarapa, others to the opposite side to Arapaoa. When the men and women belonging to Rangitane heard that the whole tribe had been killed, then they cursed Te Rauparaha, saying, "let his head be broken with (a tukituki aruhe) an instrument used for crushing fern root."

When Ngatitoa heard of this curse on Te Rauparaha, then these tribes (Ngatitoa and Ngatiawa) determined upon attacking the Middle Island.

Friend. Governor, do you and the whites hear, the reason why our Island was invaded was this curse on Te Rauparaha. Ngatitoa and Ngatiawa crossed over to Tukitukipatuaruhe. Afterwards the people of Waipapa and Kaikoura heard that Te Rauparaha was a great warrior, then Rerewaka cursed him, saying, "let Te Rauparaha's belly be ripped up with the tooth of a Manga [shark]."

Well, Te Rauparaha heard that he had been cursed. These are the reasons why the people of Ngaitahu, who were dwelling on their own land, were attacked, that is, the curse of the Manga's tooth, and the adultery of Te Kekereru with the wives of Te Rangihaeta [Te Rauparaha's lieutenant] these were the reasons why we were attacked.

The fighting party came against us, killed some, and made captives of others. Why did not Te Rauparaha and his followers first eat the men, and then go to Kaiapoi? No, the leading men of Ngaitahu were dead already, they went to Kaiapoi to fetch mere pounamus [greenstone meres], and to bring away captive the men of that place. And now Tamaiharanui, Rongotara, and Wakauira, hear of it Te Pehi, Te Pokaitara, Te Aratangata, and others also, are killed at Kaiapoi.

Where are you, all you whites! Hear the proceedings of Rawiri Puaha [Ngatitoa]. He went to the other island to devour men, subsequently he condemns it, and calls it murder, murder! Afterwards the fighting party returned to Kapiti, and dwelt there.

*The skirmish might have ended there, but Te Rauparaha and team convinced a British merchant captain to hide him and his warriors on board a sailing ship due to visit Ngai Tahu – a Maori version of the Trojan Horse.*

*Among those captured on that raid were Hakopa and Tama-i-haranui:*

But Captain Stuart's ship went and brought away Tamaiharanui, who was killed. Well, we the men of that island thought that Tamaiharanui was equal to Te Pehi [ie, the blood price had been paid] they were both chiefs. These tribes, however, did not think so. They persisted in carrying on the war, they proceeded to kill the people of Kaiapoi, Wakaraupo, and Akaroa. But, Governor, do you listen, I am now determined to revenge my dead, and seek a payment for all my lands.

Now, my Friends, it was that my fighting party came to attack the Ngatitoa and Ngatiawa; Waiharakeke and I were defeated. We fought again at Paruparu, we fought another battle at Raumoe. Friends, Governor, do all you whites of this island listen, the men of Ngaitahu put an end to this fighting. Friends, do you all attend to the contents of this paper. Te Rauparaha began hostilities against Ngaitahu; but Ngaitahu put an end to the war: wherefore, I conclude that our lands were not conquered by Ngatitoa, we still have a right to treat about our own lands.

You it was who made a mistake in giving credit to the statement of Rawiri Puaha, when he said these lands were his. No, our lands are our own. Friends, listen to the contents of this paper. I say, this mode of proceeding is wrong, men are treated as if they were land, that is, Rawiri has received the payment, and the owners of the land are treated as if they were land. Alas how utterly wrong is this mode of acting!

For these reasons it is, Governor, that I write this letter to you, that you may understand these ought to be the last payments for our lands. Cease to pay Rawiri Puaha. Rather, attend to the statements contained in this letter, and withhold any further payments for our lands. This is what I have to say to you, Governor Grey, in reference to the mistake you made as to Rawiri Puaha's dishonest claim to lands, in supposing him to be the owner of Kaiapoi, Te Kohai, Waipara, Tahatu, Matanau, Te Hurunui, Pauapirau, Wairau, and Rangatira.

Friend, Governor, I say, that the disposal of these lands rests with us and that the disposal of Kaikoura rests with Whakatau. This is all I have to say to Governor Grey. This is a protest against the dishonest proceedings of the Ngatitoa.

This letter is written by me, by your loving friend, Matiaha Tiramorehu[243]

---

243  Ngai Tahu's Treaty Settlement website claims Matiaha Tiramorehu's 1849 complaint concerned the Crown's failure to give Maori the reserve lands they had promised:
"Ngāi Tahu made its first claim against the Crown for breach of contract in 1849. Matiaha Tiramōrehu petitioned the Crown to have put aside adequate reserves of land for the iwi, as it had agreed to do under the terms of its land purchases from Ngāi Tahu." Readers can judge for themselves whether Matiaha's

*That was 1849. The Government eventually paid Tiramorehu for his land north of Kaiapoi, and attention turned to the 1848 deal where Ngaitahu had been encouraged to sell virtually the rest of the South Island to the Government.*

*Before we turn to that however, let's get a feel for how pakeha viewed the Ngaitahu tribe in Christchurch, in this report of a jubilee celebration prepared by the tribe's Kaiapoi marae in honour of Queen Victoria attaining 50 years on the throne:*

## Long May The Queen Rule Over Us, 1887[244]

The Ngaitahu tribe, of which the Kaiapoi Natives form the remainder, is supposed to be descended from the tribe which, when Abel Tasman with the *Heemskirk* touched on the shores of New Zealand in 1642, attacked one of his boat's crews. Captain Cook, in 1769, when he took possession of the Islands in the name of his Britannic Majesty George the Third, met with some of this historical tribe, but instead of raupo houses, clothing of mats, food of eels, wekas, and kakapo, they have now adopted European houses, clothing, and their articles of food.

This tribe suffered its most serious drawback at the hand of Te Rauparaha in 1827, just ten years before the Queen began her glorious reign. On the arrival of Europeans it was one of the first tribes in the colony to adopt the habits and customs of civilisation, and embraced Christianity. Among the recent leaders of the Ngaitahu there have been several eminent and good men, whose conduct towards the early European settlers from 1850 to the time when the last vestige of the splendid native bush at St. Stephen's was totally removed was most helpful.

For this, among other reasons, it is not to be wondered at that the remaining families of the Ngaitahu should meet with public sympathy, and that the gathering yesterday should have been such a successful one.

The proceedings began by the assembling of all the hapu at the schoolhouse, where a procession was marshalled by Mr George Robinson, who was decorated in a feather mat and with a taiaha of authority. The Rangiora

---

letter to the Governor covered the 'breach of contract' and 'reserves' issues the tribe later claimed it did. See http://ngaitahu.iwi.nz/ngai-tahu/the-settlement/claim-history/
244   Kaiapoi Maori Jubilee, Press, Volume XLIV, Issue 6804, 15 July 1887, Page 3
http://paperspast.natlib.govt.nz/cgi-bin/paperspast?a=d&d=CHP18870715.2.31

brass band led the way. Revs. J. W. Stack, F. R. Inwood, and G. P. Mutu, in their surplices, next the school children, carrying banners and preceded by a large banner inscribed "Long may she reign."

Then came Maori men in costume, headed by Paura Taki, Tare Tehoika, Taituah, Wiremu, Naehira, and Natanahira Waraioutu. After these came Maori women. These were succeeded by European visitors, members of the Maori Football Club, and bicyclists. The procession led the way through an arch inscribed "Wikitoria," and having passed down the village, returned to the school grounds, where an oak tree was planted by the School Committee, the National Anthem being sung and cheers given. A move was then made through the upper part of the village, which had been gaily decorated with flags, and a large triumphal arch erected, surmounted by "God Save the Queen." Arriving at the church Divine service was held.

An address was presented as follows, being drawn up by the Rev. G.P. Mutu, at the request of the Celebration Committee: –

Salutations, – We are very glad to see you here. We have had this demonstration to show our English friends that we too love our Queen, and desire to show our loyalty. Queen Victoria, we feel sure, wishes us well and desires that the statesmen of this colony should do us justice. A word about the feast. It is not our usual mode of living at Kaiapoi, but we thought it would please you all and the young Maoris to return for a day to the haka and Ngeri Paha.

In holding the fete to-day we wish redraw our European friends in closer union to us, and to cement more firmly the ties of friendship. In conclusion we would request the Hon. E. Richardson would kindly convey, to her Majesty the expression of our deep attachment and loyalty to her crown and person, desiring that she may live long to reign over us.

*What is remarkable about the jubilee celebrations is that Ngaitahu paid for the party from its own funds. Even more remarkable, there is no hint of a 'partnership' with the Crown; Ngai Tahu clearly, like virtually every other Maori tribe, saw themselves under the Crown, not co-equal with it.*

*Most remarkable of all, however, is that those sentiments were still being expressed decades after Matiaha Tiramorehu's land claims had been lodged and still remained unresolved. In fact, a list of other compensation claims had arisen as well. Clearly, Ngaitahu still believed in justice.*

*Let's retrace what happened after the initial 1849 complaint.*

*For a start, negotiator James Mackay had been sent by Lands Commissioner Donald Mclean to treat for land purchases on the West Coast – also Ngaitahu territory. You can get some sense of what the government thought would be acceptable – only small areas of reserve would be needed for Maori because they were very few in number.*

*Also note how the issue of the Te Rauparaha conquest was a factor in negotiations here as well:*

## Conquest Rights Disproven, 1906[245]

On our arrival at the Grey [district] we met with a cordially hospitable reception. Before proceeding further, I will state that the Land Purchase Commissioner McLean had no knowledge of the West Coast or the Natives who resided there. His opinion (vide his report on land purchases in the Middle Island) was that there wore about twenty-five Maoris – at any rate, a very small number – and that a moderate payment and a few acres of reserves would be sufficient for their claims.

I was directed to pay £200, and make some small reserves. There were 57 Natives then at the Grey. At the Buller I already knew there were five. In course of inquiries it was ascertained there were Natives at Arahura, Poherua, Mahitahi (since known as Bruce Bay) and Jackson's Bay, the total number being 110 men, women, and children.

We anxiously awaited a supply of provisions from Nelson. The Maoris had very limited cultivations of potatoes, and had only three axes among them to clear bush with. They generously supplied us with potatoes, dried white bait (inanga), preserved wood hens, and eels, when they caught any (scarce in the winter time).

We were delayed for a considerable period at the Grey, and when the Natives finally assembled it was found impossible to complete the purchase. I urged that they had been conquered by a division of Te Rauparaha's' invading army, and had no valid or extensive claim to the land. This was denied, they asserting that Te Aupouri, Niho, and Wiremu Te Kuihua and a fighting party of about 50 men came down the Coast, and the first place they met with any Natives was at Hokitika. They surprised a few of

---

245 First Discoveries Of Gold In N.Z., Ohinemuri Gazette, Volume XVI, Issue 2107, 21 September 1906, Page 2 http://paperspast.natlib.govt.nz/cgi-bin/paperspast?a=d&d=OG19060921.2.12

the Ngaitahu eel fishing and captured them. Among these was the chief Tuhuru, the father of Tarapuhi Te Kahuki. The fighting party refrained from killing any person, and the resident Natives gave Te Aupouri a valuable mere known as Kai Kanohi (the eater of eyes), and a quantity of unmanufactured greenstone as a ransom for their chief, Tuhuru.

I had previously seen the Kai Kanohi mere in the possession of Matenga Te Aupouri at Takaka, and was acquainted with its history. It was stated that the invaders never resided on or cultivated any of the West Coast land. It had therefore to be admitted that according to all Maori custom the conquest was a myth, and there appeared to be no alternative but to treat the purchase as a new transaction, in nowise affected by Te Rauparaha and his army's conquest of territory at Wairau. Pelorus Sound (Te Hoiere), Blind Bay (Mohua), Motueka, Takaka, Aorere, and Te Taitapu (West Coast from West Wanganui to Kahurangi Point, the latter 30 miles south of Cape Farewell, Te Reinga.)

I offered £200 and reserves at the Buller, Grey, and other places occupied by the Natives. They were were willing to accept the cash, but declined to sell any of the area between the Grey and Hokitika Rivers, extending inland from the sea shore to the sources of those and other rivers (Taramakau and Arahura). Having no authority to make any such reserves the question was adjourned until I could report to and receive fresh instructions from the Government.

*In other words, it is clear the Government recognised the "possession is nine tenths of the law" argument that Ngaitahu's West Coast hapu were raising as an argument against Ngatitoa claims. If the government knew that, then there was little moral excuse for not paying Ngaitahu for the land illegally sold by Ngatitoa on the east coast.*

*Mackay was trying to purchase 7.5 million acres (1.5 million hectares) for two hundred quid and 500 acres of reserves for the hundred or so Maori westcoasters. They in turn had wanted reserves of 200,000 acres.*

*Although critics later called the £200 offer equivalent 'to the price of a horse', that certainly wasn't the case. It was the price of a house, or more accurately, two houses back in those days.*

*Sometimes treaty breaches emerged like death by a thousand cuts. Officials and the public alike forgot the promises and began to assume they had rights across all the land, Maori or otherwise:*

## The Title To A River, 1899[246]

A curious complication is said to have arisen in connection with the dredging areas in the Arahura river-bed. When the Ngaitahu tribe of Maoris sold the West Coast lands to the Governrnent, they expressly reserved the Arahura River to themselves and their descendants for ever, and thus it never became public property in the same sense that all the other rivers and streams have done.

If such be the case it never became a portion of the Westland mining district, and the Warden had no power to deal with it in any way. It now becomes an issue whether the Governor has any power to proclaim the Arahura stream for the deposit of sludge and tailings and whether the Maoris, or their legal representatives, cannot prevent the fouling of the stream by mining operations.

The Arahura was held in the greatest regard by the early Maoris; in fact, it was to them almost a sacred river. At its upper reaches was to be found greenstone of the best quality, and the Arahura settlement was a convenient meeting-place at which were bartered birds, fish, and many articles of Maori manufacture for the much-prized greenstone.

*In 1848, Ngaitahu had been 'encouraged' to sell most of the South Island to the Crown. That transaction, recorded only vaguely at the time, lies at the heart of the Ngai Tahu treaty claims.*[247]

The following is a copy of the deed by which the Natives gave up their lands to the Government :

Whakaongo mai e nga iwi katoa. Ko matou ko –

Signed by 36 and one proxy, and by six witnesses. Hear, O all ye people! We, the chiefs and people of Ngaitahu, who have signed our names and marks to this deed on June 12th, in the year of our Lord 1848, consent to surrender for ever to William Wakefield, the agent of the New Zealand Company, established in London – that is to say their directors – our

---

246  The Title To A River, Star, Issue 6534, 11 July 1899, Page 4
http://paperspast.natlib.govt.nz/cgi-bin/paperspast?a=d&d=TS18990711.2.72
247  The Native Land Purchase Commission, Otago Witness , Issue 1434, 17 May 1879, Page 20
http://paperspast.natlib.govt.nz/cgi-bin/paperspast?a=d&d=OW18790517.2.56.3

lands and all our territorial possessions lying along the shores of this sea, commencing at Kaiapoi, at the land sold by Ngatitoa, and at the boundary of Whakatu, and thence on to Otakou, and on till it joins the boundary of the block purchased by Mr Symonds running from this sea to the mountains of Kaihuku, and on till it comes out at the other sea at the Wakatipu Waitai (Milford Haven). But the land is more accurately defined on the plan.

Our places of residence and our cultivations are to be reserved for us and our children after us and it shall be for the Governor hereafter to set apart some portion for us when the land is surveyed by the surveyors; but the greater part of the land is unreservedly given up to the Europeans for ever.

The payment made thus is L2000, to be paid to us in four instalments. Paid to us this day, five hundred, in the next instalment, five hundred; in the next, five hundred; and in the last five hundred – making a total of L2000. And the signing of our names and marks, being the token of our full consent, is done at this place, at Akaroa, on the 12th of June, 1848."

*In fact, the first land sale by Ngai Tahu had occurred at Otago in 1844, and an 1874 news report sets out a clear chronology of exactly what was sold by the tribe in total, and for how much.*

*One thing to pay close attention to in the commentary that follows is the existence of 'tenths'. In Kemp's 1848 purchase deed referenced above, Kemp had noted that some land would be set aside by surveyors for tribal reserves. The deed never specified how much.*

*The New Zealand Company had, in its negotiations with North Island tribes, specifically set aside 'tenths', or essentially one acre of land for every ten sold, to be held as tribal reserves. They did that because the North Island was comparatively heavily populated, supporting more than a hundred thousand Maori. In contrast the South Island had only 1,500 Maori, and there's conflicting evidence over whether the New Zealand Company ever offered 'tenths' to Ngai Tahu – there is no documentary evidence that it ever did.*

*However, that's what Ngai Tahu went on to claim. Some, like the writer of the analysis that follows, accused Ngai Tahu of making up the 'tenths' promise years after selling their land, and only after hearing about the deal the northern iwi had struck.*

# Taiaroa And The Claims Of The Ngaitahu Maoris[248]

There is such a mass of extraneous matter yearly accumulating on this disputed subject that it may be considered expedient and necessary to place the land claims of the Natives in this Island on a clear basis.

Fortunately there is little difficulty in so doing, save that arising from a perusal of the Parliamentary papers published by the Imperial and Colonial Parliaments during the last thirty years. The records are accessible to the students of New Zealand colonisation, and whatever his prepossessions may be previous to the task he sets himself, only one outcome is the possible result of the enquiry he is induced to institute. The Ngaitahu possessed, and ceded at different times, all the country from the Kaikouras, in the Province of Marlborough, to the river Grey on the West Coast.

This includes the whole of the Provinces of Canterbury, Otago, and Westland, save the reserves made for their benefit, which will be more particularly described hereafter. With the payments made to the Ngaitahu we propose at present only dealing, as with the others made to the Ngatiawa, Ngatitoa, Ngatimamoe, and other tribes; Hore Kerei[249], we presume, purposes not to deal, he being the mouth piece and accredited agent only of his own Iwi.

In the order, as per dates, we find the first purchase to have been made of a block of land on the 31st day of July, 1844, by the New Zealand Company, called the Otakau block, which was subsequently handed over to the Otago Association. It was purchased by Captain Symonds, Messrs Tuckett, Clarke, and Scott, for the sum of £2400.

The next purchase of importance is what is called "Kemp's purchase," the deed of sale of which was executed at Akaroa on the 12th of June, 1848, and includes the block of land from Kaiapoi and Port Chalmers on the East Coast and Arahura and Milford Haven, on the West Coast. Two straight lines were drawn across the map of the Island defining the boundaries, which map was attached to the deed of sale, and afterwards published for general information.

It will be important in the investigation of this subject, to keep these

---

248  Taiaroa And The Claims Of The'ngaitahu Maoris, Otago Witness , Issue 1169, 25 April 1874, Page 10 http://paperspast.natlib.govt.nz/cgi-bin/paperspast?a=d&d=OW18740425.2.19

249  Hori Kerei Taiaroa, MP, and son of the Chief Taiaroa who sold the land

two purchases prominently in view, as the Hon. Mr Mantell, on the 25th of September, 1872, deposed "As far as I am aware, the unfulfilled promises are those which affect the Otago block, negotiated by Captain Symonds in 1844, and the Ngaitahu block, purchased by Mr Kemp in 1848."

The Ngaitahu people, for this block purchased by Mr Kemp, received the sum of £2000. There are some interesting facts connected with this purchase. He conducted his negotiations on shipboard. He never defined nor described the amount of land to be reserved for the use of the vendors, and drew down on his head the reproach of Governor Eyre "of making a purchase without making a single reserve, or in any way indicating the number, extent, or situation of the lands to be set apart as reserves; which will I fear cause some difficulty to the Governor and New Zealand Company hereafter."

Previous to Kemp's purchase, the Ngatitoa tribe had overrun and conquered a large portion of land belonging to the Ngaitahu Iwi, the right of the possession of which, by virtue of conquest, they sold to the New Zealand Company. This block extended from Kaiapoi to the Kaikouras. Several years after the purchase, the Ngaitahu denied the right of the Ngatitoa to sell, and their claims to this portion of their estate were finally settled in 1857, by their receiving a further cash payment of £500 while Matiaha Tira Morehu of Moeraki also received the sum of £200 in satisfaction of all his claims to land north of Kaiapoi which amount was paid him by Mr Strode, R.M., Dunedin, the same year.

But all the trouble connected with Mr Kemp's purchase is not included in this brief narrative. A Company called the Nanto Bordelaise had acquired rights or reservations on Banks Peninsula, which were extinguished in December, 1856, by the Ngaitahu people receiving a further cash payment of £200 and 1200 acres of further reserved lands. The end of Mr Kemp's purchase concludes not, however, in this brief manner.

Terapuhi, Hakiha, Taetae, and others of the Ngaitahu people, residing in what is now the Province of Westland, considered that they had not been sufficiently paid for their lands in Poutini, and succeeded in May, 1861, in obtaining a further sum of £300 and about 6000 acres of additional reserves, for the extinction of their title over the piece of country west of the main range of the Island, extending from Milford Haven to the Head waters of the River Taramakau. Their title to this block had nearly all been included in the purchase of 1847.

The history ends not even here. In 1868, the Native Lands Court, sitting at Dunedin, awarded 2094 acres of Crown land in satisfaction of promises made in Kemp's deed and in the year following, about 3000 acres in the Province of Canterbury were also awarded.

On the 17th August, 1853, the deed of sale of the Murihiku block, conveying to Her Majesty "all the southern portion of the Middle Island to the south of Kemp's and Symonds' purchase"[250], excepting certain reserves named in the deed, was executed. The purchase money stipulated for was £2000, although £2600 was actually paid, the receipt for the extra £600 having been attached to the deed.

It must be borne in mind that the New Zealand Company resigned their charter, and ceased their colonising operations, in July 1850, so that all subsequent arrangements are between the Natives and the Colonial Government. With the sales at Port Cooper and Port Levy in 1849, we need not interfere.

To recapitulate. Excluding the purchase of Stewart's Island from consideration, we obtain the following information. The Ngaitahu people received the following sums for the cession of native lands in the Middle Island:

| | |
|---|---|
| July 31st, 1844 | £2400.00 |
| January 12th, 1848 | £2000.00 |
| August 10th, 1849 | £200.00 |
| September 15th, 1849 | £300.00 |
| August 17th, 1853 | £2600.00 |
| February 6th, 1855 | £100.00 |
| December 10th, 1856 | £200.00 |
| February 5th, 1857 | £200.00 |
| December 12th, 1857 | £200.00 |
| March 29th, 1859 | £300.00 |
| January 6th, 1860 | £100.00 |
| May 21st, 1860 | £300.00 |
| February, 1867 | £200.00 |
| **Total** | **£9100.00** |

With the amount of £1800 paid by Captain Wakefield in stores and specie in the year 1844 to the tribe living in the Nelson district, the Ngaitahu people are supposed to have no concern.

---

250  In other words, Southland

The investigation as to the claims of Taiaroa for unfulfilled promises to his tribe, is thus brought down to a narrow and defined basis: Were any promises made by the purchasers of the land remaining still unfulfilled, they can only pertain to the purchases of Messrs Symonds and Kemp. The language in the deed by which the Murihiku was purchased is concise and definite. It says "Those portions of land which have been set apart by Mr Mantell, and surveyed by Mr Kettle, at Tuturau, Omani, One, Aparima, Otaka, Kawakaputahuta, and Oneto, marked 1, 2, 3, 4, 5, 6, 7, are lasting possessions for ourselves and children. The only portions kept for ourselves are these just named. We agree that they shall not be sold without the Governor's consent."

The purchase money was paid, and the reserves indicated were made.

The deed of purchase called "Symonds' Deed," never having been published in the appendices to the House of Representatives, it will be expedient to recite at length. It is as follows:

"Know all men, by this document, that we the Chiefs, and others of the Ngaitahu tribe in New Zealand, who have signed our names beneath this document, acknowledge, on this thirty-first day of July, in the year of our Lord 1844, that we have given up, and absolutely surrendered, to Captain William Wakefield, agent of the New Zealand Company, and chief of its staff of officers, all our pieces of land comprised within the boundaries underwritten.

"The names of the land are Otakou, Kaukarae, Taieri, Mataura, and Kataro. The boundaries are these: The lower boundary proceeds along the coast, crossing the mouth of the river at Otako to Otupa, continuing along the sea coast to Poatiri to Tokata, thence along the summit of the ridge Kuihiteu, crossing the river Mataura, proceeding along the ridge of the Maunga Atua, Wakari and Mihiwaka, and Otuwarorau, and descending to the sea coast at Purehurehu. We also surrender all the islands of Kamaulaurua[251], Kakariri, Okaihe, Moturala, Paparoa, Matoketoke, Hakinikini, and Aonui.

"The following are the pieces of land which we have reserved for ourselves and our children: A piece of land on the seaward of Otakou named Omati, the boundary commencing at Moepuku, crossing over to Poatiri,

---

251 The letter 'L' appears in the originals of these names and reflects Ngai Tahu dialect at the time. A surviving example of the ancient tongue is Lake Waihola

and continuing along the sea coast to Wai Wakaheketeheke, crossing to Moepuku also, piece of land, Tarue, the boundary of which commences at Onumia, running in a straight line to Maitapapa, the Taieri River being another boundary also, another piece of land at the Karoro the Karoro boing the boundary above, and the ocean the outer boundary by the lower line of the native village, being about one mile in length inland. These lands we have reserved for ourselves, and we will neither sell nor lease them to any other persons without the consent of the Governor of New Zealand.

"The payment for all the lands above described is £2400, which we have this day received in the presence of these witnesses Hoani Tutawaiki Taiaroa And 21 others."

"J. J. Symonds, R.M. Frederick Tookett, George Clark, junr. David Scott."

It would be scarcely possible to consider that there could be any doubt as to the meaning of the foregoing deed but, 28 years after the date of its execution, we are told by the Hon. Mr Mantell – "It appears that, at the time of purchase, promises were made to the Natives of reserves to be selected, after the survey of lands, in the proportion defined in the New Zealand Company's scheme viz one section to every ten sections." He further adds "In making these purchases, it was clearly intended that nominally one-tenth, but virtually one-eleventh, was to be reserved for the Natives. I was instructed by the Governor to inform the Natives that the purchase money was not the only or principal consideration for the cession of their land, but that schools would be established for the instruction of themselves and their children, as well as hospitals for the treatment of their sick, besides officers who would be appointed to watch over their interests."

There is one very instructive portion of the Hon. Mr Mantell's evidence. He says "In the year 1848 my official connection with the Ngaitahu commenced." It will thus be seen that personally Mr Mantell could have known nothing as to the promises made to the Ngaitahu in 1844 [the Symonds purchase of Otago]. Until the foregoing evidence was published it was always understood that the New Zealand Company's tenths were reserved only in the Provinces of Taranaki, Wellington, and Nelson nor does there appear any collateral evidence to support the above assertion of Mr Mantell. It further appears that the "New Zealand Company did not even in these three settlements make reserves for Natives in accordance with their original scheme," for although when the Company, in June, 1839, issued proposals in London for the sale of nine-tenths of an area of 110,000 acres, and, finding the lots readily purchased, issued another prospectus in July of the same year, "no mention is made of Native reserves in these second proposals."

Had there been any claims for tenths for Native reserves in any of the land purchases of the Middle Island save in the Province of Nelson, Mr Mackay would not have ignored their existence in his elaborate paper on the origin of the New Zealand Company's 'Tenths' Native Reserves." In 1844 and 1845 there was considerable irritation between the Government and the Directors of the New Zealand Company relative to the existence of these tenths, or elevenths, supposed to be reserved by the Company. Commissioner Spain, in March, 1845, made his final award, and although the block of land bought by the New Zealand Company had been in their possession above nine months, no claims were made either by the Government or the Natives for claims under the purchase of Captain Symonds.

The stipulations under which the [Otago] block was sold were definite, and it appears probable that the claims now made were the result of after-thought, based on a knowledge of the original intention of the New Zealand Company. The Company would scarcely have made verbal promises which it ignored entirely in the deed of purchase, more especially when reservations were hinted at of an analogous character in Kemp's deed of four years later date.

Thus the question of the possession of tenths in the purchase of Captain Symonds rests mainly on the unsupported evidence of the Hon. Mr Mantell, and the fact that the purchase of this block of land was made for the New Zealand Company. What such peculiar evidence can establish will be considered in another issue.

*The first mention of the word "tenths" in any New Zealand newspaper in relation to Ngai Tahu appears in this article from early 1874, which predicts Otago Maori will likely begin to press for 'tenths' before too long. The article discloses earlier discussion that indicates 'tenths' had not previously been discussed or promised. In fact, one can see where the issue of 'tenths' might just have been lost in translation from a promise to provide ten acres per Maori:*

## Taiaroa And The Claims Of The Ngaitahu, 1874[252]

The evidence offered in support of the claims of Taiaroa is of a singular character. At the sitting of the Native Lands Court, in Dunedin, in 1868, the Hon. Mr Mantell stated that in making reserves for the Ngaitahu people the rule he adopted was to allow ten acres to each man, woman, and child but that he would recommend the Court to award fourteen acres per soul. That, acting according to the instructions of Governor Eyre, he "tried to allow as little as the Natives would take. The reserves I then made were for present wants. I left it to be determined at some future time what allowance should be made them. I often told them if they were not satisfied with my reserves they could appeal to the Government."

Four years later he stated, "As regards the first case – the Otakou block – it appears, at the time of purchase, promises were made to the Natives of reserves to be selected, after survey of lands, in the proportion defined in the New Zealand Company's scheme viz., one section to every ten sections. The Committee will see, by referring to Captain Symond's report, that he states, at the request of the principal agent of the New Zealand Company, he abstained from inserting in the deed of cession, any express stipulation with regard to further reserves. Further on, he again asserts "In making these purchases, it was clearly intended that nominally one tenth, but virtually one eleventh, was to be reserved for the Natives."

The Hon. Captain Fraser gave some peculiar evidence also before the Committee. He stated "There was some considerable discussion between the Natives and Colonel Wakefield, about the reserves they wished to have. I think, if I recollect rightly, that it was an ancient burial ground which was insisted on, and ultimately conceded by Colonel Wakefield. Mr Jones also stated that the reserve made for the Maoris by Mr Mantell was much larger than the original reserves insisted on by the Maoris.

In an earlier part of his evidence, he stated he believed "that Mr Strode and myself are the only persons in Otago who are in favour of handing over the original reserves to the Natives." His evidence, it should be remembered, is only the recollection of conversations that took place between him and Mr J. Jones.

---

252  Telegrams, Otago Daily Times , Issue 3802, 24 April 1874, Page 2
http://paperspast.natlib.govt.nz/cgi-bin/paperspast?a=d&cl=search&d=ODT18740424.2.8

The claimant himself says nothing about the reservation of "tenths" in the Otakou block, confining his statement to unfulfilled promises in Kemp's purchase, but hands in as evidence a valedictory statement made by his father on the 13th February, 1862, addressed:

"To all my Tribe, to my hapu, and to my Son: Let me bind these words to your remembrance that they may be impressed on your memory in the future, after I am dead and gone, that you may understand and judge for yourselves respecting the land that I sold to the Europeans. The European land purchasers made certain statements in all purchases of lands.

"Firstly – Be good to my nation, to the Pakeha, for it was I that brought them to this island, to Te Wai Pounamu, in former years. It was I and some other chiefs that went to Port Jackson [Sydney] and arranged a covenant there, in which we placed the whole of the Island of New Zealand under the sovereignty of the Queen, and the covenant was drawn up there, and the Governor of the Colony gave a token of honour, also the Queen's flag, to me and Tuhawaiki. The Governor gave us all authority (mana), and to us was the authority over the whole of our island, Te Wai Pounamu.

"The Queen was also to be our parent (protector), that no other of Her Majesty's subjects, or any Foreign nation, should interfere, or take or sell, or otherwise dispose of our land without our consent given to any other nation. We agreed to those arrangements of the Governor of New South Wales, and that covenant was established. After that was the Treaty of Waitangi, and I and my tribe agreed a second time.

"Secondly - After that land purchase commenced in this island, the first land we sold was Otago; it was sold to Colonel Wakefield. We pointed out all the boundaries, and all the stipulations were mentioned to Colonel Wakefield as follows : – We said 'the first payment for this land would be £100,000'. Colonel Wakefield said, 'That is too much, £2400 will be ample, and that is all the cash consideration; it had better be arranged in this manner, viz., that one acre in every ten shall be reserved for you.' We agreed to this, and said: – 'You can have the land according to these terms.'

"We do not know whether these words were written down or not, but all the people present heard these words.[253] These are the places about

---

253 The evidence from the 1800s suggests this wasn't the case. None of the other Maori present recalled 'tenths' being promised.

which we spoke, and stated that we desired to retain: Otakou, Taieri, Maranuku, Te Karoro, and other places."

The foregoing is the whole of the evidence that has been collected in support of the claims for tenths in the Otakou block. Mr Mantell being absent on the occasion of the purchase, his evidence is almost worthless; Captain Fraser narrates only what he has heard in desultory conversation; living natives present at the negotiation, who were examined in Wellington, fail to recollect anything about the promise of the reservation of the "tenths"; and the claim stands upon the unsupported testimony of Taiaroa the elder alone. His instruction to his people, and the statements it contains, deserve a little attention – for this subject has become so involved that at the present time any person can make almost any statement on the subject with impunity, without fear of contradiction.

His having placed the whole Island under the sovereignty of the Queen, by a covenant with the Governor of New South Wales, is simply nonsense, he not having the power to do so – as the powerful tribes, the Ngatiawa and Ngatitoa, held possession of the northern portion of the Island, and had done so for generations – keeping the lands of the Ngaitahu as a hunting ground, and the people themselves as a "relish" when wanted.

The connection of his tribe with the Treaty of Waitangi may be briefly narrated. On the 13th of June, 1840, Captain John Mas, Commander *H.M.S. Herald*, writes in his diary as follows:

"Arrived off Otago, but so late that we had only time to obtain the signatures of two chiefs who resided near the entrance of the harbour. Taiaroa had gone to Moeraki, I was sorry to hear, and I did not deem it advisable to enter further into the harbour, where I was told a young man, a son of Taiaroa, resides, and whose signature we might otherwise have obtained."

Tuhawaiki had signed it on the 9th, two other natives at Akaroa, and thus ends the connection of the tribe with the treaty. The declaration of sovereignty over the island took place at Cloudy Bay, four days after Taiaroa was sought for at Otago Head.

The Hon. Mr Mantell alludes in his evidence to Captain Symond's report: It would have been more pertinent had he referred to the instructions given him. He was instructed by Governor Fitzroy, on the 27th February, 1844, "to proceed to the Middle Island, and there superintend and assist the agent of the New Zealand Company in effecting the valid purchase of not more than 150,000 acres of available land. To such an extent of land the Crown's right of pre-emption will be waived, upon your report of the validity of the purchase, on certain conditions.

"You will be most careful not to countenance any, even the smallest, encroachment on, or infringement of, existing rights or claims, whether Native or other, unless clearly sanctioned by their legitimate possession You will inform the aboriginal Native population that you are sent to superintend and forward the purchase of lands which they wish to sell; and that you, on behalf of the Government, will not authorise, nor in any way sanction, any proceedings which are not honest, equitable, and in every way irreproachable."

These are the only two clauses in the instructions that at all concern the Naive race. If Mr Symonds had arranged with Captain Wakefield to exclude from the deed the mention of tenths, he was acting contrary to his instructions – a course of proceeding not likely for a moment to be tolerated by Mr Clarke, described by Colonel Wakefield as being the real Governor of New Zealand. At this period of the Colony's history, from causes too lengthy to review, the "tenths" had fallen into confusion, and claims were asserted by the Crown to the possession of all Native lands not actually in possession of the aboriginal population. Thus, on the 26th of March of the same year, when Governor Fitzroy in a proclamation waived the right of pre-emption over over certain portions of land, in condition No. 5, he stipulates "Of all land purchased from the aborigines in consequence of the Crown right of pre-emption being waived, one-tenth part of fair average value, as to position and quality, is to be conveyed by the purchaser to Her Majesty, her heirs and successors, for public purposes, especially the future benefit of the aboriginals."

It will thus be plain that the original scheme of reserving tenths by the Company, for the *sole* use of Natives, was by this authority, over certain portions of New Zealand, declared to have no [further] effect.

In the following month, by a notice published by Major Richmond, it was declared the Governor consented to waive the right of pre-emption on the part of the Crown in favour of the New Zealand Company alone. Mr Symonds started with Mr Daniel Wakefield on his mission on the 21st May, Mr Tuckett having gone from Nelson at an earlier date.

In the first deeds of cession from the Natives to the Company, where "tenths" are reserved, the following clause was inserted: "And the said

William Wakefield, on behalf of the said governors, directors, and shareholders of the New Zealand Land Company, of London, their heirs, ad. and ass., for ever, does hereby covenant, promise, and agree to and with the said chiefs, that a portion of the land ceded by them, equal to one-tenth part of the whole, will be reserved by the said governors, directors, and shareholders of the New Zealand Land Company, their heirs, ad. and ass., and held in trust by them for the future benefit of the said chiefs, their families, and heirs for ever."

In the second, and subsequent deed, instead of the word "tenths" the wording appears thus : – "A portion of the land ceded by them, *suitable and sufficient for the residence and proper maintenance of the said chiefs,*" &c., &c.

In the deed of purchase of the Otakou block neither of the above clauses appear, but the reserves are defined and accurately described. Were there no other evidence to offer in support of the position we have taken, the burden of proof would be on our side. But the testimony of Colonel Wakelield is conclusive. He writes to New Zealand Company from Nelson at length, commencing by stating that the completion of the purchase of the lands selected by Mr Tuckett for the New Edinburgh settlement had been obstructed by the bad understanding between Mr Symonds and the Company's agent.

"Upon my arrival at Otago, I found that Mr Tuckett had left but little to be done beyond completing the purchase of the land, by distributing the payments to the Natives. It remained only to verify the boundaries in the presence of some of the vendors, and of the reserves made by them for themselves and families, in order to prevent as far as possible any future question.

"For this purpose Mr Symonds proposed that we should perambulate the boundaries of the block, or so much of them as would enable us to see the principal natural limits of it. That officer, M. G. Clarke, and I, accordingly commenced our journey for that purpose, on the 18th July, accompanied by six natives, deputed by the assembled natives of the district, to point out the boundaries.

"We returned to Otago on the 26th of July. The day after our return we marked out the Government reserve at Taiaroa Head for a pilot and signal station, also the district reserved by the natives, and not included in the purchase. It embraces about four miles frontage on the eastern side of the harbour, the boundary line running across to the sea to the North of Cape Saunders, and comprises at a rough calculation ten thousand acres of land of various descriptions, well wooded, but broken by ranges of high hills. It contains the residences and cultivations of all the natives of the district of Otago, amounting to not more than forty or fifty souls.

"The deed of conveyance, a copy of which accompanies this, was prepared by Mr Symonds and Mr Clarke. When the natives were assembled at Hoputai from all parts of the coast to the number of fifty men, women, and children, the boundaries of the land to be purchased were explained to them, and time was allowed them to talk the matter over, according to their custom in such transactions, before receiving the payment. They encamped on the spot, waiting the event.

"On the 31st of July Mr Clarke addressed the Natives to the effect that they had now only to receive the payment to complete the transaction for which they had assembled, that they were about to part with the land described in the deed which, he would read to them, with all growing on it or under it – that it would be gone from them and their children for ever – that they must respect the white man's land, and that the white man would not touch that reserved by the natives.

"The deed was then read in Maori, and the Natives agreed to the boundaries and terms mentioned in it. John Tuawaiki then signed it, and was followed by all the other chiefs, and sons, and other owners of land."

In another portion of the letter, Colonel Wakefield says, "the native chiefs, in parting with their unoccupied lands, gave as their motive for so doing, and as an inducement to us to take possession of them, the convictions they labour under, that in a few years they and their tribe will be no more. The affair was concluded during the forenoon without any disagreeable occurrence, and I have never seen any more satisfactory termination of any New Zealand bargain."

Two years later, when the Crown grant was given to the New Zealand Company by Captain Gray, the boundaries of the Native Reserves as cited in the deed of cession were again inserted – no mention being made of any others. Their united area amounts to about 9300 acres. Although taking no active part in the proceedings, Mr Commissioner Spain accompanied Captain Wakefield in his southern journey, and was a spectator of the negotiations. This curtailed account of a purchase of land, connected with which there is such a mass of evidence, all tending in the one direction, will, it is to be hoped, satisfy the minds of all impartial persons, that the promises made in the cession of the Otakou Block have been fully and honourably discharged.

## *Kemp's Purchase*
In the Legislative Council last session, the Hon. Captain Fraser, in a speech containing perhaps more sentiment than fact, drew an affecting portrait of the illtreated Ngaitahu; told the Council that the Hon. Mr Mantell, failing to obtain redress for them in this Colony, carried the complaint of the Maoris to the Colonial Office in England, and failing there, threw up a valuable appointment, so that he would no longer serve under a faithless Government; gave a dissertation on Maori morality, and the wish of the Ngaitahu to preserve their children from contamination by coming into contact with those of European origin and concluded by recommending that a block of 50,000 acres in the Forks of the Hawea and Wanaka should be given them for our "unfullilled promises."

He was seconded ably by Mr Mantell. It is not at all improbable that in another year or two, tenths will also be claimed in this purchase. Taiaroa the elder, in his instructions, states "Mr Kemp said to us that ye should give up all the land, and he would take charge of it; this £2000 was an advance on the land. Mr Kemp said after that Government would make payment and return some land to us. We asked, 'What about our settlements, cultivations, sacred places, fishing grounds, and so forth?' Mr Kemp's answer was, 'The Government will agree to all these requests, your cultivations will not be taken from you'. Mr Kemp also said to us, 'If you do not give up your land, soldiers will be sent to take possession of it', and on that we gave our final consent to the sale."

Prior to the despatch of Mr Kemp to purchase this land, the actual terms of the purchase had been arranged by Sir George Grey with the chiefs of the Ngaitahu. In a despatch to Earl Grey, the Governor says: – "I found upon conversing with the chiefs of the Middle Island, that they all acquiesced in the propriety of an immediate settlement of their claims to land upon the following basis: that the requisite reserves for their present and reasonable future wants should be set apart for themselves and their descendants, and should be registered as reserves for such purposes. The purchase money to be £2000."

This arrangement took place several months previous to Mr Kemp's negotiation. In the deed of cession, the following passage occurs in reference to the reserves spoken of by the Governor: "Our places of residence and our cultivations are to be reserved for us and our children after us and it shall be for the Governor hereafter to set apart some portion for us when the land is surveyed but the greater part is given up to the Europeans for ever."

Writing to W. Gisborne, Esq., from Wellington, June 20, 1848, Mr H. T. Kemp remarks, "In obedience to the Lieutenant-Governor's instructions, their pahs and cultivations have been guaranteed to them as expressed in the deed of title. They are, generally speaking, of small extent. Beyond these I have not felt myself authorised in making any guarantee, and with the consent of the people, have thought it better to leave the subject to be considered and decided on between the Governor and the Company. The Natives clearly admit they have sold the whole of Banks Peninsula to the French Company."

About September, 1848, Mr Mantell appears on the scene to complete the arrangements left unaccomplished by Mr Kemp, which he succeeded in doing by the end of January following.

On the 5th of September he clears that ground before the enquiry. Speaking of some Natives at Akaroa, who wished to repudiate the sale and resist the surveys, he says "I feel that a survey by force, even against one man, or concession to intimidation, would be inconsistent with my duty to Her Majesty's Government."

Proceeding to Kaiapoi to mark out the reserves, he writes, "I have with their almost universal approbation[254], reserved for their use a block containing about 500 acres of bush and 2140 acres of open land, old kumara gardens, and swamps enclosing all their cultivations.

"I have further guaranteed that the site of the ancient pah, Kaiapoi, shall be reserved to Her Majesty's Government, to be held sacred from both Europeans and Natives. I also reserved an ancient pah, 5 acres in extent, on the north bank of the Waimakariri.

"I have in each of these cases left plans with the resident Natives, all the Natives present agreeing to the limits as I described them."

At Te Tamatu, where he was met by Taiaroa and Maopa, he laid out reserves containing 80 acres; at Arowhenua, 376 acres; at Te Umukaka,

---

254 Approval, endorsement and encouragement

187 acres; at Waitemate, 17 acres; at Timaru, 20 acres and on the north bank of the Waitaki, 389 acres.

Before crossing the Canterbury boundary, we will note how he was guided by the principle he laid down of giving 10 acres to each soul. He reserved 3,714 acres of land for the use of 372 Natives. The custom was to take the census before making the surveys.

At Kakanui, he gave to 12 souls, 75 acres; at Moeraki, 600 acres to 87 Natives; at Waikouaiti, 1800 acres to 121 souls; and at Puraukanui, to 45 Natives, 270 acres. The average acreage per soul in this allotment will be found to be the same as across the Waitaki. The only difficulty he experienced was at Waikouaiti, where a dispute arose as to the boundaries of the reserve. The block of 1800 acres then marked off was afterwards increased to 2394 acres – the difference having been referred to His Excellency for decision.

Mr Mantell had, however, promised some Natives who lived 30 miles inland up the Waitaki, that a reserve should be hereafter made them, "which promise was subsequently carried into effect by 138 acres being surveyed for that purpose. Thus, when these two claims were settled, the Native title over the whole of the purchase, excepting Banks Peninsula, was supposed to be extinguished. Including these two reserves, the Natives retained 7090 acres.

Col. Godfrey had awarded 30 000 acres of land on Banks Peninsula to the Nanto Bordelaise Company, which the Government willed should be taken in the neighborhood of Akaroa. The Ngaitahu claimed that they had £5000 still to receive from the Company, but as the occupation by the French was subsequent to Sir George Gipps' proclamation of sovereignty, early in 1840, over New Zealand, the claim of the Company was declared null and Ports Cooper and Levy, being needed for the Canterbury Settlement, were sold, with the adjoining lands, to the New Zealand Company for £500 in 1849, the Natives reserving for their own use 859 acres at Port Cooper, and 1381 acres at Port Levy. The New Zealand Company having purchased the claims of the Nanto Bordelaise, and the title of the aboriginal owners not having been declared to be extinct, they sold for £150 – but were paid £200 – "the remainder of their lands in Banks Peninsula," making further reserves of 1298 acres.

Then the question of "unfulfilled promises" cropped up from the ambiguous wording of the deed of purchase, and for the final extinction of their claims in the Province of Canterbury they were awarded in 1868, by the

Native Lands Court and the Provincial Government, 2844 acres – or, in another form, the Natives in the Province of Canterbury possess 10,076 acres of land to a population of about 400 souls, or at the rate of 25 acres per inhabitant.

In Otago the reserves given by Mr Mantell amounted to 3377 acres in Kemp's purchase, which was supplemented by the Native Lands Court in 1868 granting further reserves amounting to 2094 acres. Including the small remnant of the Ngatimamoe that still survive, with the tribe of which Taiaroa appears to be the recognised head, we find, excluding the few members that live north of the Hurunui among the Ngatiawa, that the Ngaitahu tribe – the total population of which most probably does not exceed 1400 souls – in Westland, Canterbury, Otago, Stewart's Island, and Ruapuke, own 42,250 acres of land, averaging about 30 acres per man, woman, and child; and that they have received in payment for the lands they have sold at different times – excluding the Princes Street Reserve [in Dunedin] the sum of £17,100.

The bald outline of facts we have presented to our readers on this subject will enable them to form their own conclusions as to the justness of the claim H. K. Taiaroa yearly brings before the House of Representatives, and the Hon. Wi Tako Ngatata before the Legislative Council. Very few, even of our leading politicians, have an intimate knowledge of the details we have been at some considerable trouble to collect; while members, who, during the session have to sit at three or four Committees during the morning, have neither leisure nor inclination to wade through the mass of printed evidence, that would alone enable them to form a correct opinion as to the justice or injustice of the claims for compensation.

*It may have been a long article, but it's also an important one. The direct quotes of the men who negotiated the land purchases don't disclose any discussion at the time of one acre for every ten, but they do show reserve planning of ten acres for every Maori.*

*Newspaper articles covering the complaints of Ngaitahu do not begin raising the "tenths" issue until the 1870s, but the only person who claims to have clearly heard any discussion was Ngai Tahu's Otago chief, Taiaroa – no other direct witnesses supported his recollection.*

*The question of what Ngai Tahu were originally promised is important. If you read Ngai Tahu's version of events to the Waitangi Tribunal, they say:*

In 1849 Tiramorehu wrote a petition to Queen Victoria. The petition was signed by all the leading Ngāi Tahu chiefs of the time. They asked that the Crown put aside adequate reserves of land for the iwi, as agreed to under the terms of its land purchases. In the 20 years from 1844, Ngāi Tahu signed land sale contracts with the Crown for some 34.5 million acres, approximately 80% of the South Island, Te Waipounamu. The Crown failed to allocate one-tenth of the land to the iwi, nor did it pay a fair price, as it agreed."[255]

*Now remember, this is from Ngai Tahu's official treaty settlement website. Unfortunately, it is also wrong. Matiaha Tiramorehu did not petition Queen Victoria in 1849. He did write to the Governor, suggesting the reserves were too small, but readers will note there was absolutely no mention of a promise of 'tenths', which one would have expected Ngai Tahu's most articulate chief to have raised if he remembered such a promise a mere one year after the event. Instead, he complains that the Government surveyor had insisted on small reserves during negotiations:*

## Ngai Tahu Letter To Governor Eyre, 1849[256]

MOERAKI, 22ND OCTOBER, 1849: Listen to these my words relative to the part (of land) which was made sacred to yourself and Governor Grey by Mr. Mantell, also to the part which was reserved for the Maoris: The owners of the land are discontented with the portions allotted to them by Mr. Mantell.

You are aware when Mantell first commenced his work in this place, his first mistake was at Kaiapoi, viz., he would not listen to what the owners of the land wished to say to him; they strenuously urged that the part that should be reserved for the Maoris ought to be large, but Mantell paid no attention to their wishes; it was thus he did wrong in the commencement of his work, and continued to do so in all his arrangements in regard to the portions which were reserved for the Maoris.

It is in consequence of this I write to you, my esteemed friend, Governor Eyre: – pay attention. The principal cause of all the disputes in this Island

---

255 http://ngaitahu.iwi.nz/ngai-tahu/ko-au-matiaha-tiramorehu/
256 http://nzetc.victoria.ac.nz//tm/scholarly/tei-Mac01Comp-t1-g1-t6-g1-t10.html

is that of your having given the payment of a part of our Island to the Ngatitoas, it is this which has caused all the disputes amongst the Natives of this Island: – but you, Governor Eyre, are aware of the cause of all the disturbance of that Island, it is the same here, and there will ere long be ruptures among us.

These are my reasons for writing to request of you that the boundaries of Moeraki may be extended, that we may have plenty of land to cultivate wheat and potatoes, also land where our pigs, cattle, and sheep can run at large; it will not be long before we purchase both cattle and sheep, and what land have we now in the small pieces which are reserved by Mantell for us fit for such a purpose; each allotment which Mantell has set aside for the Maoris is about as large as one white man's residence. We are conjecturing who could have given Mantell his instructions so to act; do you, Governor Eyre, think that I should tell him to reserve for the multitude a piece of land only large enough for one man? No; moreover the Natives will never consent to it. There are many people, and but a small quantity of land for them.

I imagined that it was by your instructions that Mantell reserved such small patches for the Maoris. I also remember the conversation that Governor Grey had at Akaroa with the Natives of Port Levy; Ngaituahuriri spoke to the Governor concerning the payment for Kaikoura and Kaiapoi; he (the Governor) told the Ngaitahu Tribe that (the payment for) Kaiapoi should not be given to the Ngatitoas, but that for Kaikoura was already gone to them. Upon which Te Uki said to the Governor, Do not hide from us what you may have wrongly done with our place or country, but tell us that we may all know what you have done. After which conversation Governor Grey asked Ngaituahuriri if he would part with some of his land; upon which the Ngaitahu Tribe hearing, gave their consent that Kaiapoi should be given up to the Governor, relying implicitly on his former promises; but no, it (the payment for Kaiapoi) has been given to the Ngatitoas.

When Mr. Kemp came here, he placed the boundary of the Ngatitoa's land at Kaiapoi; this mistake caused our hearts to be darkened. Since then Mantell arrived here; and on their (the Maoris) seeing the portions which he reserved for them, began to quarrel.

However, I considered at that time that it was for all Ngaitahu to complain; but now, I myself will speak. The white man's transactions are bad, – there are in consequence great disturbances already amongst the Natives of this Island; therefore I earnestly request that some person may be sent here directly to alter all the boundaries, Moeraki included; that there may be a large block reserved for us, is the constant topic of our conversation. Extend the boundaries at Moeraki.

Therefore, let not the white people say it was through any fault of the Maoris that this disturbance has arisen; – no, it was yours; still, should I ever hear anything wrong, I will let you know of it. This is all I have to say.
From
Matiaha Tiramorehu

*Surveyor Walter Mantell was sent Tiramorehu's complaint for comment, and at this point stands by his decision to allocate reserves the way he did:*

Mr. Mantell to the Hon. the Colonial Secretary[257]
Wellington, 24th January, 1850.

Sir, –
I have the honor to acknowledge the receipt this day of your letter of the 24th December, ultimo, enclosing one from Matiaha Tiramorehu, relative to the Moeraki and other reserves, which with its translation I return.

In obedience to your directions, I forward a table showing the proportion between population and land reserved at the places in question. By this you will perceive that the wants of the Natives are amply provided for in the reserves which I made, the boundaries of which, at the time of the survey, were in each case approved by them.
I have, &c.,
Walter Mantell,
Late Commissioner

*Leaving aside the merits of either the Government or Ngai Tahu's claims on whether the reserves were large enough, these documents clearly destroy any suggestion emerging from poor memories three decades later that Ngai Tahu had actually, genuinely been promised reserves totalling 3.4 million acres in return for selling 34 million acres of land to the Crown.*

---

257  Ibid

*This means, of course, that the evidence given to the Waitangi Tribunal and which it upheld, about the so called theft of 3.4 million acres, was utterly wrong, and the use of that to justify a massive treaty settlement in 1998 was also wrong.*

*However, in all fairness, the evidence does suggest Ngai Tahu deserved the settlement it received. The Government, you see, admitted in its own internal correspondence at the time that it had acted dishonourably in the way it purchased the South Island.*

*First, there were allegations the Government had not 'negotiated' a fair price for the land but simply made a 'take it or leave it' offer.*

## At The Royal Commission, 1879[258]

A chief named Tikao objected to accept so small a sum as £2,000, but Mr Kemp said if the Kaiapoi Natives did not accept it the money would be paid over to the Ngatitoa. The deed was then signed, ample reserves being promised. Mr Mantell in the following year renewed these promises, and also promised that schools and hospitals would be provided for the Natives. Matahia Tiramorehu, another chief who signed the deed, gave corroborative evidence, adding that the deed was signed after Mr Kemp had told them that if they did not cede the land he would bring down soldiers to occupy it. None of the promises made as to reserves, schools, and hospitals, had been fulfilled.

*Walter Mantell, you'll recall, had already admitted that part of the deal was to build schools to educate Maori and hospitals to take care of their sick:*

"I was instructed by the Governor to inform the Natives that the purchase money was not the only or principal consideration for the cession of their land, but that schools would be established for the instruction of themselves and their children, as well as hospitals for the treatment of their sick, besides officers who would be appointed to watch over their interests."

In 1864, an internal government report lamented that Ngai Tahu's reserves were not large enough to financially sustain them and that the tribe was lapsing into disarray:

---

258  The Native Land Purchase Commission, Otago Witness , Issue 1434, 17 May 1879, Page 20
http://paperspast.natlib.govt.nz/cgi-bin/paperspast?a=d&d=OW18790517.2.56.3

# A Tribe Taken Advantage Of, 1864[259]

Copy of a report by Mr. T. Clarke, R.M., on the condition of the Natives in the Southern Provinces.
Auckland, September 29th, 1864.

Sir, –

In compliance with that portion of your instructions requiring me to enquire into the condition of the Natives of the Southern Provinces, I have the honour to report shortly the result of my observations and enquiries.

I much regret that it is not in my power to give any very flattering account of the Kaitahu [a variant on Ngaitahu] tribes. I have visited some of their "Kaikas," and conversed with some of their principal men, and I can only say that as a rule they are in a most unsatisfactory condition. Taking them as a people they are the most inert and listless I ever met, whether this arises from the frequent use of ardent spirits – to which the Natives are much addicted – (the law for preventing the supply of spirits to Natives being in these Provinces a dead letter), or to the almost total neglect of their welfare by the Government, I am not prepared to say, perhaps to both. Certain it is, however, there is a very marked contrast in these and the tribes occupying the North Island.

In discussions with those Natives in the Northern Island who have shewn a disposition to question the advantage to themselves of the presence of a large European population, the state of these [southern] Natives has frequently been held up as a proof to the contrary. They have been described as a people contented and happy, living in the midst of plenty and enjoying the benefits of civilization. If Aparima which abuts on the township of Riverton, may be taken as a sample, I am bound in truth to state from the result of my own observation that the very opposite is the case; as a people they are squalid, miserable and ignorant.

It has I think been found in every country where a civilized people has been brought in close contact with an uncivilized, that the latter have always shewn a greater predilection for adopting the evil practices of the dissolute and abandoned, rather than follow the example of the moral and good. These people are no exception to this rule. But when it is

---

259  http://nzetc.victoria.ac.nz//tm/scholarly/tei-Mac02Comp-t1-g1-t9-g1-t2.html

remembered that their earliest association was with the class of Europeans who enjoy an unenviable reputation for recklessness and debauchery, the surprise is that they are not much worse.

Formerly the Wesleyan, and latterly the German Missionaries have done much to check these evil influences and have in many ways benefited these people. But drunkenness is still of frequent occurrence, and to this, perhaps, amongst other causes may be attributed the great mortality which has taken place within the last 13 years. It is a melancholy fact that the aboriginal race is fast disappearing from these Provinces.

No schools exist in these Provinces; the Wesleyan and Maori Missionary Society of Otago have suspended operations, and the German Missionary Society is, from lack of means, relaxing its efforts, and now a strong appeal is made to the Government to step in and succour this small remnant of a once numerous and powerful tribe.

Some of their chiefs are fully alive to their wretched condition. They scruple not to lay the whole blame on the Government. I refer to the alleged promises made by the Government through their agents at the cession of the lands in these Provinces to which I shall do myself the honour particularly to draw your attention in another letter.

The question may suggest itself, if these chiefs are sincere in their regrets at their present low state, how is it that they have not exerted themselves to raise their people from their degraded condition? They answer that they have placed full reliance upon the Government giving full effect to its engagements; that the Government promised to undertake the task of ameliorating their condition, as part of the consideration for their lands; that, after waiting in vain for these benefits, they concluded in their own minds that Government had forgotten them.

They then wrote to the Governor, asking him to send a Pakeha to watch over their interests, and to advise them; no Pakeha ever was sent. They have asked for schools for their children; none have ever been established. Despairing of any assistance from the Government, they have, at the instance of the Rev. R. F. Reimenschneider (a German Missionary) built a church, and are erecting a school-house at their own expense.

The Government have assisted in building school-houses at Moeraki and Waikouaiti, and have very lately paid two-thirds of the price for the erection of a church and school-house at Riverton, but further than this, I am not aware that anything has been done.

A number of gentlemen in Dunedin, sensible of the neglected state of the Natives and anxious to improve their condition, formed themselves into a Society for that purpose; but their benevolent intentions on behalf of the Natives have, from a combination of difficulties, been frustrated, and not the least of these difficulties was the want of pecuniary means. Their applications to the public have been either coldly met or wholly unreciprocated.

The agents for this Society have been told that the Natives hold large reserves, which are, for the most part, lying waste (the Natives occupying only small portions) which if let would bring in ample means. Upon this ground assistance has been refused. The fact that the Natives cannot deal with their own reserves does not appear to have occurred to these objectors.

The application of this Society to the General Government has, practically, shared the same fate. The consequence is that the operations of the Society have been suspended.

Another grievance is that the Natives are, practically, excluded from our Courts from the want of a person to lay their causes of complaint intelligibly before the Magistrate.

Another cause of grievance (in my opinion a very reasonable one) is the want of an officer whose duty it should be to advise and watch over Native interests.

It will, perhaps, be expected of me that, as I have been making myself acquainted with some of the principal evils under which these Katimamoe and Kaitahu tribes are laboring, I should point out what, in my opinion, is the best mode of remedying, or at least mitigating those evils.

I should, first of all, remark that I would not for one moment advocate a system having a tendency to spoil the Natives, making them simple dependents on the bounty of the Government. All that I would ask of the Government is to fulfil their first arrangements, and carry them out in their full integrity. Put within the reach of the Natives the means of raising them from their present low condition, let their desire for knowledge be satisfied, and let them see that we are anxious to discharge our moral obligations, and give practical proof of the desire so often sounded in their ears – that of considering them as one people with ourselves.

- Firstly. I would suggest that an officer be appointed, with as little delay as possible, whose individual duty it shall be to look after the interests of Natives residing in the Provinces of Otago and Southland, also

to hold the appointment of Commissioner of Native Reserves. It is impossible for the present Assistant Native Secretaries, from the nature of their other duties, to give the Natives that attention they require.
- Secondly. I would suggest the appointment of properly qualified persons, who have a good general knowledge of the language, to be permanently attached to the Resident Magistrates' Courts, to be officers of those Courts. Two interpreters would, I think, be sufficient – one for Dunedin and Port Chalmers, and the other for Invercargill and the Bluff.
- Thirdly. That Medical men be appointed to attend upon the Native sick. The services of three medical men would be required – one for Moeraki, Waitaki and Waikouaiti, one for Purakaunui, Otakou and Taiari, and one for the different places in the Southland Province.
- Fourthly. That schools be established and schoolmasters appointed at the following places: – Moeraki, Waikouaiti, Otakou Heads, Ruapuke, and Aparima. In these schools the English language should be taught, and to be open to half-castes and Maoris alike.
- Fifthly. With regard to the Native reserves, I would suggest that the Natives be induced to hand over all those portions which they do not require for their own use into the hands of the Commissioner of Native Reserves, to be dealt with by him for the benefit of the Native owners. I feel sure that a good income would be realized, which, if judiciously dispensed, would greatly benefit the Natives.

I would in conclusion earnestly beg the Government to lose no time in giving effect to these suggestions, or to any other which they may think fit to adopt, whereby these people may be benefited.

I have, &c.,

H. T. Clarke.

The Honorable the Colonial Secretary Native Department

*There were many documents and reports into Ngai Tahu's perilous state over the ensuing century, nearly all recording that the tribe had been unfairly treated and recommending compensation that the government promised but never delivered. Although admittedly the false claims about the 'stolen' 3.4 million acres of 'promised' tenths had woven themselves irreversibly into media and official coverage, even that error does not negate the basics. The $170 million*

*Waitangi settlement has re-energised the tribe, and arguably fairly reflects the contribution Ngai Tahu's land deals made to the future of New Zealand as a whole.*

*As the tribe themselves noted repeatedly, they were loyal New Zealanders despite their unresolved disappointments over the land transactions.*

Chapter 19

# The Cultural Impact Of Mr Selfridge

*Recently the subject of a TV drama series a century after its establishment, the cultural influence of the British department store Selfridges had a larger impact on emerging New Zealand business life than might at first be assumed.*

*Not only did the opening of Selfridges attract headlines in London – the colonies were equally excited, with newspapers New Zealand-wide printing the good news:*

## Selfridge's, 1909[260]

Oxford Street, London, between Bond Street and Marble Arch.

Twelve months ago this building was not begun. To-day it stands complete; a world's record in swift construction; a splendid testimony to the capability of British labour; a monument in steel and stone to the power of will.

In that main artery of London traffic, Oxford Street, and in the heart of the shopping district, the great building conspicuously occupies an acre of land, while the floorage made available for selling purposes by such an ample site is six acres in extent – an area equal to all the street-level floors of Regent Street from end to end.

---

260  Selfridge's, Grey River Argus, 3 April 1909, Page 4
http://paperspast.natlib.govt.nz/cgi-bin/paperspast?a=d&d=GRA19090403.2.30

The building is a modern fireproof structure of steel and Portland stone. It rests upon foundation walls which, 70 feet below the surface, are 27 feet thick. Its floors of ferro-concrete are eight in number, five above and three below the level of the street. Nine passenger lifts and five separate fireproof stairways connect the floors, and everything that thought, experience, and skill can devise for the comfort, convenience, and safety of the people is an accomplished fact at "Selfridge's."

A hundred different departments are here established, and in general merchandise, in all that Men, Women, and Children wear, and in almost everything that enters into the affairs of daily life (excepting provisions, wines, etc), Messrs Selfridge and Co will aim to have and hold first rank in public favour.

The spacious Reception Rooms welcome all visitors; the Library and Silence Room give restful seclusion; a "First-Aid" ward, fully equipped with a trained nurse in attendance, provides for any indisposition or mishap; the "Bureau de Change" negotiates letters of Credit, etc; Colonial Rooms with registers for visitors will be appreciated by friends from overseas.

The Bureau of Information, the Railway, Steamship, and Theatre Booking Offices, and Parcel and Cloak Check Desks, are one and all conveniences open to everyone, with gratuities neither expected nor allowed.

The General Post Office has established here a Post, Telegraph, Savings Bank, and Money Order Office, a boon that will be valued. The Luncheon Hall is finely appointed, and will have an excellent Cuisine. Adjoining is the pretty Tea-Garden open to the sky, and a luxurious smoking lounge for gentlemen.

The telegraphic address is "Selfridge, London" the Selfridge telephone number is "Gerrard One" and there is telephonic communication between every counter and any part of the British Isles.

In every sense of the word, "Selfridge's" is complete. It is the pleasant resort, as well as the most convenient shopping place in Great Britain. And you are invited to make it you rendezvous whenever you are in London.

*Harry Gordon Selfridge, the brash American figurehead of the eponymous store, was soon capturing headlines of his own in New Zealand as even the tiniest provincial newspapers followed his exploits. He was, for example, one of the first to fly business class:*

## Selfridge Flies To Business Meeting, 1919[261]

LONDON, JUNE 28: Captain Gatherwood, who recently won the aerial Derby, piloted Mr Gordon Selfridge, founder and head of the great firm of Selfridge and Co., from London to Dublin and back in 6 hours 40 minutes.

The distance is 700 miles, and Mr Selfridge, who wanted to transact urgent business, explained that he made the long journey in perfect comfort. If he had gone in the ordinary way by train and steamer it would have taken him 20 hours.

The achievement, Mr Selfridge says, gives a hint to hurried business men of the advantages to be derived from the further development of aeroplanes in the immediate future.

## Selfridge On Advertising During Hard Times, 1918[262]

The "Chicago Tribune" recently published – as a cable message from Charles N. Wheeler, London correspondent – a remarkable interview on advertising with Mr Harry Gordon Selfridge, proprietor of an American-plan department store in London.

The interview includes the following statements:

"The day after war was declared I increased our advertising space. From that day I have been buying all the advertising space available.

"I would do more advertising today if I could get the space. We are limited only by the limitations of our newspapers. We are taking, right now, every inch they will give us and at rates that would make us in the States turn somersaults and fall over backwards.

"The first four months of this year have been the biggest four months in our history. Now more than at any other time it is necessary to push the display advertising."

---

261 'Plane In' Business: Mr Selfridge's Trial, Poverty Bay Herald, Volume XLVI, Issue 14963, 16 July 1919, Page 6
http://paperspast.natlib.govt.nz/cgi-bin/paperspast?a=d&d=PBH19190716.2.62.18
262 Selfridge Is Buying All Space Available, Ashburton Guardian, Volume XXXIX, Issue 9467, 3 December 1918, Page 8
http://paperspast.natlib.govt.nz/cgi-bin/paperspast?a=d&d=AG19181203.2.34

# How Smart Advertising Pays, 1913[263]

## *The Case Of Selfridge's*

Clever advertising pays. Every business man will tell you this, but not all of them put the precept into practice. If they did they would be richer, their turnover would be greater, and the public would probably be getting a better article at a cheaper price.

Selfridge's have surprised London last month by announcing a net profit on the year of £104,000. It is not an enormous amount, seeing that £800,000 is invested in their business, but it is extraordinary when it is remembered that Selfridge's have only been four years in London.

They broke all the canons of shop-keeping on the outset of their career by building their giant emporium far away from the ordinary avenues of shop-keeping trade, and then by brainy advertising they drew the public to their doors, till there is no institution in London at the present moment which is better known than Selfridge's.

What they have accomplished in four years is un-exampled in this city (says the *Sydney Sun's* London correspondent), and suggests untold possibilities in the immediate future. But had Selfridge's built the biggest dry goods palace in London, and fitted it with the best selection of goods in the world at the most moderate prices, they would have had very few customers if they had not legitimately exploited every avenue of smart advertisement.

Other firms have found the wisdom of following their example. The other day, Waring's, one of the biggest furniture department stores in the world, changed hands with a stock of something like half a million pounds on its books. The new company, determined to rid themselves of most of this, opened an advertising campaign. They paid a man skilled in catching the public eye £500 for the skeleton of a scheme of advertising that would appeal to all sections of the public.

Their shop was crowded and besieged by thousands of purchasers for a month on end. When the sale was finished they had cleared far more than the most sanguine amongst them had anticipated. Of course, they could not have done it had the furniture they offered not been up to the

---

263   How Smart Advertising Pays, Marlborough Express, Volume XLVII, Issue 96, 24 April 1913, Page 2
http://paperspast.natlib.govt.nz/cgi-bin/paperspast?a=d&d=MEX19130424.2.9

standard which they stated, but given fair value the public can, by judicious advertising, be always relied upon for generous support in this or in every other city.

## Business Life: The Modern Shop Girl, 1911[264]

Brains are not the secret of success. The secret of success is personality, declares Mr. James de Conlay, in the January *London Magazine*, in an article chiefly dealing with the shop girl.

To millions of people, he says, "the shop girl is simply a human automaton, who passes things over the counter and wishes them 'Good-day'," and then he shows how wrongly people judge and what an important creature "(and in some cases what an ideal creature) the shop girl really is. Mr de Conlay has an amusing way of putting things.

Because the counters of the London shops are a certain standard height, the shop girl must be neither short nor tall. She has to be what may be conveniently termed "stock size."

It may be imagined, he says, that provided a girl has a fair appearance and an average stock of brains she can be dumped behind a counter and told to serve either ribbons, laces or underwear, but that is a vast mistake, for there is no business in the world so highly specialised as the drapery houses of London, which represent not so much a trade as a profession.

This he attributes largely to the influence of America and the new ideas introduced into London by Mr. Selfridge. Notably, for the first time in their lives English people were permitted to walk about a shop without being pestered to buy something. The secret, however, why Selfridge's is "somehow different" from other places, lies, he says, not in the shop itself, but in the people who serve in it. They are chosen for their personalities.

Incidentally he gives a staggering list of what is required of the modern shop girl: She has to meet a myriad requirements even down to her teeth. "It is held that a person who is slovenly with her teeth, will be slovenly in business, and modern business has no-use for slovens."

---

264   Business Life, New Zealand Herald, Volume XLVIII, Issue 14623, 8 March 1911, Page 10
http://paperspast.natlib.govt.nz/cgi-bin/paperspast?a=d&d=NZH19110308.2.115

## University Qualifications Useless In Business, 1913[265]

Times-Sydney Sun Special Cable. London, September 22. The proposed college where superfluous girls can be fitted for occupation in business does not find general favour. Among the opponents of the scheme are Sir Thomas Lipton, Sir Joseph Lyons (chairman of Messrs. J. Lyons and Co., Ltd.), Sir T. R. Dewar (managing director of Messrs. John Dewar and Sons), and Mr. H. Selfridge (of Selfridge's stores, London).

Sir T. Lipton says the ordinary educated girl is more likely to be contented in business than the college girl. His experience was that few college men were successful in business, and the same applied to women. Sir Joseph Lyons considers that positions are rarely found in business for college girls without displacing men. He thinks the outlook suggests a grim sex war.

## The World's Policemen, 1916[266]

*Mr. Selfridge's Plea For A Closer Union With The U.S.*
An eloquent plea for a closer union between the United States and Great Britain is made by Mr Gordon Selfridge (of London) in an interview with Mr Edward Marshall which appears in the American newspapers.

"With all my heart," says Mr Selfridge, "I want a fuller understanding, closer sympathies, and governmental co-operation between America and England. I want my country to learn much from England – first of all, frankness, then calmness, honesty of underlying purpose, and unalterable determination. I want to see these two great English-speaking nations joined in bonds of union. It would be to our good, England's good, and the good of the whole world.

"We are the two great peace-lovers among the nations. We could make ourselves so strong and so representative of right that by our worthy influence, and if that were not effective, by our irresistible power, we could dominate the world, compelling decency, decorum, and progress.

"We have been the world's policemen. We should be big enough and

---

265  Women In Business, New Zealand Herald, Volume L, Issue 15414, 24 September 1913, Page 9
http://paperspast.natlib.govt.nz/cgi-bin/paperspast?a=d&d=NZH19130924.2.40
266  The World's Policemen, Feilding Star, Volume XII, Issue 2998, 21 July 1916, Page 2
http://paperspast.natlib.govt.nz/cgi-bin/paperspast?a=d&d=FS19160721.2.13

strong enough and clever enough, if we only joined hands for the purpose, to keep the world in a progressive tranquility such as it has never enjoyed. I believe the thought is far from Utopian indeed, I think it might and will be realised."

## Selfridge Opines On Car Ownership, 1927[267]

The dictum of an English County Court Judge that nobody is justified in owing a motor-car with a salary or income below £1500 has aroused a sharp controversy.

Mr. Gordon Selfridge, the well-known merchant, expresses the opinion that a careful man with £500 a year can safely invest in a motor-car. Sir Josiah Stamp, president of executive of the London, Midland, and Scottish Railway, says that it should be possible for a man with £600 or £700 to run a car, but below this other claims on income ought to come first.

The Automobile Association says thousands of its members do not earn £500 annually. A second-hand car can be purchased for £50, and a man and his family can get an astonishing amount of pleasure for 40s a week. There are two hundred omnibus drivers in London alone who own motorcars. They say they have given up paying doctors' bills and spend the money in running cars.

## Miss Sherlock Holmes: Female Head Of Selfridge's Secret Police, 1913[268]

Many telegrams were received by Mr H. Gordon Selfridge recently congratulating him on the successful result of the shop-lifting case in the courts.

One of the first came from Mr Richard Burbidge, of Harrod's. There are few problems which confront the large storekeeper more difficult than the problem of the shop thief, for it is necessary for retail firms not only to have a watch kept on their own property, but also to see that their customers are protected from pick-pockets.

---

267 How Much A Year? Evening Post, Volume CIV, Issue 68, 17 September 1927, Page 9
http://paperspast.natlib.govt.nz/cgi-bin/paperspast?a=d&d=EP19270917.2.29
268 Miss Sherlock Holmes, Northern Advocate, 1 May 1913, Page 3
http://paperspast.natlib.govt.nz/cgi-bin/paperspast?a=d&d=NA19130501.2.6

Every large store has its detective department, thoroughly organised, working in such a way that mistakes are never made. It is not an offensive but a defensive department – the aim of the storekeeper is not to arrest but to prevent shop-lifters coming to his shop.

"I am, of course, glad," said Mr Selfridge to an "Express" representative, "that the public understand how vital it is that their interests and ours should be guarded. I look to the cooperation of every shopper to help us in our difficult and delicate task of eliminating these parasites who prey on society."

A large department store is like the principal shopping thoroughfare of an important suburb. You would never leave it unpoliced. The only difference is that the ratepayers pay to be protected against thieves, while the large shopkeeper has to bear the cost of his own police system.

## *Guests Of The House*

It must not be thought that every customer that goes into a large store is watched by secret eyes, and followed from floor to floor. The average shopper is easily recognised. Nothing is likely to disturb the serenity and pleasure of her shopping. Nevertheless, among the vast crowd of innocent shoppers, people of dishonest intent come and go, just as they do in every crowded street of London.

Few people, for instance, have the sensation of being watched walk down Regent Street or Bond Street, yet plain-clothes policemen and detectives are there every day on the look-out for any one whose movements appear suspicious.

"Those who come to our store," Mr Selfridge said, "are, in a sense, guests of our house. We must place detectives here and there to see that they are not preyed upon, and if occasionally one who is equivalent to an uninvited guest slips in, and tries to rob us, we must act accordingly.

"The reputation of a great house depends on honesty. We should be bad citizens of a civilised State did we not strive to the best of our ability to assist the State in bringing dishonest people to heel, even though it cost us the expenditure of much time and money, and the risk of misunderstanding by some people.

"Come down and see our secret service department. Here is the room where the manager keeps a black list of every known shop-lifter. It is a black book with two photographs, full-face and profile, of each of these particular criminals. A record is written against each photograph.

"These women come in all sorts of disguises," an "Express" representative was told; "but their faces are known to our secret service staff."

## Chief Lady Detective

Then Mr Selfridge pressed a button and asked for Miss X. Presently a neatly dressed, business-like woman came into the room. She wore a large black hat with an ostrich feather curling above the brim; a black veil did not conceal the keen, steady blue eyes and the strong chin of an altogether dominant face for a woman. Her costume was a well-fitting suit of blue serge. She carried a black bag in her hand. She looked an ordinary unassuming shopper of the middle-class type. There was nothing in her appearance to attract special attention.

She is the head of the Selfridge secret service. She sat down, and as one looked at her she gave the impression of a woman of absolute capability and self assurance. If Sir Arthur Conan Doyle had wanted a type for a feminine Sherlock Holmes he could have taken her face, that held resolution and knowledge behind its pleasant smile.

"How do I work?" she said. "Well, I don't think anybody need be afraid that I don't know my business. I have been a detective for twenty-one years. I was on railway service for quite a long time, and then I have acted for a famous firm of solicitors.

"You see me to-day in this dress, wandering about the shop, but tomorrow I may pass you by and even speak to you without your guessing my identity. I change my disguises according to the class of shop thief I want to catch, for, of course, I know nearly all the regular ones.

"One day I am a fashionable lady; another day an old woman; a third day I may be a foreigner; and once I was a man. My hair is sometimes black, sometimes brown, and at other times golden. I have studied the art of disguising not only my face and figure, but my voice."

## Four Classes Of Thieves

"The average customer does not bother me at all. I can tell at a glance when my services will be required. You may roughly divide shop-thieves into four classes: The professional shop-lifter. The woman who has a mania for stealing, though she can pay for the things. The woman who yields to a sudden impulse. The poor woman who steals for the first time out of necessity.

The third class is the most difficult to detect, and the most readily forgiven. She did not come in with intent to steal. A rich piece of brocade, or a lace handkerchief, is before her, and some impulse urges her to take it. Many such women have been known to come back, confess their theft, and beg for forgiveness.

With the professional shop-lifter it is a game of 'catch-me-if-you-can.' Just as the burglar goes on with his risky profession, although he knows he is a marked man if caught, so the professional shop-lifter comes out marauding, ready to risk another term of imprisonment if she is caught.

"I can easily tell when any one acts in a markedly suspicious manner. The first thing a thief does is to look about, left and right, to see that she is not being watched; or she resorts to the hundred and one known tricks with muff and reticule.

"The professional shop-lifter of the lower class is not an easy person to arrest. I have even known them to carry scissors to stab the arm with or pepper to throw in the eyes. Of course, I keep a look-out on male pickpockets in the interests of the customers, and I never forget a face."

## Chapter 20

# Call Of The Wild

*Few things send tingles up the back of the spine as much as the thought of being stalked by a beast of prey. In New Zealand in the 21st century, such things don't happen – if you leave aside the ongoing reports of big cats in the South Island high country.*

*However, go back a century ago and the world was still industrialising. The lines between civilisation and the wild were blurred, and travelling circuses packed to the rafters with leopards, lions, tigers, bears and elephants blurred those lines even more.*

*You will quickly discover a number of very good reasons why dangerous animals are no longer subjected to the ignominy of becoming circus animals.*

*You couldn't turn a newspaper page, somewhere in New Zealand, without weekly discovering some new report about some unfortunate coming face to face with a fanged executioner, usually overseas but sometimes in New Zealand.*

*Please remember, these events took place a long, long time ago. You are reading reportage from a different era, with different values (which is probably the point that makes this book different). All involved, animal and human, have passed away decades ago. This is an insight into the way things were, not the way things are. In many cases, it is also a paean to human foolishness:*

## Leopard On The Loose In Central Auckland, 1925[269]

Escapes of wild animals from a Zoo possess a thrill which can never be equalled by escapes of prisoners from gaol or dangerous lunatics from custody. Probably the danger is considerably exaggerated, but it is the danger of an unknown quantity.

The female leopard which escaped from the Auckland Zoo three days ago, has aroused an interest in the whole of the Western Springs district and the combined efforts of hunters and beaters have failed to locate the animal. There have been similar exciting escapes from zoos and menageries before, and they have generally had a tame ending.

The lion which escaped from another Auckland Zoo was eventually bailed up in a paddock by a cow, thus providing an inglorious ending to its dash for freedom and casting a slur on the proverbial reputation of a lion for bravery.

It may be that some of our noted big-game hunters will yet have to be requisitioned to track the beast to its lair. Has a certain member of the Bench been consulted? Already a domestic cat which does not usually stay away from home has disappeared, and fears have been expressed that it may have fallen a victim to the leopard's hunger.

Many males, not quite so unaccustomed to absences from home, and often at a loss for a satisfactory, if untruthful, explanation, will now be able to say that they have been hunting the elusive leopard. Baited traps have been set in likely spots and every device known to man has been used to capture the escaped animal.

Meanwhile parents fear for their children, and children fear for their domestic pets, so that the capture of the leopard would be a real relief, and it is to be hoped that the vigorous efforts now being made will result in this wandering female being brought back safely to the respectable paths of zoo domesticity.

*The leopard was on the run in Auckland city for a month, presumably living on food scraps and the occasional pet. At one point police thought they had the animal bailed up in bush at Western Springs, but when they sent a police*

---

269  An Elusive Leopard, Auckland Star, Volume LVI, Issue 222, 19 September 1925, Page 8
http://paperspast.natlib.govt.nz/cgi-bin/paperspast?a=d&cl=search&d=AS19250919.2.22

tracking dog in to find it the dog never returned. Police decided discretion was the better part of valour.

Finally, in mid-October, the big cat turned up, miles away from the zoo, having managed to elude searchers for weeks.

## An Inglorious End: Leopard Found In Harbour, 1925[270]

### *Floating In The Tamaki, No Clue To Mystery*

The body of the leopard which escaped from the Auckland Zoo twenty-five days ago, was found floating in the Tamaki River yesterday afternoon. This is the inglorious end to an escapade which ruffled the whole community, and the fact that the appearance of the animal gives no clue to how its end was brought about only deepens the mystery, which has enshrouded its liberty.

The ordinary symptoms of drowning were absent from the body, which a fishing party, Messrs. M. and E. Goldsboro, R. Smith and S. Wrathall espied in Karaka Bay, round the point from St. Helier's, and later brought to the shore.

The intrepid hunters who scoured the countryside in the neighbourhood of the Zoo with clubs and such weapons will probably have a qualm when they realise from our photograph the proportions of the animal which they endeavoured so confidently to capture. It had been described as resembling a large cat, but though there is a point of likeness in the sleek, lines of the animal, a much more apt comparison is to say that it has a cat's head and a setter's body. Its length from head to tail-tip was 6ft 2ins.

The search for the animal had a serious and an equally diverting aspect, but it is quite apparent that had any of the clubmen brought it to bay, in the excitable days following its escape, they would have realised the temerity of their action.

But now it is all over. Hundreds of people have seen the dead body and have realised that the days of practical joking as to its capture are over. It took quite a lot of persistence on the part of the finders to convince the police and the Zoo authorities that this, the first, and let one hope the last, leopard to roam the city, was actually mort, and that the need of beaters,

---

270  An Inglorious End, Auckland Star, Volume LVI, Issue 241, 12 October 1925, Page 10
http://paperspast.natlib.govt.nz/cgi-bin/paperspast?a=d&cl=search&d=AS19251012.2.112

cages, traps and other subterfuges of the keepers, no longer existed.

The residents of St. Helier's, however, appreciated the fact that the authorities did not come post-haste to recover the body, and even before the animal, limp and lifeless in the fishing party's boat, had been brought to the shore, the news of the catch had spread. An excited crowd cheered as it was brought ashore and then a regular pilgrimage set in to the back of a local store, its temporary vault.

To aid those who really wish to convince themselves (let it be hoped they will refrain from forcing their views through the Press), it may be stated that the body showed no signs of decomposition, nor were there any marks on it, and it was evident that its immersion had been a short one. Just how it got down to the Tamaki is the nicest point of the mystery, but it apparently walked farther than it floated.

## Cow Kills Panther, 1939[271]

A remarkable story of how a cow killed a full-grown panther comes from Gudalur, in the Nilgiri Hills, and is vouched for by local huntsmen. The cow and its calf were tethered outside a house at night. One morning a dead panther was found nearby, gored through the heart, and the cow's horns were covered with blood.

## Natives Fight Enraged Panther, 1929[272]

A gruelling fight between a panther and four Mahratta wrestlers is reported from the Poona district, writes an Anglo-Indian correspondent to the "Daily Chronicle".

Passing through some fields the wrestlers unwittingly disturbed a panther with a cub. The mother sprang at one man and began to maul him. Another wrestler seized the animal round the middle and swung it round. It bit one of his hands to pulp, and tore the muscles of both arms.

A third wrestler, who had a small axe, ran up and struck the panther on

---

271  Cow And Panther, Evening Post, Volume CXXVII, Issue 22, 27 January 1939, Page 11
http://paperspast.natlib.govt.nz/cgi-bin/paperspast?a=d&d=EP19390127.2.137
272  Natives Fight Enraged Panther, Evening Post, Volume CVII, Issue 130, 6 June 1929, Page 14
http://paperspast.natlib.govt.nz/cgi-bin/paperspast?a=d&d=EP19290606.2.141

the middle of the back, inflicting a severe wound, but the brute retorted by tearing the villager's chest open and inflicting other injuries.

Seizing the axe, the fourth man split open the panther's skull, but not before a stroke from the animal's claws had ripped off part of his scalp. One of the four wounded wrestlers has died.

## Five Lions Escape, Panic In Theatre, 1914[273]

NEW YORK, DEC. 17. Five lions escaped from the Eighty-sixth Street Theatre during a performance. The audience fled in a panic.

The police opened a revolver fusillade amid the crowd, killing one lion and wounding a policeman seriously. The lions then attacked the police, clawing several badly. The lions fled to different parts of the building.

One lion escaped into the street, and knocked down a photographer named Tooman who was running from another lion which was inside his photographic gallery, which is over the theatre. Finally all the lions were rounded up and shot.

## Tiger Attacks N.S.W. Teacher, 1903[274]

SYDNEY, FEBRUARY 24. An animal supposed to be a tiger attacked a teacher who was riding through the bush near Marulan, injuring him and his horse.

## Menagerie Breaks Loose In NSW: Lion In A Hen-House, 1910[275]

SYDNEY, JULY 8. While a performance of Wirth's Circus was in progress at Murrurundi a lion, two lionesses, and two wolves escaped.

The wolves and a lioness were captured before they had got clear of the circus grounds, but not before the lioness had attacked and injured a

---

273 Five Lions Escape, Timaru Herald, Volume CI, Issue 15534, 19 December 1914, Page 10
http://paperspast.natlib.govt.nz/cgi-bin/paperspast?a=d&d=THD19141219.2.47
274 Tiger Attacks N.S.W. Teacher, Wanganui Herald, Volume XXXVII, Issue 10882, 24 February 1903, Page 5
http://paperspast.natlib.govt.nz/cgi-bin/paperspast?a=d&cl=search&d=WH19030224.2.28
275 Big Game Hunting, Auckland Star, Volume XLI, Issue 161, 9 July 1910, Page 5
http://paperspast.natlib.govt.nz/cgi-bin/paperspast?a=d&d=AS19100709.2.16

pony. The circus hands and a number of residents set out in chase of the others, and after a long search found the lion in a hen-house.

A cage drawn by an elephant was sent and the lion recaged. The other lioness was discovered prowling about in the main street, and it was surrounded, and a cage being brought it was driven in. There was much excitement in the township while the chase was in progress, though the circus audience remained quiet.

The lions mauled several horses, almost killing one.

*Wirth's Circus had its fair share of incidents in New Zealand as well:*

## Fight Between Panthers, 1904[276]

AUCKLAND, FEB 1. At Wirth's Circus at Whangarei a fight took place between the panthers, the male panther killing and half eating the female.

*In another local circus performance, OSH would have had a fit at the big cat roaming loose on the stage, within one leap of the audience:*

## Leopard Loose On Stage In NZ, 1920[277]

This panther (pictured) was captured in the jungles of India at the early age of six months. It is claimed to be the only tame panther in the world. It was recently exhibited throughout New Zealand by the Silvester Astras Company, the animal being loose on the stage whilst Astras, blindfolded, gave her telepathic mild-reading act.

## Evidently You Can Hide Your Lion Eyes,1919[278]

*Lion In The Hills, Uncanny Noises At Night*
SYDNEY, AUG. 1. A lion is reported to be roaming at large in the hills

---

276 Fight Between Panthers, West Coast Times , Issue 13099, 2 February 1904, Page 4
http://paperspast.natlib.govt.nz/cgi-bin/paperspast?a=d&d=WCT19040202.2.12.7
277 A Tame Panther, Free Lance, Volume XXI, Issue 1092, 7 April 1920, Page 15
http://paperspast.natlib.govt.nz/cgi-bin/paperspast?a=d&d=NZFL19200407.2.39
278 "Lion" In The Hills, Poverty Bay Herald, Volume XLVI, Issue 14989, 16 August 1919, Page 3
http://paperspast.natlib.govt.nz/cgi-bin/paperspast?a=d&d=PBH19190816.2.27

around the village of Yeovil. A well-known resident, while fox hunting, ran across the tracks of a strange animal. Soon afterwards he saw a lion at close quarters, but not having sufficient heavy ammunition he did not shoot.

He ran for assistance, and parties of hunters were organised. They saw the lion but were unable to bag him. Uncanny howls have been heard by a number of settlers in the vicinity at night, and the unusual tracks of a large animal have been seen by numerous people. A monster hunting party is being organised to beat the bush thoroughly. It is thought that the lion is identical with an animal which is reported to have escaped from a circus at Peak Hill a few weeks ago.

## Boy's Tussle With Lion, 1945[279]

Depositing his overcoat on his father's knee, a boy aged 15 raced down the aisle at a Manchester circus, jumped into the ring, and sprang on the back of a five-year-old forest-bred lion.

He seized a tuft of the lion's mane and tried to hang on, but the lion pulled him to the ground. The boy's parents screamed, but the people in the gallery thought it was part of the act. When attendants and the lion's

---

279  Drama At A Circus, Evening Post, Volume CXXXIX, Issue 3, 4 January 1945, Page 6
http://paperspast.natlib.govt.nz/cgi-bin/paperspast?a=d&d=EP19450104.2.110

trainer – a young woman – rushed to rescue the boy there were shouts of "Let them fight it out!"

The boy escaped minus the seat of his pants and a slightly lacerated leg. The trainer, who was billed to wrestle with the lion, was bitten.

## That Lion In The Mirror? It's Real, 1935[280]

Terror seized the inhabitants of Drosendorf, a little town in Lower Austria, when a lion escaped from a travelling circus. They fled from the streets to the nearest shelter and left the lion to rush down the deserted streets alone.

Its keeper tore after it, but in vain - the beast would pay no heed to his calls or threats. Suddenly it caught sight of its own image in the mirror of a shop front. It stopped immediately. Then with a great roar the lion sprang at his "enemy."

With a crash of broken glass, it found itself inside the shop, which, fortunately, was empty. It stood there cowed and intimidated by its strange surroundings. It was bleeding from its badly-cut paws. Apparently all its adventurous spirit left it, for when its keeper arrived on the scene it immediately allowed itself to be captured without resistance, and followed its keeper home.

## New Zealand Tiger Hunter Mostly 'Armless'[281]

CALCUTTA, FRIDAY. Mr Leopold Acland, a New Zealand landowner, wounded a tiger in the Khalna district of India. The tiger disappeared in the jungle, but suddenly reappeared and fell on Mr Acland.

Another of the party shot and killed the tiger. While dragging Mr Acland by the arm to the jungle the limb was amputated by the tiger.

---

280  The Lion And The Mirror, Evening Post, Volume CXX, Issue 136, 5 December 1935, Page 7
http://paperspast.natlib.govt.nz/cgi-bin/paperspast?a=d&d=EP19351205.2.39
281  Sensational Tiger Shooting, Nelson Evening Mail, Volume XLII, 18 April 1908, Page 2
http://paperspast.natlib.govt.nz/cgi-bin/paperspast?a=d&d=NEM19080418.2.27

## Why Tiger-Hunting Is Shortsighted Endeavour, 1886[282]

A Madras letter says that Mr Robinson, head assistant collector, Kistna, was killed on the 27th of April near the village of Remedichella by a tiger. He was out after a tiger that had been wounded by a shikaree.

The tiger lay in a brushwood. Mr Robinson, who was short sighted, advanced near the bushes, closely followed by the deputy collector, when suddenly the tiger was seen by all but Mr Robinson, crouching in the bushes.

Mr Robinson had requested the first shot, consequently no one fired, but called his attention to the spot. Mr Robinson went forward a few paces, when suddenly the tiger raised itself from the bushes, and Mr Robinson fired and missed.

The tiger sprang at his assailant's shoulders, and Mr Robinson clutched the brute with both arms round its shoulders, turning his head away with a smothered cry. The tiger's jaws closed over the side of Mr Robinson's head, crunching the bone. The deputy-collector killed the tiger as the two fell together.

## Auckland Audience Prepares To Flee As Tiger Struggles Loose, 1902[283]

AUCKLAND, JUNE 20. An exciting scene was witnessed at Wirth's Circus last night, during the act where Rougal had two tigers harnessed to a chariot, which they pull round the ring. One tiger refused duty, and struggled to get out of the harness. It seemed for a moment as if the tiger would have the best of it.

Some of the audience made for the door, while the majority rose from their seats in readiness to escape. The trainer realised that his power over the beast was at stake, and pulled the tiger to its feet, adjusted the harness and completed the act.

---

282 Terrible Scene At A Tiger Hunt, Tuapeka Times, Volume XIX, Issue 1277, 25 August 1886, Page 6
http://paperspast.natlib.govt.nz/cgi-bin/paperspast?a=d&cl=search&d=TT18860825.2.50
283 A Man And A Tiger, Wanganui Chronicle, Volume XXXXVII, Issue 11678, 21 June 1902, Page 5
http://paperspast.natlib.govt.nz/cgi-bin/paperspast?a=d&cl=search&d=WC19020621.2.17.2.1

## The Cheetah And The Child, 1910[284]

It would create a longing in the breast of old Anglo-Indians to be back in India if they knew of the havoc tigers and leopards are playing in some parts of Bengal and the United Provinces, writes a correspondent.

Near the Teral Jungles the tigers seem to have grown very bold, and recently there were reports of three or four men having been killed by a single man eater.

In the Nadia district in Bengal the conditions, according to a correspondent, are worse. The village of Guptipara is infested with tigers, and the villagers are forced to remain indoors after dusk. This state of affairs is possibly due to the fact that there are very few Anglo-Indian sportsmen nowadays who go out after big game. Besides the risk, it is an expensive hobby and takes up too much time.

The natives are also inclined to exaggerate in these things, and it is possible that the passing of a tiger through a village has been magnified, in some cases, into a raid.

A curious story comes from Ceylon, for instance, where a cheetah had carried away a child, and the mother found it safe in the den. The missing child was of course taken home, but the cheetah apparently had become attached to the child, and visited the house at night. It is stated – and the correspondent vouches for the truth of the story that the cheetah roused the whole neighbourhood by its attempts to enter the house.

A true incident is, however, reported from Ajodhya, where a Hindu priest was made a prisoner, with his family, in a temple by a leopard. The animal entered the priest's home, but the latter took refuge in the temple. The leopard climbed up a tamarind tree near the temple and kept watch. It was shot by a government official.

## Racing Cheetahs, Greyhounds Defeated, 1937[285]

Eight cheetahs brought to England for racing purposes by Mr. K. C. Gandar Dower, the big-game, hunter and athlete, are now so fully trained

---

284 The Cheetah And The Child, Auckland Star, Volume XLI, Issue 43, 19 February 1910, Page 17
http://paperspast.natlib.govt.nz/cgi-bin/paperspast?a=d&d=AS19100219.2.112
285 Racing Cheetahs, Evening Post, Volume CXXIV, Issue 157, 31 December 1937, Page 4
http://paperspast.natlib.govt.nz/cgi-bin/paperspast?a=d&d=EP19371231.2.12

that they race against greyhounds in practice at the Harringay dog track, says a writer in the "Daily Telegraph."

It has been found that a racing greyhound needs 40 yards start on a cheetah in a race of 440 yards, or once round the Harringay track. While the greyhounds' fastest speed is usually between 36 and 39 m.p.h., the cheetahs have been timed to do laps at 42 m.p.h. [68km/h]

Over longer distances the dogs would probably do better, since the cheetah, reputed to be the fastest four-legged animal, is essentially a sprinter and appears to be unable to get his second wind.

Mr. Gandar Dower brought ten of the animals to England from Kenya, where he trapped them, but two of them died from some form of poisoning. The remainder have surprised their owner and trainers by their docility and intelligence. They were first trained in a private paddock to race after a dead rabbit towed behind a car.

Since they came out of quarantine they have been "boxed" regularly in their cages to Harringay, where they have been trained to follow an electric hare with a piece of rabbit attached to it. The animals are of both sexes, and all were fully-grown when captured.

Mr. Gandar Dower believes that one reared in captivity would not be suitable for racing, as it would not be so fast and might be treacherous. Hitherto the cheetahs have been raced together and matched singly against greyhounds. The greyhound is the more difficult of the two to manage and is the worse tempered.

If the dog gets the electric hare the cheetah leaves him alone. On the other hand, if the cheetah catches the hare, the dog will sometimes show fight. The cheetah then gives him a cuff with its paw and the dog retires. I am told that there is a dog in the stables where the cheetahs are quartered, and that they are extremely fond of it. They are docile with human beings, even with strangers.

All answer to their own names. At the end of a race the trainer shouts for Gussy or Maurice or Louis, and the animal trots back to him; No decision has yet been made as to when or where the cheetahs will first be raced in public. Apart from their tremendous speed they are worth watching, for they move with perfect grace both on the flat and over hurdles.

# Last Days Of The Raj: Cheetah Hunting, 1913[286]

## *The Sport Of Kings*

The old Indian sports are slowly dying out; such a spectacle as a fight to the death between a tiger and an elephant, with a maharajah and gaily-attired horde of retainers lining the battlements, bright eyes peeping through the lattice-work, behind which are the purdah women, is a thing of the past, but still here and there in the native States of the great peninsula can be seen sports such as were known before ever the invading Moghul armies swept over the border to claim the land for their own.

In Jaipur, the capital of Rajputana, the ruler still keeps an arena within the Hawa Mahal (or Palace of the Winds), where most of the male animals to be found in the State are pitted one against the other on public holidays. Who that has seen two rams rushing furiously together, and heard the crash as their foreheads meet, can ever forget it? Wild boars, sambhur (a species of small deer); buffaloes; goats, quails, and partridges contest with one another with apparently great enjoyment to themselves; little harm is done to the contestants, but there is plenty of excitement round the ring, and bets are freely made as to which animal will, through sheer exhaustion, throw up the sponge.

One can see, too, in Jaipur, a sight to be witnessed nowhere else in India, for are not the Maharajah's dancing horses famous throughout the world? And what are these long, lithe leopards which, with silk hoods drawn over their eyes, tug at leashes, kept for? These are the famous hunting cheetahs, reserved for the sport of kings.

Picture to yourselves a wide, rolling plain, crossed here and there by nullahs, burned brown by the sun, the only sign of vegetation being patches of sage-brush. Away on the horizon herds of deer may be seen browsing. In the foreground appears a cart, on which is crouched a cheetah, sniffing suspiciously, but unable to see whither his course is leading, as a bandage is tied over his eyes.

A knot of horsemen is in attendance, and at the bidding of the huntsman in charge the cart proceeds to wend its way to windward of the feeding herd. From the knoll where the horsemen wait, one can note that the herd

---

286  Cheetah Hunting, Oamaru Mail, Volume XXXVIII, Issue 11831, 17 January 1913, Page 2
http://paperspast.natlib.govt.nz/cgi-bin/paperspast?a=d&d=OAM19130117.2.12

is becoming uneasy as the cart approaches nearer and nearer.

Slowly and with infinite caution the cart arrives at a spot almost a hundred yards distant from where the chief of the herd is keeping watch and ward. Nearer it cannot go for suddenly the alarm is given, and, with one bound, the deer are off. Not alone, however, for simultaneously the cheetah is unhooded, and makes for the leader.

Then ensues a race such as can be seen only once or twice in a lifetime. Over two hundred yards the cheetah is the fastest thing on earth, and if he can overtake the deer, the chase is at an end, for struggle as he may the pursuer flies remorselessly on his quarry's throat; and sucks his lifeblood. More than two hundred yards, and the cheetah will give up the chase, and return to his masters. Where there is cover to be found, it is interesting to watch the cheetah stalking his prey from bush to bush and from clump of grass to clump of grass, its long, yellow body scarcely noticed against the plain as it writhes its way closer.

So firm a grip does the cheetah take of the throat of the deer that only when a large wooden ladle, filled with the blood and entrails of its victim, is pushed between its jaws is it possible to drag away the carcass.

## Hunting Cheetahs, 1908[287]

It possesses the enormous bound of the leopard, as well as the freedom of limb action of the greyhound; and this unique combination of leaping and galloping in the same action is the cause of its extraordinary speed. The limbs are long and slim, the figure is slender, with a deep chest and small loins – in these respects the cheetah resembles the greyhound, its length, head and body, is about four and a half feet; tail, two and a half feet. Its height varies from thirty to thirty-three inches.

The cheetah, therefore, is nearly as tall as a small tiger, but because of its extreme slimness, its weight is about one fifth that of the tiger. In fact, its average weight at full growth is no more than sixty pounds – about the same as that of a large English bull-dog. Curiously, its jaws are short, like the bulldog's not long like the greyhound's. In character the cheetah is a wild animal, powerful and dangerous. His training also includes taming.

---

[287] Hunting Cheetahs, Timaru Herald, Volume XIIC, Issue 13564, 7 April 1908, Page 7
http://paperspast.natlib.govt.nz/cgi-bin/paperspast?a=d&d=THD19080407.2.56

Once really tame, the cheetah becomes a member of the family. In India there is a close intimacy between animals and their keepers. A mahout sleeps with his elephant. So also the keeper of the cheetah. The animal is made to wear a hood, to accustom him to the hunting operations in which he is destined to take part.

When ready for work, a pair of cheetahs will be placed on the head of a trained elephant, and behind them sit the sportsmen. When antelopes or other prey are within reach the cheetahs are released, and they crawl slowly along the ground, and using any cover they can find. When the antelope is still for a moment, intent on browsing, the cheetah takes short rushes from cover to cover.

In this manner he generally succeeds in approaching undetected to within a hundred yards of the prey. Then, with one grand rush, bounding and galloping in one action apparently, he bursts into the open. If the prey had been any other animal but an antelope there would be no race, for the cheetah would be upon it before it had fairly started. But, accustomed to a life of constant peril in the jungle, an antelope will be browsing peacefully the first half of a second, and leaping through the air the next. Because of its extreme vigilance and remarkable quickness in starting, it will in most cases be in full flight the moment the cheetah has broken cover. Then there is a real race; short, but intense.

## Children Fight Off Puma, 1918[288]

The Albert Medal has been awarded to Doreen Ashburnham, aged 11, and Anthony Farrer, aged 8, residing at Cowichan Lake, Vancouver Island.

The children left their homes for the purpose of ponies. Suddenly a 7ft puma attacked them. The puma sprang and knocked down the girl, but the boy attacked the beast, which was on the girl's back, with his fists and a riding bridle.

The beast turned upon the boy. Doreen, jumping to her feet, fought the beast with her clenched hands, actually putting her arm into the puma's mouth to prevent it biting Anthony.

Thus, she got the creature off. Standing on his hindquarters, the puma

---

288  Fight With A Puma, Mount Ida Chronicle, Volume XLV, 18 January 1918, Page 1
http://paperspast.natlib.govt.nz/cgi-bin/paperspast?a=d&d=MIC19180118.2.2

fought her until it became frightened by a sudden noise and slunk off. The children, badly injured, reached home. The puma was killed later.

## The Elephant In The Room, 1912[289]

An elephant paid a visit to a tobacco shop near the Gare de Lyon, swallowed several pounds of snuff and 200 or 300 cigars, and wrecked the shop.

M. and Mme. Vaux were sleeping in their bedroom on the ground floor just behind the shop – which is also a restaurant – when Mme. Vaux awoke and said she heard burglars.

M. Vaux got out of bed and picked up a revolver. Just then the trunk and head of an elephant appeared through the wall, most of which fell on Mme. Vaux, and husband and wife, in their night attire, climbed out of the window at the back and disappeared.

The elephant, which had escaped from a circus proprietor, had been frightened by a dog, and lost his temper with a carrot hung outside the tobacco shop as a sign, because it was painted tin and was not good to eat.

In less than a quarter of an hour he succeeded in leaving nothing standing except the walls, and only the outer four of those. He then followed his keeper quietly enough to the circus.

## Jumbo Rampages Through Sydney, 1927[290]

(FROM OUR OWN CORRESPONDENT.) SYDNEY, MAY 13. Quite a deal of consternation and not a small amount of damage was caused at Newtown, Sydney, this week when a full-grown female elephant from Wirth's menagerie escaped and roamed the streets for hours.

The first intimation of the escape was the discovery by her keepers that chains had been snapped like so much twine and that the side of a shed in which the elephant was housed was pushed down.

Looming suddenly out of dark lanes, she startled many pedestrians who fled to the police station and told weird tales of a ghostly apparition.

---

289  Elephant In A Bedroom, Bay Of Plenty Times, Volume XLI, Issue 5900, 23 December 1912, Page 5 http://paperspast.natlib.govt.nz/cgi-bin/paperspast?a=d&cl=search&d=BOPT19121223.2.40
290  Elephant At Large, Auckland Star, Volume LVIII, Issue 116, 19 May 1927, Page 10 http://paperspast.natlib.govt.nz/cgi-bin/paperspast?a=d&cl=search&d=AS19270519.2.116

Their experiences, however, were nothing to that of a householder who, hearing a tearing, rending noise in his front garden, ran downstairs and found that his front fence had been trampled down. It was dark and he received the greatest fright of his life when, as he stood looking for the reason of the fence's fall, one of the branches of a tree, three feet from his head, was torn down.

It was only then that be saw the huge shape standing in the shadows. The sight terrified him. He ran inside and it was ten minutes before he could pluck up courage to investigate again.

By that time the elephant's keepers were on the trail. It was clearly defined, for fences and shrubbery had been trampled down during the elephant's progress. A singular feature was that the elephant had maintained the "keep to the left" rule and, when it was necessary for it to turn down a street, had always turned to the left. Keepers attributed this peculiarity to training of the circus ring.

The big elephant submitted quietly to recapture, was taken back and secured with extra chains.

## Lion Vs Elephant, 1886[291]

A terrific encounter took place one day lately at the winter quarters of Forepaugh's menagerie, in Philadelphia, between the elephant Bolivar and an untamed Nubian lion named Prince, resulting in the death of the latter.

The lion was a splendid specimen of his species. He had been imported only a few weeks before and was worth $2,000. He was confined in an unusually strong cage in the animal house and four weeks ago the course of training began.

The lion was of too ferocious a disposition to permit of the entrance of the trainer into the cage until the animal had been sufficiently subdued with the prod and lash. In the afternoon the trainer unlocked the door for the first time and entered. For a few minutes all went well.

Prince growled ominously, however, when the pistol was fired over his head, and the trainer kept himself on the alert anticipating an attack. At

---

291 ENcounter Between An Elephant And A Lion, Bruce Herald, Volume XVII, Issue 1727, 26 February 1886, Page 5
http://paperspast.natlib.govt.nz/cgi-bin/paperspast?a=d&cl=search&d=BH18860226.2.28

last he struck the lion with his whip, and the enraged beast raised his powerful paw and struck at him. The man jumped aside, and perhaps escaped disembowelment, but sustained a fearful laceration of the thigh and leg.

Then the lion prepared to spring at him and the trainer jumped backward with such force as to break the bars of the cage from their fastenings. He fell out backward on the tan-covered ground, and for a moment was stunned. This proved to be a fortunate accident, for the lion bounced through the open cage door, and alighting a considerable distance beyond where the man lay, did not turn back, but rushed out of the building.

He pursued his way through the ring barn and entered the open door of the elephant house. Bolivar stood nodding where he was chained to a stake near the door. Prince hesitated for a moment, and then lay back on his haunches. He crept slowly forward until he was within reach of the elephant. Then he raised his paw and struck at the supine trunk. The tough skin was somewhat torn and the pachyderm became instantly fully awake, and, raising his trunk, made a blow at the lion but the latter escaped it by springing backward.

Vainly did Bolivar endeavour to break away from his fastenings. All his strength was insufficient to tear up the stake, and it was too short to break. He bellowed with rage, and his shrill shrieks were taken up by twenty of his fellows.

The combined roar made it sound as though pandemonium had broken loose. Prince crouched again and prepared to spring. Quick as a lightning flash was the movement which landed him on the elephant's head. But he had to deal with a power greater than his own over which his only advantage was his agility.

Bolivar easily shook him off and tossed him to some distance. The excitement at this point became intense. Both the elephant and the lion were fearfully enraged. Bolivar trumpeted loudly and Prince roared like thunder in anger and pain.

Again the twenty other elephants in the stable added to the excitement, and trumpeted in chorus. The sound was terrible, and it was this that first attracted the attention of the few men who were at the time around the grounds. Armed with pitchforks and such other weapons as they could find, they rushed to the elephant house, keeping a sharp lookout, fearing lest a stampede of the elephants had taken place, or that one by some means had broken loose and was on a rampage.

One man of greater temerity than the rest made his way to the door. As if spellbound the wounded trainer, who had limped his way to the door, was already standing there watching the contest and unconscious of the danger to which his position had exposed him.

The contest was quickly decided. The lion prepared for another spring. He lay back on his haunches, and with ears flattened against his head and eyes gleaming like balls of fire, crept forward stealthily, cautiously measuring the distance. With a suppressed growl the lithe, tawny form shot through the air.

The elephant's trunk was then turned over his back, and his little eyes were snapping viciously. With a motion so quick as to be almost imperceptible the proboscis was lowered and elevated twice, and then came down with terrific force, striking the lion as he was in mid-air.

Before he could recover the elephant dealt him a terrific blow on the side, and reaching forward the full length of his chain he drew the lion toward him, and lifting his free foot he leaned his whole weight on his fallen foe. The effect was to crush in the ribs of the conquered monarch of the forest. In this manner he trampled all over the lion and pierced him with his tusks until life was gone.

Then he raised it with his trunk and tossed it to the other end of the stable. In half an hour all the elephants had become pacified. Their keepers had been sent for and succeeded in quieting them. The dead lion's body was removed. Bolivar sustained no serious injury, except a slight contusion on the head and the trunk. He was unusually vicious that day and had to be hobbled with a double chain. – *S.F Bulletin*.

# Chapter 21

# The Tarawera Eruption

On June 10, 1886, New Zealand's biggest volcanic eruption in modern times claimed the lives of between 120 and 153 people. No one knows for sure, because the majority of victims were unidentified Maori villagers. All were buried, Pompeii-style, in rivers of mud and choking volcanic ash.

The volcano was not known to be active, or even in fact a volcano. Explorers had documented Mt Tarawera as a 'flat-top' mountain, and Maori had no oral tradition regarding the mountain. That assumption had been based on understandable ignorance of the geology. In fact, Lake Rotomahana was one of Tarawera's craters, filled with water and thus deceptively tranquil.

Scientists estimate a 1315AD eruption of Tarawera may have helped propel the globe into the Little Ice Age, because of the volume of ash and gas it spewed out.

Of course, Tarawera is itself dwarfed by the much larger Taupo supervolcano, which has not erupted in 2,000 years. Nonetheless, the events of 1886 serve as a chilling reminder that New Zealand's big North Island volcanoes are only ever a heartbeat away from changing our lives forever.

## Taupo Awoken By Massive Explosion, 1886[292]

The following report has been received by Captain Edwin, from Taupo:

---

292  Messages to Captain Edwin. Star, Issue 5641, 10 June 1886, Page 3
http://paperspast.natlib.govt.nz/cgi-bin/paperspast?a=d&d=TS18860610.2.23

"At 2 a.m. a terrific report awoke everybody in Taupo, when an immense flame was observed, with a continuous shower of meteors shot through the air and heavy shocks of earthquakes followed in quick succession.

"All this has been going on ever since, and we now learn Mount Tarawera, at Rotorua, has broken out in active eruption. C. J. Morton."

From Gisborne, Captain Edwin has received a telegram giving the following particulars:

"Strong gale from south-west. Gloomy, threatening, and very dark." I hear, here at Wellington, that the explosions were heard as far as Blenheim and Kaikoura.

AUCKLAND, JUNE 10. A Rotorua telegram states, "We have all passed a fearful night here, the earth having been in a continual quake since midnight. At 2.10 a.m. there was a heavy quake, then a fearful roar which made everyone run out of their houses, and a grand but yet terrible sight presented itself.

"Mount Tarawera, close to Rotomahana, became suddenly an active volcano, belching out fire and lava to a great height. The eruption appears to have extended to several places southwards.

"A dense mass of ashes came pouring down, and were accompanied by a suffocating smell. An immense black cloud, which extended in line from Taheke to Paeroa mountain, was one continual mass of electricity all night, and is still the same.

"Judging from the quantities of dust here it is feared the results will be serious to the people at Wairoa and the natives round Tarawera Lake. Hundreds of new boiling springs have broken out all round here, some in the middle of the road."

A Tauranga telegram says: – "The panic is increasing, and everybody is anxious to leave." (Special to the *Star*)

## Great Loss Of Life, Buildings Destroyed, 1886[293]

We are indebted to the Chief Postmaster for a copy of the following telegram, received from the Wellington office at 10-52.

"Re Eruption. Tauranga reports that 2.15 a.m. loud reports and heavy earthquakes began and continued till 5 a.m. Tauranga is in darkness, and

---

293   Numerous Earthquakes, Marlborough Express, Volume XXII, Issue 136, 10 June 1886, Page 2
http://paperspast.natlib.govt.nz/cgi-bin/paperspast?a=d&d=MEX18860610.2.9

thick clouds of sulphurous matter, gypsum, etc, in the air.

"Mount Tarawera and Rotomahana are reported to have broken out, and the eruption is going on continuously. We have no communications at present with Taupo and Tarawera. From Rotorua there are fearful reports of loss of life at Wairoa. Only five persons have arrived here safe as yet, but they state that the whole of the Hasgard family (schoolmaster at Wairoa) are missing, and have been buried alive beneath the schoolhouse, which was set on fire by lightning, and subsequently buried with ashes and mud from the volcano.

"McRae's hotel at Tarawera is a complete wreck. Great loss of life amongst the natives. Fourteen as yet found dead."

LATER, WELLINGTON, JUNE 10, 11. A.M. "Wairoa, (10 miles from Ohinemutu and six miles from Mount Tarawera) is covered with blue mud 10 feet deep. Houses buried up to the eaves."

## Large Loss Of Life Feared, 1886[294]

WELLINGTON, JUNE 10. The Secretary to the Post Office has received the following telegram:

"Rotorua. Between the roar of thunder, the roaring of two or three different craters, the stench, and the continual quaking of the earth, all is dire confusion. Several families left their homes in their night dresses, with whatever they could seize in the hurry, and made for Tauranga. Others, more lucky, got horses and left for Oxford.

"The fearful aspect of affairs is just as bad now (8 a.m.) as during all the night. I have sent my family to Oxford this morning, and if matters don't improve during the day, I shall follow them for a day or two." E. D. Danskt, Postmaster Rotorua.

## The Expeditions To The Terraces, 1886[295]

14th June. Several parties started yesterday to inspect the immediate scene

---

294  Details from Rotorua, Star, Issue 5641, 10 June 1886, Page 3
http://paperspast.natlib.govt.nz/cgi-bin/paperspast?a=d&d=TS18860610.2.18.5
295  The Expeditions To The Terraces, Evening Post, Volume XXXII, Issue 24, 15 June 1886, Page 2
http://paperspast.natlib.govt.nz/cgi-bin/paperspast?a=d&d=EP18860615.2.29

of the volcano, Stewart's party having gone round by the south, Warbrick's by the direct route from Wairoa, and Mitchell's party also by the south.

A lady (Mrs Robert Graham, of Auckland) accompanied the latter party, and she bravely rode across the devastated region as far as the horses could well go, and then travelled on foot to within a short distance of the old site of Rotomahana, for the lake of that name is no more, and its place is a raised plain of sand, pumice and dust, in which numerous geysers, steam, flames, and black mud are issuing continually.

The Pink Terrace is occupied by a great mud geyser, and the noble White Terrace is obliterated and gone. Lake Tarawera appeared quite free from clouds or steam, and Te Ariki was easily approachable by boat, but the unfortunate inhabitants around that lake must all have days ago been suffocated in the dust and mud which covers the whole of that region.

The mountain range of Wahanga, Ruawahia, and Tarawera frowned preternaturally over the scene, their sides bathed in white dust, and only a little smoke and steam issuing from the summit. The southern end of Tarawera mountain seemed to have been blown away, and a pumice mound or cone was formed above.

Other parties start to-day to further inspect the scene, and Dr. Hector goes by boat to Te Ariki, with a large party, to discover the fate of the natives who, thought to number 100, are supposed to be smothered in that locality.

## The Volcano As Seen From Taranaki[296]

The *Taranaki Herald* has the following:

The dense column of smoke and vapour ascending from Mount Tarawera has been visible from New Plymouth, and on Sunday (13), crowds of persons were to be seen on the various hills surrounding the town gazing at the majestic column ascending high up from the horizon.

Mr Humphries, Chief Surveyor, took observations with his instruments, with which he was able to compute accurately the exact height of the rising vapour. On applying at his office yesterday, he courteously furnished us with the result of his observations.

---

296   The Volcano As Seen From Taranaki, Oamaru Mail, Volume X, Issue 3555, 29 June 1886, Page 4
http://paperspast.natlib.govt.nz/cgi-bin/paperspast?a=d&d=EP18860615.2.29

He found that the column ascended a height of 23,000 feet above the top of Mount Tarawera. The width of the column was from 1.5 miles to 2 miles, which shows the immense amount of smoke and steam being emitted from the mountain and its surroundings. The top of the cloud was tinged a rose color, and gradually deepened till, at the horizon, the whole was of a deep roseate hue, being, probably, the reflection of the fire underneath the horizon.

Owing to the curvature of the earth, 12 000 feet of the base of the column was hidden from view, but the portion visible indicated that the volcano was very active. Occasionally large volumes appeared to be belched forth, and would alter the shape from time to time.

## Tongariro And Ruapehu Burst Into Life, 1886[297]

### *Threatening Symptoms*
Colonel McDonnell, writing from Masterton to Mr T. W. Gudgeon, Auckland, says:

"I only returned yesterday from Karioi, a station belonging to Morrin, Studholm, and Co at the foot of Ruapehu Mountain.

"On Sunday week I rode over the Owhaoko Ranges, which are snow covered. From Owhaoko, though 80 odd miles distant, as the crow flies, from Tarawera, I could see the volume of steam and smoke rising heavenwards.

"The mountain Tongariro, or really Ngaruhoe, has altered in shape. It must be 100 miles from Tarawera and 10 from Ruapehu. As I remember it, it was shaped as a perfect cone; now it is like a cone with part of the top and one side gone. I think the top must have caved in. The mountain seems to have lost about one-fourth or one-fifth of its height.

"Ruapehu, ever known as an extinct volcano, showed signs of life, and emitted steam, smoke, and jots of fire, and now there are several boiling springs on the north-western slopes, on the Wanganui side. I don't expect this mountain will explode, but goodbye to Taupo and Wanganui if so."

The remarks about Ruapehu agree to some extent with the statement of Mr Cussen, surveyor, to the effect that the crater of Ruapehu is now a

---

297 Tongariro And Ruapehu Active, Auckland Star, Volume XVII, Issue 151, 30 June 1886, Page 2
http://paperspast.natlib.govt.nz/cgi-bin/paperspast?a=d&d=AS18860630.2.20

lake of boiling water, which is constantly being added to by the melting of the snow around the summit of the hill. Scientific men should examine these volcanoes without delay.

## Tarawera Is New Zealand's Vesuvius, 1886[298]

Since the Tarawera outburst, much has been written about volcanoes, but scarcely anything has been published relating to similar eruptions of mud, or as to the subterranean transmission of the sound to great distances, such as appears to have taken place in this instance.

In a dissertation given by Humboldt before the Academy of Berlin in January, 1823, the subjoined facts are cited, and we need scarcely add that the professor's testimony is almost beyond question. He visited volcanoes all over the globe and studied them carefully. In 1797 the volcano of Pasto, east of the Guaytara river [South America], emitted for three months uninterruptedly a lofty column of smoke, which column disappeared at the instant when at a distance of 240 geographical miles, the great earthquake of Riobamba and the immense eruption of mud called moya, took place, causing the death of from 30,000 to 40,000 persons.

In like manner, when the long-tranquil volcano of the Island of St. Vincent broke out on the 30th April, 1811, a loud subterranean noise was heard at the same moment in South America which spread terror and dismay over a district of 35,000 English geographical square miles.

The sound travelled at least 628 English geographical miles in a straight line, and "was certainly not propagated through the air, and must have proceeded from a subterranean cause."

At the earthquake of Lisbon in 1755, not only were the Swiss lakes and the sea on the coast of Sweden violently agitated, but in the West Indian Islands, where the tide never exceeds 30 inches, the sea suddenly rose 20 feet. These instances prove that volcanic forces do not act superficially, but from great depths in the interior of the earth, and affect simultaneously widely distant points of the earth's surface.

In Naples, during the eruption of Vesuvius, in October 1822, the whole of the country round was darkened for several hours, so that lanterns were

---

298  Volcanic Outbursts, Hawera & Normanby Star, Volume VII, Issue 1343, 26 June 1886, Page 2
http://paperspast.natlib.govt.nz/cgi-bin/paperspast?a=d&d=HNS18860626.2.6

carried in the middle of the day, "as has often been done in Quito during the eruption of Pinchincha."

At Vesuvius, eruptions of lava are less dreaded than those of ashes. Another phenomenon which was observed at Tarawera was also noted at Vesuvius. The hot aqueous vapors which rose from the crater during the eruption formed, in cooling, a dense cloud, surrounding the fire and ashes, which rose to a height or about 10,000 feet.

Flashes of forked lightning issuing from the column of ashes darted in every direction, and the rolling thunders were distinctly distinguished from the sounds which proceeded from the volcano. The describer adds, "In no other eruption had the play of electric light formed so striking a feature."

Torrents of mud are ascribed to two separate causes. One is the volcanic thunderstorm, which envelopes with cloud the cone of ashes, and which is accompanied by violent rain in its immediate vicinity. The rain descends in the form of torrents of mud in all directions which the terrified husbandman imagines to consist of "waters which have risen from the volcano and have overflowed the crater."

The other cause of mud eruptions which is pointed out is that vast cavities often exist on the slopes at the foot of volcanoes, which communicate with mountain torrents and underground reservoirs of water. When earthquake shocks, which in the Andes usually precede eruptions, convulse the entire massif of the volcano, these subterranean reservoirs are opened, and there issue from them water, fishes, and tufaceous mud.

On some occasions there is ejected an otherwise unknown fish, the Pimelodes Cyclopum, which was first described by Humboldt. On June 19th, 1698, a mountain north of Chimborazo, named Carguairazo, above 19,000 feet high, fell in and the country for nearly thirty geographical square miles was covered with mud and fishes. Seven years earlier a putrid fever in Ibarra was ascribed to a similar eruption of fish from the volcano of Imbaburu.

Elsewhere Professor Humboldt discusses the phases of volcanic activity, and remarks that both at Vesuvius in Pliny's time, and at Jorullo in September, 1759, the revival of a long-extinct volcano began, as did Tarawera, with a tremendous ejection of ashes. The younger Pliny, whose father was killed by the eruption which the latter describes, relates that at an early stage the ashes had accumulated to the depth of four or five feet.

Judging by the latest reports from Tarawera, it seems that one can scarcely look forward to a speedy tranquilisation of the disturbances. They may become less violent, but it will probably be a long while before things settle down so as to render Rotorua a comfortable place of residence.

Chapter 22

# Climate Change 150 Years Ago

*The city of Christchurch has been getting more than its fair share of brutal weather events in the wake of the devastating 2011 earthquake, which appears to have lowered large portions of the city.*

*Interestingly, the flooding of Christchurch and in fact the rest of New Zealand is not unprecedented, as these reports show – our climate has always suffered extremes, but the results were far more tragic back then than now:*

## Hurricane Destroys New Zealand, Many Lives Lost, 1868[299]

Warning of the approaching storm appears to have been given on the morning of the 2nd instant, when the barometer suddenly fell, and the wind commenced to rise. Heavy rain continued to pour down from the evening of the 2nd until the evening of the 4th almost without intermission.

The wind also increased and on the night of the 4th and morning of the 5th blew a perfect hurricane. In addition to a large number of other vessels, there were no less than five English ships in port, and at one time it was feared the damage in the harbour would have been even greater than it was.

The schooner *Iona*, a fine vessel belonging to Lyttelton, was driven ashore, and became a total wreck. The *Iona* was loaded with a cargo of

---

299 The Late Heavy Gale. Taranaki Herald, Volume XVI, Issue 813, 29 February 1868, Page 1

flour and wheat for Hokitika, the whole of which was lost. Another fine schooner also owned by a Lyttelton firm, named the *Three Sisters*, was likewise driven ashore, and broken up in a very short time. The *Three Sisters* was in ballast when she went ashore, and fortunately no lives were lost from either vessels.

The ships *Melitia*, *Glenmark*, *Mermaid*, and *Beautiful Star* drifted at least half-a-mile, but none of them had gone ashore when the *Kauri* left. Three or four small cutters and schooners were driven ashore and became total wrecks, whilst a large number have escaped with loss of bulwarks, and their sterns being broken in.

The Auckland schooner *William and Julia* had arrived from Kaiapoi, but rode out the gale without sustaining any damage. It is generally supposed that several vessels have suffered at Kaiapoi, but the heavy fresh in the rivers had completely stopped communication with that port.

Nearly every bridge in the province had been carried away, and a large number of houses were under water. Every available boat was out night and day to remove families from their houses.

Communication by road was entirely cut off, and the whole of the swamp had about five or six feet of water. The telegraph had also been broken down. The water was about five feet higher than it was ever known to be before, and was still rising.

No loss of life has been reported although one or two persons had a very narrow escape. The destruction to property is immense, and it is estimated that about 1,000 sheep and cattle have been drowned.

The *Lyttelton Times* says "again has the result of a fresh in our principal rivers made itself felt, but instead of the damage being, as hitherto, chiefly confined to one locality, it has on this occasion ranged over a large portion of the Province." On the morning of the 4th by one o'clock, the banks below Madras Street Bridge had been stopped, and the road on either side became flooded.

Shortly before three, the overflow commenced at the bottom of Gloucester Street, the river being level with the buttresses of the Government foot bridge, Lane's Mill, and Montreal Street bridges, and flowing over the flooring of Worcester Street bridge. At seven o'clock, the whole of the block containing the Post-office and Market-place was knee-deep under water, and communication with both the Victoria and Colombo street bridges was entirely cut off for pedestrians.

At half-past twelve this morning (5th) the overflow appeared to have reached its full height, and shortly after it very visibly began to retire from the higher ground. Before this, the Post-office was from three to four feet under water, whilst the flow near the Government foot bridge had made its way up Gloucester Street, and effected a junction with that proceeding from the Market-place.

Mr. Hargreaves' office was the highest point reached in Cathedral Square, and Dr. Deamer's residence the highest in Armagh Street. Cabs were plying to and fro at the Colombo Street bridge the greater portion of the night, and we may mention that one man in attempting to cross it in the earlier part of the evening was very nearly drowned.

The morning coach from Christchurch was unable to get beyond Trelearen's, the road thence almost to Kaiapoi being entirely under water. But since then several persons have been through from Christchurch, and it is beyond doubt that the swing bridge has been carried away. The Girder Bridge, on the Rangiora Drain road, is reported to have been similarly destroyed, but no certainty exists upon the matter.

White's Bridge, at Felton's Ferry, at 6 o'clock last evening, was safe and as the river was then falling very fast, no anxiety on this account need be entertained. In Kaiapoi itself, the inundation has been much more serious and wide-spread than on any previous occasion. On the Rangiora Drain Road, in the area forming the original swamp, and in the Church Bush, almost the whole of the farms are flooded, and the destruction to crops alone must be very extensive.

The Kaiapoi Island is completely overrun, and the country below Kaiapoi towards the beach has also suffered very considerably. Near Fendaltown, where the river Avon forms a sort of basin by being backed up with flax and toi-toi, the water rose yesterday morning upwards of four feet in a quarter of an hour. A large quantity of land in the neighbourhood was completely flooded, Mr. Barry alone losing between 300 and 400 sheep, besides a number of cattle.

At the Selwyn, the bridge – Mr. Doyle's costly structure – is a complete wreck, and about 200 yards of the embankment on this side of the river has also been washed away. The piling put up since the former flood remains good.

The river near the Coal track is reported to be higher than known for the past fourteen years. The whole bed, between one and two miles wide, is one sheet of water, but there is no news of any overflow.

OAMARU: The gale at Oamaru, on the night of the 4th instant, must have been fearful. Between seven and eight o'clock p.m., the *Star of Tasmania* went ashore falling seaward. Two sailors and two children, passengers, were drowned. The rest of the crew were rescued about midnight. About 0 o'clock the *Water Nymph* went ashore, about a quarter of a mile to the north of the *Star*. All hands saved.

A schooner, supposed to be the *Otago*, went ashore in two pieces. The *Star of Tasmania* is an entire wreck, her bows only remaining. The *Water Nymph* is breaking up. The jetty is totally wrecked. All the surf boats are smashed. The bodies of the two sailors and children are found.

At Totara the floods swept away several houses. Nine persons were drowned. Seven of the bodies have been recovered. At Kakanui, the fellmongery establishment and houses were swept away. No lives were lost. This information was received from the Rev. Mr. Gillies, who communicated it to Sergeant Moore, of the Police, when returning from Oamaru, at the Pleasant Hirer.

Another account states that the *Star of Tasmania* when it struck beach almost waterlogged – hit ground with terrific force, stem-on, slewed round broadside on beach, next wave knocked her over and tore hole through her side; two children, named Baker, going home to their parents, were drowned in their berths and three sailors jumped overboard, and strove to swim ashore – back wash was too much.

Fears are entertained about the *Miskin* and *Wainui* boats absent North Coast.

DUNEDIN. Heavy floods over Province commenced on the 4th inst. The Dunedin streets were in many parts flooded, causing great damage. The bridge 'Water of Leith' was washed away. In the country districts the destruction was greater – Tokomairiro country under water: a young man, named Draper, was drowned in attempting to save cattle. Lawrence partly under water; Waitahuna Flat covered. Roads and bridges throughout the districts much damaged; floods highest ever known there.

Internal communication almost entirely stopped. Mails conveyed in boat nine miles to Waipora township. Taieri one unbroken sheet of water: many houses washed away. Taieri bridges cost over £20,000, and approaches greatly injured. A son of Mr Grant, West Taieri, lost his life attempting to go to his father's assistance. A man, known as German Charlie, drowned. Losses in this district beyond comprehension – farms completely destroyed, loss of stock inestimable.

Palmerston inundated, flour mills washed away; Runciman (proprietor), wife, three children, two men, and female servant clung to water-wheel during the night, seven rescued next morning – man, Gray, swam with rope. At Dunstan, Manaheirika River three feet higher than great flood in September, 1866. Six hours river covered with wreck of farms, &c.

Floods in Oamaru district, frightful. Rumored at Totara station eleven lives lost: a man, named Lowden, wife and family, residing on station, were asleep in bed when the water came upon them, all drowned. Floods north of Palmerston reported very destructive. The rain just commenced to fall again in torrents.

PICTON. The *Marlborough Press* states that on Saturday the 1st instant, about 7.45 a.m., was heard the booming mournful rumble which always precedes an earthquake! Before the sound of that approach had passed away, the earthquake was felt, coming from a S.W. direction, and the earth could, during its progress, be plainly seen to move.

The oscillations of the houses were visible to those outside, while those inside were fully alive to the fact that something more than common was going on. But little actual damage was done by the shock. The earthquake was the severest that has been felt in the province for some years, and lasted a few seconds.

About 12.30 p.m. it commenced to rain, and continued without intermission during the remainder of the day and night following. During Sunday, (the 2nd,) the rain and wind continued from the S.E. with little intermission, causing Taylor river to rise suddenly.

On Monday the river rose higher, submerging all Blenhiem to a depth of 18 to 24 inches – deeper than any flood which has occurred here before. At present it would be impossible to compute the value of the property injured or destroyed.

Few, if any, who are living near the banks of the Waitohi, have escaped without adding to the general loss. Mr. Esson, has lost a stack of hay, cow-sheds, outhouses, and fences valued at not less than £200; besides this many others have assisted to swell the amount of property destroyed, until it would be hard to say how many hundreds or thousands of pounds will replace the articles damaged at what in future, will be known as the great flood.

The rain on Monday began to abate, and on Tuesday morning parties crossed the river without much difficulty and up to the time of writing, it presents no appearance of being again likely to rise.

All communication being stopped, we are unable to state how far the ravages of the storm have been felt; but we have received intelligence that the road as far as the Half-way House is quite impassable for vehicles or horses, and that the whole of the bridges are washed away. Several large landslips have taken place; these, together with trees lying across the road, will make it a matter of impossibility to travel between Picton and Blenheim for some time.

The floods of the Wairau have done immense damage, drowning sheep and cattle by thousands, and destroying the crops. The flood was higher than any previous one in the memory of the settlement, and washed away the Boulder-bank on Wednesday-night, thus fortunately affording an outlet for the waters.

The body of a sailor was found on the bank and was taken in by the *Lyttelton*.

AUCKLAND. During the recent stormy weather about £1,000 of damage was done to the Otea Copper Mine in Mine Bay, Great Barrier. A quantity of the machinery was washed away, and other damage done to the amount above stated.

Chapter 23

# Educating Pita

One of the most enduring myths of modern times is that Maori were punished for speaking Maori in school, because of deliberate Pakeha domination of the education system. In fact, it was initially the decision of Maori parents in the 1860s and 70s who were, for the first time, trying to get their children a 'proper' education.

Indeed, part of the Ngai Tahu settlement we dealt with earlier hinged on the failure to provide schooling of a British standard to Ngai Tahu children.

For Maori children still in their tribal villages, the schools were outposts of England, of the new culture of the world opening up to them. They could, and did, speak Maori at home and in daily village life, which is precisely why their parents did not want them speaking Maori in school. Of what use, they thought, is an education if you come out of it still ignorant of the English language?

In the same way that children are today dropped in Maori immersion schools and taught only in Maori in order to teach them the language, so too 140 years ago were non-English speaking Maori children sent to schools and taught to learn, read, write and think only in English.

Maori, ironically, saw far earlier than other cultures, that English was going to be the language of the future, the language of commerce and education. Today, children across Scandinavia and many other European nations are taught in English, and the practice is growing in Asia, for precisely that same reason.

Maori wanted their children to become as westernised as a Londoner, in *order to take full advantage of what they felt the British Empire had to offer.*

*It was Pakeha who were constantly seeking more Maori culture to be displayed, and sometimes they were rebuked by Maori for doing so:*

## Maori Anger At Return Of Old Ways, 1891[300]

A great Maori festival is announced to be held on St Patrick's Day at Onawe, a peninsular in Akaroa harbour, in memory of "the great defeat of the Ngaitahu by Te Rauparaha, at that storied spot. A bullock is to be cooked whole in a Maori oven; there are to be races, and games, and a Maori war-dance and the ancient Maori fortifications, which are in a good state of preservation, will be duly labelled with cards, and orally explained."

The announcements of this festival have stirred up the feelings of some of the Maoris, and Te Taka, of Kaiapoi, in a letter to the *Press*, thus protests against it:

"Friend, I have been told that it is the purpose of your newspaper to discourage everything that tends to degrade people. Friend I ask you then to discourage what the Akaroa pakehas propose to do.

In obedience to the chiefs, of the governors and bishops and clergymen and magistrates, we have abandoned the customs of our ancestors, and adopted the customs of the white people. Why then do the white people ask us to revive customs we have abandoned, in accordance with the advice of their best men?

We have taught our children to accept the instruction imparted in the schools, and to conform in everything to the manners and customs of the English, and now the English are asking them to do the very things we were told not to do, and which we have advised our children to cast aside for ever, because they were degrading customs.

I suppose it is that the white people may have the opportunity of ridiculing our old customs, and making us Maoris the subjects of their mockery that your children may laugh at our old ways and customs, that they may twit us with being cannibals, and tearing our food with our teeth like dogs.

My friend, a few years ago we Maoris should have resented the proposal made by the English settlers at Akaroa as a curse, an insult only to be

---

300  A Civilised Maori, Timaru Herald, Volume LII, Issue 5091, 14 March 1891, Page 4
http://paperspast.natlib.govt.nz/cgi-bin/paperspast?a=d&d=THD18910314.2.27

atoned for by blood. For no greater insult can be offered to a Maori than to cook food on a place sacred to the dead.

Friend, this is a proposal on the part of the Pakehas to disgrace us Maoris, to lower us in the estimation of all people by enticing our young people to behave shamefully for their amusement."

*You can feel the pain and the hurt in the letter, not just the breach of tapu surrounding cooking on a battleground, but also the bewilderment: for half a century Maori had rapidly westernised and decided that many former cultural practices were reflections of a primitive past, and not where Maori wished to position themselves in the modern world. Yet here were those old ways being resurrected for cultural entertainment.*

*At a deeper level, the letter represented a fork in the road for Maori: was their best option to become brown Westerners, or was there still room for tribal customs?*

*Pakeha, wanting perhaps romantically to recreate the days of the noble savage, sought a greater expression of Maori culture and language, while Maori who had fought for the right to a British education saw it as a backward step:*

## The Maori Language In School, 1932[301]

"I have Maori children in my care who can hardly speak a word of their native tongue," said a Wanganui school teacher. "When I question them on the subject they say that their parents will not allow them to speak it. It is a great pity that some Maori parents are ashamed of their language, and I would emphasise the need of introducing the teaching of Maori into our education curriculum in some way if the native tongue is not to die out altogether."

## Maori Schools Punish Pupils For Speaking Te Reo, 1935[302]

Sir, – I would like to support Tamaiwahanehua's suggestion for the teaching of the Maori language in the schools of New Zealand. It would at least be

---

301 The Maori Language, New Zealand Herald, Volume LXIX, Issue 21311, 12 October 1932, Page 12
http://paperspast.natlib.govt.nz/cgi-bin/paperspast?a=d&cl=search&d=NZH19321012.2.125
302 The Maori Language, New Zealand Herald, Volume LXXII, Issue 22052, 7 March 1935, Page 13
http://paperspast.natlib.govt.nz/cgi-bin/paperspast?a=d&cl=search&d=NZH19350307.2.149.7

as useful to us as the knowledge of French and Latin that is drilled into our children at present, only to be forgotten as soon as they leave school.

During a recent visit to Rotorua I was appalled to find that no effort at all is made in the native school at Whakarewarewa to teach the Maori children their own language, and what is more, they are actually punished if they speak Maori in the school or school grounds. Surely it is time something was done to help them in what is almost the only heritage we have left them, their language.

Signed, Pakeha

*Perhaps the real issue lay somewhere in between. Maori children were educated officially in only a couple of ways – through ordinary state schools or native schools. The state schools tended to be in towns and cities, and as more Maori bought houses and worked in town, they grew up alongside pakeha and sent their kids to pakeha schools.*

*Naturally, everyone at state schools was being taught in English, and because of their urbanisation the families were often speaking English at home. These are the children, the Wanganui teacher remarked, who knew no Maori.*

*The Maori still living in villages were catered to by native schools. They, of course, were surrounded by Te Reo in their family lives, so the philosophy of the native schools was to expose them to the one thing the village and family were not providing: English, and turn them into little Englanders...*

## The Education Of The Maori, 1906[303]

"The object of the whole system of native education," says Inspector Bird, "is to Anglicise or Europeanise the Maori. To do that, he must become thoroughly acquainted with the English language. The Maori child thinks in Maori, and so long as he does that he will be a Maori. You want to teach him to speak and think in English, and when he can do this he is quite on a level with the ordinary Pakeha child.

"The only difference between a Maori child and a European child is the language. If you were to attempt to teach a Maori child in nothing but Maori, you would be carrying coals to Newcastle. He has already got

---

303 The Education Of The Maori, Timaru Herald, Volume LXXXIII, Issue 12898, 8 February 1906, Page 7
http://paperspast.natlib.govt.nz/cgi-bin/paperspast?a=d&d=THD19060208.2.44

Maori ideas in his head, and if he has no other language than Maori in which to express his thoughts, how is he going to get on when he finds himself called to deal with Europeans?

"The aim of the system is to 'Anglicise the Maori', and the fate of every successful native school is to become a board school that comes under the Board of Education for the district. The latest instance is the native school at Te Kuiti (King Country), which passes to the control of the Auckland Board of Education.

"The most intelligent Maoris who have children attending school are themselves fully alive to the advantages their children reap by being able to understand English, and they frequently ask that even more insistence shall be laid upon the teaching of English to their children.

"English is taught to the child through conversations on various topics, and care is generally taken that the topic chosen is something actually connected with everyday life. The children usually suit words to actions which they or their class mates perform, and it is quite possible that the average Maori child knows more English than a stranger may imagine. In other respects, the system of native schools approaches very near to that of public schools. Beyond Standard II, the syllabus is the same as in public schools, and work in the native school does not, as some people imagine, stop at Standard II or III."

*An example of one of these native schools was Whakarewarewa, in the heart of the Rotorua tourist district:*

## Whakarewarewa Maori School: First Year Of Operation, 1903[304]

The following particulars respecting the Whakarewarewa Maori School will be interesting to those who desire to see our Maori young people fitted for something better than even the fascinating haka and poi dance.

It was supposed, previous to the opening of the school, now just over a year ago, that considerable difficulty would be experienced in inducing the boys and girls of Whakarewarewa to leave their pleasant and profitable occupa-

---

304  Whakarewarewa Maori School, New Zealand Herald, Volume XL, Issue 12308, 27 June 1903, Page 6 http://paperspast.natlib.govt.nz/cgi-bin/paperspast?a=d&d=NZH19030627.2.79

tion of dancing, diving, etc., for the dull routine of school work, but the groundlessness of such fears is amply shown by the statistics of attendance.

All children of school age in the neighbourhood are on the roll, together with a good many who are over that age, and it is a rare thing for any to be absent even for a half-day. For the last six months, with an average roll number of 53, the average attendance has been over 56. This, of course, speaks well for the general healthiness of the scholars, but it also shows a remarkable willingness to face such inconveniences as frosts, storms, etc.

With only two or three exceptions, the children were quite new to school life, so that the work of the year has consisted chiefly in preparing for a Standard I. pass, but this, though not a very formidable undertaking for European children, means a very great deal to the young Maori. He has to learn to read, write, and speak a foreign language (more than half the sounds of which he has never uttered, and does not know how to utter), and whatever else he has to learn is taught him in this foreign language.

It is not uncommon to meet with people who have very inadequate notions of the requirements for a Maori school Standard I. pass, and it would be well if such persons could hear what the demands of the inspectors at an examination actually are, especially in English, reading, and spelling. Writing, drawing, formal arithmetic, singing, sewing, etc., do not present so much difficulty to the Maori mind, and in fairly equipped schools are generally well done.

At the examination of the Whakarewarewa school (held on the 10th inst.) 42 scholars were presented for a standard pass, not one of whom failed; and the preparatories, out of 28 possible marks, gained 26. Taking the school as a whole, out of 322 possible examination marks 311.5 were gained, the gross (or general merit) percentage being 95.1.

The history of the school during the year has not been altogether uneventful, the long illness of the head-teacher (the Rev. H. W Burgoyne) being, however, the only disagreeable incident.

Visitors to the school, more or less distinguished, have been many, amongst them being His Excellency the Governor and the Premier, Mr. Seddon having visited the school on two occasions. The number on the roll at present is 67.

*Many pakeha, and a growing number of Maori, felt by the 1930s that the pendulum had swung too far, that Maori children were losing their cultural identity.*

## All New Zealanders Should Be Bi-Lingual, 1934[305]

A prominent Maori of Wanganui complains that many of the young people of his race cannot speak their own language. Much has been said in recent times about the desirability of preserving the Maori tongue, and our present Governor-General loses no opportunity of counselling the people, and especially the younger generation, to treasure as part of their lives the language, legends, songs and artcraft of the race.

But the predominantly pakeha element in their early environment makes it difficult for the native youth in many parts, especially in the neighbourhood of the towns, to acquire, or retain, a knowledge of the speech of their forbears.

At school they are not taught to read or write Maori, and even in the playground the native school teachers discourage the speaking of Maori. The mother tongue is not considered worth perpetuating. There are exceptions. I know a Maori college where the headmaster and teachers recognise the necessity for handing on the native language in as accurate a form as possible, and they give some attention to Maori in classic and unspoiled texts such as the originals of the legends dictated to Sir George Grey and his interpreters, or written for him by the chiefs of over eighty years ago.

In this way a corrective is given to the modern tendency to make every second word in Maori pidgin-English. But generally there is a lack of perception of either the utility or beauty of Maori, and a generation is growing up in ignorance of the best things in the literature of the race.

I have known Maori parents to lament the fact that the pakeha schools make the children unwilling to speak Maori even at home.

My own idea is that every New Zealander, at any rate to the native-born, whether pakeha or Maori, should be to a certain extent bi-lingual. A thorough schooling in English is, of course, indispensable for the Maori of to-day, but this need not suffer if a little time were devoted to the tongue of the people. Both teachers and pupils in all schools would be the better for some instruction in the elements of Maori.

The steady increase in the native population justifies an educational policy which shall recognise Maori as a necessary part of a rightly-balanced cultural training suited to the requirements of the country.

---

305 Their Native Tongue, Auckland Star, Volume LXV, Issue 78, 3 April 1934, Page 6
http://paperspast.natlib.govt.nz/cgi-bin/paperspast?a=d&cl=search&d=AS19340403.2.57

# Losing Racial Pride, 1925[306]

Fears that the Maori was losing his racial pride were voiced by Mr. W. N. Coughlan, president of the Native School Teachers' Association, at the annual conference yesterday.

Some of the younger Maoris, said Mr. Coughlan, refrained from doing things which were considered merely Maori. That was a great pity, as a race, when it lost its racial pride, was not of much consequence. Every effort should be made to foster racial pride among the Maoris.

He moved that the association recommend the Department of Education to allow teachers reasonable liberty to introduce into their programme of work suitable Maori folk songs, handwork, a simple war dance, the haka, and poi movements. It was decided to send a letter embodying the motion to the department. Mr. Coughlan also expressed the opinion that there was a danger of the Maori language dying out. Some Maoris could speak English only.

Sir James Carroll, whom he had met a few days before, deplored the fact that the young natives of to-day did not speak proper Maori but employed a type of pidgin English. It would be no hardship on young Maoris if they were compelled to learn their, language. It was decided to ask the Senate of the University of New Zealand to make it compulsory for all Maoris sitting for the matriculation examination [University Entrance] to take Maori as a language. It was further resolved that the Senate be asked to set a high standard in the examination.

*The education establishment by the 1930s was in favour of encouraging Maori, not squashing it, but what authorities could not agree on was what constituted 'authentic' te reo. Imagine your surprise, for example, when you discover in the following article that the 'f' sound used in every Maori word with a "wh" in it, should not actually be there and was only added to make the words easier for pakehas to say.*

*To put it even more plainly: the most common manifestation of 'authentic' Maori language in radio and TV broadcasts every day in New Zealand, turns out to be a pidgin-English version of Maori. Go figure.*

---

306  Losing Racial Pride, New Zealand Herald, Volume LXII, Issue 18918, 16 January 1925, Page 12
http://paperspast.natlib.govt.nz/cgi-bin/paperspast?a=d&cl=search&d=NZH19250116.2.151

## Will Someone Tell National Radio How To Speak Maori? 1928[307]

### Common Errors Corrected, Peculiarities Of Structure: Address By Noted Scholar

"You will not mind my saying it is positively criminal to talk about 'Otahu'; it is so much easier and prettier to say 'Otahuhu'," said Archdeacon H. W. Williams, when addressing a meeting of the anthropology and Maori race section of the Auckland Institute last evening.

'Rotomahana' was another word which he quoted as "euphonious when properly pronounced and dreadful when it is not.

"I am rather a grumbler," the archdeacon continued, "but if you look in the railway guide or the newspapers you will almost invariably find words like Miti Miti as two words. Part of the genius of the Maori language is a fondness for duplicating syllables, and the word should, of course, be 'Mitimiti'. You might as well write Auck Land as Miti Miti.

"Another dreadful one that appears in the Railway Guide is 'Ho Ho' instead of Hoho." The fame of Archdeacon Williams as a Maori scholar drew a large audience to the University College to hear him on the subject of Maori Language and Literature. Among those present were pupils of St. Stephen's School for Maori Boys.

Mr. A. T. Pycroft, who presided, recalled the fact that the archdeacon was one of the third generation of a family who had devoted much time to the study of the Maori language. *Williams' Maori Dictionary*, well known to all interested in the Maori race, was first completed some 90 years ago, and it was mainly owing to the work of their guest that we had now a complete dictionary.

### Language or Dialect

At the outset, Archdeacon Williams disclaimed any intention of giving a lecture on his subject, and said he was rather going to have a little chat about it. Maori was one of a group of languages, and it always seemed to him a little questionable whether one should not speak rather of the Maori dialect than of the Maori language. One thing all these Polynesian

---

307 Maori Language, New Zealand Herald, Volume LXV, Issue 20020, 9 August 1928, Page 12
http://paperspast.natlib.govt.nz/cgi-bin/paperspast?a=d&d=NZH19280809.2.123

languages had in common was a very limited phonology. The only pair of "voiced" and "voiceless" letters in Maori was "f" and "v."

In all the Island names "g" should be pronounced as "ng," as in Pago Pago.

One had to be careful in pronouncing "wh" in Maori. It was not "f," and when it was sounded that way it was as a concession to the weakness of the pakeha, who had difficulty in pronouncing it.

"Nga" also troubled English people when it came at the beginning of the word. It was only stage fright, he thought. "We English almost made it a point of honour not to pronounce correctly any sound which did not occur in our own language."

A Maori learning English was inclined to make the English "r" into an "l," although he could sound "r" quite well.[308] This was a curious instance of compensation in the matter of phonetics. The Maori ng was not the ng of "finger," [with the word turning on a hard 'g'] but the ng of "singer," and should be so sounded in words like "Mangere."

## *Few Possible Syllables*

The lecturer explained the sound value of five long and short vowels in Maori, and pointed out the language had only a possible 55 syllables. Of these only 51 were actually used, and hence it was inevitable that there was much repetition of sounds in Maori words. The Maori 55 syllables compared with a possible total of over 80,000 syllables in English.

The main thing in speaking Maori was to keep the vowels perfectly pure, and to give each vowel its full value in whatever part of a word it occurred. In the matter of accent Maori words tended to break up into groups of two syllables. There had been a tendency among philologists to lean too much on similarity in words between Maori and Indonesian languages, for there was a great dissimilarity in grammar. Unfortunately the study of the relationship of Maori with Polynesian languages had still to be worked out.

It was rather a slur on our English scholarship that practically all the valuable books on these languages were brought out either by Dutch or Germans.

---

308   Again, more proof that authentic pre-European Maori probably pronounced the word 'aroha' the Hawaiian way: 'aloha'

## *The Word for "Flea"*

In the Malayan languages there were not only prefixes or suffixes, but also infixes or syllables inserted in the middle of the word. He knew of only one word in Maori that might possibly be an example of an infixed particle, but he was not sure of that. As far back as 1814 it was stated by the Maoris that they had no fleas until the pakeha came.

Now the common Maori word for flea was "puruhi," and it was an interesting question whether this was derived from the word flea. He thought it might have been. In almost all the Island languages they had been rather at a loss for a name for the flea, and this seemed to bear out the Maori claim.

When he was asked, he usually said the chief difficulty of Maori was its extreme simplicity. He was convinced Maori grammar was the most straightforward and intelligible of all Island grammars. There was no declension of nouns and no inflections, speaking generally. There was no verb 'to be' or verb 'to have', and many sentences had no verb in them. They got on very well without. "Ko" was not the verb to be as was sometimes stated. Several of the prepositions had a sort of time sense about them which seemed peculiar to Europeans. The only inflection in the Maori verb was the change from the active to the passive.

## *Influence of Bible Translation*

A good deal of Maori had now been committed to print. At the end of 1834, Colenso arrived at the Bay of Islands with a properly equipped printing-press, and they might take that as the beginning of Maori literature. He took his hat off to those early missionaries for the wonderful way they translated the Bible, but there still were quite a number of blemishes. There were many revisions, but the Bible was treated with great reverence, and there was a disinclination to change a form once fixed. Thus a well-known text was made to mean "The harvest is great, but the labourers are uncertain what they are going to do."

The Maoris having only the Maori Bible as a model, were inclined when writing to assimilate their style to that in the translation and fall into its errors. A certain number of Maori newspapers were run at different times, many of them with most interesting histories. The trouble was that when they sat down to write, the Maoris used much worse Maori than they did in speaking.

The free use of a blackboard added much to the practical helpfulness of the discourse.

*One could be a pedant and insist on the removal of the amateur pidgin-English 'f' in Whakatane or whanau, but in some respects the evolution of Maori into its modern form is not only healthy in a language, but a further example of a blended nation. After all, when Europeans first arrived in New Zealand the Maori 'H' – as in Hone Heke – was in many regions actually a 'Sh', as in Shone Sheke. Do we really want to go back to pure te reo from 200 years ago?*

Chapter 24

# Life In New Zealand – Part 4

## The Story Of The Jolly Justice, 1870[309]

A story is told which goes to show the position the Commission of the Peace holds in the estimation of our leading men. A gentleman, a Justice of the Peace, learning that a certain person had been appointed to the Commission, went straight to a member of the then Government, and complained that a "most improper appointment" had been made, and asked that it might be cancelled, on the ground that the new J.P. had been found in a state of helpless intoxication under a verandah.

"D – n it," replied the member of the Government, "the Commission cannot be lower than it is."

What came of the remonstrance is not told, but we suppose on the principle that matters could not be much 'worse than they were', the appointment stood good, irrespective of justice being found snoring off the effects of a narcotic under the verandah.

The Commission has fallen upon evil times in the outlying districts. Loud and many are the complaints that come from Marton, one of the most prosperous agricultural communities in the Colony, respecting the

---

309  The Evening Herald. Tuesday, July 12, 1870, Wanganui Herald, Volume IV, Issue 905, 12 July 1870, Page 2
http://paperspast.natlib.govt.nz/cgi-bin/paperspast?a=d&d=WH18700712.2.8

way justice is administered there. On the last court day no magistrates made their appearance, although there were several cases to be heard, and the Commission was once more brought into contempt.

On a former occasion, one magistrate only appeared, the other magistrates remaining away because the one sitting had made himself obnoxious.

Marton is becoming a bye-word for the disgraceful "incidents" and "scenes" that are continually occurring among its magistracy. One member of that community, a J P., has managed to bring himself into such public odium, that his brother magistrates will hold no communication with him and this, we believe, is the cause of all the magisterial scandal that has taken place.

The Government should certainly adopt some plan that would cause a more harmonious co-operation among the magistrates, or provide for the due and regular administration of justice.

## Mostly About Women, 1891[310]

Women are loveliest in womanly attire. Women have three ages: Their real age, the age they profess, and the age they would like to be. Woman may indeed have a sphere that is boundless, but she has to stop when she comes to a barbed-wire fence.

Persian woman have little education, and are reared in seclusion and ignorance, knowing nothing beyond the walls of their houses. Hindoo women are forbidden to read or write. Indeed those who dare to indulge in such luxuries are often accidentally missing.

Mrs Emson, of New York, is said to have the most perfectly-formed foot in that city. She can tread on eggs without crushing them, so beautifully is her instep arched. During the past two years, there have been several women committed for trial on criminal charges at Wellington, but not one has been convicted. Female jurymen wanted, evidently.

A medical college has been opened for women at Queen Margaret, College, Glasgow. It is said that the demand in the Old World for highly competent women in medicine is rapidly increasing.

Miss Nelly Kelly is a regular first wire operator of the American Associated Press, and receives £6 a week, the same salary as is paid to first wire men. She is

---

310  Mostly About Women, Observer, Volume XI, Issue 636, 7 March 1891, Page 9
http://paperspast.natlib.govt.nz/cgi-bin/paperspast?a=d&d=TO18910307.2.42

said to be the only telegraph woman in the United States holding such a place.

At Hutt, Wellington, the other day, a young woman named Emily Maidment did a heroic and daring act which deserves to be recorded. This girl was driving a cart, when she saw approaching two runaway horses dragging a mail coach, with no one in charge. She at once leapt from the cart, ran and caught a rein that was dragging on the ground, and by wrapping the rein round her body managed to stop the runaways.

## The Dread Cannibal, Richards, 1884[311]

A coloured man, named Richards, who formerly resided in Olneyville, Rhode Island, but has since removed to another part of that State, has often made his hearers roar with laughter by the story of how he acted the cannibal for two years in a well-known American show which travelled in England.

Richards was kept shut up in a cage as a dangerous wild animal, and was expected to glare fiercely at the spectators, and every now and then make a grab at anyone who too closely approached his cage. He was taught a sort of gibberish, which he repeated occasionally to the horror and terror of the lookers-on, who probably imagined that he was expressing a preference in his own native tongue for human tender loin or infantile veal.

The keeper would describe to the spectators what a terribly ferocious creature the cannibal was, and how long it had taken to subdue him, at the same time exhibiting a formidable weapon of iron which he said had been used to bring the cannibal to terms.

Richards was naturally as harmless as a child, and about as far from the general idea of a cannibal as could well be imagined. He received £5 a week and board – not human flesh, but ordinary diet – for his masquerade, and while in England married a white wife.

## Getting A Taste For Religion, 1888[312]

ARRIVED: the *Taupo* from New Hebrides [now Vanuatu]. She brings

---

311   A Sham Cannibal, New Zealand Herald, Volume XXI, Issue 6972, 22 March 1884, Page 2
http://paperspast.natlib.govt.nz/cgi-bin/paperspast?a=d&d=NZH18840322.2.55.24
312   A Cannibal Island, Poverty Bay Herald, Volume XV, Issue 5113, 8 March 1888, Page 2
http://paperspast.natlib.govt.nz/cgi-bin/paperspast?a=d&d=PBH18880308.2.8

news to the effect that the Rev. Robertson is the only European living at Erromongo. He is the fourth missionary stationed there, the natives having devoured all his predecessors.

## Dr Livingstone Nowhere To Be Seen, Call Peter Jackson, 1889[313]

April 6. H. M. Stanley, the explorer, in a letter to the Royal Geographical Society, describes the regions in which he has been travelling. He states that there are cannibal tribes in the forests in the interior, and that dwarfs are extremely numerous, who are experts in the use of poisoned arrows.

## Female Madness, Bedlamites At Large, Priceless Orchids Damaged, 1913[314]

LONDON, FEB 8. Suffragettes at night entered two orchid houses at Kew Gardens, smashed 30 windows, and uprooted priceless orchids. Great damage was done.

One woman smashed two £80 windows at Selfridge's stores. Suffragettes cut 30 telephone wires, including the trunk line to Dumbarton, and five telegraph wires between Birmingham and Coventry.

## WWII Bombings Make Middle East Look Like A Picnic, 1945[315]

LONDON, APRIL 26. Tonight, Mr. Churchill confirmed that Hitler's rocket war had ceased. It is revealed that V 2 rocket bombs killed a total of 2754 people and that 6523 persons were seriously injured.

The first rocket fell on the evening of September 8 at Epping. About 1200 V2s (long-range rockets) fell in southern England and London,

---

313  H. M. Stanley, Colonist, Volume XXXII, Issue 5463, 8 April 1889, Page 3
http://paperspast.natlib.govt.nz/cgi-bin/paperspast?a=d&d=TC18890408.2.28
314  Female Madness, Marlborough Express, Volume XLVII, Issue 35, 10 February 1913, Page 5
http://paperspast.natlib.govt.nz/cgi-bin/paperspast?a=d&d=MEX19130210.2.17
315  Rocket War Finished, Evening Post, Volume CXXXIX, Issue 98, 27 April 1945, Page 7
http://paperspast.natlib.govt.nz/cgi-bin/paperspast?a=d&d=EP19450427.2.69

which was the target for the rockets, as for the earlier flying bombs, says the Press Association.

The V bombs are finished, but the scars and the sorrow they have caused remain. They caused havoc on the way to London by falling short, especially in Essex, Hertfordshire, and Kent.

The attack reached its crescendo during one week in February in which 71 bombs dropped in southern England. Totals of from 50 to 60 a week were common throughout January, February, and March.

The worst incidents were, first, at New Cross where 167 people were killed when a rocket fell on a crowded chain store at lunch time; secondly, at Stepney, where a block of flats was reduced to rubble and 133 were killed; thirdly, at Farringdon Market near Ludgate Circus, on a day in March when the stalls were crowded with shoppers and 115 were killed; fourthly, at Deptford, where a surface shelter was wrecked and 50 nearby flats destroyed and more than 50 were killed. In a single day, in one London suburb, 1000 houses were damaged in rocket attacks.

Among the buildings destroyed was Whitefields Tabernacle in Tottenham Court Road.

## *Selfridge's Hit*

Seven American soldiers were killed when a rocket fell on the side of Selfridge's store in Oxford Street and a taxicab was blown into the shop. The occupants of the cab were never found. A rocket fell near the Hyde Park speakers' corner at Marble Arch, which is crowded on Sunday afternoons, but was practically deserted when the rocket came down at 7.39 a.m. Only one person was killed. The doctors' quarters at Chelsea Royal Hospital, in which army pensioners live, received a direct hit.

Some rockets burst in the air. The last rocket fell at Orpington on the evening of March 27. The earlier rockets were radio controlled until they started falling towards southern England and the latest type had an automatic device to cut out its fuel supply at a determined height. A new type of flying-bomb is believed to have been launched against England early in March. Airmen estimated its speed at 800 miles an hour.

## Tuatara in Wellington, 1908[316]

Some interesting investigations have been carried out by Mr Hector McLeod on the site of the Maori pa once situated on Palmer Head, near Seatoun, in Wellington Harbour. Oruaiti pa, as it was called, was built by the chief Te Rerewa, of the Rangitane tribe, and was the citadel of a populous village that was situated on the Seatoun flat.

"In those days naval battles were fought in Evans Bay, and natives came across from the Wairarapa," says the Wellington Post. "The highlands of the South Island were visible on fine days, and in the South Island was the precious coveted greenstone. The holders of Oruaiti learned that there were things as precious as greenstone in the South Island from some Maori voyagers who were blown across the Straits by a fierce southerly. These men, when they landed, were detected by women, and would have been massacred on the spot, but that they told such amazing stories of the fertility of the land in the Marlborough Sounds country, of the abundance and high quality of the fern-root, and that the country was a most desirable one to possess.

" Their reports were found to be true by the Ngaitahu, who raided the land across the Straits and made it their own, subduing the Mamoe."

Tradition records that the Wanganui Natives travelled south with the idea of subduing the Oruaiti pa, and were themselves routed and slaughtered in Worser Bay, five hundred of them falling in one day. In the early days of European settlement various articles of Maori manufacture, such as stone axes and chisels, flint scrapers and bone fish-hooks, were found on the site of the old pa, but these have now all disappeared. Pieces of moa bone and moa eggshells have been picked up on the Miramar peninsula, and three people claim to have seen a live specimen of the tuatara lizard. Mr McLeod states that he saw one of the lizards quite recently, so that apparently some of the curious creatures have escaped the massacre that followed the introduction of pigs to New Zealand. Fifty years ago the lizards were plentiful, but since then they have practically disappeared from the mainland.

---

316 The Oruaiti Pa, Manawatu Standard, Volume XLI, Issue 8542, 24 March 1908, Page 7

Chapter 25

# All That Glitters: The Goldrush

*While Gabriel Read holds a place in official New Zealand history and school text books as the first man to find gold, the story – as always – wasn't quite that simple. Although history has long since forgotten them, a number of other actors took the stage before Read, and the old newspapers tell their stories:*[317]

Mr Gabriel Read is popularly known as the first discoverer of gold in the province of Otago, but, like many other popular delusions which may for a time remain unchallenged, such is not the fact, as the following evidence will prove, the truth of which can be easily attested, as, with the exception of Capt. Cargill and Mr Valpy, the parties named still occupy influential positions in our midst.

In the course of his many peregrinations throughout the length and breadth of Otago the writer of this article had the good fortune, during the past year, to meet and enjoy a lengthened personal conversation with Mr John Sinclair, of the Tois Tois, who had the honor[318], although as yet he has enjoyed none of the reward and glory of being the real discoverer

---

317  The Pioneer Of Gold Discovery In Otago. Timaru Herald, Volume XII, Issue 499, 9 March 1870, Page 4 http://paperspast.natlib.govt.nz/cgi-bin/paperspast?a=d&d=THD18700309.2.22
318  Keen-eyed readers may have noticed the Americanised spellings of words like "neighbour" and "honour" in the old news articles. This implies the early settlers spelt that way, which in turn raises questions about how and why we later switched to the versions we now use.

of gold in this province. The following are the facts, shortly stated:

In 1853 (eight years before Gabriel Read's discovery) Mr Sinclair accompanied Mr Valpy, who was then the holder of the Tuapeka run, in a journey thither, and being a native of Breadalbane (Perthshire), where minerals abound, he has always been in the habit, when travelling, of observing the nature of the country traversed, and its mineral resources, and all the more so that the Australian gold discoveries were creating so much sensation.

Having camped for the night on the banks of the Tuapeka stream, nearly opposite Gabriel's Gully, he awoke early in the morning, and while washing in the stream observed signs of gold. He then determined to visit the locality shortly thereafter with shovel and tin dish to prospect the ground. Becoming himself the holder of the adjoining Waipori run, during the same year he returned to Tuapeka, and spent two hours in digging upon the banks of the Tuapeka river, washing the proceeds roughly in a tin dish and, observing that gold was present in the soil, he placed the washings in his handkerchief, which he conveyed home to the Waipori station where the more careful washing process was completed - the result being 2 ozs. 10 dwts. of gold dust for his two hours work.

With this prospect he next morning set out for Dunedin, and at once called upon Mr. J. H. Harris, whom he requested to accompany him to his Honor the Superintendent (Capt. Cargill) and on obtaining an interview, and exhibiting the prospect (Mr Macandrew happened also to be present in the room) Capt. Cargill at once declared that if the discovery of gold was one made known it would ruin the province forever, as strangers would rush the country, and carry off the benefits to the ruin of the settlers. Knowing that Mr Sinclair, whom he accompanied to Otago in the *John Wickcliffe*, was a freemason, he strongly urged secrecy, which Mr Sinclair promised, and to which promise he proved faithful throughout.

From that time Mr Sinclair continued to prospect various parts of the province, and having removed to his present station at the Toi Tois, in his occasional trips to Dunedin he continued to prospect likely ground, and discovered gold, less or more, in every place he tried.

In Mackay's Otago Almanac for 1864, the credit is given to Mr Lizard of being the first to find gold in Otago, but it now appears that during a visit to Mr Sinclair he was informed of the exact spot where gold would be found, and where, upon his return he made the discovery. Upon one occasion, in talking of the Australian goldfields in the long-room of the

Clutha- Ferry Hotel, a discussion took place upon the existence of gold in Otago, and to the surprise of all present Mr Sinclair undertook to show gold in less than a quarter of an hour and going to the crossing place where he had before obtained prospects, he returned within the specified time with several specks of the precious metal.

Mr Sinclair informs us that about the time of Gabriel Read claiming the reward, he reminded those in power of his prior claims. He was then invited to a public dinner in Dunedin, but residing so far distant from the metropolis, and being so far advanced in years, he declined the honor. Surely it now becomes us as a Province to make Mr Sinclair some tangible presentation, which might be handed down to future generations, in commemoration of his valuable discovery, and faithful adherence to his promise not to reveal the fact.

*OK, so it wasn't Gabriel Read in May 1861 who found the first gold in Otago, it was John Sinclair in 1853 – who in turn was ordered by Otago's then provincial governor, Captain Cargill, to keep the discovery secret for the good of the colony. At least, that's how Sinclair's friends tell it. Sinclair wasn't the only candidate put forward as the first discoverer of gold, however:*[319]

Sir, – By referring to the report of Mr. Alexander Garvie you will see it is dated 15th July, 1858, and in it will be found the announcement of gold having been discovered in the Clutha River above the junction of the Manuherikia (the very spot to which the present rush is directed) and the Tuapeka, Mapuherikia, Pomahaka, and Waitahuna. All that I had to do with the above report was the foot note dated, as you mention, viz., the 10th August, 1859, in which the south branch of the Tokomairiro river was indicated as a payable gold-field (now the Woolshed diggings).

...While Mr. Garvie was exploring further down, I penetrated into the Upper Clutha district by the Lindis Pass, and published the fact of gold being present in the Lindis River, under date July 1858, at a point 22 miles above the present Hartley diggings. I take no credit to myself for this, as I did not test its capabilities, but simply announced the fact. On the contrary, Mr. Garvie suggested the probable payable nature of the ground,

---

319  Original Correspondence, Otago Daily Times, Issue 210, 22 August 1862, Page 5
http://paperspast.natlib.govt.nz/cgi-bin/paperspast?a=d&d=ODT18620822.2.21

if worked by a wholesale system of working. He suggested the same of the Tuapeka, to which Mr. T. Gabriel Read's name is now solely attached.

Yours, &c. J. Thomson,
Chief Surveyor
Dunedin, 20th August, 1862

*So now it seems clear that Dunedin's Chief Surveyor had filed reports as early as 1858 confirming the presence of gold in Otago. Nobody, however, had reckoned on the legend of Black Peter to add some colour to the mix:*[320]

Mr Vincent Pyke, M.H.R., makes the following appeal in the Dunedin evening papers of Saturday – "There is a man living amongst us who may fairly claim to be the father of Goldmining in New Zealand. His name is Edward Peters, native of Bombay, better known, perhaps, as 'Black Peter' by old residents. He was the first man to demonstrate, by actual discovery, the existence of payable gold-workings in Otago but be was poor, humble, and ignorant, and old not know how to torn his discoveries to profitable account. Wherefore he has been neglected, and the value of his work has been ignored except by the few who are acquainted with the facts; and the honours and the rewards that should have been his have been awarded to others.

"Writing in 1858, Mr J T. Thomson, then Chief Surveyor, says in a footnote, to his Report on the Reconnaissance Survey of the South-eastern District of Otago: – 'The best sample of gold yet brought into town was found in the Tokomairiro River (south branch). This sample indicates a workable goldfield'.

"The locality referred to is now known as the Woolshed Creek, and the finder was Black Peter. For this statement I had the personal assurance of the late Mr John Hardy, CE. In 1860 Mr John L. Gillies, when searching for some vagrant cattle, came upon Black Peter working for gold in a bend of the Tuapeka stream at what is now called Evans Flat. His only implements were a tin dish and a sheath-knife, *but he had found the gold.*

"Mr Gillies stayed with him nearly all day, and himself washed out some penny weights of gold with the same simple appliances. When Mr Gillies

---

320　The Story of Black Peter. Southland Times, Issue 9079, 1 December 1885, Page 2
http://paperspast.natlib.govt.nz/cgi-bin/paperspast?a=d&d=ST18851201.2.17

returned to Tokomairiro he took this gold with him and subsequently communicated the circumstances to Mr Gabriel Read. Mr Read thereupon shouldered his swag and went prospecting upon the hint thus given.

"This was in May, 1861. He followed the track of Black Peter, pursued the stream up to a shepherd's hut on the run then occupied by Messrs Davy and Bowler, crossed over the range, and discovered the auriferous deposits in Gabriel's Gully. The shepherd was Mr Munro, who still resides in the neighbourhood. I have no desire to detract from the credit due to Mr Read, but there can be no question that Black Peter was the original discoverer both of the Woolshed and the Tuapeka goldfields.

"From this start all the gold-digging and mining that has taken place in New Zealand, and all the consequent access of trade and population, most undoubtedly originated. Black Peter is now old, infirm, and crippled – a confirmed invalid in fact and unable to earn sufficient to supply himself with scanty sustenance. His pitiful case was brought under the notice of Mr J.O. Brown and myself by a lady resident at Balclutha, where poor Edward Peters is living rather starving. A memorial in his behalf, setting forth his work in the past,' and his wants in the present day, was presented to 'Parliament and duly considered by the Goldfields Committee, with the result that a sum of fifty pounds was placed on the Appropriation Act for his benefit, 'conditionally on an equal sum being raised by private subscription'.

"I am now assured by the lady who generously espoused his cause that she is unable to collect the insignificant sum necessary to secure the Government subsidy. Therefore, I appeal to the public, who have so greatly benefited by the labours of Black Peter, to come forward and contribute to the fund now being raised in his behalf. The time is approaching when the subsidy will lapse. I hope, therefore, it will be remembered that 'they give twice who give quickly'.

"Subscriptions will be gladly received by the managers of the *Evening Star* and *Evening Herald*, and duly acknowledged."

*There are several variations on who first tipped Gabriel Read off, however. Black Peter features in some of those stories, and some not:*[321]

---

321  A Miner's Reminiscence of" Gabriels", Southland Times , Issue 14020, 7 April 1898, Page 3 http://paperspast.natlib.govt.nz/cgi-bin/paperspast?a=d&d=ST18980407.2.24

In 1860 John Little Gillies started from Tokomairiro to look for two horses which he had heard were up Tuapeka Flat. On his way he called upon, and stopped all night with, a shepherd named Munro.

In the morning Gillies went to wash at the creek, and, being an old Australian digger, his attention was drawn to the promising-looking wash in the creek. He took a milk dish and washed a prospect, which looked promising. However, being pressed for time, he went no further just then, but got the horses and returned home.

About twelve months later Gabriel Read was leaving the employ of Mr Hardy, of Toko, intending to go home. He was advised, however, by Mr Gillies to go and give the ground where he (Gillies) had obtained the good prospect a trial. A party was formed, comprising Gabriel Read, Brookes, Hardy's son, and others, and having procured pack horses a start was made for the ground. On their way they camped in the middle of what is now known as Gabriel's Gully.

During the time his mates were boiling the billy, Gabriel took his sheath knife and pannikin and began picking the gold out of the crevices in the creek. A start was made right away. They worked about two weeks and then returned for "tucker" and made their find known. A month later there were about 1000 men on the ground, and goods of all descriptions were at fabulous prices. Flour, £24 per 200lb sack; tin basin, £1; bucket, £1; pair boots, £5; cartage, £100 a ton and over. One well known Southland gentlemen, Mr John McQueen, made £100 one day with a team of bullocks."

*Another version puts Black Peter front and centre again:*[322]

In issue of January 24 I read a review by "J.C." of a publication entitled "Early Days in Central Otago: Being Tales of Times Gone By." As the book may be treated as authentic history, I wish to state a few facts as a correction, in connection with the discovery of gold at Gabriel's Gully.

Messrs. Musgrave and Murray, who settled in the district in 1858, held a large portion of the country as a sheep run, lying between their homestead (adjacent to the present Mount Stuart railway station) and Waitahuna. Mr. Thomas Murray, when staying a night at Esdaile's (his out-station shepherd)

---

322   The Otago Gold Diggings. Auckland Star, Volume LXII, Issue 52, 3 March 1931, Page 9
http://paperspast.natlib.govt.nz/cgi-bin/paperspast?a=d&d=AS19310303.2.111.4

hut, met John Peters, known as Black Peter, there, on his way to Dunedin.

During the evening chat Peters showed him a parcel of gold dust and intimated the object of his journey. From Peters' description of the locality where he gathered the gold, Mr. Murray thought it to be in the vicinity of what is known as Munro's Gully, Mr. Munro, a resident there, having spoken of seeing shining material in the sheep tracks at the creek crossings.

The following Sunday Mr. Murray attended church at Tokomairiro (Milton), and during the usual conversation following the service, the only opportunity the settlers then had of meeting together and discussing business and topics of the day, he mentioned Black Peter's mission to Dunedin. There were present Messrs. Peter McGill, John L. Gillies, John Hardy, and, I think, the fifth member of the party was Mr. James Adams. Mr. Hardy said he had a man working for him who had experience on the Californian goldfields, and suggested that the five present should fit him out and send him in search for the position of Peter's find. This man was Gabriel Read.

He was equipped, and dispatched from Mr. Murray's homestead with his bullock team. Mr. Peter Robertson was at that time head shepherd for Messrs. Musgrave and Murray, and lived near their woolshed, which gave the name to the Woolshed Diggings, as many of the diggers on their tramp to Waitahuna, Tuapeka and Dunstan made for the woolshed to get a night's shelter.

Read did not do much for himself in the way of making a fortune, and the £500 offered by the Provincial Council was very tardily handed over to him. Not long afterwards he was prospecting on the Woolshed, and I remember well a piece of blue pug he gave to my father. It was studded with brilliants. I spent some time a few years later endeavouring to locate the source of this, thinking they might be diamonds, as I had found pure Oriental rubies in the same locality, their quality being vouched for by Professor Ulrich, of the Dunedin University.

Yours etc

John M. Murray

*Apart from the possibility of finding rubies and diamonds still at Tuapeka, perhaps one of the more intriguing stories is one suggesting the very first gold found in New Zealand may still be in someone's jewellery box somewhere as an old family heirloom from grandma:*[323]

---

323   Gabriel's Gully Gold, Hutt News, Volume 10, Issue 6, 8 July 1936, Page 2

How Gabriel Read was enabled to make his dramatic discovery of gold which started the Gabriel's Gully rush in 1861, is told by a resident of Dunedin, who has furnished some interesting details of an expedition made by three men in the Tuapeka district for the purpose of finding crossing over the Molyneux [Clutha] River. Instead, they found some gold, which is still in existence in a shape of a ring, while their discovery was made known to Read, who soon afterwards imparted the knowledge to the whole province. The Dunedin resident is a grandson of one of the men.

Mr. William Dawson, together with Edward Peters and another man, were sent by Mr. William Anderson, of Inchclutha, with a mob of sheep to find a crossing of the Molyneux. They were unsuccessful in their quest and on the return journey the party camped one night at the mouth of a gully. Mr. Dawson went to a nearby creek to obtain water and on his return stated that there was some good "hearth" clay in the stream, and had he been nearer home he would have taken some home.

Peters, or 'Black Peter', as he was commonly known, had had considerable experience of gold mining in Victoria and California and realised at once that the type of clay was a gold bearing one. After tea he took the basin in which the dishes had been washed up, and walked down to the creek, the others following later.

He worked for some time, but as it commenced to rain the other members of the party returned to the camp. About half an hour later Peters came back to the tent, and, holding out his hand, said: "I got it." The other men had not seen raw gold before and were inclined to be incredulous, but Peters assured them that he had found the precious metal, and he gave his "find" to Mr. Dawson to have a ring made for his wife.

This ring of pure gold was worn by Mrs. Dawson up to the time of her death in 1915, and it is now in the possession of her son, Mr. G. T. Dawson, of Timaru. Peters and the third member of the party returned to the locality after the sheep had been taken back to Inchclutha, and secured more gold. They then left for Dunedin and while staying at an hotel in Milton they showed their specimens of gold to a man who was also a guest, at the same time telling him where they had discovered it. The man proved to be Gabriel Read, who lost no time in using the information given, and after prospecting the district thoroughly he made

http://paperspast.natlib.govt.nz/cgi-bin/paperspast?a=d&d=HN19360708.2.4

a report to the Superintendent of the Province (Major Richardson), and within a few weeks there had commenced the great Gabriel's Gully rush.

*Another historian also talks of a band of gold:*[324]

When [Read] came to Otago he heard that a man called Black Peter had found some gold at Woolshed Creek and Tuapeka, and he tramped away inland. The Otago Provincial Government had offered a reward of 500 pounds for the discovery of a remunerative gold field. In the rocky wilds of Tuapeka, Read spent a night in the hut of a hospitable shepherd, Peter Robertson. He made no secret of his search. The shepherd's wife laughed at his hopes, and advised him to go away home again.

He laughingly promised her some of the first gold he got. He was as good as his word, for from the first gold he won in Gabriel's Gully he handed over to Mrs. Robertson a handful of dust, from which were made three rings, one of which is still in the possession of the family. Read made his great discovery in a stream-bed in a place which soon became famous. After sinking two and a quarter feet he came to a soft slate, and, to quote his own words, "saw the gold shining like the stars in Orion on a dark frosty night."

*The bitter irony in all of this is that Gabriel Read made very little money from his gold-strike either. He handed his gold to the Otago provincial administration for the good of the public, and accepted in return the 500 pound 'finder's fee' for locating a commercial goldfield. Neighbouring Southland and Canterbury paid out twice that amount – a thousand pounds – to the finder of each field. When Read died in Tasmania in 1894, he'd been in a home for the mentally-ill for some years:*[325]

The Hobart Mercury of the 5th inst. has the following: On Friday last, in the picturesque little graveyard at New Norfolk, the remains of sturdy old Gabriel Read were laid in mother earth, all the aged man could return to

---

324   The Days Of Gold, Auckland Star, Volume LXII, Issue 20, 24 January 1931, Page 7
http://paperspast.natlib.govt.nz/cgi-bin/paperspast?a=d&d=AS19310124.2.185.57
325   The Discoverer Of Gabriel's Gully. Otago Witness , Issue 2126, 22 November 1894, Page 17
http://paperspast.natlib.govt.nz/cgi-bin/paperspast?a=d&d=OW18941122.2.51.1

the bounteous parent whoso golden riches have made his name famous wherever the mining tale is told. For Gabriel Read was the lucky discoveror of the first payable goldfield in the province of Otago, New Zealand; after him Gabriel's Gully, within the courses of the Waitahuna and Tuapeka rivers, was named and as he was no niggard with his knowledge: to him the world, and especially New Zealand, owes the wea.lth which made many others rich, and entirely changed for many years the character of a district which had been doomed to scanty agriculture, but through him became an Eldorado.

Read's statement, it is chronicled, was at first received with incredulity. The news seemed too good to be true. Prospectors had been seeking gold for 10 years, and reputed discoveries had been numerous and frequent, but nothing had come of them.

Then the rush set in, for Read's generous act had opened to the public what might have remained hidden for years. "Off to the diggings" was the cry on every hand, and the least to benefit by them and their riches was, perhaps, Gabriel Read himself. Always a wanderer, he continued a prospector, opening up fresh localities in the same province, during which he received two sums of £500 as a tribute from the nation that had received so much from his enterprise and bounty.

Gabriel Read's life was, however, in the main a sad one. A native of this colony, a fall in the hunting field at an early age inflicted on him traumatic injuries from which he never recovered, and made him subject to fits of violence and eccentricity which were a great source of trouble to himself and his friends. Of late years his wanderings ceased, but he had the benefit of unremitting care and attention, and passed away quietly at a green old age to the land of riches immeasurable and without alloy. Many a comrade of his in the old days, and many a fortunate digger who had reaped some of the good luck to which he sowed, will join with his Tasmanian friends in saying 'Peace to his ashes.'

*At the time of his death, Gabriel Read's estate was diminished, less than 90 pounds left to his widow. Yet Read's commercialisation of the Otago goldfields boosted the population of the province by "sevenfold" over the years of the rushes, and "For three years nine months after the gully was discovered*

*1,699,667 ounces of gold passed through the Customs at Dunedin*[326]*" – a haul which when valued at today's rates of up to NZ$2000 an ounce equates to many billions in today's money. At its peak, the Tuapeka region alone had 30,000 residents compared to the 12,000 living in Dunedin city.*

---

326  Marching To Gabriel's. Poverty Bay Herald, Volume XLI, Issue 13392, 28 May 1914, Page 7
http://paperspast.natlib.govt.nz/cgi-bin/paperspast?a=d&d=PBH19140528.2.68

Chapter 26

# Land Of Hope And Dreams

*Our journey through Our Stories began with the colonisation of Auckland in 1842. Over the past few hundred pages we have criss-crossed the islands and the barriers of time to enjoy immersion in our past.*

*Perhaps it is fitting then, for the final word to come from Wellington, the site of the first official colony, and an Evening Post retrospective on that city's first 50 years:*

## Looking Ahead, 1890[327]

"New Zealand has completed the first fifty years of its existence as a colony, and has entered on its second half-century," remarked "The Post" in reference to the Jubilee celebrations of January 1890.

"Fifty years ago the noble but savage Maori was undisputed owner of the wild but fertile lands where now prosperous and growing cities, towns, and villages stand, or which yield their crop of grain, wool, or meat to the hardworking settler, or their treasures of mineral, wealth to the-hardy miners.

White men there were undoubtedly scattered here and there—in the main not very creditable specimens of their race, but the Maoris liked to

---

327  Fifty Years Ago, Evening Post, Volume CXXIX, Issue 23, 27 January 1940, Page 11
http://paperspast.natlib.govt.nz/cgi-bin/paperspast?a=d&d=EP19400127.2.60

have a few white men, and it was the ambition of every tribe to have a pakeha or two affiliated, as it were, to it.

There were noble and earnest men who had already laboured in the mission field, and here and there were scattered a few whaling stations, alternately the scene of the hardest labour and the wildest dissipation. At Kororareka, where there was already a British Resident established, there was assembled a strange community of generally disreputable people. Ticket-of-leave men and escaped convicts from Sydney, deserters from English ships, fugitives from justice, pakeha-Maoris of the most debased character, and others, constituted a community the like of which has now no parallel on the earth's face, and made beautiful Kororareka what it was officially described as, 'a perfect Pandemonium'.

Of course, there were a few respectable people there, thrown there by some evil fate, but their numbers were few and their life must have been one of daily peril and much misery. A few vain attempts had been made towards systematic colonisation in the extreme north, but they were unsuccessful and were quickly abandoned. Nothing in the nature of colonisation had really been achieved.

There were none in New Zealand then imbued with the hope of building up a national existence, who looked to the land as their home, and whose fondest hope was that they and their descendants would continue to live and labour in it. Even the missionaries scarcely looked upon it as their permanent abiding place.

Such cultivation as it was carried on was of the rudest kind, and chiefly, if not entirely, by the Natives, while the livestock was limited to one line, pigs; of anything but aristocratic lineage and appearance.

Such was New Zealand on January 21 in the year of grace, one thousand eight hundred and forty.

### *The Aurora Arrives*

But a new era was at hand. As the rays of the next morning's sun tipped Aorangi, the good, ship *Aurora*, well-named after the rosy goddess of the morn, was ploughing the waters of Cook Strait approaching Port Nicholson, laden with the dawn of a higher future of settlement, civilisation, and prosperity. Those who were on board the Aurora on that memorable occasion and now survive, may well look around them today with feelings of astonishment, not unmingled with pride, at the fruits of their enterprise surrounding them on every side, and also a feeling of deep thankfulness to that Providence which has so greatly blessed their adventure.

Probably none of them, even in their wildest anticipations or dreams, ever pictured such progress as has been achieved, or imagined that fifty years would produce such marvellous transformations. Indeed, they could not.

### *Then And Now*
Let us think what the scene was then, and compare it with the one which now meets the eye on entering Port Nicholson. Forest-clad hills on every side extending to the water's very edge. No sign of human habitation save the great war pah of Te Puni's, where Petone now stands, and the smaller pahs at Te Aro and Pipitea. The waters of the harbour broken only (save that the *Tory* lay off Somes Island) by great war canoes, manned by savages, tattooed warriors, naked, or next door to it. No sign of horse, sheep, or cow, or what they would deem cultivation. Everything around them wild, unpromising, and astounding in its novelty.

It is a wonder that the hearts of the boldest of them did not fail, or that they ever allowed the ships that brought them to depart, and leave them alone in the strange land which they had ventured so far to subdue. And let it be remembered that the gallant little band included women and children - thereby greatly intensifying the responsibility and anxiety of the male members of the expedition. Their hearts, however, failed them not, and they entered steadily on the work that they had come here to do.

### *After Fifty Years*
It was impossible for them to imagine the wonders that a few decades would effect. How their hearts would have been inspired with fresh hope and courage could a vision of Wellington as it stands today have been vouchsafed them, with its network of streets and fine buildings, its railways and tramways, its busy wharves, and the noble steamships and sailing vessels which frequent them; and, above all, that wonder of wonders, the electric cable, which brings us within a few hours communication with the rest of the world.

These were wonders undreamt of on board the Aurora. And what of the possible developments of the next fifty years? Amongst the children taking part in the present celebrations will be many who will probably live to witness the completion of New Zealand's first century of life. What changes will they not see!

It will be for those who live to see the century of the colony to look back and note what has been achieved, and draw wondering comparison between what is now and what will be then.

We must be content to know that New Zealand has now an assured career progress open before her, and that there-is ample room for the most extraordinary development which we can even dream of now as being possible. When the next great halting place in New Zealand's history is reached, and the Centenary is celebrated instead of the Jubilee, it will be a pleasant thing for many an old man and woman then to recall the events of 50 years before, and tell their children and grandchildren how the Jubilee was celebrated in 1890, and how they remember seeing some at least of the noble band of pioneer settlers, the full benefit of whose heroic enterprise the then living generations will be reaping and enjoying.

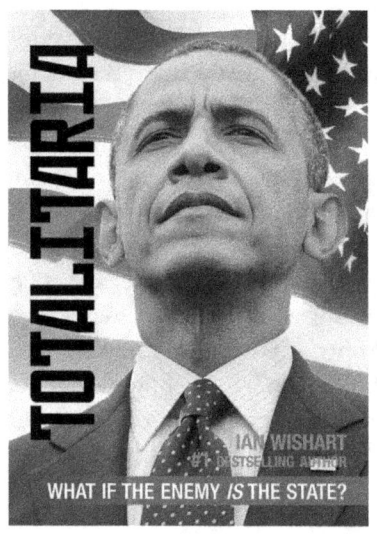

## THE CRITICS ON THE GREAT DIVIDE

"I can recommend it, I think it is a fascinating read and I think everybody should be reading it."
– Doris Mousdale, Newstalk ZB

Ian Wishart's new book is excellent, easy and informative reading…based on documentary evidence. Good reading.
– Roger Bailey, SunLive

There can be simply no doubt that The Great Divide must find a place…on the bookshelves of every educated New Zealander. In short – read it."
– Bruce Moon

## FIVE STAR REVIEWS ON AMAZON

Reading the footnotes will open your eyes. The research he has done is fantastic. The is a book to read and pass to people close to you!

Ian Wishart has clearly put a phenomenal amount time and research into this book. He has footnotes of references for nearly every statement he makes (which I truly appreciate). It is also reassuring to see how the conclusions that took me years to reach are so articulately and comprehensively laid out in print.

### www.ianwishart.com

www.ingramcontent.com/pod-product-compliance
Lightning Source LLC
Chambersburg PA
CBHW071953220426
43662CB00009B/1114